ANTICIPATORY BREACH

This work examines in detail the English doctrine of anticipatory breach, a hugely important subject in terms of both contract theory and commercial practice. It fills a significant gap in the existing literature with a comprehensive, systematic and in-depth treatment of the subject. The book not only restates the doctrine of anticipatory breach but also rejuvenates it, developing the proposition that the doctrine is essentially a mechanism for sanctioning present contractual remedies for future breaches. This proposition is developed in four Parts consisting of nine Chapters, which cover between them various aspects of the doctrine of anticipatory breach: historical genesis, theoretical characterisations, terminology, the constitution of an anticipatory breach, the defence of anticipated breach, the principle of election, the peculiarities of a right to claim damages, the assessment of damages, the victim's ability to continue with its performance and to claim the contract price when it is due, etc. Above all the book presents a carefully engineered critical review of the doctrine of anticipatory breach as it stands, challenging the misconceptions with which it was historically associated, the obscurity and precariousness of its theoretical foundation and the resulting inconsistency and inflexibility in its application. Instead, the author argues for a reformulation which follows a more rational, coherent and refined theoretical framework. This book is written in clear, straightforward language, and will appeal to academics, practitioners and law students alike.

Anticipatory Breach

QIAO LIU

HART PUBLISHING
OXFORD AND PORTLAND, OREGON
2011

Published in the United Kingdom by Hart Publishing Ltd
16C Worcester Place, Oxford, OX1 2JW
Telephone: +44 (0)1865 517530
Fax: +44 (0)1865 510710
E-mail: mail@hartpub.co.uk
Website: http://www.hartpub.co.uk

Published in North America (US and Canada) by
Hart Publishing
c/o International Specialized Book Services
920 NE 58th Avenue, Suite 300
Portland, OR 97213-3786
USA
Tel: +1 503 287 3093 or toll-free: (1) 800 944 6190
Fax: +1 503 280 8832
E-mail: orders@isbs.com
Website: http://www.isbs.com

British Library Cataloguing in Publication Data
Data Available

ISBN: 978-1-84946-112-2

Typeset by Compuscript Ltd, Shannon
Printed and bound in Great Britain by
Lightning Source UK Ltd

To my parents, Helene and Charlie

FOREWORD BY THE HON JUSTICE WILLIAM GUMMOW AC JUSTICE OF THE HIGH COURT OF AUSTRALIA

The author challenges the confident statement by no less an authority than Lord Wilberforce[1] that anticipatory breach 'is one of the more perspicuous braches of the law of contract and the modern position is clear'. The author is right to do so.

The doctrine is usually associated with *Hochster v De la Tour*.[2] On a motion before the Court of Queen's Bench in arrest of judgment recovered by the plaintiff, the question identified by Lord Campbell CJ was:

> Whether, if there be an agreement between A and B, whereby B engages to employ A on and from a future day for a given period of time, to travel with him into a foreign country as a courier, and to start with him in that capacity on that day, A being to receive a monthly salary during the continuance of such service, B may, before the day, refuse to perform the agreement and break and renounce it, so as to entitle A before the day to commence an action against B to recover damages for breach of the agreement; A having been ready and willing to perform it, till it was broken and renounced by B.[3]

The plaintiff's declaration was that the defendant had 'wrongfully wholly broke, put an end to and determined his said promise and engagement', to the damage of the plaintiff.[4]

One reason why the courts, particularly the English courts, appear to have given up the inquiry as to the doctrinal basis for anticipatory breach, leaving it as but a manifestation of commercial convenience, may lie in a failing appreciation of the pleading system from which sprang the issues in the mid-19th century cases such as *Hochster*.

A starting point is the proposition that absent proof of readiness and willingness, the plaintiff had no cause of action for breach of contract. The analysis by Mason CJ (who had the advantage of practising at a Bar in a jurisdiction which retained a strict pleading system) is worth repeating here. In *Foran v Wight*[5] he said:

> The prevailing rules and forms of common law pleading in the eighteenth and nineteenth centuries, which necessarily reflected the principles of substantive law as applied by the courts, demonstrated that the courts treated readiness and willingness as being

[1] *Federal Commerce & Navigation Co Ltd v Molena Alpha Inc* [1979] AC 757 at 778.
[2] (1853) 2 El & Bl 678 [118 ER 922].
[3] (1853) 2 El & Bl 678 at 687–688 [118 ER 922 at 925].
[4] (1853) 2 El & Bl 678 at 680 [118 ER 922 at 923].
[5] (1989) 168 CLR 385 at 402; [1989] HCA 51.

> material to the existence of the plaintiff's cause of action. The plaintiff was required to aver in his declaration the material elements in his cause of action. These elements included satisfaction or performance of all conditions precedent. Thus the plaintiff was required to aver performance of any condition precedent to, or concurrent with, performance of the defendant's promise. Just as the plaintiff was required to plead and prove readiness and willingness in a suit for specific performance, so at common law he had to plead and prove that he was ready and willing in an action for damages for breach of contract. It followed that proof that the plaintiff was ready and willing to perform his obligation on which performance of the defendant's promise was expressed to be conditioned was regarded as being essential to the plaintiff's cause of action.

The state of the law preceding the decision in *Hochster* was further explained as follows by Dixon CJ in *Peter Turnbull & Co Pty Ltd v Mundus Trading Co (Australasia) Pty Ltd*:[6]

> Now long before the doctrine of anticipatory breach of contract was developed it was always the law that, if a contracting party prevented the fulfilment by the opposite party to the contract of a condition precedent therein expressed or implied, it was equal to performance thereof: *Hotham v East India Co.*[7] But a plaintiff may be dispensed from performing a condition by the defendant expressly or impliedly intimating that it is useless for him to perform it and requesting him not to do so. If the plaintiff acts upon the intimation it is just as effectual as actual prevention.

Counsel in *Hochster* no doubt understood this, but Lord Campbell had been hostile to the submission that to preserve his remedy the plaintiff 'was bound to remain idle'.[8] The point the defendant unsuccessfully urged was that the conduct of the defendant had been no more than evidence of a dispensation of the necessity for the plaintiff to show readiness and willingness to perform, which dispensation the defendant might retract at any time before the time for performance arrived, so that an action instituted in the meantime was premature.

In Chancery, were the contract one susceptible of specific performance, a decree might be made in such circumstances before the arrival of the performance date.[9] But *Hochster* was a contract of personal service on a three month tour of Europe, and the case was an action at law for damages.

There would be no conceptual difficulty in the anticipatory breach cases if, as a matter of implication by law, the parties had a 'right to the maintenance of the contractual relations up to the time for performance, as well as to a performance of the contract when due'. That statement by the Supreme Court in *Roehm v Horst*[10] has been taken up in the United States, with the result that the anticipatory

[6] (1954) 90 CLR 235 at 246–247; [1954] HCA 25. See also at 253 per Kitto J and see further *Foran v Wight* (1989) 168 CLR 385 at 402–403 per Mason CJ.

[7] (1787) 1 TR 638 [99 ER 1295].

[8] (1853) 2 El & Bl 678 at 686 [118 ER 922 at 925].

[9] *Hasham v Zenab* [1960] AC 316 at 329–330.

[10] 178 US 1 at 19 (1900).

breach is repudiation of an implied term.[11] But this approach has not been adopted in other common law jurisdictions.

What does appear settled is that it is sufficient that, viewed objectively, the conduct of the relevant party is such as to convey to a reasonable person in the situation of the other party, the repudiation or disavowal either of the contract as a whole or of a fundamental obligation under it.[12] The author rightly is exercised by the apparent qualification associated with the House of Lords decision in *Woodar Investment Development Ltd v Wimpey Construction UK Ltd.*[13] In that case the bona fide belief by a party that it had an express power to terminate answered an allegation against it of absence of readiness and willingness to perform.

The conceptual difficulty which continues to lie at the root of the anticipatory breach doctrine was identified by McArthur J in *Y P Barley Producers Ltd v E C Robertson Pty Ltd.*[14] After referring to statements in judgments by such significant figures as Lord Esher MR, Bowen LJ and Lord Wrenbury, his Honour asked how an act not itself a breach of contract could be converted into a breach of contract by the election of the other party to the contract.[15] He answered that the action was 'an artificial cause of action' whereby '[t]he repudiation accepted and acted upon by the other party gives such party the right to at once bring an action for damages as for a breach of contract'.[16]

In like vein, the author of this work takes as his theme the proposition that the doctrine of anticipatory breach is a device to recognise as a contractual wrong words or conduct that relate essentially to an obligation the time for performance of which has yet to arrive and which effects an acceleration of legal remedies for the anticipated actual breach of that obligation; this acceleration of remedies is justifiable only where the anticipated breach is fundamental and, if it is so, where to hold the innocent party to the contract would encourage a waste of resources and an augmentation of losses. Further, the notion of 'election' is said to have no part to play here; the issue is whether the innocent party has effectively terminated the contract by acceptance and whether that termination is justifiable by the anticipatory breach relied upon to support the termination.

The author has considered decisions from England, Australia, Canada and the United States. The vexing decision of the House of Lords in *White and Carter (Councils) Ltd v McGregor*,[17] in which Lord Reid gave the leading speech, is assigned to Scotland.

11 *Restatement, Second, Contracts §253; Farnsworth on Contracts*, 3rd ed (2004), vol II at §8.20; *Equitable Trust Co of New York v Western Pacific Railway Co* 244 F 485 (1917) per Judge Learned Hand.

12 *Laurinda Pty Ltd v Capalaba Park Shopping Centre Pty Ltd* (1989) 166 CLR 623 at 657–658; [1989] HCA 23.

13 [1980] 1 WLR 277.

14 [1927] VLR 194.

15 [1927] VLR 194 at 207.

16 [1927] VLR 194 at 208.

17 [1962] AC 413.

Contract law is a field replete with terms in common usage but having distinct meanings which are insufficiently appreciated. The author picks his way carefully between the senses in which the courts have used the terms 'rescind', 'repudiate', 'elect', 'fundamental' and the like.

It is a truism insufficiently remarked that the search for the answers to what present as difficult issues of law must begin with an appreciation of the fundamental principles involved. When they have slipped from sight, more often than not, there ensues a line of unsatisfactory and self-contradictory authority. The course of authority over a century and a half in which the doctrine of anticipatory breach has been developed reveals a related but distinct failure. This lies in the absence in the foundation 19th century cases to expound a clear doctrinal basis whereby the common law developed this aspect of contract law.

This is the state of affairs to which the author responds. He is to be congratulated on the result.

Canberra
September 2010

ACKNOWLEDGEMENTS

In completing my DPhil thesis in Oxford and turning it into this book, I am indebted to many people. I wish to express my appreciation to all those who have offered their guidance, assistance and support to me in this long and important chapter of my life. All of them cannot be named. My deepest appreciation goes to my DPhil supervisor and friend Professor Ewan McKendrick. He played a crucial role in my success in completing both a MPhil degree with a historical study on *Hochster v De la Tour* and also the DPhil degree, which was awarded on my thesis entitled 'The Doctrine of Anticipatory Breach: A Critical Analysis' as it stands and with a recommendation for its publication as a book. I also owe special gratitude to my mentor, friend and former colleague Professor Charles Rickett, who has given me invaluable advice and encouragement since I moved to Australia. I am grateful for the generous support and encouragement from Professor Jill Poole and Professor Adrian Chandler during my time at Bristol. I appreciate the guidance from Associate Professor Louise Gullifer and Professor Mindy Chen-Wishart when I was a MJur student at Oxford. Their excellent tutorials (on Commercial Law and Contract respectively) inspired my passion for legal research and led me to a Distinction in my first British law degree. I am grateful to Justice Gummow of the High Court of Australia, who not only kindly agreed to write a foreword for this book, but also made valuable suggestions for its improvement. Finally, I thank Mr Richard Hart and his highly efficient team for their support and assistance in the editing and publishing of this book.

I also acknowledge with gratitude the following institutions, which have been of significant help to my DPhil research. My appreciation goes to the University of Oxford and its Faculty of Law for the wonderful opportunity they gave to me to pursue my academic interest in a surrounding of world-class scholars and facilities, and for awarding me the Shell Centenary Scholarship and the Winter Williams Scholarship; to Linacre College for providing me with a home, in both the material and the spiritual sense, and for awarding me the Heselton Legal Research Scholarship; to St Anne's College for accommodating me and giving me all the help I ever needed in my first year in Oxford; to the Sino-British Educational Trust, the Great Britain-China Fellowship Trust, Hong Kong Oxford Bursaries and Wing Yip Brothers' Bursaries for providing financial assistance which enabled me to complete my DPhil degree; to the School of Law in the Leicester University for offering me my first teaching post (as a part-time tutor) in English contract law; to the Department of Law of the University of the West of England and TC Beirne School of Law of the University of Queensland for supporting my research.

My ultimate gratitude is owed to my family: my parents, my wife and my son, Charlie, who have brought immense joy and motivation to my work. Without their support, encouragement and love I would not have been able to complete this book.

Portions of some chapters of this book have appeared or will appear in the *Modern Law Review* ((2011) Vol 74), the *Cambridge Law Journal* ([2007] Vol 56), the *Legal Studies* ((2005) Vol 25), the *Lloyd's Maritime and Commercial Law Quarterly* ([2006], [2007], [2010]) and the *Canadian Business Law Journal* ((2008) Vol 46). I thank the publishers of these journals for kindly granting me the permission to reprint some parts of the articles.

Qiao Liu
Xi'an, China
07 Oct 2010

CONTENTS

Foreword vii
Acknowledgements xi
List of abbreviations xv
Table of cases xvii
Table of statutes and codes xxxv

Introduction 1

Part I Demystifying Anticipatory Breach 7

Chapter 1 The Genesis of Anticipatory Breach 9
Section A A Re-examination of *Hochster v De la Tour* 10
Section B The Gestation of the 'Implied Promise' Theory 14
Section C The Rise of the Principle of Election 22

Chapter 2 A Redefinition of Anticipatory Breach 26
Section A Two Enquiries 26
Section B Nomenclature 39

Part II Establishing Anticipatory Breach 45

Chapter 3 A Critique of the Prevailing Test 47
Section A The Dichotomy of English Law 47
Section B The Decline of the Renunciation Approach 52
Section C The Defects of the Renunciation Approach 65

Chapter 4 The Making of a Unifying Test 70
Section A The Rise of the Fundamental Breach Approach 70
Section B The Principle of Inferred Fundamental Breach: The Dual Tests 73
Section C Two Evidential Modes of Establishing Anticipatory Breach 85

Chapter 5 Anticipated Breach as Defence 93
Section A The *Braithwaite* Conundrum 93
Section B The Waiver Theory 100
Section C The Averment of Willingness and Readiness 105

Part III 'Election' Following Anticipatory Breach 113

Chapter 6 Unlocking the Enigma of Acceptance 115
  Section A The Constitution of Acceptance 115
  Section B The Nature of Acceptance 121

Chapter 7 The Use and Misuse of 'Affirmation' 129
  Section A The Orthodox Test and Its Attempted Salvation 129
  Section B Revitalising Affirmation: an Estoppel View 141

Part IV Remedying Anticipatory Breach 153

Chapter 8 Claiming Damages 155
  Section A The Right to Claim Damages 155
  Section B Assessing Damages 167

Chapter 9 Specific Relief 193
  Section A A Claim for the Contract Price 193
  Section B Specific Performance and Injunctions 217

Conclusion 220

Bibliography 228

Index 234

LIST OF ABBREVIATIONS

ACTSC:	Australian Central Territory Supreme Court
ACWS:	All Canada Weekly Summaries
All ER (D):	All England Direct Law Reports (Digests)
All ER Rep Ext:	All England Law Reports Reprints Extension
ALJ:	Australian Law Journal
ALJR:	Australian Law Journal Reports
ALR:	Australian Law Reports
ANZ ConvR:	Australian and New Zealand Conveyancing Reports
ANZ Ins Cas:	Australian and New Zealand Insurance Cases
BCLC:	Butterworths Company Law Cases
BCLR:	British Columbia Law Reports
BCSC:	British Columbia Supreme Court
BLR:	Building Law Reports
CE:	Court of Exchequer
CISG:	United Nations Convention on Contracts for the International Sale of Goods 1980
Com Cas:	Reports of Commercial Cases
Con LR:	Construction Law Reports
CSIH:	Court of Session Inner House
CSOH:	Court of Session Outer House
D:	Dunlop, Bell & Murray's Reports, Session Cases (2nd Series)
DLR:	Dominion Law Reports
EAT:	Employment Appeals Tribunal
EC:	Court of Exchequer Chamber
EG:	Estates Gazette
EGLR:	Estates Gazette Law Reports
FAMCA:	Family Court of Australia
FCA:	Federal Court of Australia
FCC:	Federal Court of Canada
FCR:	Federal Court Reports (Australia)
FSR:	Fleet Street Reports
GWD:	Greens Weekly Digest
HCA:	High Court of Australia
LGLR:	Local Government Reports
LJC:	Lord Justice-Clerk
LJ Ch:	Law Journal Reports, Chancery New Series
LJKB:	Law Journal Reports, King's Bench New Series
LJR:	Law Journal Reports
LKSC:	Supreme Court of Sri Lanka (Decisions from the Sri Lanka Law Reports)

Lloyd's Rep Med:	Lloyd's Law Reports Medical
Lloyd's Rep PN:	Lloyd's Law Reports Professional Negligence
LT:	Law Times Reports
Mass:	Massachusetts Reports
MULR:	Melbourne University Law Review
NCLJ:	North Carolina Law Journal
NE:	North Eastern Reporter (USA)
NI:	Northern Ireland Law Reports
NLR:	New Law Reports (Sri Lanka)
NSWCA:	New South Wales Court of Appeal
NSWLR:	New South Wales Law Reports
NY:	New York Reports
NZCLC:	New Zealand Company Law Cases
NZLR:	New Zealand Law Reports
OR:	Ontario Reports
PECL:	The Principles of European Contract Law 2002
PICC:	UNIDROIT Principles of International Commercial Contracts 2004
PRNZ:	Procedure Reports of New Zealand
R (HL):	Rettie, Crawford & Melville, Session Cases (4th Series)
SCC:	Supreme Court of Canada
SCLR:	Scottish Civil Law Reports
SCR:	Supreme Court Reports (Canada)
SCV:	Supreme Court of Victoria
SGHC:	Singapore High Court
SLR:	Singapore Law Reports
Sol Jo LB:	Solicitors Journal, Lawyers Brief
SR (NSW):	New South Wales State Reports
TCC:	Technology & Construction Court (of Queen's Bench Division)
TCLR:	Technology and Construction Law Reports
TLR:	Times Law Reports
UCC:	Uniform Commercial Code (USA)
UCLA LR:	University of California at Los Angeles Law Review
VLR:	Victorian Law Reports
VSCA:	Victoria Court of Appeal
WASC:	Western Australia Supreme Court
WN (NSW):	Weekly Notes New South Wales
WWR:	Western Weekly Reports (Canada)

TABLE OF CASES

England

Abrahams v Performing Right Society [1995] ICR 1028 (CA) 210
Abrahams v Reiach (Herbert) Ltd [1922] 1 KB 477 (CA) 183
Abram Steamship Co Ltd v Westville Shipping Co Ltd [1923] AC 773 (HL) 124
Afovos Shipping Co SA v Romano Pagnan and Pietro Pagnan (Trading As R Pagnan & F lli) (The 'Afovos') [1983] 1 WLR 195 (HL) 39, 71, 72, 81, 83, 222
Afovos, The (See *Afovos Shipping v Romano Pagnan*)
A-G v Pritchard (1928) 97 LJKB 561, 44 TLR 490 126
Agra Bank ex p Tondeur, Re (1867–68) LR 5 Eq 160 64
Aktor, The (See *PT Berlian v Nuse Shipping*)
Al Hofuf, The (See *Scandinavian Trading v Zodiac*)
Alaskan Trader, The (See *Clea Shipping v Bulk Oil*)
Albion Sugar Co Ltd v William Tankers Ltd and Davies (The 'John S Darbyshire') [1977] 2 Lloyd's Rep 457 (Com Ct) 90
Alfred C Toepfer International GmbH v Itex Itagrani Export SA [1993] 1 Lloyd's Rep 360 (Com Ct) 77
Alfred C Toepfer v Peter Cremer [1975] 2 Lloyd's Rep 118 (CA) 58, 77
Allen v Robles [1969] 1 WLR 1193 (CA) 135
Allied Marine Transport Ltd v Vale do Rio Doce Navegacao SA [1985] 1 WLR 925 (CA) 118
Alma Shipping Corp of Monrovia, The v Mantovani (The 'Dione') [1975] 1 Lloyd's Rep 115 (CA) 115
Amory v Brodrick (1822) 5 B & A 712, 106 ER 1351 17
Anchor Line Ltd v Keith Rowell Ltd (The 'Hazelmoor') [1980] 2 Lloyd's Rep 351 (CA) 66
Anderson v Equitable Life Assurance Society (1926) 134 LT 557 (CA) 126
Angelia, The (See *Trade and Transport Inc v Iino Kaiun*)
Anglia Television v Reed [1972] 1 QB 60 (CA) 170
Anglo-African Shipping Co of New York Inc v J Mortner Ltd [1962] 1 Lloyd's Rep 81 (QB) 214
Appleby v Myers (1867) LR 2 CP 651 12
Applied Computer Expertise Ltd v Parallellweb Ltd (unreported, Com Ct, 18 September 2001), [2001] All ER (D) 42 (Sep) 78, 163, 189
Artpower Ltd v Bespoke Couture Ltd [2006] EWCA Civ 1696, 150 Sol Jo LB 1463 123
Aspdin v Austin (1844) 5 QB 671, 114 ER 1402 20
Attica Sea Carriers Corp v Ferrostaal Poseidon Bulk Reederei GMBH (The 'Puerto Buitrago') [1976] 1 Lloyd's Rep 250 (CA) 196, 201, 203, 207, 208, 212

Avery v Bowden (1855) 5 El & Bl 714, 119 ER 647 ....22, 23, 156, 159, 221
Baillie v Kell & Hogg (1838) 4 Bing NC 638, 132 ER 934....................89
Banco de Portugal v Waterlow [1932] AC 452 (HL)....................170
Bank Line Ltd v Arthur Capel & Co [1919] AC 435 (HL) 87, 181
Barber & Co ex p Agra Bank, Re (1869–70) LR 9 Eq 725....................64
Barrick v Buba (1857) 2 CB NS 563, 140 ER 536....................23, 59
Beach v Reed Corrugated Cases Ltd [1956] 1 WLR 807 (QB)....................183
Bell v Peter Browne & Co [1990] 2 QB 495 (CA)....................35, 53
Benjamin Scarf v Alfred George Jardine (1881–1882)
LR 7 App Cas 345 (HL)....................124, 125, 135
Bentsen v Taylor, Sons & Co (No 2) [1893] 2 QB 274 (CA)....................149
Berkeley Community Villages Ltd v Pullen [2007]
EWHC 1330 (Ch), [2007] 3 EGLR 101....................218
Berners v Fleming [1925] 1 Ch 264 (CA)....................135
Birmingham & District Land Co v London & North Western Rly Co (1888)
40 Ch D 268 (CA)....................151
Blackburn v Smith (1848) 2 Exch 783, 154 ER 707....................142
Bliss v South East Thames Regional Health Authority [1987] ICR 700 (CA)....................58
Bold v Brough, Nicholson & Hall Ltd [1964] 1 WLR 201 (QB)....................186
Borag, The (See *Compania Financiera v Hamoor*)
Boston Deep Sea Fishing & Ice Co v Ansell (1888) 39 Ch D 339 (CA)....................90
Bowdell v Parsons (1808) 10 East 359, 103 ER 811....................17
Boyo v Lambeth LBC [1994] ICR 727 (CA)....................116, 125, 161, 197
Brace v Calder [1895] 2 QB 253 (CA)....................64
Bradley v Newsom, Sons & Co [1919] AC 16 (HL)....................33, 35
Bradshaw v Porter, cited in (1680) 2 Lev 245, 83 ER 540....................32
Braithwaite v Foreign Hardware Co [1905] 2 KB 543 (CA)....................90, 105, 175, 187
Bremer Handelsgesellschaft mbH v JH Rayner & Co Ltd [1979]
2 Ll Rep 216 (CA)....................78
Bremer Handelsgesellschaft v Vanden Avenne-Izegem [1978]
2 Lloyd's Rep 109 (HL)....................144
Bremer Vulkan Schiffbau und Maschinenfabrik v South India
Shipping Corp Ltd [1981] AC 909 (HL)....................41
Brimnes, The (See *Tenax Steamship v Owners of Brimnes*)
British & Beningtons Ltd v North West Cachar Tea Co [1923]
AC 48 (HL)....................57, 61, 81, 88, 93, 100, 109, 187
British Aircraft Corp v Austin [1978] IRLR 332 (EAT)....................32
British Electrical and Associated Industries (Cardiff) Ld v Patley Pressing Ld
[1953] 1 WLR 280 (QB)....................30
British Waggon Co v Lea & Co (1879–80) LR 5 QBD 149....................64
British Westinghouse Electric & Manufacturing Co Ltd v Underground
Electric Railways Co of London Ltd [1912] AC 673 (HL)....................179
Brown v Muller (1871–72) LR 7 Ex 319....................168, 171, 172
BS & N Ltd (BVI) v Micado Shipping Ltd (Malta), The Seaflower (No 2)
[2000] 2 All ER (Comm) 169, [2000] 2 Lloyd's Rep 37 (QB)....................180, 181, 182, 189
Burton v Pinkerton (1866–67) LR 2 Ex 340 (CE)....................63
Bwllfa and Merthyr Dare Steam Collieries (1891) Ltd v Pontypridd
Waterworks Co [1903] AC 426 (HL)....................181

C & P Haulage v Middleton [1983] 1 WLR 1461 (CA) 170
Caines v Smith (1847) 15 M & W 189, 153 ER 816 17
Campbell Mostyn (Provisions) Ltd v Barnett Trading Co [1954] 1 Lloyd's Rep 65 (CA) 178
Cantor Fitzgerald International v Callaghan [1999] ICR 639 (CA) 141
Cargo Ships El Yam Ltd v Invoeren Transport Onderneming Invotra NV [1958] 1 Lloyd's Rep 39 (Com Ct) 58, 61, 87
Carillion JM Ltd v Bath & North East Somerset Council [2009] EWHC 166 (TCC), [2009] All ER (D) 62 (Feb) 131
Carswell v Collard (The 'Victoria') [1893] AC 635 (HL) 63
CCC Films (London) v Impact Quadrant Films [1985] QB 16 170
Cehave NV v Bremer Handelsgesellschaft MBH (The 'Hansa Nord') [1976] QB 44 (CA) 39
Central Estates (Belgravia) Ltd v Woolgar (No 2) [1972] 1 WLR 1048 (CA) 141
Central London Property Trust v High Trees House [1947] KB 130 ....145, 150
Cerberus Software v Rowley [2001] ICR 376 (CA) 210
Chandler v Webster [1904] 1 KB 493 (CA) 12
Chaplin v Hicks [1911] 2 KB 786 (CA) 188, 189
Chappell v Times Newspapers Ltd [1975] ICR 145 (CA) 198
Charles Rickards Ltd v Oppenhaim [1950] 1 KB 616 (CA) 135, 149
Cheikh Boutros Selim El-Khoury v Ceylon Shipping Lines Ltd (The 'Madeleine') [1967] 2 Lloyd's Rep 224 (Com Ct) 81, 82
Cherry v Thompson (1871–72) LR 7 QB 573 29
Chilean Nitrate Sales Corp v Marine Transportation Co Ltd & Pansuiza Compania de Navègacion SA; Marine Transportation Co Ltd v Pansuiza Compania de Navègacion SA (The 'Hermosa') [1982] 1 Lloyd's Rep 570 (CA) 40, 59, 74, 76, 84, 91, 222, 279
China National Foreign Trade Transportation Corp v Evlogia Shipping Co SA of Panama (The 'Mihalios Xilas') [1979] 1 WLR 1018 (HL) 100, 124
Christie & Vesey Ltd v Maatschappij Tot Exploitatie Van Schepen en Andere Zaken, Helvetia NV (The 'Helvetia-S') [1960] 1 Lloyd's Rep 540 (Com Ct) 81
City of London v Goree (1677) 2 Lev 174, 83 ER 505 32
Clarke v Dickson (1858) El Bl & El 148, 120 ER 463 40
Clarkson Booker Ltd v Andjel [1964] 2 QB 775 (CA) 124
Clayton v Oliver [1930] AC 209 (HL) 160
Clea Shipping Corp v Bulk Oil International Ltd (The 'Alaskan Trader') (No 2) [1984] 1 All ER 129 (QB) 195, 200, 203, 206, 211
Clough v London & North Western Railway Co (1871) LR 7 Ex 26 (EC) 125, 135
Cockburn v Alexander (1848) 6 CB 791, 136 ER 1459 182
Coggs v Barnard (1703) 2 Ld Ray 909, 92 ER 107 32
Combe v Combe [1951] 2 KB 215 (CA) 150
Compania Financiera Soleada SA v Hamoor Tanker Corp Inc (The Borag) [1981] 1 WLR 274, [1981] 1 Lloyd's Rep 483 (CA) 178
Concord Trust v The Law Debenture Trust Corp [2005] UKHL 27, [2005] 1 WLR 1591 ....38, 69

Continental Contractors Ltd and Ernest Beck & Co Ltd v Medway Oil & Storage Co Ltd (1925) 23 Ll L Rep 124 (CA) 61, 99
Continental Contractors Ltd and Ernest Beck & Co Ltd v Medway Oil & Storage Co Ltd (1926) 25 Ll L Rep 288 (HL) 61
Cornwall v Henson [1900] 2 Ch 298 (CA) 54
Cort v Ambergate Nottingham and Boston and Eastern Junction Railway Company (1851) 17 QB 127, 117 ER 1229 ....19, 101, 103, 106
Cussons v Skinner (1843) 11 M & W 161, 152 ER 758 ....89, 90
Cyril Leonard & Co v Simo Securities Trust Ltd [1972] 1 WLR 80 (CA) 90, 121
D & C Builders v Rees [1966] 2 QB 617 (CA) 150
Dalkia Utilities Services Plc v Celtech International Ltd [2006] EWHC 63 (Comm), [2006] 1 Lloyd's Rep 599 ....57, 71, 118
Dampskibsselskabet 'Norden' A/S v Andres & Cie SA [2003] EWHC 84 (Comm), [2003] 1 Lloyd's Rep 287 178
Danube & Black Sea Railway & Kustendjie Harbour Co Ltd v Xenos (1863) 11 CB NS 152, 142 ER 753 ....23, 117, 132
Davidson v Gwynne (1810) 12 East 381, 104 ER 149 70
Davis Contractors Ltd v Fareham Urban DC [1956] AC 696 (HL) 33, 37, 124
De Bernardy v Harding (1853) 8 Exch 822, 155 ER 1586 ....11, 120
De Medina v Norman (1842) 9 M & W 820, 152 ER 347 60
Decro-Wall International SA v Practitioners in Marketing Ltd [1971] 1 WLR 361 (CA) 49, 55, 118, 196, 199, 218
Deeny v Gooda Walker (No 3) [1995] 1 WLR 1206 (Com Ct) 163
Denmark Productions Ltd v Boscobel Productions Ltd [1969] 1 QB 699 (CA) 90, 120, 198, 218
Denton v Great Northern Ply Co (1856) 5 El & Bl 860, 119 ER 701 32
Dietman v Brent LBC [1987] ICR 737 (QB) 117, 197, 208
Dione, The (See *Alma Shipping v Mantovani*)
Doctor Grenville v The College of Physicians (1796) 12 Mod 386, 88 ER 1398 89
Domb v Isoz [1980] Ch 548 (CA) 117
Dunn v Sayles (1844) 5 QB 685, 114 ER 1408 20
Dynamic, The (See *Ocean Marine v Koch*)
Earls Terrace Properties Ltd v Nilsson Design Ltd [2004] EWHC 136 (TCC), [2004] BLR 273 179
Edwards Re ex p Chalmers (1872–73) LR 8 Ch App 289 (CA) 19, 64, 106
Ehrensperger v Anderson (1848) 3 Exch 148, 154 ER 793 ....59, 120
Elderton v Emmens (1853) 13 CB 495, 138 ER 1292 ....20, 21, 32
Elena d'Amico, The (See *Koch Marine v D'Amica*)
Ellen v Topp (1851) 6 Exch 424, 155 ER 609 106
Ellis & Co's Trustee v Dixon-Johnson [1924] 2 Ch 451 (CA) 70, 115, 168
Embiricos v Sydney Reid & Co [1914] 3 KB 45 86
Entores v Miles Far East Corp [1955] 2 QB 327 (CA) 120
Erlanger v New Sombrero Phosphate Co (1877–78) LR 3 App Cas 1218 (HL) 40
Essex Line Ltd v Societe Charbonniere de Reception en Commun [1939] 64 Ll L Rep 295 (KB) 57
Establissements Chainbaux SARL v Harbormaster Ltd [1955] 1 Lloyd's Rep 303 (QB) 101

Ets Soules & Cie v International Trade Development Co Ltd [1980] 1 Lloyd's Rep 129 (CA)....160
Evening Standard Co Ltd v Henderson [1987] ICR 588 (CA)....208
Federal Commerce & Navigation Ltd v Molena Alpha Inc [1979] AC 757 (HL)....47, 48, 49, 58, 72, 83, 222
Fenton Insurance Co Ltd v Gothaer Versicherungsbank VVaG [1991] 1 Lloyd's Rep 172 (Com Ct)....24, 77
Fercometal Sarl v MSC Mediterranean Shipping Co SA (The 'Simona') [1989] AC 788 (HL)....81, 95, 99, 104, 134, 149, 187
Fibrosa Spolka Akcyjna v Fairbairn Lawson Combe Barbour Ltd [1943] AC 32 (HL)....12, 156
Financial Techniques (Planning Services) Ltd v Hughes [1981] IRLR 32 (CA)....58
Financings Ltd v Baldock [1963] 2 QB 104 (CA)....80
First National Bank v Thompson [1996] Ch 231 (CA)....40
Ford v Tiley (1827) 6 B & C 325, 108 ER 472; [1827] 5 LJR 171....17, 60
Forsikringsaktieselskapet Vesta v Butcher [1989] AC 852 (CA)....186
Fratelli Sorrentino v Buerger [1915] 3 KB 367 (CA)....64
Freeth v Burr (1874) LR 9 CP 208....52, 53, 54, 55, 66
Frost v Knight (1871–72) LR 7 Ex 111 (EC)....24, 27, 28, 34, 35, 115, 129, 130, 160, 171, 175, 177, 218
Garnac Grain Co Inc v HMF Faure & Fairclough Ltd [1968] AC 1130 (HL)....57, 117, 118, 168
Gator Shipping Corp v Trans-Asiatic Oil Ltd SA and Occidental Shipping Establishment (The 'Odenfeld') [1978] 2 Lloyd's Rep 357 (Com Ct)....120, 196, 199, 200, 207, 208, 211, 213
Gebruder Metelmann GmbH & Co v NBR (London) Ltd [1984] 1 Lloyd's Rep 614 (CA)....170
Geipel v Smith (1872) LR 7 QB 404....87, 181
Gilbert Ash (Northern) Ltd v Modern Engineering (Bristol) Ltd [1974] AC 689 (HL)....155
Glencore Grain Rotterdam BV v Lebanese Organisation for International Commerce (The 'Lorico') [1997] 2 Lloyd's Rep 386 (CA)....91, 101, 149
Golden Strait Corp v Nippon Yusen Kubishka Kaisha (The 'Golden Victory') [2007] UKHL 12, [2007] 2 AC 353....160, 177–82, 225
Golding v London & Edinburgh Insurance Co Ltd (1932) 43 Ll L Rep 487 (CA)....30
Goodhart v Hyett (1883) 25 Ch D 182....219
Goodman v Pocock (1850) 15 QB 576, 117 ER 577....11, 121, 126
Great Peace Shipping Ltd v Tsavliris Salvage (International) Ltd (The 'Great Peace') [2002] EWCA Civ 1407, [2003] QB 679....37
Greenaway Harrison Ltd v Wiles [1994] IRLR 380 (EAT)....78
Greenhalgh v Mallard [1947] 2 All ER 255 (CA)....36
Gregos, The (See *Torvald v Arni Maritime*)
Griffith v Selby (1854) 9 Exch 393, 156 ER 167....106

Gulf Agri Trade Fzco v Aston Agro Industraial AG [2008] EWHC 1252 (Comm), [2008] 2 Lloyd's Rep 376 ....48, 61, 67
Gunton v Richmond-upon-Thames LBC [1981] Ch 448 (CA) 53, 78, 161, 182, 197, 198, 199
Guy-Pell v Foster [1930] 2 Ch 169 (CA) 34, 93, 118
Hadley v Baxendale (1854) 9 Exch 341, 156 ER 145 168
Halkett v Earl of Dudley [1907] 1 Ch 590 135
Hammersely v De Biel (1845) 12 Cl & Fin 45, 8 ER 1312 32
Hansa Nord, The (See *Cehave v Bremer Handelsgesellschaft*)
Harnor v Groves (1855) 15 CB 667, 139 ER 587 142
Haseltine Lake & Co v Dowler [1981] ICR 222 (EAT) 78
Hatten Wyatt Solicitors v Mamedu (unreported, EAT, 20 November 2007) 20
Hazelmoor, The (See *Anchor Line v Keith Rowell*)
HB Property Developments Ltd v Secretary of State for the Environment (1998) 78 P & CR 108 (CA) 125
Heisler v Anglo-Dal Ltd [1954] 1 WLR 1273 (CA) 91
Helvetia-S, The (See *Christie & Vesey v Maatschappij*)
Henderson v Henderson (1843) 3 Hare 100, 67 ER 313 36
Henderson-Williams (t/a F Henderson-Williams & Co) v Davis (unreported, CA, 17 June 1999) 36
Hermosa, The (See *Chilean Nitrate v Marine Transportation*)
Heyman v Darwin Ltd [1942] AC 350 (HL) 24, 30, 40, 59, 122, 124
HIH Casualty & General Insurance Ltd v Axa Corporate Solutions [2002] 2 All ER (Comm) 1053 (CA) 144
Hill v Parsons [1972] Ch 305 (CA) 198, 208
Hitchin v Campbell (1746–1779) 2 Black W 827, 96 ER 487 126
Hoare v Rennie (1859) 5 H & N 19, 157 ER 1083 54
Hochster v De la Tour (1853) 2 El & Bl 678, 118 ER 922 ....1, 9–22, 24, 27, 32, 33, 54, 120, 121, 129, 156, 161–62, 171, 181, 220–21
Holland v Bennett [1902] 1 KB 867 (CA) 29
Holt & Anor v Faulks & Anor [2001] BCC 50 (Ch) 64
Honck v Muller (1881) 7 QBD 92 (CA) 54
Hongkong Fir Shipping Co Ltd v Kawasaki Kisen Kaisha Ltd [1962] 2 QB 26 (CA) 49, 63, 70–71, 87, 199
Hounslow LBC v Twickenham Garden Developments Ltd [1971] Ch 233 ....196, 206
Howard v Pickford Tool Co Ltd [1951] 1 KB 417 (CA) 24, 30, 141, 198
HSS Hire Services Group plc v BMB Builders Merchants Ltd, Grafton Group (UK) plc [2004] EWHC 2013 (QB) 40, 64, 183
Hulle v Heightman (1802) 2 East 145, 102 ER 324 121
Hunt v Silk (1804) 5 East 449, 102 ER 1142 142
Huntington v Imagine Group Holdings Ltd [2008] EWCA Civ 159, [2008] All ER (D) 40 (Feb) 57
Hussey v Eels [1990] 2 QB 227 (CA) 179
Hvalfangerselskapet Polaris A/S v Unilever Ltd, Lever Bros Ltd (1932) 42 Ll L Rep 215 (CA) 58, 115
Hyundai Heavy Industries Co Ltd v Papadopoulos [1980] 1 WLR 1129 (HL) 35
Imperial Group Pension Trust Ltd v Imperial Tobacco Ltd [1991] 1 WLR 589 (Ch) 32

Inchbald v The Western Neilgherry Coffee, Tea, and Cinchona Plantation Co Ltd (1864) 17 CB NS 733, 144 ER 293 ....19, 106
Insurance Corp of the Channel Islands, Royal Insurance (UK) Ltd v Royal Hotel Ltd [1998] Lloyd's Rep IR 151 (Com Ct) 143
Internet Broadcasting Corp v MAR LLC [2009] EWHC 844 (Ch), [2009] All ER (D) 177 (Apr) 72
Interoffice Telephones Ltd v Robert Freeman Co Ltd [1958] 1 QB 190 (CA) 162
Irani v Southampton and South West Hampshire Health Authority [1985] ICR 590 (Ch) 208
Ivory v Palmer [1975] ICR 340 (CA) 117, 208
J Rosenthal & Sons Ltd v Esmail [1965] 1 WLR 1117 (HL) 53
Jackson v Union Marine Insurance Co Ltd (1874) LR 10 CP 125 (EC) 198
Jaks (UK) Ltd v Cera Investment Bank SA [1998] 2 Lloyd's Rep 89 (QB) 57
James Schaffer LD v Findlay Durham & Brodie [1953] 1 WLR 106 (CA) 58, 66, 78
James v Heim Gallery Ltd (1980) 41 P & CR 269 (CA) 144
Jewelowski v Propp [1944] KB 510 172
John S Darbyshire, The (See *Albion Sugar v William Tankers*)
Johnson v Agnew [1980] AC 367 (HL) 41, 122, 127, 137, 143, 178, 218
Johnstone v Milling (1886) 16 QBD 460 (CA) 24, 54, 57, 68, 70, 115, 117, 129, 159
Jones v Barkley (1781) 2 Doug 684, 99 ER 434 ....18, 19, 106
Kaines (UK) Ltd v Osterreichische Warrenhandelsgesellschaft Austrowaren Gesellschaft GmbH [1993] 2 Lloyd's Rep 1 (CA) 156, 170, 172, 177, 178
Kammins Ballrooms Co Ltd v Zenith Investments (Torquay) Ltd [1971] AC 850 (HL) 101, 124, 125
Kanchenjunga, The (See *Motor Oil v Shipping Corp of India*)
Keys v Harwood (1846) 2 CB 905, 135 ER 1201 11
Kingston v Preston cited in (1773) 2 Doug 689, 691, 99 ER 437, 438 (Lord Mansfield), *sub nom Anon* (1773) Lofft 194, 98 ER 606 106
Koch Marine Inc v D'Amica Societa di Navigazione ARL (The 'Elena d'Amico') [1980] 1 Lloyd's Rep 75 (Com Ct) 172, 178
Laird v Pim (1841) 7 M & W 474, 151 ER 852 19
Lavarack v Woods of Colchester Ltd [1967] 1 QB 278 (CA) 173, 179, 183, 184, 185, 188
Lawrence and Another Assignees of W Okill, a Bankrupt v Knowles (1839) 5 Bing NC 399, 132 ER 1152 106
Lefevre v White [1990] 1 Lloyd's Rep 569 (QB) 120
Leigh v Paterson (1818) 8 Taunt 540, 129 ER 493 ....124, 171
Lewis v Motorworld Carages Ltd [1986] ICR 157 (CA) 32, 76, 85
Lilley v Elwin (1848) 11 QB 742, 116 ER 652 11
Littlehampton Book Services Ltd v Dorling Kindersley Ltd (unreported, Com Ct, 17 May 2001), [2001] All ER (D) 224 (May) 75, 93, 182
Liverpool CC v Irwin [1977] AC 239 (HL) 33, 38
Lombard North Central plc v Butterworth [1987] QB 527 (CA) 41, 80
London Transport Executive v Clarke [1981] ICR 355 (CA) 161, 198, 199
Longden v British Coal Corp [1998] AC 653 (HL) 178
Lorico, The (See *Glencore Grain v Lebanese Organisation*)
Lovelock v Franklyn (1846) 8 QB 371, 115 ER 916 ....10, 16, 21
Lumley v Gye (1852) 2 El & Bl 216, 118 ER 749 27

Lumley v Wagner (1852) 1 De GM & G 604, 42 ER 687 208
M & J Polymers Ltd v Imerys Minerals Ltd [2008] EWHC 344 (Comm), [2008] 1 All ER (Comm) 893 ....56, 77
Mackay v Dick (1881) 6 App Cas 251 (HL) 198
Madeleine, The (See *Cheikh Boutros v Ceylon Shipping*)
Mahmud v Bank of Credit and Commerce International SA [1998] AC 20 (HL) 32
Main's Case, Sir Anthony (1596) 5 Co Rep 20b, 77 ER 80 ....15–19, 21, 27, 31, 60, 101, 106, 220–1
Manx Electricity v J P Morgan Chase Bank [2003] EWCA Civ 1324, [2003] BLR 477 ....29, 157, 160
Maple Flock Co Ltd v Universal Furniture Products (Wembley) Ltd [1934] 1 KB 148 (CA) 53, 55, 56, 74, 76
Marbé v George Edwardes [1928] 1 KB 269 (CA) 160
Maredelanto Compania Naviera SA v BergbauHandel GMBH (The 'Mihalis Angelos') [1971] 1 QB 164 (CA) 33, 35, 78, 81, 90, 118, 174–7, 180, 182
Marks v Lilley [1959] 1 WLR 749 (Ch) 217
Marsh v National Autistic Society [1993] ICR 453 (EAT) 198
Masood v Zahoor [2008] EWHC 1034 (Ch) 200
Matthews v Smallwood [1910] 1 Ch 777 ....124, 125
Measures Bros Ltd v Measures [1910] 2 Ch 248 (CA) 64
Melachrino v Nickoll & Knight [1920] 1 KB 693 ....163, 169, 171, 178, 179
Mercer v Whall (1845) 5 QB 447, 114 ER 1318 90
Mersey Steel and Iron Co v Naylor Benzon & Co (1884) 9 App Cas 434 (HL) 50, 52, 53–5, 59, 67, 70
Mess v Duffus (1901) 6 Com Cas 165 64
Michael v Hart & Co [1902] 1 KB 482 (CA) 34, 168, 185
Mihalios Xilas, The (See *China National Foreign Trade Transportation v Evlogia Shipping*)
Mihalis Angelos, The (See *Maredelanto Compania Naviera SA v BergbauHandel*)
Millar's Karri and Jarrah Co (1902) v Weddel, Turner & Co [1908–10] All ER Rep Ext 1274 (KB) 53, 55
Miller v Minister of Pensions [1947] 2 All ER 372 (KB) 77, 188
Millett v Van Heek and Co [1921] 2 KB 369 (CA) 34, 170
Ministry of Sound (Ireland) Ltd v World Online Ltd [2003] EWHC 2178 (Ch), [2003] 2 All ER (Comm) 823 ....196, 197, 200, 202, 204–5, 207, 213–4
Moorcock, The (1889) 14 PD 64 (CA) 33, 38
Morgan v Bain (1874) LR 10 CP 15 64
Morrow v Safeway Stores Ltd [2002] IRLR 9 (EAT) 32
Moschi v Lep Air Services Ltd [1973] AC 331 (HL) 35, 120
Motor Oil Hellas (Corinth) Refineries SA v Shipping Corp of India, (The 'Kanchenjunga') [1990] 1 Lloyd's Rep 391 (HL) 124, 125, 126, 135, 143, 149, 151, 159
Ms E A Nelson v Kingston Cables Distributors Ltd, Independent, 12 June 2000 (EAT) 40, 78
MSC Mediterranean Shipping Co SA v BRE-Metro Ltd [1985] 2 Lloyd's Rep 239 (Com Ct) 120

Mulvenna v Royal Bank of Scotland plc [2003] EWCA Civ 1112, [2003] All ER (D) 183, 184
Never-Stop Railway (Wembley) Ltd v British Empire Exhibition (1924) Inc [1926] Ch 877 78
New Zealand Shipping Co Ltd v Société des Ateliers et Chantiers de France [1919] AC 1 (HL) 124
Nichols v Raynbred (1615) Hob 89, 80 ER 238....204
Nickoll & Knight v Ashton Edridge & Co (1900) 2 QB 298....171
North Down Hotels Ltd v Province-Wide Filling Stations Ltd [1993] NI 261 (Ch)....144
North Sea Energy Holdings NV v Petroleum Authority of Thailand [1999] 1 Lloyd's Rep 483 (CA)....100, 184
North-Western Cachar Tea Co Ltd v British & Beningtons Ltd (1922) 10 Ll L Rep 381 (CA)....35
Norwest Holst Group Administration Ltd v Harrison [1985] ICR 668 (CA).....35, 53, 116–7
Norwich Union Life Insurance Society v Low Profile Fashions Ltd [1992] 1 EGLR 86 (CA)....202
Nottingham Building Society v Eurodynamics Systems Plc [1995] FSR 605 (CA)....92
O'Neil v Armstrong, Mitchell & Co [1895] 2 QB 418 (CA) 63
Ocean Marine Navigation Ltd v Koch Carbon Inc (The 'Dynamic') [2003] EWHC 1936 (Comm), [2003] 2 Lloyd's Rep 693....203, 207, 211, 213, 216
Odenfeld, The (See *Gator Shipping v Trans-Asiatic Oil*)
Oliver Ashworth (Holdings) Ltd v Ballard (Kent) Ltd [2000] Ch 12 (CA)....100, 124–6, 153
Omilaju v Waltham Forest LBC (No 2) [2004] EWCA Civ 1493, [2005] ICR 481....85
Omnium v Sutherland [1919] 1 KB 618 (CA)....61
Page One Records Ltd v Britton [1968] 1 WLR 157 (Ch)....208
Panchaud Freres SA v Etablissements General Grain Co [1970] 1 Lloyd's Rep 53 (CA)....91, 101, 149
Paula Lee Ltd v Robert Zehil Ltd [1983] 2 All ER 390 (QB) 184
Payzu Ltd v Saunders [1919] 2 KB 581 (CA)....54
Pearl Mill Co Ltd v Ivy Tannery Co Ltd [1919] 1 KB 78....126
Peeters v Opie (1671) 2 Wms Saund 35, 85 ER 1144....19, 106
Perar BV v General Surety & Guarantee Co Ltd [1994] 43 Con LR 110 (CA)....64
Peter Dumenil & Co Ltd v James Ruddin Ltd [1953] 1 WLR 815 (CA) 59
Peyman v Lanjani [1985] Ch 457 (CA) 125, 148
Phillpotts v Evans (1839) 5 M & W 475, 151 ER 200....10, 18, 171
Photo Production Ltd v Securicor Transport Ltd [1980] AC 827 (HL) 28, 35, 49, 71, 72, 122, 123, 159
Planché v Colburn (1831) 8 Bing 14, 131 ER 305; (1831) 5 Carr & P, 172 ER 876....11, 12, 13, 22, 156, 221
Portaga Comercio Internacional SA v Federative Republic of Brazil (unreported, Com Ct, 5 February 1998)....78, 199
Post Chaser, The (See *Societe Italo-Belge v Palm*)
Post Office v Roberts [1980] IRLR 347 (EAT) 32
Poussard v Spiers & Pond (1876) 1 QBD 410 ....198, 199
Prickett v Badger (1856) 1 CB NS 296, 140 ER 123 11
Proctor & Gamble (Health and Beauty Care) Ltd v Carrier Holdings Ltd [2003] EWHC 83 (TCC), [2003] BLR 255....156

Pro Victor, The (See *SK Shipping v Petroexport*)
PT Berlian Laju Tanker Tbk v Nuse Shipping Ltd (The 'Aktor') [2008] EWHC 1330 (Comm), [2008] 2 All ER (Comm) 784, [2008] 2 Lloyd's Rep 246 83
Puerto Buitrago, The (See *Attica Sea Carriers v Ferrostaal Poseidon*)
R Pagnan & Fratelli v Corbisa Industrial Agropacuaria Limitada [1970] 1 WLR 1306 (CA) 179
R v East Berkshire Health Authority, ex parte Walsh [1984] ICR 743 (CA) 198
Rees v Lines (1837) 8 Carr & P 126, 173 ER 427 59
Regent International Hotels (UK) Ltd v Pageguide Ltd (unreported, QB, 6 March 1985) 199
Reichman v Beveridge [2006] EWCA Civ 1659, [2006] All ER (D) 207, 208, 209, 211, 213
Reid v Explosives Co Ltd (1887) LR 19 QBD 264 (CA) 64
Reid v Hoskins (1855) 5 El & Bl 729, 119 ER 653 ....22, 23, 156, 159, 221
Rhymney Rail Co v Brecon & Merthyr Tydfil Rail Co [1900-03] All ER Rep 582 (CA), (1900) 69 LJ Ch 813 70
Rice (t/a Garden Guardian) v Great Yarmouth BC [2003] TCLR 1, (2001) 3 LGLR 4 (CA) 42
Richardson v Dunn (1841) 2 QB 218, 114 ER 85 130
Ridgway v The Hungerford Market Co (1835) 3 Ad & E 171, 111 ER 378 89
Rigby v Ferodo Ltd [1988] ICR 29 (HL) 198
Ripley v McClure (1849) 4 Exch 345, 154 ER 1245 ....10, 18, 101
Robert A Munro & Co v Meyer [1930] 2 KB 312 55
Robert Cort & Son Ltd v Charman [1981] ICR 816 (EAT) 197
Robophone Facilities v Blank [1966] 1 WLR 1428 (CA) 155, 162
Robson & Sharpe v Drummond (1831) 2 B & Ad 303, 109 ER 1156 ....61, 63
Roper v Johnson (1873) LR 8 CP 167 ....34, 168, 172
Roth & Co v Taysen Townsend & Co (1895) 1 Com Cas 240 (QB) 171
Royscot Commercial Leasing Ltd v Ismail (unreported, CA, 29 April 1993) 210
Rubel Bronze & Metal Co Ltd v Vos, re an arbitration [1918] 1 KB 315 ....56, 70
Rust v Abbey Life Assurance Co Ltd [1979] 2 Lloyd's Rep 334 (CA) 120
RV Ward Ltd v Bignall [1967] 1 QB 534 (CA) 120
Safehaven Investments Inc v Springbok Ltd (1996) 71 P & CR 59 (Ch) 136, 224
Sanders v Ernest A Neale Ltd [1974] ICR 565 (NIRC) 197
Sands v Clarke (1849) 8 CB 751, 137 ER 703 11
Santa Clara, The (See *Vitol v Norelf*)
Sarker v South Tees Acute Hospitals NHS Trust [1997] ICR 673 (EAT) 20
Scandinavian Trading Co A/B v Zodiac Petroleum SA & William Hudson Ltd (The 'Al Hofuf') [1981] 1 Lloyd's Rep 81 (QB) 57, 90, 94
Scandinavian Trading Tanker Co AB v Flota Petrolera Ecuatoriana (The 'Scaptrade') [1983] QB 529 (CA), [1983] 1 Lloyd's Rep 146 203
The Scaptrade (See *Scandinavian Trading Tanker v Flota*)
Sheffield v Conrad (1987) 22 Con LR 108 (CA) 90, 91
Shell UK Ltd v Lostock Garage Ltd [1976] 1 WLR 1187 (CA) 38
Shindler v Northern Raincoat Co Ltd [1960] 1 WLR 1038 (Manchester Assizes) 163, 210
Shirlaw v Southern Foundries (1926) Ltd [1939] 2 KB 206 (CA) 38
Short v Stone (1846) 8 QB 358, 115 ER 911 ....10, 17
Shuttleworth v Garnet (1688) 3 Mod 239, 87 ER 156 32

Shyam Jewellers Ltd v Cheeseman [2001] EWCA Civ 1818, [2001] All ER (D) 423 (Nov) 56, 74, 75
Simona, The (See *Fercometal Sarl v MSC Mediterranean Shipping*)
Sinason-Teicher Inter-American Grain Corp v Oilcakes and Oilseeds Trading Co Ltd [1954] 1 WLR 1394 (CA) 78, 101
Sir Anthony Main's Case (See *Main's Case*)
SK Shipping (S) PTE Ltd v Petroexport Ltd (The 'Pro Victor') [2009] EWHC 2974 (Comm) 61, 63, 75–6, 78, 79, 85
Slade's Case (1602) 4 Co Rep 91a, 76 ER 1072........32
Smethurst v Mitchell (1859) 1 El & El 622, 120 ER 1043........135
Smith v Butler [1900] 1 QB 694 (CA)........42
Smith v Hodson (1790) 4 TR 211, 100 ER 979........145
Societe Italo-Belge pour le Commerce et l'Industrie v Palm and Vegetable Oils (Malyasia) Sdn Bhd (The 'Post Chaser') [1982] 1 All ER 19 (Com Ct)........150
Societe Maritime et Commerciale v Venus Steam Shipping Co Ltd (1904) 9 Com Cas 289........78
Solholt, The (See *Sotiros Shipping v Sameiet Solholt*)
Sorgato v Khalili (unreported, QB, 30 July 1992)........210
Sotiros Shipping Inc v Sameiet Solholt (The 'Solholt') [1983] 1 Lloyd's Rep 605 (CA)........171, 210
South West Water Services Ltd v International Computers Ltd [1999] BLR 420, [2001] Lloyd's Rep PN 353 (TCC)........70
Spettabile Consorzio Veneziano di Armamento E Navigazione v Northumberland Shipbuilding Co Ltd [1918-19] All ER Rep 963 (CA)........53, 57, 78
Stanton v Richardson (1871-72) LR 7 CP 421........63
Startup v Cortazzi (1835) 2 Cr, M & R 165, 150 ER 71........171
State Securities plc v Initial Industry Ltd (unreported, Ch, 29 January 2004), [2004] All ER (D) 317 (Jan)........80
State Trading Corp of India Ltd v M Golodetz Ltd [1989] 2 Lloyd's Rep 277 (CA)........100, 120, 122
Stevens & Cutting Ltd v Anderson [1990] 1 EGLR 95, [1990] 11 EG 70 (CA)........125
Stocznia Gdanska SA v Latvian Shipping Co, Latreefer Inc [1995] 2 Lloyd's Rep 592 (Com Ct)........133, 203, 215
Stocznia Gdanska SA v Latvian Shipping Co, Latreefer Inc [1996] 2 Lloyd's Rep 132 (CA)........133, 215, 216
Stocznia Gdanska SA v Latvian Shipping Co, Latreefer Inc [1997] 2 Lloyd's Rep 228........118, 120, 134, 135, 138, 143, 146
Stocznia Gdanska SA v Latvian Shipping Co, Latreefer Inc [1998] 1 WLR 574 (HL)........36, 133, 134, 155, 215
Stocznia Gdanska SA v Latvian Shipping Co, Latreefer Inc [2001] 1 Lloyd's Rep 537 (Com Ct)........58, 118, 134, 135, 138, 140, 148, 209
Stocznia Gdanska SA v Latvian Shipping Co, Latreefer Inc [2002] EWCA Civ 889, [2002] 2 All ER (Comm) 768........80, 133, 134, 135, 138, 139, 141, 143, 146

Stocznia Gdynia SA v Gearbulk Holdings Ltd [2009] EWCA Civ 75, [2009] 1 Lloyd's Rep 461 ....118, 142, 155
Sudan Import & Export Co (Khartoum) Ltd v Societe Generale de Compensation [1958] 1 Lloyd's Rep 310 (CA) 141, 145, 159
Suisse Atlantique Société d'Armement Maritime SA v NV Rotterdamsche Kolen Centrale [1967] 1 AC 361 (HL) 83, 160
Superhulls Cover Case, The (See *Youell v Bland Welch*)
Sweet & Maxwell v Universal News [1964] 3 All ER 30 (CA) 58
Synge v Synge [1894] 1 QB 466 (CA) 170
Talbot v Berkshire CC [1994] QB 290 (CA) 36
Taylor v Caldwell (1863) 3 B & S 826, 122 ER 826 33
Taylor v National Union of Seaman [1967] 1 WLR 532 (Ch) 208
Taylor v Oakes Roncoroni & Co [1922] All ER Rep Ext 866, (1922) 27 Com Cas 261 (CA) 55, 90, 91, 95–7, 100, 120, 125, 127, 133, 223
Technocrats International Inc v Fredic Ltd [2004] EWHC 692 (QB), [2005] 1 BCLC 467 28
Telephone Rentals plc v Burges Salmon & Co (unreported, CA, 9 April 1987) 206
Temperton v Russell [1893] 1 QB 715 (CA) 27
Tenax Steamship Co v Owners of the Motor Vessel Brimnes (The 'Brimnes') [1975] QB 929 (CA) 120
Texaco Ltd v The Eurogulf Shipping Co Ltd [1987] 2 Lloyd's Rep 541 (Com Ct) 78
Thomas Marshall (Exports) Ltd v Guinle [1979] Ch 227 ....65, 83, 197
Thorpe v Fasey [1949] Ch 649 ....66, 72
Tilcon Ltd v Land & Real Estate Investments Ltd [1987] 1 WLR 46 (CA) 29, 118
Toller v Law Accident Insurance Society Ltd (1936) 55 Ll L Rep 258 (CA) 40
Tool Metal Manufacturing Co Ltd v Tungsten Electric Co Ltd (No 3) [1955] 1 WLR 761 (HL) 151
Torvald Klaveness A/S v Arni Maritime Corp (The 'Gregos') [1994] 1 WLR 1465 (HL) 71, 78, 83
Trade and Transport Inc v Iino Kaiun Kaisha Ltd (The 'Angelia') [1973] 1 WLR 210 (QB) 63, 73, 89, 176
Trans Trust SPRL v Danubian Trading Co LD [1952] 2 QB 297 (CA) 163
Trollope v Caplan [1936] 2 KB 382 (CA) 189
Turnor v Goodwin (1714) Fort 145, 92 ER 796 106
UCB Bank plc v Hepherd Winstanley and Pugh, The Times, 25 August 1999 (CA) 186
United Australia Ltd v Barclays Bank Ltd [1941] AC 1 (HL) 126
United Dominions Trust (Commercial) Ltd v Ennis [1968] 1 QB 54 (CA) 142, 155
Universal Cargo Carriers Corp v Citati (No 1) [1957] 2 QB 401 ....1, 59, 61, 63, 65, 73, 75, 79, 83, 86–92, 121, 160, 175, 223
Universal Cargo Carriers Corp v Pedro Citati (No 2) [1957] 2 Lloyd's Rep 311 (Com Ct) 89
Urquhart Lindsay & Co Ltd v Eastern Bank Ltd [1922] 1 KB 318 ....54, 159
Veracruz I, The (See *Veracruz Transportation v VC Shipping*)
Veracruz Transportation Inc v VC Shipping Co Inc and Den Norske Bank A/S (The 'Veracruz I') [1992] 1 Lloyd's Rep 353 (CA) 219

Victoria, The (See *Carswell v Collard*)
Vine v National Dock Labour Board [1957] AC 488 (HL)....197, 198
Vitol SA v Norelf Ltd (The 'Santa Clara') [1996] AC 800 (HL)....116–20
Vynior's Case (1609) 8 Co Rep 81b, 77 ER 597....15, 32
Warburton v Storr (1825) 4 B & C 103, 107 ER 997....15, 16
Warlow v Harrison (1859) 1 El & El 309, 120 ER 925....32
Warner Brothers Pictures v Nelson [1937] 1 KB 209....208
Watts, Watts Ltd v Mitsui Ltd [1917] AC 227 (HL)....173
WE Cox Toner (International) Ltd v Crook [1981] IRLR 443 (EAT)....141
West v Stowel (1577) 2 Leo 154, 74 ER 437....204
Weston v Downes (1778) 1 Doug 23, 99 ER 19....12
White & Carter (Councils) Ltd v Harding (CA 21 May 1958)....193, 194, 196, 200–3, 205
Wilkinson v Verity (1871) LR 6 CP 206....23, 156
William Cory & Son Ltd v City of London Corp [1951] 2 KB 476 (CA)....38
Williams v Carwardine (1833) 5 Car & P 566, 172 ER 1101....120
Winch v Keely (1787) 1 TR 619, 99 ER 1284....27
Withers v General Theatre Corp Ltd [1933] 2 KB 536 (CA)....183
Withers v Reynolds (1831) 2 B & Ad 882, 109 ER 1370....19, 54, 106
WJ Alan & Co Ltd v El Nasr Export and Import Co [1972] 2 QB 189 (CA)....150
Woodar Investment Development Ltd v Wimpey Construction UK Ltd [1980] 1 WLR 277 (HL)....49, 50, 57, 58, 59, 60, 65, 78, 222
Woodhouse AC Israel Cocoa SA v Nigerian Produce Marketing Co Ltd [1972] AC 741 (HL)....148
Woods v WM Car Services (Peterborough) Ltd [1982] ICR 693 (CA)....32, 73
Wyvil v Stapleton (1724) 1 Str 615, 93 ER 735....19
Youell v Bland Welch & Co Ltd (the 'Superhulls Cover' Case) (No 2) [1990] 2 Lloyd's Rep 431 (Com Ct)....144
Yukong Line Ltd of Korea v Rendsburg Investments Corp of Liberia [1996] 2 Lloyd's Rep 604 (Com Ct)....125, 131, 132, 139, 141, 143, 144, 148, 224

Australia

Agricultural & Rural Finance v Gardiner [2008] HCA 57, (2008) 251 ALR 322....101, 124
Austral Standard Cables Pty Ltd v Walker Nominees Pty Ltd (1922) 26 NSWLR 524 (NSWCA)....150
Automatic Fire Sprinklers Proprietary Ltd v Watson (1946) 72 CLR 435 (HCA)....205
Bowes v Chaleyer (1923) 32 CLR 159 (HCA)....42
BP Refinery (Westernport) Pty Ltd v Shire of Hastings (1977) 180 CLR 266 (PC Australia)....38
Brisbane CC v A-G of Queensland [1979] AC 411, (1978) 19 ALR 681 (PC Australia)....36
Carr v JA Berriman Pty Ltd (1953) 89 CLR 327 (HCA)....48, 76, 130, 139
Champtaloup v Thomas [1976] 2 NSWLR 264 (NSWCA)....142
CIC Insurance Ltd v Bankstown Football Club Ltd (1994-1995) 8 ANZ Ins Cas 61-232 (NSWCA)....160

Coastal Estates Pty Ltd v Melevende [1965] VR 433 (SCV Full Ct)....................................125
Commonwealth of Australia, The v Amann Aviation Pty Ltd [1991] 174 CLR 64 (HCA)....................................170, 180, 184, 185, 188–91
Commonwealth of Australia, The v Verwayen [1990] 170 CLR 394 (HCA).......101, 126, 150
Craine v The Colonial Mutual Fire Insurance Co Ltd [1920] 28 CLR 305 (HCA)....................................141, 146
DTR Nominees Pty Ltd v Mona Homes Pty Ltd (1978) 138 CLR 423 (HCA) 48, 186
Farrow Mortgage Services Pty Ltd v Edgar (1993) 114 ALR 1 (FCA) 118
Finlayson v Finlayson (2002) 29 Fam LR 460 (FAMCA)....................................75
Foran v Wight [1989] 168 CLR 385 (HCA).................................... 80, 81, 96, 102–4, 107–9, 148, 150
GEC Marconi Systems Pty Ltd v BHP Information Technology Pty Ltd [2003] FCA 50 (2003) 128 FCR 1....................................124, 142
Hecec Australia Pty Ltd v Hydro-Electric Corp [1999] FCA 822, (1999) ATPR 46-196....................................24, 156
Henry Dean & Sons (Sydney) Ltd v P O'Day Pty Ltd (1927) 39 CLR 330 (HCA)....................................90
Holland v Wiltshire (1954) 90 CLR 409 (HCA) 117, 120
Immer (No 145) Pty Ltd v The United Church in Australia Property T rust (NSW) [1992–1993] 182 CLR 26 (HCA) 126, 141, 142
J & S Chan Pty Ltd v McKenzie [1994] ANZ ConvR 610 (ACTSC)....................................208
Koompahtoo Local Aboriginal Land Council v Sanpine Pty Ltd [2007] HCA 61, (2007) 233 CLR 115....................................41
Larking v Great Western (Nepean) Gravel Ltd (1940) 64 CLR 221 (HCA) 138
Larratt v Bankers & Traders' Insurance Co Ltd (1941) 41 SR (NSW) 215 (NSWSC) 142
Laurinda Pty Ltd v Capalaba Park Shopping Centre Pty Ltd (1989) 166 CLR 623 (HCA)....................................48
Legione v Hateley (1983) 152 CLR 406 (HCA) 148
Lion White Lead Ltd v Rogers (1918) 25 CLR 533 (HCA) 120
Luna Park (NSW) Ltd v Tramways Advertising Proprietary Ltd (1938) 61 CLR 286 (HCA)....................................33, 55
Mackenzie v Rees (1941) 65 CLR 1 (HCA)....................................164
Majik Markets Pty Ltd v S & M Motor Repairs Pty Ltd (No 1) (1987) 10 NSWLR 49 (NSWSC)....................................120
McDonald v Dennys Lascelles Ltd (1933) 48 CLR 457 (HCA)....................................122
McRae & Anor v Bolaro Pty Ltd [2000] VSCA 72 (unreported, 5 May 2000)..................136
McRae v Commonwealth Disposals Commission (1951) 84 CLR 377 (HCA) 189
Metro Meat Ltd v Fares Rural Co Pty Ltd [1985] 2 Lloyd's Rep 13 (PC Australia) 83
Net Parts International Pty Ltd v Kenoss Pty Ltd [2008] NSWCA 324 (unreported, 4 December 2008) 120
O'Connor v SP Bray Ltd (1936) 36 SR (NSW) 248 (NSWSC) 126
Ogle v Comboyuro Investments Pty Ltd [1976] 136 CLR 444 (HCA).........139, 143, 159, 218
Peter Turnbull & Co Pty Ltd v Mundus Trading Co (Australasia) Pty Ltd [1954] HCA 25, (1954) 90 CLR 235.................................... 1, 18, 32, 36, 102–4, 111, 115, 117, 150
Progressive Mailing House Pty Ltd v Tabali Pty Ltd (1985) 157 CLR 17 (HCA)....................................159, 167, 208

R v Clarke (1927) 40 CLR 227 (HCA) 120
Rawson v Hobbs [1961] 107 CLR 466 (HCA) 108, 118
Sargent v ASL Developments Ltd (1974) 131 CLR 634 (HCA) 124, 127, 142, 145, 146
Shepherd v Felt and Textiles of Australia Ltd (1931) 45 CLR 359 (HCA) 90
Shevill v Builders Licensing Board (1982) 149 CLR 620 (HCA) 80
Sunbird Plaza Pty Ltd v Maloney [1988] HCA 11, (1988) 166 CLR 245 .... 35, 90, 143, 159
Tramways Advertising Pty Ltd v Luna Park (NSW) Ltd (1938) 38 SR (NSW) 632 (NSWSC Full Ct) 33
Tropical Traders Ltd v Goonan (1964) 111 CLR 41 (HCA) 135, 145
Turner v Bladin (1951) 82 CLR 463 (HCA) 218
Turner v Labafox International Pty Ltd (1974) 131 CLR 660 (HCA) 125
Waltons Stores (Interstate) Ltd v Maher (1988) 164 CLR 387 (HCA) 150
Winterton Constructions Pty Ltd v Hambros Australia Ltd (1992) 39 FCR 97 (FCA) 64
Wood Factory Pty Ltd v Kiritos Pty Ltd (1985) 2 NSWLR 105 (NSWCA) 79, 120
Wright Prospecting Pty Ltd v Hancock Prospecting Pty Ltd (1) [2007] WASC 78 (27 March 2007) 35
YP Barley Producers Ltd v E C Robertson Pty Ltd [1927] VLR 194 (SC) 1, 94, 159

Scotland

Blyth v Scottish Liberal Club 1982 SC 140 (SD) 58
Edinburgh Grain Ltd (in liquidation) v Marshall Food Group Ltd 1999 SLT 15 (CSOH) 64
ERDC Construction Ltd v HM Love & Co 1994 SC 620 (SD) 156
Forslind v Bechely-Crundall 1922 SC (HL) 173, 1922 SLT 496 .... 9, 54, 62, 73, 76
Howie v Anderson (1848) 10 D 355 171
Hutchison v Graham's Executrix 2006 SCLR 587, 2006 GWD 14-259 (CSOH) 36
James McKelvie & Co v Murray & Co Ltd (1928) 31 Ll L Rep 80 (CSOH) 57
Langford & Co Ltd v Dutch 1952 SC 15 (CSIH) 18 .... 194, 205, 211
Miller Fabrications Ltd v J & D Pierce (Contracts) Ltd [2010] CSIH 27, 2010 GWD 15-283 68
Monklands DC v Ravenstone Securities 1980 SLT (Notes) 30 (CSOH) 29
Ross v MacFarlane (1893) 1 SLT 175 (CSOH), aff'd (1894) 1 SLT 463 (SD) 64
Salaried Staff London Loan Co Ltd v Swears & Wells Ltd 1985 SC 189, 1985 SLT 326 (CSIH) 203
White & Carter (Councils) Ltd v McGregor [1962] AC 413 (HL Sc), 1962 SC (HL) 1 .... 193–7, 199–203, 205, 209, 210, 211, 213–6, 226
White & Carter (Councils) Ltd v McGregor 1960 SC 276 (CSIH) 194

Canada

American National Red Cross v Geddes Bros (1920) 61 SCR 143 (SCC) 120
Asamera Oil Corp v Sea Oil & General Corp [1979] 1 SCR 633, (1978) 89 DLR (3d) 1 (SCC) 202
Connaught Laboratories Ltd v R [1978] FCJ No 605 (FCC) 50
Cromwell v Morris (1917) 34 DLR 305 (Alberta SC) 1

Highway Properties Ltd v Kelly, Douglas & Co Ltd (1971) 17 DLR (3d) 710 (SCC) 208
Kloepfer Wholesale Hardware & Automotive Co v Roy [1952] 2 SCR 465 (SCC) 218
McCallum v Zivojinovic (1977) 79 DLR (3d) 133, 16 OR (2d) 721 (CA) 48
McGibbon et al v Popoff [1977] 4 WWR 685 (BCSC) 218
Morrison-Knudsen Co Inc v British Columbia Hydro and Power Authority (1978) 85 DLR (3d) 186 (BCCA) 156
Pompeani v Bonik Inc (1997) 35 OR (3d) 417 (Ontario CA) 48
Roberto v Bumb [1943] 2 DLR 613 (Ontario CA) 218
Sanko Iris and Sanko Venus, The (See *Sanko Steamship v Eacom*)
Sanko Steamship Co v Eacom Timber Sales Ltd (The 'Sanko Iris' and 'Sanko Venus') (1986) 32 DLR (4th) 269, 8 BCLR (2d) 69 (BCSC), [1987] 1 Lloyd's Rep 487 ......48, 87
Saskatchewan River Bungalows Ltd v Maritime Life Assurance Co (1994) 115 DLR (4th) 478 (SCC) 149
Spirent Communications of Ottawa Ltd v Quake Technologies (Canada) Inc (2008) 291 DLR (4th) 163, 88 OR (3d) 721 (Ontario CA) 71, 84, 85
United Food and Commercial Workers International Union v Finnamore 2005 BCSC 1454, (2005) 143 ACWS (3d) 669 48

United States of America

Clark v Marsiglia 1 Denio 317 (NY 1845) 209
General American Tank Car Corp v Goree (No 2114) 296 F 32 (4th Cir 1924) 164
John A Nichols v The Scranton Steel Co 137 NY 471 (1893) 165
John Heard v Charles E Bowers 40 Mass 455 (1839) 60
Long Island Rail Road Co v Northville Industries Corp 362 NE (2d) 558 (1977) 164
Rockingham County v Luten Bridge Co 35 F 2d 301 (1929) 209
Roehm v Horst 178 US 1, 20 S Ct 780 (1900) 1, 34, 43, 165
Thomas J Daniels v Samuel F J Newton 114 Mass 530 (1874) 165

New Zealand

Brooklands Motor Co Ltd (in receivership) v Bridge Wholesale Acceptance Corp (Australia) Ltd (1994) 7 NZCLC 260 (HC) 9, 77
Chatfield v Jones [1990] 3 NZLR 285 (CA) 120, 143
Dymocks Franchise Systems (NSW) Pty Ltd v Todd [2002] UKPC 50, [2002] 2 All ER (Comm) 849 (PC New Zealand) 68
Hughes v Huppert [1991] 1 NZLR 474 (HC) 143
Ken & Ken Corp Ltd v Kenji Umezaki [2005] NZHC 479 77
Starlight Enterprises Ltd v Lapco Enterprises Ltd [1979] 2 NZLR 744 (CA) 9

Other Jurisdictions

A-G of Belize v Belize Telecom Ltd [2009] UKPC 11, [2009] 2 All ER 1127 (PC Belize) 38
Ajayi v RT Briscoe (Nigeria) Ltd [1964] 1 WLR 1326 (PC Nigeria) 151
AKAS Jamal v Moolla Dawood, Sons & Co [1916] 1 AC 175 (PC Burma) 178

Bahamas, The (See *Sentinel International v Cordes*)
Hirji Mulji v Cheong Yue Steamship Co Ltd [1926] AC 497 (PC Hong Kong) 87, 124, 181
Jerome Francis v The Municipal Councillors of Kuala Lumpur [1962] 1 WLR 1411 (PC Federated Malay States) 197
Khatijabai Jiwa Hasham v Zenab (AS Legal Representative of HG Harji) [1960] AC 316 (PC Eastern Africa) 29
Martin v Stout [1925] AC 359 (PC Egypt) 29
MP-Bilt Pte Ltd v Oey Widarto [1999] 3 SLR 592, [1999] SGHC 70 216
PR of Tang Man Sit v Capacious Investments Ltd [1996] 1 AC 514 (PC Hong Kong) 126
Sarat Chunder Dey v Gopal Chunder Laha (1892) LR 19 Ind App 203 (PC Bengal) 144
Sentinel International Ltd v Cordes (The 'Bahamas') [2008] UKPC 60, [2008] All ER (D) 141 (Dec) 50
Sinhalese Film Industrial Corp Ltd v Madanayake—NLR—289 of 74 [1971] LKSC 1, (1971) 74 NLR 289 (PC Sri Lanka) 13
Spiricor of Saint Lucia Ltd v AG of St Lucia (PC St Lucia 1 December 1999) 75
Tai Hing Cotton Mill Ltd v Kamsing Knitting Factory (A Firm) [1979] AC 91 (PC Hong Kong) 34, 163, 169, 170, 182
Vaswani v Italian Motors (Sales and Services) Ltd [1996] 1 WLR 270 (PC Hong Kong) 58

TABLE OF STATUTES AND CODES

CISG art 25 ... 72
CISG art 71 ... 78
Contractual Remedies Act 1979 (NZ) ss 7(2), 7(3)(c) ... 9, 77
CPR 17.1(2) ... 90
CPR 3.1(2) ... 162
Hong Kong Sale of Goods Ordinance s 53(3) ... 169
Law Reform (Contributory Negligence and Apportionment of Liability) Act 2001 (SA) ss 3, 7(2) ... 186
Law Reform (Contributory Negligence) Act 1945 s 1(1) ... 186
PECL art 8:105 ... 78
PECL arts 8:103, 9:304 ... 72
PICC art 7.3.3 ... 72
PICC art 7.3.4 ... 78
Restatement (First) of Contracts § 318 ... 162
Restatement (Second) of Contracts § 257 ... 209
Restatement (Second) of Contracts § 251 ... 78
Restatement (Second) of Contracts § 318 ... 166
Restatement (Second) of Contracts § 347 ... 179
Restatement (Second) of Contracts § 360 ... 218
RSC Ord 18 r 7(4) ... 107
RSC Ord 25 r5 ... 141
SGA 1979 s 31(2) ... 41, 55
SGA 1979 s 35(1) ... 91
SGA 1979 s 49(1) ... 205
SGA 1979 s 51(3) ... 169
SGA 1979 ss 11, 61(1) ... 41
Trade Union and Labour Relations Act 1974 ... 197
UCC § 2-609 ... 78
UCC §1-207 ... 142

Introduction

A legal system cannot always leave a wrong unremedied until it actually materialises. It is sometimes necessary to act in anticipation of a wrong. Preventive measures are commonplace. A person may be convicted for preparing for a crime. An injunction may be granted on the ground of an anticipated tort or breach of contract. However, the law may in appropriate circumstances go beyond merely preventive measures and offer full remedies as if the anticipated wrong had occurred. In the law of contract, a breach that lies in the future may attract such 'accelerated' remedies. This is accommodated under the doctrine of anticipatory breach, an ingenious invention of English courts that has been well received across the common law world. This book presents a systematic treatment of this doctrine. In this Introduction a sketch of the book will be drawn: its scope, significance, structure and approach. We attempt first to describe in general terms the type of factual situations with which this book deals. To prevent this description from becoming too abstract, we begin with three illustrative cases.

In our first case,[1] on 1 January, A and B enter into a contract of personal service, under which A agrees to start working for B on 1 July for three months. On 1 February B informs A orally that his service is no longer needed.

In our second case,[2] on 1 January, A and B enter into a voyage charter, under which B agrees to load his cargo onto A's vessel within seven working days from receiving a notice of readiness to load. B receives the notice on 1 July but provides no cargo. On 8 July, when cargo has still not been supplied and only two working days are left for completing the loading, A accepts an offer from a third party and sails the vessel away for another voyage.

In our third case,[3] on 1 January, A and B enter into a package holiday contract, under which B agrees to provide travelling and accommodation services to A for a two-week holiday commencing on 1 July. By the end of April, A learns that B's financial position is starting to deteriorate and that he has defaulted on several similar contracts. A telephones B in order to raise his concerns. B reassures him that he is not in financial difficulty and that he will be able to perform the contract with A.

[1] A simplified version of *Hochster v De la Tour* (1853) 2 El & Bl 678, 118 ER 922.

[2] A simplified version of *Universal Cargo Carriers Corp v Citati (No 1)* [1957] 2 QB 401.

[3] For a similar but more unusual scenario, R Goode, 'International Restatements of Contract and English Contract Law' (1997) *Uniform Law Review* 231, 240.

These three cases well illustrate both the core idea and the borderline of the doctrine of anticipatory breach. There are some common threads running through these cases, although apparent differences are also present. In the first case, B orally refuses to perform the contract before the employment commences. If he does not retract this refusal and persists in not honouring the contract, A will undoubtedly be entitled to damages on 1 July on the ground of B's actual non-performance and to terminate the contract sometime afterwards when the prolonged non-performance becomes sufficiently serious. Neither of these remedies is available to A before 1 July, given that no actual non-performance has occurred on B's part. This would mean that, despite B's unequivocal refusal to go on with the contract on 1 February, A has to stay idle and may not seek alternative employment until sometime after 1 July. This seems to cause injustice to A as he is forced to endure the financial and mental consequences of being tied to an empty contract and not being able to enter into alternative employment before 1 July. In light of this, it seems that A should at least be granted a right to walk away from the contract immediately after 1 February.

In the second case, the situation is more complex. There is no doubt that B is in breach of the contract from 1 July onwards for failing to provide a cargo and will again be in breach on 10 July, when the lay days end, for failing to complete loading. Yet for either breach A's only remedy may be damages. A may not on either date instruct the master to sail away unless either breach can be said to be either of a condition (used in its strict sense) or of sufficient seriousness. If A is not entitled to terminate the contract, the vessel will be running in vain until the delay becomes so protracted as to justify a withdrawal from the contract. A will be forced to wait without knowing how long the delay might be and even whether B will eventually supply a cargo at all. This is demonstrably harsh and hugely wasteful. A must be allowed to call off the charter and accept the alternative offer to employ its vessel.

The third case is at the same time similar to and also fundamentally different from the first two cases. A's concerns are aroused not by B's words or conduct in relation to the particular contract between them, but by a suspected general deterioration in B's financial position. Compared to the first two cases, the third case is less clear-cut. The deterioration may not adversely or seriously affect the performance of the particular contract. It may result merely in a postponement or minor alterations to the itinerary. A's suspicion may turn out to be unfounded. In these circumstances, it may be precipitous to allow A immediately to walk away from the contract. Nevertheless, there are good reasons for affording A some kind of protection. Should B cancel the contract shortly before 1 July, it might be too late for A to make alternative arrangements with another travel agency. His holiday would be completely ruined. He might not get full compensation for all his losses. The appropriate remedy seems not to be to grant A a right of immediate termination, but to grant it only when B fails to supply adequate assurance of its performance within a reasonable time after A requests it to do so. We may refer to this as an 'insecurity of performance' case.

The English doctrine of anticipatory breach addresses the first two cases but is silent on the third. The key question underpinning the doctrine is one of constitution, namely, whether, when a contracting party's words or conduct before the time set for its performance suggest a likely breach at that time, the prospect and nature of the 'anticipated' breach is such that it entitles the other party immediately to terminate the contract and sue for damages. In essence, the doctrine is not only 'a method of giving present damages for a future breach',[4] but also a mechanism that enables present termination for such a breach. It prescribes the circumstances and manner in which present remedies (including both a termination of the contract and a claim for expectation damages) may be sanctioned for one or more future breaches. The doctrine does not cover all cases where a future breach is 'anticipated'. It does not involve any halfway house such as a 'suspension' of contract performance or an order that the party whose conduct is complained of must provide adequate assurance for its future performance. It concerns only the most drastic cases where an immediate right of termination arises because a future breach is 'anticipated'. This book confines itself to this natural ambit of the doctrine. It considers not only the question of constitution but also many other connected questions. For example, in the first case, the question may be asked whether A may, despite B's refusal to use his services, keep himself at B's disposal during the contract period and claim the agreed remuneration at the end of that period. In the second case, there is also the issue whether A may accept the third party's offer even though at that time A does not know that B has no cargo and is unsure of when B may complete loading the vessel. It is suggested that the question of constitution, as well as all those connected questions, can be answered satisfactorily under the umbrella of a general theory that expounds the theoretical and practical foundations of the doctrine of anticipatory breach.

It is not open to doubt that the doctrine of anticipatory breach has an important place in the law of contract. Its theoretical significance is obvious. The very idea of granting contractual remedies for a future breach has been revolutionary. A series of enquiries come out of it. On what ground, and how, may an unaccrued contractual obligation be enforced? Is an anticipatory breach a present or a future breach? What distinguishes an anticipatory breach from an actual breach? Does the concept of 'anticipatory breach' involve an acceleration of the anticipated breach or legal remedies for it? What is the justification for such acceleration? On the other hand, the practical significance of the doctrine of anticipatory breach may at first sight appear to be seriously circumscribed. In the case of a discrete commercial contract, such as a contract for the sale of goods, it is true that the courts are rarely called on to adjudicate a claim brought before the time for performance has arrived. The same cannot, however, be said of long-term contracts such as employment, construction or insurance contracts. It is not uncommon that a claim under those contracts is adjudicated before the time

[4] M Mustill, 'Anticipatory Breach of Contract: The Common Law at Work' in *Butterworth Lectures 1989–1990* (London, Butterworths, 1990) 1, 19.

for the defendant's performance arrives. More importantly, the playing field of anticipatory breach is not in fact confined to cases where the matter is tried before the time for performance. An anticipatory breach is necessarily in issue wherever an attempt is made to justify the termination of a contract in view of anticipated breach(es). The fact that the matter is tried after the time for performance does not obviate the need to invoke the doctrine of anticipatory breach. In the second case discussed above, for example, the issue of anticipatory breach would arise even if A does not accept the third party's offer until several days after the lay days end. At that time B is already in breach of contract—it has failed to complete loading within the lay days. Yet for that breach A's only remedy lies in damages (commonly in the form of demurrage). If the legitimacy of A's withdrawal of the vessel is disputed, it is necessary for the court to anticipate, from the time of withdrawal rather than from the time of trial, a future point of time when B's prolonged delay becomes serious enough to justify the withdrawal. Thus, since A's withdrawal of the vessel occurs prior to that future point of time, A may invoke the doctrine of anticipatory breach to support its claim for damages irrespective of whether the action is brought or the matter is tried before that time.

Notwithstanding its obvious significance, the doctrine of anticipatory breach has, surprisingly, not as yet been subject to an in-depth and systematic treatment. This book attempts to fill the gap and to conduct a comprehensive study with a view not only to restating but also to rejuvenating the doctrine. It will do so in four Parts, which are further divided in total into nine Chapters. In Part I, 'Demystifying Anticipatory Breach', our task is to resolve some fundamental theoretical issues and dispel some myths that have long surrounded the doctrine of anticipatory breach. Chapter 1 is an historical account of how the idea of anticipatory breach evolved in the late 19th century and how that development has influenced the modern doctrine of anticipatory breach. Based on this historical survey, Chapter 2 explores the nature of anticipatory breach in the light of two competing theories that have since emerged in the case law, and it elucidates some of the confusing terminology used in this area of law.

Part II, entitled 'Establishing Anticipatory Breach', develops a unified and apposite legal test as to what constitutes an anticipatory breach. Chapter 3 exposes the problems associated with two contradictory tests under the existing law. In particular, the orthodox 'renunciation' approach is put under critical review. Chapter 4 devises and adopts a principle of 'inferred fundamental breach' as the single test for all types of anticipatory breach. Chapter 5 is devoted to the related issue whether, and how, a party in breach of contract might rely upon the other party's future, anticipated breach(es) to exonerate itself from liability. The Chapter reveals that the party in breach might so exonerate itself even in circumstances where it cannot be shown that the second party commits an anticipatory breach.

In Part III, '"Election" Following Anticipatory Breach', we turn to the so-called 'principle of election'. According to that principle, the victim must 'elect' either to 'accept' the anticipatory breach or to 'affirm' the contract and this 'election' determines what legal remedies are available to it. 'Election' is thus an issue preceding 'remedy'. Chapter 6 explores what constitutes an effective 'acceptance' and whether it might be characterised as an act of 'election'. Chapter 7 investigates the constitution of an 'affirmation' and probes the doctrinal basis on which it operates. These two Chapters together cast serious doubt on the use of the term 'election' in this context and propose to reshape the law according to a more fundamental and rational doctrine.

Part IV, entitled 'Remedying Anticipatory Breach', assesses the principal remedies available to the victim of an anticipatory breach. Chapter 8 deals with the victim's claim for damages. It is focused on two distinct issues. The first issue is whether it is justifiable to make the victim's right of action for damages dependent on its acceptance of the anticipatory breach and to allow that right of action to accrue immediately following the acceptance. The second issue is concerned with the time by reference to which damages must be assessed and the question whether, and to what extent, a supervening event might be taken into account in that assessment. Chapter 9 is entitled 'Specific Relief'. Its main part concentrates on the circumstances in which, following an anticipatory breach, the victim may continue its performance under the contract and thereby earn the contract price. Chapter 9 is followed by a Conclusion, which summarises and synthesises the whole book.

Part I

Demystifying Anticipatory Breach

This Part attempts to dispel some misconceptions about anticipatory breach and to explore its true nature. Chapter 1 traces the historical origin of two such misconceptions: the 'implied promise' theory and the breach-conversion rule. Chapter 2 rejects both of them and builds a theoretical framework on the basis of an appraisal of two competing theories that seek to explain the legal nature of anticipatory breach.

1

The Genesis of Anticipatory Breach

The doctrine of anticipatory breach, despite its universal acceptance in common law jurisdictions,[5] is deeply affected by myths and confusions. Many of these myths and confusions can be traced back to the early days of the doctrine's development. There can be no denial that the doctrine as enunciated in the landmark case of *Hochster v De la Tour*[6] makes good practical sense. Yet the path to a satisfactory rationalisation of that doctrine has not been a smooth one. In fact, the law has taken wrong turns and made misleading deviations. Our eyes will be focused mainly on the 19th century, for it was then that the doctrine took a distinctive shape in two vital respects. The first was the characterisation of an anticipatory breach as a present actual breach of an implied promise. The second, somewhat contradictory, respect was the inception of a 'principle of election' that made the constitution of an anticipatory breach dependent on an 'election' to

[5] Eg USA federal law: *Roehm v Horst* 178 US 1, 20 S Ct 780 (1900); US State law: all but two States (Massachusetts and Nebraska) have adopted the doctrine, see KA Rowley, 'A Brief History of Anticipatory Breach in American Contract Law' (2000–2001) 69 *University of Cincinnati Law Review* 565, 600; AL Corbin, *Corbin on Contracts*, Interim edn (Matthew Bender, 2007) vol 10 'Breach of Contract' § 959 fn 2; Canadian law: *Cromwell v Morris* (1917) 34 DLR 305 (Alberta SC); GHL Fridman, *The Law of Contract*, 5th edn (Toronto, Thomson, 2006) 605 *et seq*; Australian law: *YP Barley Producers Ltd v E C Robertson Pty Ltd* [1927] VLR 194 (SCV); *Peter Turnbull & Co Pty Ltd v Mundus Trading Co (Australasia) Pty Ltd* [1954] HCA 25, (1954) 90 CLR 235; JW Carter, E Peden and GJ Tolhurst, *Contract Law in Australia*, 5th edn (LexisNexis, 2007) chs 29, 30; New Zealand law: Contractual Remedies Act 1979 ss 7(2), 7(3)(c); *Starlight Enterprises Ltd v Lapco Enterprises Ltd* [1979] 2 NZLR 744 (CA); *Brooklands Motor Co Ltd (in receivership) v Bridge Wholesale Acceptance Corp (Australia) Ltd* (1994) 7 NZCLC 260, 449 (HC); JF Burrows, J Finn and S Todd, *Law of Contract in New Zealand*, 3rd edn (Wellington, LexisNexis, 2007) ch 18. In civilian jurisdictions, the scene is quite different. The doctrine is not adopted in France: S Whittaker, 'How Does French Law Deal with Anticipatory Breaches of Contract?' (1996) 45 *ICLQ* 662; D Harris and D Tallon (eds), *Contract Law Today: Anglo-French Comparisons* (Oxford, Clarendon, 1989) 294–5; M Franklin, 'Equity as Form: A Study of Frost v Knight' (1955–1956) 30 *Tulane Law Review* 175. In Germany, a breach characterised as anticipatory in common law countries is sometimes remedied in a similar way: BGB §323 IV; BS Markesinis, H Unberath and A Johnston, *The German Law of Contract: A Comparative Treatise*, 2nd edn (Oxford, Hart Publishing, 2006) 430–31; BS Markesinis, W Lorenz and G Dannemann, *The Law of Contracts and Restitution: A Comparative Introduction*, German Law of Obligations Series (Oxford, Clarendon, 1997) 491 *et seq*. Scotland embraces a similar doctrine of anticipatory breach as the English one: *Forslind v Bechely-Crundall* 1922 SC (HL) 173, 179 (Viscount Haldane), 1922 SLT 496 (unless indicated otherwise, the Session Cases report will be cited hereafter); DM Walker, *Principles of Scottish Private Law*, 4th edn (Oxford, Clarendon, 1988) vol II 144–6; WW McBryde, *The Law of Contract in Scotland*, 3rd edn (Edinburgh, W Green, 2007) [20–22] *et seq*. Generally, GH Treitel, *Remedies for Breach of Contract: A Comparative Account* (Oxford, Clarendon, 1988) 379–81.

[6] n 1.

accept that breach. Both respects have important implications for the theoretical foundation of the doctrine. Before an historical survey is conducted, it is necessary to analyse carefully the ground-breaking decision in *Hochster.*

A. A Re-examination of *Hochster v De la Tour*

Hochster was decided at a time described by Atiyah as 'the age of freedom of contract'.[7] By an agreement on 12 April 1852 the defendant agreed to employ the claimant as a courier for a three-month trip to Europe commencing on 1 June 1852. On 1 May the defendant wrote to the claimant saying that he had changed his mind and that the claimant's service was not required. The claimant instituted an action for damages on 22 May. Between 22 May and 1 June, the claimant obtained another engagement with Lord Ashburton on equally good terms but this did not commence until 4 July. It was held by Lord Campbell CJ on behalf of the Court of Queen's Bench that the claimant was entitled to succeed in an action for damages.

It was not disputed before the court that the claimant should be given an exit from the contract following the defendant's renunciation. The legal combat converged on the issue whether the renunciation constituted an actionable breach. The central difficulty stemmed from a 'serious' question posed by counsel for the claimant as to 'whether in law it is possible to break a contract before the day for its performance comes'.[8] At the time when the claimant commenced the action, the performance date fixed by the contract was still 10 days away. Had the claimant relied upon an actual breach by the defendant of his obligation to employ as the cause of action, the action would have been premature and summarily dismissed. The claimant submitted that the renunciation was itself the cause of action. However, no direct prior authority could be furnished in his favour. In a previous line of cases, a party's act incapacitating it from carrying out the contract before the date for performance had been held to constitute a breach.[9] The relevance of these 'disablement' cases to *Hochster* hinged, however, on whether they evidenced a general doctrine of anticipatory breach that accommodated both disablement and renunciation.[10] A formidable obstacle to the claimant was a ruling of Parke B on two prior occasions that a renunciation before the date for performance was not in itself a breach.[11]

[7] PS Atiyah, *The Rise and Fall of Freedom of Contract* (Oxford, Clarendon, 1979) 426.

[8] *Hochster* (n 1) 682, 923.

[9] *Ibid* 684–6, 924–5, citing *Short v Stone* (1846) 8 QB 358, 115 ER 911; *Lovelock v Franklyn* (1846) 8 QB 371, 115 ER 916.

[10] *Ibid* 684, 924.

[11] *Phillpotts v Evans* (1839) 5 M & W 475, 478, 151 ER 200, 202; *Ripley v McClure* (1849) 4 Exch 345, 359, 154 ER 1245, 1251.

It was against this background of the general absence of decisive direct authority that *Planché v Colburn*,[12] a case arguably quite off the mark, came into reckoning. In that case, C engaged P to write a book for publication and undertook to pay P £100 upon delivery of the completed manuscript. P carried out considerable work but, before he completed the manuscript, C altered the publication plan and proposed to publish the manuscript in a new series of books, which was designated for a wholly different audience. C told P that if P did not accept this new arrangement he would pay neither £100 nor any remuneration for P's work done. P rejected the proposal and sued C for compensation for work done. In a judgment delivered by Tindal CJ, with which the other three judges concurred, it was held that P was entitled to compensation for work done, without tendering or delivering the completed manuscript. The jury accordingly awarded P £50. One difficulty in evaluating the significance of this decision lies in ascertaining the nature of the damages award of £50. P raised three counts in his declaration: assumpsit for damages for breach of contract; debt; and quantum meruit (then known as a common money count for work and labour). The case was reported in two nominate reports but neither made it entirely clear on which count the award of £50 was made, particularly whether it was, in modern terms, damages for breach of contract or restitution for unjust enrichment. Although Tindal CJ stated that, by refusing to proceed, C had 'broken' his contract with P,[13] the reasoning was too compressed to be conclusive. After all, at the time when the case was decided, the law of unjust enrichment was still in embryonic form and quantum meruit could be seen either as a measure of contractual damages or as a restitutionary remedy independent of the contract.[14] At any rate, the issue whether C's obligation to pay £100 could be broken before it was due to be performed was never presented or argued before the court in *Planché v Colburn*.

[12] *Planché v Colburn* (1831) 8 Bing 14, 131 ER 305. Also, (1831) 5 Carr & P, 172 ER 876. The Bingham report will be cited hereafter.

[13] *Ibid* 15–16, 306.

[14] For the contractual view, SJ Stoljar, *The Law of Quasi-Contract*, 2nd edn (Law Book, 1989) 231 *et seq*; P Jaffey, *The Nature and Scope of Restitution* (Oxford, Hart Publishing, 2000) ch 3; A Burrows, *The Law of Restitution*, 2nd edn (London, Butterworths, 2002) 17, 343 fn 4. For the restitutionary view, G Jones (ed), *Goff and Jones: The Law of Restitution*, 7th edn (London, Sweet & Maxwell, 2007) [1–022], [20–023]; P Birks, *An Introduction to the Law of Restitution* (Oxford, Clarendon, 1985) 232; J Beatson (ed), *Anson's Law of Contract*, 28th edn (Oxford, OUP, 2002) 650; PH Winfield, *The Province of the Law of Tort* (Cambridge, CUP, 1931) 158; Mustill (n 4) 34. It was the latter view that subsequently prevailed: *Keys v Harwood* (1846) 2 CB 905, 135 ER 1201; *Lilley v Elwin* (1848) 11 QB 742, 755, 116 ER 652, 657 (Coleridge J); *Sands v Clarke* (1849) 8 CB 751, 137 ER 703; *Goodman v Pocock* (1850) 15 QB 576, 117 ER 577; *De Bernardy v Harding* (1853) 8 Exch 822, 155 ER 1586; *Prickett v Badger* (1856) 1 CB NS 296, 304, 140 ER 123, 126 (Williams J); 306, 127 (Crowder J). Also, TW Chitty, AT Denning and CP Harvey (eds), *Smith's Leading Cases*, 13th edn (London, Sweet & Maxwell, 1929) vol II, 23 *cf* 39; DJ Ibbetson, *A Historical Introduction to the Law of Obligation* (Oxford, OUP, 1999) 281; JH Baker, 'The Use of Assumpsit for Restitutionary Money Claims 1600–1800' in EJH Schrage (ed), *Unjust Enrichment: The Comparative Legal History of the Law of Restitution*, 2nd edn (Berlin, Duncker and Humblot, 1999) 31, 38.

Curiously, a tangential feature of the decision in *Planché v Colburn* was seized upon by counsel for both parties in *Hochster*, and the case seems eventually to have had an impact on both the outcome in *Hochster* and the future development of the doctrine of anticipatory breach. It was the law at the time that a contract should be *rescinded*, namely, brought to an end both retrospectively and prospectively, before a claim for quantum meruit could be sustained and that a mere discharge of the contract, which determined the contract prospectively only, was not sufficient.[15] The rule persisted until it was removed by the House of Lords in the mid 20th century,[16] with the consequence that only from that date could the termination or discharge of a contract also trigger a restitutionary claim. In this context, Tindal CJ's observation in *Planché v Colburn* that P's claim for quantum meruit was sustainable only because the special contract between the parties had ceased to exist[17] attracted attention from both sides in *Hochster*. It was upon the interpretation of this observation that the two sides were demonstrably at odds. Counsel for the claimant submitted that P was entitled to, and did, treat himself as discharged from the contract by reason of C's renunciation and was entitled to succeed in a claim for contractual damages, which, measured by quantum meruit, amounted to £50. Therefore it was argued that *Planché* was an authority for the claimant. In contrast, counsel for the defendant contended that the contract in *Planché* was 'rescinded' and therefore the quantum meruit recovery rested upon a liability independent of the contract. In addition, the rescission of a contract seemed then to be understood as a process not of unilateral determination but as a process that required 'mutual consent'.[18] Counsel for the defendant thus advanced an 'offer to rescind' theory and argued that the defendant's renunciation was 'no more than an offer to rescind' the contract.[19] As a result, only two options were open to the claimant: he could either accept this offer or ignore it. If he chose to accept it, the defendant's renunciation would be completed as a breach. But then the whole contract would be wiped out *ab initio* and all claims under the contract, including a claim for contractual damages, would consequently be forfeited. If he ignored it, the situation would be the same as if there had been no renunciation.[20]

The court in *Hochster* rejected the defendant's 'offer to rescind' theory. Obviously, the theory would cause manifest injustice to the claimant. He would be put in an extremely unfair position. If the claimant accepted the 'offer', he would be deprived of a right to sue for contractual damages which would otherwise have been available if he had not accepted the breach and the defendant had persisted in his refusal to perform when the date for performance arrived. More

[15] *Weston v Downes* (1778) 1 Doug 23, 99 ER 19; *Appleby v Myers* (1867) LR 2 CP 651, 659 (Blackburn J); *Chandler v Webster* [1904] 1 KB 493 (CA) 499 (Collins MR).

[16] *Fibrosa Spolka Akcyjna v Fairbairn Lawson Combe Barbour Ltd* [1943] AC 32 (HL).

[17] *Planché* (n 12) 16, 306.

[18] *Hochster* (n 1) 685, 924 (Crompton J in colloquy).

[19] *Ibid* 686, 925.

[20] *Ibid* 688, 925.

importantly, since the contract in *Hochster*, unlike that in *Planché*, was still wholly executory and a claim for quantum meruit was unavailable to the claimant, to deny the claimant contractual damages would leave him with no legal remedy whatsoever. On the other hand, if the claimant ignored the 'offer', the defendant would not even be in breach and the claimant would have to waste his resources on a futile contract as he would be bound by the contract to remain ready to perform. It would indeed lead to anomalous results had such an unbalanced theory been endorsed in *Hochster*. As a result, it has been suggested that counsel for the defendant made a bad move by gambling on the theory and should have instead contended that the claimant was entitled to treat himself as discharged from the contract but that he could not claim damages until the date for performance.[21] In this sense, the 'offer to rescind' theory has been said to have changed 'the line of Anglo-American contract law for the foreseeable future'.[22] This statement might, however, be considered to be somewhat exaggerated, as the court's reasoning in *Hochster* could not be said to follow necessarily from its rejection of that theory.

Lord Campbell CJ responded to the above problems by taking two significant steps. First, his Lordship was quite certain that there were strong policy reasons for giving the claimant a power to discharge/terminate the contract:

> [I]nstead of remaining idle and laying out money in preparations which must be useless, [the claimant] is at liberty to seek service under another employer, which would go in mitigation of the damages to which he would otherwise be entitled for a breach of the contract.[23]

His Lordship formulated an 'implied promise' theory to justify the claimant's right of termination. It was held that every anticipatory breach, whether it was by way of renunciation or disablement, was a present breach of an implied promise that a party would do nothing to the prejudice of the other inconsistent with the relationship constituted by the terms of their contract.[24] In other words, both parties impliedly promised to maintain 'willingness and readiness' to perform the contract. His Lordship seemed in this way not only to have solved the paradox of how one could presently break a future obligation but also to have created a general doctrine that united disablement with renunciation. Section B herein explores whether this 'implied promise' theory was historically well founded.

Secondly, although Lord Campbell did not adopt the 'offer to rescind' theory, his reliance on *Planché* as an authority seemed to suggest that an actual termination of the contract was essential to the constitution of an anticipatory breach.[25] His Lordship endorsed the claimant's interpretation of *Planché*, namely, that P

[21] *Corbin on Contracts* (n 5) § 960; Mustill (n 4) 41.

[22] Mustill, *ibid*. The Privy Council rejected the theory in a subsequent case: *Sinhalese Film Industrial Corp Ltd v Madanayake—NLR—289 of 74* [1971] LKSC 1, (1971) 74 NLR 289 (PC Sri Lanka) 291 (Lord Diplock).

[23] *Hochster* (n 1) 690, 926.

[24] *Ibid* 689, 926.

[25] *Ibid* 693, 927.

had treated himself as discharged from the contract and had succeeded on his first count, a claim for damages for breach of contract. In his opinion, an immediate action for contractual damages necessarily followed a discharge of the contract.[26] This was a strong signal indicating that Lord Campbell might have incorporated Tindal CJ's above-mentioned observation into *Hochster*, thereby taking the view that the claimant's action should succeed only because he had 'accepted' the defendant's anticipatory breach. This constituted the germ of an important yet controversial part of the 'principle of election' that emerged later. Section C herein explains how that part of the principle subsequently took root in a series of late-19th-century cases.

B. The Gestation of the 'Implied Promise' Theory

1. Pre-*Hochster* Disablement Cases

By adopting the 'implied promise' theory in *Hochster*, Lord Campbell managed to turn a number of earlier disablement cases into a firm judicial basis for the doctrine of anticipatory breach. It was held to have been settled in those cases that a disablement, or self-created incapacity, constituted a breach of an implied yet present obligation to maintain readiness to perform the contract.[27] His Lordship argued that, had the defendant, instead of renouncing the contract, embarked on a voyage for Australia on 1 May, so as to render it impossible for him to perform the contract on 1 June, the claimant would have been entitled to bring an action before 1 June according to this well-established rule of law.[28]

It is submitted that his Lordship might have assumed too much and that the earlier disablement cases did not in fact support the 'implied promise' theory. The 'implied promise' theory seemed to have its origin in penal bond cases. In those cases there was usually only one promisor and one promisee. The promisee when enforcing the promise would sue in debt for a fixed sum of money (the penalty) that the promisor was obliged to pay on a penal bond, which payment was defeasible by a condition subsequent that the promisor should perform its promise.[29] Where the promise was subject to a condition precedent to be fulfilled by the promisee but, before that condition could be fulfilled, the promisor disabled itself from performing the promise, a question arose whether the promisee might claim the penalty without fulfilling the condition precedent. One approach taken by the courts was to hold that since the disablement 'prevented' the promisee from

[26] *Ibid* 693–4, 927–8.

[27] *Ibid* 686, 690, 925, 926.

[28] *Ibid* 690, 926.

[29] AWB Simpson, *A History of the Common Law of Contract* (Oxford, Clarendon, 1975) 90, 107; Mustill (n 4) 17. Generally, AL Corbin, 'Conditions in the Law of Contracts' (1918–1919) 28 *Yale Law Journal* 739; GH Treitel, '"Conditions" and "Conditions Precedent"' (1990) 106 *LQR* 185.

fulfilling the condition precedent, the condition was thus exempted, the promise became immediately due to be performed and the promisee might enforce the penalty on the ground of an actual non-performance of that promise. Thus, in *Sir Anthony Main's Case*,[30] under a lease of 21 years the lessor executed a penal bond to secure its promise to grant the lessee a new lease for a further 21 years on condition that the lessee should surrender the current lease before its expiration and during the lessor's lifetime. Before the current lease expired and the lessee could surrender it, the lessor granted an interest to a third party for 80 years. It was held that the lessor was liable on the bond as the condition precedent to his promise, namely, the lessee's surrender of the current lease, was 'dispensed with'.[31] Not every condition precedent, however, could be said to have been exempted by a disablement. It was in cases where such an exemption was impossible that the need seemed to arise for resort to an 'implied promise' theory. In *Vynior's Case*,[32] therefore, the promise was to observe an arbitral award if and when the award was made by a specified third party at or before a future date. The promisor revoked the third party's authority to arbitrate before the future date arrived and before any award could be made. The reasoning in *Main's Case* was obviously inapplicable as, without the award, the promise to observe it could not be due to be performed. It was thus held that the promisor broke an implied promise not to revoke the arbitrator's authority before an award was made. This decision, however, rested upon a rather unusual rationale. The implied promise was held to be extractable only from an 'ancient form' assumed by the express promise to observe, a specific undertaking by the promisor to 'stand to, abide, observe, perform, fulfil and keep' the award.[33] For this reason, the value of the decision in *Vynior's Case* was negligible. In *Warburton v Storr*,[34] a much later but almost identical case, where that exact combination of words was not used in the bond, Abbott CJ simply relied upon a statement in *Vynior's Case* that a promisor should not be allowed to take advantage of a condition precedent, even if the latter was set solely for its benefit, to the promise which it disabled itself from performing.[35] The Chief Justice went on to state 'a well-known and established rule of law' that 'if a party covenants to do a certain thing, and afterwards, by his own act, disables himself from performing it, that is in itself a breach of the covenant'.[36] This 'rule of law', in fact, had little to do with the 'implied promise' theory.[37] In penal bond cases there was no need to establish a breach of promise as such. The appropriate action was one for debt. The courts were never confronted with the issue whether the promisee might sue in damages for what was essentially a future breach. The

30 *Sir Anthony Main's Case* (1596) 5 Co Rep 20b, 77 ER 80.
31 *Ibid* 21a, 81.
32 *Vynior's Case* (1609) 8 Co Rep 81b, 77 ER 597.
33 *Ibid* 82b, 601.
34 *Warburton v Storr* (1825) 4 B & C 103, 107 ER 997.
35 *Ibid* 107, 999, citing *Vynior's Case* (n 32) 82b, 601.
36 *Ibid* 106, 999.
37 *Cf* PM Nienaber, 'The Effect of Anticipatory Breach: Principle and Policy' [1962] *CLJ* 213, 217.

'breach' in Abbott CJ's statement referred merely to a failure of the condition subsequent on the bond. It was quite unnecessary to engineer something like the 'implied promise' theory. The form of action dominating at the time thus prevented that theory from being developed. In *Warburton*, indeed, counsel for the promisor conceded that he might have been liable for a breach of an implied promise not to revoke the third party's authority, had the promisee brought an action in assumpsit.[38] We must, therefore, turn to some early-19th-century cases where a proper action for breach of contract was brought.

In respect of those breach of contract cases, there were two points to be made. The first point is that the need to resort to the 'implied promise' theory arose where a party sued for the other party's disablement without performing what was not only a condition precedent to, but also a consideration or agreed equivalent for, the other party's disabled performance. In such a situation the reasoning in *Main's Case* could not apply as it could not be said that as a result of the claimant being somehow 'exempted' from its performance the defendant was thus bound immediately to perform its part. The adoption of the 'implied promise' theory in such cases was nevertheless only partial and conditional. In *Lovelock v Franklyn*,[39] the defendant agreed to assign a property to the claimant on condition that the claimant should first pay for it within seven years from a named day. Before the seven years expired and before the claimant made any payment the defendant assigned the property to a stranger. The claimant sued the defendant for breach of contract. Lord Denman CJ held, without making any mention of the reasoning in *Main's Case*, that the defendant had broken an implied promise to keep ready to perform, because he had incapacitated himself from performing the contract 'at the very time when he may be called on and should be ready' to assign.[40] Although it was not made clear what special facts in that case necessitated the implication of the promise,[41] this decision came fairly close to the 'implied promise' theory in *Hochster*. There was, however, an important difference. Lord Denman distinguished *Lovelock* from a case '[w]here a party agrees to sell, or to lease, on a given future day'. In such a case the party 'may have all the intermediate time open to him for acquiring the means of performing his contract' and 'of rehabilitating himself before the time of performance', hence 'the contract is not broken by something which may merely prevent the performance in the mean time'.[42]

This distinction illuminates our second point. *Lovelock* was exceptional among pre-*Hochster* cases in its adoption of the 'implied promise' theory. In the majority of those cases, where a condition precedent to the disabled party's performance was, unlike in *Hochster*, not a 'definite and absolute' time but 'some act or request' of the other party and therefore capable of being 'dispensed with' by

[38] *Warburton* (n 34) 104, 998.
[39] n 9.
[40] *Ibid* 378, 919.
[41] P Mitchell, '*Hochster v De La Tour* (1853)' in C Mitchell and P Mitchell (eds), *Landmark Cases in the Law of Contract* (Oxford, Hart Publishing, 2008) 139.
[42] *Lovelock* (n 9) 378, 918–19.

the disablement according to the reasoning in *Main's Case*, the 'implied promise' theory found no place.[43] This was so despite the fact that that theory might be said to have at least notionally avoided the problem of enlarging the defendant's contractual obligation without its consent. Instead of working the immediate accrual of a future obligation, the theory manufactured a connected, yet distinct, present implied obligation. The courts before *Hochster*, however, generally failed to take notice of the potential significance of that theory. A good example was *Ford v Tiley*.[44] Tiley promised to grant Ford a lease of a house for 14 or 21 years on condition that Tiley should become possessed of the house, which condition could not be satisfied before midsummer 1827 due to third parties' interests in the house. In June 1825, Tiley leased the house to a third party for 23 years. In 1826 Ford sued Tiley for breach of contract. Bayley J held Tiley liable. A crucial point concerned the obligation held to have been broken by Tiley. The reporter's note in the Law Journal Reports indicated that when the case was retried it was decided that Tiley had broken a special clause in the agreement that neither party should 'run from' the agreement or do anything to prevent the lease from being executed by all necessary parties.[45] If so, no question of breaching a future obligation arose. However, Bayley J also hinted that Tiley might be in breach of his express obligation to grant the lease to Ford. The underlying reasoning, which again echoed that in *Main's Case*, seemed to be that Tiley's disablement exempted the condition precedent, namely, Tiley's becoming in possession of the house.[46] Tiley's obligation to grant the lease consequently became immediately due. Bayley J concluded that Ford's action was not premature. The decision was open to the criticism that it altered considerably the contract expectation as Tiley was made to account for Ford's loss at a time when Tiley would not be liable to perform under the contract. It did, however, mean that, even if it had not been for the reporter's note in the Law Journal Reports, *Ford* would have been unlikely to represent, as Sir Michael Mustill once suggested, the first appearance at common law of the doctrine of anticipatory breach.[47]

In summary, the above survey of pre-*Hochster* disablement cases shows that there was in fact no well-established rule of law that could support the 'implied promise' theory advanced by Lord Campbell in *Hochster*. The courts either resorted to the reasoning in *Main's Case*, thus obliterating the need to invoke that theory, or, when they did imply a promise, they restricted the implication of the promise to special circumstances and failed to associate it ineluctably with the

[43] PA Moses, 'The Doctrine of Anticipatory Breach of Contracts, Theoretically and Historically Considered' (1900–1901) 1 *North Carolina Law Journal* 321, 325. Relevant cases include: *Bowdell v Parsons* (1808) 10 East 359, 103 ER 811; *Amory v Brodrick* (1822) 5 B & A 712, 106 ER 1351; *Short v Stone* (n 9); *Caines v Smith* (1847) 15 M & W 189, 153 ER 816. Also, Mustill (n 4) 20.

[44] *Ford v Tiley* (1827) 6 B & C 325, 108 ER 472.

[45] *Ford v Tiley* [1827] 5 LJR 171 fn 1. *ibid* 329, 473.

[46] *Ford v Tiley* (n 44) 327, 473.

[47] Mustill (n 4) 21.

disabled future performance. Next we turn to pre-*Hochster* renunciation cases in search for a basis for the 'implied promise' theory.

2. Pre-*Hochster* Renunciation Cases

In its nature, the 'implied promise' theory should not discriminate between a renunciation and a disablement. For a considerable period of time both before and after *Hochster*, in fact, both types of conduct were viewed as resting upon a manifestation of intention. However, while some sign of the 'implied promise' theory could be captured in several disablement cases preceding *Hochster*, that theory seemed to be entirely foreign to pre-*Hochster* renunciation cases. As mentioned above, in two of those cases,[48] Parke B stated obiter in an unmistakable fashion that a renunciation prior to the time for performance was not a breach and thus did not constitute a cause of action for damages. Both cases involved a refusal by a buyer to accept the goods under a sales contract when the goods were still in transit to the discharging port. In both cases the buyer committed an actual non-performance of his express obligation to accept and pay for the goods as he persisted in his refusal even when the seller tendered the goods. Furthermore, since the seller's claim was brought well after the date for delivery, there was no question of premature action. Parke B nevertheless remarked that the renunciation was a 'mere nullity'[49] and 'nothing more than an expression of an intention to break the contract, not final, and capable of being retracted'.[50]

Nevertheless, the reasoning in *Main's Case* was still utilised in some cases to facilitate a quicker, and ultimately fairer, resolution of a dispute. In this context the concept of 'prevention' was extended to accommodate the act of renunciation.[51] In *Jones v Barkley*,[52] under a contract for the sale of a property, the sellers were obliged to assign the property to the buyer after a fixed future date. The buyer's obligation to pay fell due only when the assignment was completed. When the sellers duly offered to assign and tendered a draft for that purpose, the buyer refused to proceed with the contract. It was held by Lord Mansfield that the buyer was not entitled to rely upon the non-assignment as a defence as his renunciation had prevented the sellers from assigning the property and the assignment was therefore exempted.[53] This decision, however, highlighted a difficulty mentioned earlier in respect of the exemption of a condition that also constituted the consideration under the contract. As a result of applying the reasoning in *Main's Case*, Lord Mansfield seemed to have endorsed an exotic theory that the assignment should be treated as if it had been 'constructively performed' in law. The effect

[48] *Phillpotts v Evans* (n 11); *Ripley v McClure* (n 11).

[49] *Phillpotts v Evans ibid* 478, 202.

[50] *Ripley v McClure* (n 11) 359, 1251.

[51] Mitchell (n 41) 141–2. It was thus said that a renunciation if acted upon 'is just as effectual as actual prevention', *Peter Turnbull* (n 5) 247 (Dixon CJ).

[52] *Jones v Barkley* (1781) 2 Doug 685, 99 ER 434.

[53] *Ibid* 694, 440.

was that only the buyer was liable to perform the contract. As the reporter's note disclosed, the sellers were awarded £611 as damages, which equalled the full contract price payable by the buyer.[54] This theory of 'constructive performance' had had its mark in earlier cases[55] but had the effect of turning a reciprocal exchange into a gift.[56] In a similar later case, *Laird v Pim*,[57] the injustice of the theory was acknowledged[58] but the court eventually felt bound by *Jones v Barkley* as an 'express authority'.[59] The theory of constructive performance was an unfortunate development. Although it was by no means compelled by the reasoning in *Main's Case*, it did instance a difficulty caused by the latter. Another difficulty was also discerned by the court in *Laird v Pim*, where it was pointed out that, since in *Jones v Barkley* the assignment was required only after a fixed future date, had the buyer renounced the contract before that date, the sellers would not have been entitled to bring an action for damages for the renunciation.[60]

In view of these difficulties in applying the reasoning in *Main's Case*, it was suggested by Dawson that the renunciation in cases like *Jones v Barkley* should be regarded as a breach of an implied promise not to hinder or prevent the victim from fulfilling the condition precedent, namely, the assignment of the property in that case.[61] This implied promise was said not to be broken until the condition was actually prevented by a discharge of the victim from the contract. This suggestion was consistent with both the 'implied promise' theory in *Hochster* and the principle of election established thereafter. It was, however, clear that no pre-*Hochster* renunciation case had adopted the suggestion. In *Cort v Ambergate Nottingham & Boston & Eastern Junction Railway Co*,[62] a case resembling *Hochster* in most respects, Lord Campbell held that the vendors of certain chairs were entitled to damages for their loss of profit without manufacturing or supplying the chairs, where the purchasers were bound to pay only upon delivery and renounced the contract before any chair was manufactured, because the renunciation 'prevented' and 'discharged' the vendors from their further performance of the contract.[63] Apparently, the vendors neither treated themselves as discharged from the contract nor commenced the action until after the expected date for delivery had passed. They were thus not suing for a breach of a future obligation. There was

[54] *Ibid* 695, 440, fn 3.

[55] Eg *Peeters v Opie* (1671) 2 Wms Saund 350, 85 ER 1144. For the civilian origin of the theory and a similar doctrine of constructive service in employment cases, Mitchell (n 41) 142, 144–6, 155–6.

[56] Generally, Atiyah (n 7) 210.

[57] *Laird v Pim* (1841) 7 M & W 474, 151 ER 852.

[58] *Ibid* 478, 854 (Parke B).

[59] *Ibid* 484, 856 (Lord Abinger CB); 485, 857 (Parke B).

[60] *Ibid* 483, 856 (Lord Abinger and Parke B in argument).

[61] F Dawson, 'Metaphors and Anticipatory Breach of Contract' [1981] *CLJ* 83, 95.

[62] *Cort v Ambergate Nottingham & Boston & Eastern Junction Railway Co* (1851) 17 QB 127, 117 ER 1229.

[63] *Ibid* 142, 145, 148, 1235–7. Also, *Wyvil v Stapleton* (1724) 1 Str 615, 93 ER 735; *Withers v Reynolds* (1831) 2 B & Ad 882, 109 ER 1370; *Inchbald v The Western Neilgherry Coffee, Tea, and Cinchona Plantation Co Ltd* (1864) 17 CB NS 733, 144 ER 293; *Re Edwards ex p Chalmers* (1872–73) LR 8 Ch App 289 (CA).

also no indication in the case that the purchasers had made and broken an implied promise. Therefore, the case, like many others, could not assist the 'implied promise' theory. In fact, as will be shown in the next subsection, only limited support for that theory could be found, and that only in a special area of law.

3. Wrongful Dismissal in Employment Contracts

Hochster was a case involving a relationship of master and servant. In modern terms, the contract in that case was a contract of personal service (or an employment contract) and the defendant's renunciation was a wrongful dismissal of the claimant.[64] If confined to such an area, the 'implied promise' theory was amply justified by the law at the time. Just a few years before *Hochster* was decided, the employment relationship had undergone a transformation from one of 'service and pay' to a 'continuing employment' relationship. Under a 'service and pay' relationship, a contract of personal service was viewed as a mere exchange of service for remuneration. The only obligation of an employer under the contract was to pay wages at the specified date; a wrongful dismissal constituted no breach at all.[65] The only remedy a wrongfully dismissed employee had was to sue the employer for an actual failure to pay when the payment fell due, provided that he averred his own willingness and readiness to serve.[66] This state of law was far from satisfactory. The employee was effectively required to remain ready to serve during the whole period in which the contract was expected to last and to bring a claim for every individual instalment of wages when it fell due. If he was successful, the employer would be liable to pay in full on the footing that the service had been constructively provided.

The solution the law came up with was to adopt a two-tiered structure for a contract of personal service.[67] The 'service and pay' relation only formed the first tier. The second tier was a continuing employment relationship under which the employer impliedly promised to retain the employee while the employee impliedly promised to serve the employer during the term fixed by the contract. In the leading case *Elderton v Emmens*,[68] Elderton was the 'permanent attorney and solicitor'

[64] The decision in *Hochster* has been applied in the modern context to contracts of employment: *Sarker v South Tees Acute Hospitals NHS Trust* [1997] ICR 673 (EAT); *Hatten Wyatt Solicitors v Mamedu* (unreported, EAT, 20 November 2007).

[65] *Aspdin v Austin* (1844) 5 QB 671, 684, 114 ER 1402, 1408 (Lord Denman CJ). Also, *Dunn v Sayles* (1844) 5 QB 685, 114 ER 1408.

[66] *Aspdin v Austin ibid* 684–5, 1408.

[67] MR Freedland, *The Contract of Employment* (Oxford, Clarendon, 1976) 19–20. In a completely restructured new edition, *Personal Employment Contract* (Oxford, Clarendon, 2003) 361, 362, 393–5, Freedland again suggested that the wrongfulness of a dismissal might lie in a breach of an implied duty to give reasonable notice, an implied duty of mutual trust and confidence or an implied mutual duty of efficient dispute resolution. Undoubtedly, none of these suggested obligations might be implied if the contract in question is not an employment contract.

[68] *Elderton v Emmens* (1853) 13 CB 495, 138 ER 1292, aff'g (1848) 6 CB 160, 136 ER 1213, rev'g (1847) 4 CB 479, 136 ER 594.

of a company of which Emmens was the legal representative. Elderton was paid reasonable rewards for his service. On 30 November 1844 the old employment contract was replaced with a new one under which Elderton would from 1 January 1845 be paid a fixed annual salary in return for the same service. Elderton was wrongfully dismissed on 25 May 1845 and he sued for breach of contract. The company's promise to pay the salary being unenforceable because of the lack of a valid consideration, Elderton argued that the dismissal amounted to a breach by the company of an implied promise to employ and retain him for at least one year and entitled him immediately to claim damages. Following an initial rejection, this argument was accepted upon appeal by the Exchequer Chamber and then by the House of Lords.[69] The implied promise to 'employ' was of course not a promise to supply Elderton with any particular work but a promise 'to engage in his service', namely, to maintain him in employment.[70] As summed up by Crompton J in the House of Lords:

> [W]herever there is a contract for hiring or employment on the one part, and service for wages or salary on the other, for a specified time, there is an engagement on the part of the employer to keep the employed in the relation in question during that time, and not merely to pay him the wages for the services at the end.[71]

Thus, a promise to employ could equally be implied from the contract in *Hochster*. Lord Campbell relied upon the decision of the Exchequer Chamber in *Elderton v Emmens* in his judgment.[72] It appears that Lord Campbell could have reached the same conclusion as he did solely on the basis of the principle in *Elderton v Emmens*. Yet he decided to create a general 'implied promise' theory, applicable to all types of contract, and regarded it as the solution to the problem of erecting a present liability for a future breach. In terms of the development of precedent, this was, it is submitted, an unwarranted extension of the principle in *Elderton v Emmens*.

To conclude the current section on the pre-*Hochster* cases, it seemed to have been realised in some of those cases that, where the reasoning in *Main's Case* was either unworkable or unapplied, the only way to combine justice with logic was to succumb to the 'implied promise' theory. Reading between the lines in some judgments, especially that in *Lovelock v Franklyn*, we can sense that the theory was brewing. Yet it was not until *Hochster* itself that the final and decisive step was taken to complete the theory as an alternative to a direct recognition that a future breach might be currently actionable. *Hochster* also extended, unwarrantedly, the principle in *Elderton v Emmens* to the general law of contract. In all, the 'implied promise' theory cannot be said to be supported by the main body of case law that existed before *Hochster* was decided.

[69] *Ibid* 506, 508, 510, 1297, 1298, 1299 (Crompton J); 511, 1299 (Martin B); 517, 1301 (Wightman J); 518, 1302 (Erle J); 521, 1303 (Platt B); 530, 1306 (Coleridge J); 531, 532–3, 1307 (Parke B); 539–40, 1310 (Lord Truro); *cf* 512, 1299 (Talfourd J); 526–7, 1305 (Maule J).

[70] *Elderton v Emmens* (1848) 6 CB 160, 176, 136 ER 1213, 1219 (Parke B).

[71] *Elderton v Emmens* (n 68) 506, 1297.

[72] *Hochster* (n 1) 689, 926.

C. The Rise of the Principle of Election

As mentioned earlier, Lord Campbell's reasoning in *Hochster*, especially his reliance on *Planché v Colburn*, sowed the seed for the proposition that in the case of anticipatory breach, termination of contract was essential to the constitution of the breach and thus to a claim for damages. In a series of late-19th-century cases, this was installed as an integral part of the principle of election.

The first of this chain of cases was *Avery v Bowden*.[73] By a charterparty B agreed to load a cargo at Odessa on board a ship owned by A. The ship, registered in the UK, arrived at Odessa on 11 March 1854. Four or five days later, in communication with B's agent at the port, the master was told that there was no cargo for the ship and she should leave. On 1 April it became known at Odessa that war had been declared between the UK and Russia, the State in possession of Odessa. The master continued to demand cargo until 17 April, when the ship eventually sailed away in ballast before the lay days expired. In its claim for damages, A had to rely upon the words of B's agent in the middle of March as the cause of action, for the contract was frustrated on 1 April by the declaration of war and by then B's obligation to complete loading a cargo had not as yet matured. The case was tried in the same court as *Hochster* had been, with Lord Campbell also delivering the judgment of the court. It was held that the words of B's agent did not amount to a renunciation of the contract.[74] On appeal, the decision was affirmed by the Exchequer Chamber on the same ground.[75] This formed the *ratio* of both *Avery v Bowden* and a jointly decided case with similar facts, *Reid v Hoskins*.[76]

Nevertheless, it was not that *ratio*, but two similar dicta from Lord Campbell in both cases, that later gained prominence. In *Avery*, counsel for the defendant (B) argued that the breach in *Hochster* was 'complete' only if and when the victim took it as putting an end to the contract.[77] Lord Campbell saw no difficulty in accepting this argument and stated that had the language of the defendant's agent been stronger and thus constituted a renunciation, 'according to our decision in *Hochster v De La Tour*', the master of the ship might not have treated it as a breach and sued for damages after he 'still continued to insist upon having a cargo in fulfilment of the charter party'.[78] Accordingly, acceptance of an anticipatory breach was regarded as a prerequisite for the breach to be constituted and for a right of action for damages to arise. Lord Campbell's dicta subsequently obtained general circulation and were treated as the *ratio* of both *Avery* and *Reid*.

[73] *Avery v Bowden* (1855) 5 El & Bl 714, 119 ER 647.

[74] *Ibid* 727–8, 652–3.

[75] *Avery v Bowden* (1856) 6 El & Bl 962, 973, 119 ER 1122, 1126 (Pollock CB); 975, 1127 (Alderson B).

[76] *Reid v Hoskins* (1855) 5 El & Bl 729, 119 ER 653, aff'd (1856) 6 El & Bl 953, 119 ER 1119.

[77] *Avery v Bowden* (n 73) 722, 650.

[78] *Ibid* 728–9, 652–3. Also, *Reid v Hoskins* (n 76) 744, 659.

The reason appeared to be a mistake in the reporting of the cases.[79] The reporter's headnote for the decision of the Court of Queen's Bench in both cases cited Lord Campbell's dictum as the sole ground of the decision and entirely omitted the correct *ratio*, namely, that there was no renunciation.[80] The headnote was then repeated in the law report of the decision of the Exchequer Chamber,[81] despite the fact that none of the appellate judges, with the exception of Cresswell J,[82] commented on the dictum.

In the aftermath of *Avery* and *Reid*, Lord Campbell's dicta were quickly endorsed as binding law.[83] If the victim of an anticipatory breach accepted it, the breach became a cause of action.[84] Conversely, in *Wilkinson v Verity*,[85] where a bailee wrongfully sold the goods in custody to a third party without either the authorisation or knowledge of the bailor and when the bailment ended refused a demand of the bailor for the return of the goods, Willes J in reliance on Lord Campbell's dicta stated that the wrongful disposition was not 'of itself a violation and breach of the contract' unless and until it was treated as such by the bailor.[86] Consequently, the Statute of Limitations did not start to run until the bailee refused to return the goods, when the actual non-delivery constituted a cause of action. The principle of election was neatly summed up by Cockburn CJ in *Frost v Knight*:

> The promisee, if he pleases, may treat the notice of intention as inoperative, and await the time when the contract is to be executed, and then hold the other party responsible for all the consequences of non-performance: but in that case he keeps the contract alive for the benefit of the other party as well as his own; he remains subject to all his own obligations and liabilities under it, and enables the other party not only to complete the contract, if so advised, notwithstanding his previous repudiation of it, but also to take advantage of any supervening circumstance which would justify him in declining to complete it.
>
> On the other hand, the promisee may, if he thinks proper, treat the repudiation of the other party as a wrongful putting an end to the contract, and may at once bring his

[79] L Vold, 'Anticipatory Breach of Contracts and Necessity of Election' (1927–1928) 26 *Michigan Law Review* 502, 519.

[80] In *Avery* (n 73), the concluding part of the headnote reads: 'Held that the refusal of the agent before the time for loading had expired, not being acted on as a renunciation of the contract, was not a cause of action; and that the plea was therefore proved.' In *Reid* (n 76), the concluding part of the headnote reads: '… supposing the language of M [the agent] to have amounted to a renunciation of the contract giving the plaintiff a right to elect to treat the contract at an end (and semble that it did not), this would not constitute a breach until the election was exercised on behalf of the plaintiff.'

[81] *Avery v Bowden* (1856) 6 El & Bl 953, 119 ER 1119. *Reid v Hoskins* shared the same headnote.

[82] *Ibid* 974–5, 1127. The dictum was held to be an alternative ground for refusing the action.

[83] *Barrick v Buba* (1857) 2 CB NS 563, 579–80, 140 ER 536, 543–4 (Cockburn CJ). In this case, however, it was found, and indicated correctly in the headnote, that there was no renunciation.

[84] *Danube & Black Sea Railway & Kustendjie Harbour Co Ltd v Xenos* (1863) 11 CB NS 152, 175–7, 142 ER 753; 762–3 (Erle CJ); 178–9, 764 (Williams J); 180–1, 764 (Byles J); 181, 765 (Keating J); aff'd (1863) 13 CB NS 825, 143 ER 325.

[85] *Wilkinson v Verity* (1870–71) LR 6 CP 206.

[86] *Ibid* 209.

> action as on a breach of it; and in such action he will be entitled to such damages as would have arisen from the non-performance of the contract at the appointed time, subject, however, to abatement in respect of any circumstances which may have afforded him the means of mitigating his loss.[87]

This passage was echoed in *Johnstone v Milling*,[88] where the Court of Appeal went even further:

> [A] renunciation of a contract, or, in other words, a total refusal to perform it by one party before the time for performance arrives, does not, by itself, amount to a breach of contract but may be so acted upon and adopted by the other party as a rescission of the contract as to give an immediate right of action.[89]
>
> [A] declaration of intention by the promisor not to carry out the contract … is not in itself and unless acted on by the promisee a breach of the contract; … it only becomes a breach when it is converted by force of what follows it into a wrongful renunciation of the contract.[90]

These statements were reminiscent of the 'offer to rescind' theory, which, although rejected in *Hochster*, might still 'rule us from the grave'.[91] But they actually assumed a new, different form. An anticipatory breach was recognised as a wrong, but an 'acceptance' was required to convert it into a fully fledged breach.[92] This rule formed part of the principle of election. We refer to it as the 'breach-conversion rule'. It has received the imprimatur of the House of Lords—an anticipatory breach was 'only complete and enforceable at the moment of rescission so that breach and termination of the contract are simultaneous'.[93] In its most extreme form, the rule was stated to be that '[a]n unaccepted repudiation is a thing writ in water and of no value to anybody; it confers no legal rights of any sort or kind'.[94]

In this Chapter, we have examined the historical development of two aspects of the doctrine of anticipatory breach: the 'implied promise' theory and the breach-conversion rule. Both of them have been found to be problematic. The former was invented by the court in *Hochster* on a precarious judicial basis, whilst the latter gained prominence by reason of an error in law reporting. There was a

[87] *Frost v Knight* (1871–72) LR 7 Ex 111 (EC) 112–13, rev'g (1869–70) LR 5 Ex 322 (CE). Also, 118 (Byles J).

[88] *Johnstone v Milling* (1886) 16 QBD 460 (CA).

[89] *Ibid* 467 (Lord Esher MR).

[90] *Ibid* 472–3 (Bowen LJ). Bowen LJ described an unaccepted anticipatory breach as a '*brutum fulmen*' (empty threat). Also, 470 (Cotton LJ).

[91] AH Chaytor and WJ Whittaker (eds), FW Maitland, *The Forms of Action at Common Law* (Cambridge, CUP, 1965) 2.

[92] Eg GED Pont (ed), *Halsbury's Laws of Australia* (Sydney, Butterworths, 1992) vol 6 [110–8200] (looseleaf): 'an anticipatory breach arises where, prior to the time appointed for performance by the promisor, the promisee justifiably terminates the performance of the contract for the promisor's repudiation or inability to perform', cited with approval *Hecec Australia Pty Ltd v Hydro-Electric Corp* [1999] FCA 822, (1999) ATPR 46–196 [62].

[93] *Heyman v Darwin Ltd* [1942] AC 350 (HL) 382 (Lord Wright).

[94] *Howard v Pickford Tool Co Ltd* [1951] 1 KB 417 (CA) 421 (Asquith LJ). Also, *Fenton Insurance Co Ltd v Gothaer Versicherungsbank VVaG* [1991] 1 Lloyd's Rep 172 (Com Ct) 180 (Potter J).

bizarre inconsistency between the two. An anticipatory breach was somehow seen as at once both an actual breach of an implied promise and an incomplete breach unless and until 'accepted' by its victim. The breach-conversion rule could be said to have sabotaged, to some extent, the 'implied promise' theory's enterprise to create a presently enforceable obligation. Their co-existence under the existing law renders the foundation of anticipatory breach unintelligible and unstable. It is thus time to instil new life into the doctrine of anticipatory breach. This is the task of the next Chapter.

2

A Redefinition of Anticipatory Breach

Although the doctrine of anticipatory breach has been historically tainted with theoretical difficulties, such as the fastening of the existence of a breach to the necessity of an option to terminate the contract, it does not follow that it thus 'cannot be rationalised, but must be seen as a piece of positive law, firmly established but not anchored in or deducible from the ordinary course of the law of contract'.[95] This Chapter proposes to lay down a new and rational theoretical foundation for the doctrine. Section A attempts to explore, by making two principal enquiries, what, in nature, characterises the type of legal wrong that is referred to as 'anticipatory breach'. Section B then appraises whether the term 'anticipatory breach' is an appropriate label for that type of legal wrong.

A. Two Enquiries

1. Is an Anticipatory Breach a Breach of Contract?

At first sight, this seems to be a paradoxical and redundant question. How can an anticipatory breach not be a breach of contract? Yet, terminology is not decisive. It has been advocated that what is dubbed 'anticipatory breach' should not be regarded as a breach of contract, or at least not as a complete breach of contract. An anticipatory breach is a civil wrong, viz a breach of a non-criminal common law duty.[96] Curiously, in an article that appeared in the Harvard Law Review about 80 years ago, it was suggested that that duty was best viewed as tortious rather than contractual in nature.[97] The author's argument was essentially based on a theory that contractual rights in 'intangible advantageous relations', assignable and pledgable as 'business credit', should be regarded as entitled to the same protection as actual property.[98] An anticipatory breach, consequently,

[95] M Mustill, '*The Golden Victory*—Some Reflections' (2008) 124 *LQR* 569, 584.

[96] Generally, P Birks, 'The Concept of a Civil Wrong' in D Owen (ed), *Philosophical Foundations of Tort Law* (Oxford, Clarendon, 1995).

[97] L Vold, 'The Tort Aspect of Anticipatory Breach of Contracts' (1927–1928) 41 *Harvard Law Review* 340.

[98] *Ibid* 353, 355. Also, Atiyah (n 7) 429; *Corbin on Contracts* (n 5) § 856.

was seen as detached from any non-performance (including mal-performance) of the contract and as constituting an infringement of the victim's property. The proprietary view of contractual rights was adopted in the 19th-century courts. It seemed to be supported not only by the fact that 'choses in action',[99] including contractual rights, had become assignable, but also by the development of a tortious liability for 'interference with a contractual relationship'.[100] The leading case on the latter development, *Lumley v Gye*,[101] was actually decided in the same court in the same month of the same year as *Hochster*. It is thus reasonable to suspect that Lord Campbell, when delivering the judgment in *Hochster*, might have been under some influence from this 'contractual property' theory. In *Lumley v Gye*, a theatre owner was held to be entitled to institute a claim in tort, before its contractual employment of a singer was set to start, for damages against a rival theatre owner who enticed away the singer. The defendant's act was regarded as an infringement of the claimant's intangible property right.[102] This tortious liability was later extended to an interference with 'mere economic expectancies'.[103] It was thus said that if a contractual right could generally be characterised as property, then no one, be it a stranger or a contracting party, might without justification impair it.[104] The impact of the 'contractual property' theory on the doctrine of anticipatory breach was most visible in *Frost v Knight*.[105] A man promised to marry a woman as soon as the man's father died. During his father's lifetime the man refused absolutely to marry the woman and was therefore sued by her. It was held that the defendant was liable for breach of promise. To say that he had actually broken his promise to marry would be stretching the reasoning in *Main's Case* too far. The promise simply could not be said to have fallen due to be performed while the father was still alive. Lord Cockburn CJ, instead, in reliance on *Hochster*, reasoned that the renunciation impaired 'an inchoate right to the performance of the bargain', 'a right to have the contract kept open as a subsisting and effective contract', and thus constituted 'a violation of the contract *in omnibus*' or 'a breach of the entire contract'.[106] As his Lordship explained, the 'unimpaired and unimpeached efficacy' of a contract depended precisely on the fact that a party's 'rights acquired under it may be dealt with by him in various ways for his benefit and advantage'.[107] Clearly, his Lordship was stating a

[99] Eg *Winch v Keely* (1787) 1 TR 619, 99 ER 1284.

[100] Eg PW Lee, 'Inducing Breach of Contract, Conversion and Contract as Property' (2009) 29 OJLS 511.

[101] *Lumley v Gye* (1852) 2 El & Bl 216, 118 ER 749.

[102] *Ibid* 232, 755 (Erle J). Also, Note, 'Tortious Interference with Contractual Relations in the Nineteenth Century: The Transformation of Property, Contract, and Tort' (1979–1980) 93 *Harvard Law Review* 1510, 1524.

[103] *Temperton v Russell* [1893] 1 QB 715 (CA). Also, BL Fine, 'An Analysis of the Formation of Property Rights Underlying Tortious Interference with Contracts and Other Economic Relations' (1983) 50 *University of Chicago Law Review* 1116.

[104] Vold (n 97) 361.

[105] n 87.

[106] *Ibid* 114.

[107] *Ibid*.

general principle of contract law, rather than a rule applicable only to a promise creating a personal status of betrothal.[108] This explicit reliance on the 'contractual property' theory is, however, misplaced. The theory entirely overlooks the vital difference between suing the contracting counter party and a party not privy to the contract for an interference with the contractual relationship. In the former case, even if the victim's contractual rights are treated as its property, a liability does not flow from an infringement of that property unless contract law dictates it. The infringement must constitute a breach of a 'primary contractual obligation', namely, an obligation that arises from the conclusion of the contract.[109] No anticipatory breach can be found if no contravention of a primary contractual obligation is involved.[110] The difficulty in applying the 'contractual property' theory to a contracting party, rather than a third party, is that it cannot sufficiently explain why contractual remedies, such as termination of contract and expectation damages, are available to the victim. At any rate, the theory tends unjustifiably to stretch, outflank and undermine the contractual obligations voluntarily assumed by the party engaging in the 'infringement'. In particular, if that party is bound to perform only in the future, a present primary contractual obligation cannot spring magically from a perception of the victim's contractual rights as property. What the court in *Frost v Knight* failed to establish was what exact primary contractual obligation was breached by the defendant's renunciation. For this reason, the proprietary or tortious view of an anticipatory breach must be seriously doubted.

A second theory that makes a dent in the characterisation of an anticipatory breach as a breach of contract is the breach-conversion rule. Under this rule, an anticipatory breach is complete as a breach of contract only if and when it is accepted. To a large number of scholars, the logic of this rule is clearly unsound.[111] The key point is that the rule is in direct collision with the natural meaning of the term 'breach'. A breach is a contractual wrong. It is all about what a contracting party does. How the other party reacts is entirely irrelevant to the question whether a breach has or has not been committed. Therefore, whether an anticipatory breach constitutes a breach cannot depend on an 'acceptance' by the victim of it as such. The difficulty with the rule can be seen in a growing number of cases. Although the courts seem generally to acquiesce in the rule, some judges have openly challenged it. Dillon LJ, for example, stated that in anticipatory breach cases the only cause of action the victim had was that arising

[108] *Ibid* (Cockburn CJ); 118 (Byles J).

[109] *Photo Production Ltd v Securicor Transport Ltd* [1980] AC 827 (HL) 848 (Lord Diplock). A 'secondary contractual obligation', in contrast, arises from a non-performance of a primary contractual obligation.

[110] Eg *Technocrats International Inc v Fredic Ltd* [2004] EWHC 692 (QB), [2005] 1 BCLC 467.

[111] HR Limburg, 'Anticipatory Breach of Contracts' (1924–1925) 10 *Cornell LQ* 135, 140, 148*ff*; Vold (n 79) 508*ff*; Nienaber (n 37) 221; JC Smith, 'Anticipatory Breach of Contract' in EZ Lomnicka and CGJ Morse (eds), *Contemporary Issues in Commercial Law* (London, Sweet & Maxwell, 1997) 180; *Corbin on Contracts* (n 5) § 1320. *cf* Dawson (n 61) 95, 102.

from the anticipatory breach itself and acceptance of that breach was 'a matter going to remedy rather than a fresh fact necessary to complete a new cause of action'.[112] More recently, in *Manx Electricity v J P Morgan Chase Bank*,[113] a clear distinction was drawn between the constitution of a breach and the accrual of a right of action for damages. Accordingly, an anticipatory breach was itself a breach but was not 'actionable' in damages unless and until accepted.[114] In that case, the victim, the employer under a construction contract, was not suing in damages for the contractor's anticipatory breach. Instead, it sought to recover under a performance bond issued by a third-party bank who undertook to reimburse the employer in the event that the contractor defaulted. Despite the fact that the employer had not accepted the anticipatory breach, both the Commercial Court and the Court of Appeal rejected the bank's application for a preliminary judgment to strike out the claim. Clearly, the anticipatory breach on its own was considered to constitute a 'default' by the contractor that would activate the bond. Indeed, for this purpose, that breach was explicitly recognised as equivalent to an actual breach.[115] More commonly, however, the obsoleteness of the breach-conversion rule is only implicit in the decisions. For example, it is well established that the victim of an anticipatory breach might sue for specific performance when, and only when, the breach remains unaccepted.[116] The breach itself was evidently the cause of action. In addition, the rule might not sit easily with a line of cases in which the place where an anticipatory breach was committed, rather than the place where it was accepted, was held to be the place of breach and therefore only the court situated there had jurisdiction over the dispute.[117] The rule could also sometimes give rise to odd results in a 'chain contract' scenario. Where S agrees to sell goods to B1 who then agrees to sell them to B2, S's renunciation of the contract prior to the date of delivery may well lead to a renunciation by B1 of its contract with B2. If B2 'accepts' B1's renunciation before B1 'accepts' S's, according to the breach-conversion rule B1, as opposed to S, would be the first in time to have committed an anticipatory breach. Consequently B1 would be precluded from claiming an indemnity by S against any claim which might be brought against B1 by B2, for B1's 'earlier' breach could not have been caused by S's 'later' breach. Obviously, this is a ludicrous argument. It was rejected on the

[112] *Tilcon Ltd v Land & Real Estate Investments Ltd* [1987] 1 WLR 46 (CA) 53. Similarly, in Scotland, in *Monklands DC v Ravenstone Securities* 1980 SLT (Notes) 30 (CSOH), Lord Dunpark rejected as 'self-contradictory' the contention that an anticipatory breach was not per se a breach of contract and was convertible into a breach only by acceptance.

[113] *Manx Electricity v J P Morgan Chase Bank* [2003] EWCA Civ 1324, [2003] BLR 477.

[114] *Ibid* [38]ff (Rix LJ).

[115] The unaccepted anticipatory breach was stated by Tomlinson J to be an 'outstanding breach' (cited *ibid* [32]) and by Rix LJ to be an 'actual repudiatory breach' (*ibid* [36]).

[116] *Khatijabai Jiwa Hasham v Zenab (AS Legal Representative of HG Harji)* [1960] AC 316 (PC Eastern Africa).

[117] *Cherry v Thompson* (1871–72) LR 7 QB 573; *Holland v Bennett* [1902] 1 KB 867 (CA); *Mutzenbecher v La Aseguradora Espanola* [1906] 1 KB 254 (CA); *Martin v Stout* [1925] AC 359 (PC Egypt).

ground that the breach-conversion rule did not apply to the above scenario.[118] The better view is that the rule itself must be rejected.

The rather dramatic statement of Asquith LJ in *Howard v Pickford* that an anticipatory breach was 'a thing writ in water'[119] has been widely considered to be a vivid depiction of the breach-conversion rule. Literally, that statement went further than the rule itself. It denied an unaccepted anticipatory breach not merely of the status of a breach, but also of any legal significance. In this sense, the statement was probably an over-generalisation.[120] In truth, it is submitted, it was meant to be something quite different from the breach-conversion rule. It should be read as merely an antidote to the proposition that an anticipatory breach might by itself bring a contract to an end. This was evidenced by the facts of *Howard v Pickford* itself, where the court disallowed an action for a declaration that a wrongful dismissal, unaccepted, had released the employee from the contract. Also bearing witness to the above interpretation were two prior cases cited by the court,[121] where an unaccepted anticipatory breach was held to be wholly nugatory and ineffective in law.[122] These observations, when put into their correct context, only reasserted that an acceptance was necessary for the contract to be dissolved. Nevertheless, Asquith LJ's statement was subsequently divested of this apparently more faithful interpretation and was simply deemed to be identical to the breach-conversion rule. The use of metaphor in that statement was excessive and misleading. It must be abandoned along with the breach-conversion rule itself. In conclusion, an anticipatory breach is best seen as a freestanding breach of contract whose constitution does not depend either on its victim's infringed rights being characterised as proprietary or on its victim's acceptance of the breach as such.

2. Is Anticipatory Breach Distinct from Actual Breach?

The second enquiry is whether an anticipatory breach is a distinct type of breach from an actual breach. There are two competing theories in this regard. One insists that an anticipatory breach is nothing but a special type of actual breach, to be specific, an actual breach of a present implied obligation, whilst the other argues that it is distinct from an actual breach and is embodied in a legal inference. In this subsection these two theories must be explained and compared.

[118] *British Electrical and Associated Industries (Cardiff) Ld v Patley Pressing Ld* [1953] 1 WLR 280 (QB) 286 (McNair J).

[119] *Howard v Pickford* (n 94) 421.

[120] Mustill (n 4) 61–2.

[121] *Howard v Pickford* (n 94) 421 (Evershed MR).

[122] *Golding v London & Edinburgh Insurance Co Ltd* (1932) 43 Ll L Rep 487 (CA) 488 (Scrutton LJ); *Heyman v Darwin* (n 93) 361 (Lord Simon LC).

The Actual Breach Analysis

A breach of contract is normally conceived of as an actual breach, namely, a non-performance of a primary contractual obligation which has already fallen due to be performed. Every contractual obligation has a 'due time' for performance. The due time can be either actual time ascertainable by the calendar or clock or by reference to a contingency, or notional time to be determined according to the particular circumstances of a case, such as 'a reasonable time'. The significance of 'due time' lies in the fact that the obligor is not legally bound to perform the obligation before that time arrives. A mere failure to perform the obligation before its due time is not an actual breach. It is, indeed, no breach at all. To illustrate, a contract for the sale of goods concluded on 1 January provides that the seller (A) must deliver goods to the buyer (B) on 1 April and B must pay A within three days after taking delivery. If on 1 February no goods are delivered, A is not thereby in 'breach' of its obligation to deliver. Likewise, if on 5 April B fails to pay because A has not delivered the goods, B's failure cannot be said to constitute a 'breach' of its obligation to pay. Where, however, on 1 February A definitely refuses to deliver the goods or B definitely refuses to pay, should such a refusal be recognised as a breach of the contract? If yes, what breach? One school of thought views it as but a special type of actual breach. This 'actual breach' analysis can be stated as follows. There can be no other way to breach a contractual obligation than 'actually' to breach it. Accordingly, there is no such a thing as an '*anticipatory* breach'. It is nonsensical to say that a contractual obligation can be 'anticipatorily' breached before its due time arrives. A party's definite refusal to perform a contractual obligation before its due time arrives, if it is to be a breach at all, can only be an actual breach. The actual breach must be a present breach, namely, a breach that occurs at the present time, for without a present breach no present remedies are available. Therefore, it cannot be a breach of the obligation that still lies in the future. An actual breach of a future obligation, by definition, occurs only when the obligation falls due to be performed and is thus a future breach. The refusal must be a present, actual breach, namely, an actual breach of a present obligation. The key to this analysis is that a present obligation must be found to form the subject of the breach.

Our historical survey in Chapter 1 has shown that two main methods have been employed to analyse a renunciation or disablement as an actual breach. The breach was either of an accelerated future obligation or of a separate implied obligation that was presently due.[123] The first method finds its origin in the reasoning in *Main's Case*,[124] which states that a promise subject to a condition precedent should immediately become due as a renunciation or disablement waives or dispenses with the condition. Its arena of operation is, however, seriously restricted. It does not apply where the only condition is the arrival of a future time. It may also cause difficulties in modern, bilateral contract cases. In our above illustration,

[123] Mustill (n 4) 1, 38.
[124] n 30.

for example, it is difficult to see how a renunciation on 1 February by B of the obligation to pay might dispense with A's delivery of the goods and thereby make B's obligation accrue immediately on that date. This may involve not only a false assumption as to A's 'constructive' delivery but also an enlargement of B's obligation to pay without its consent. Even where the condition is a non-promissory one, it may not always be possible to say that the promise can be made unconditional by the renunciation or disablement. For example, a promise to abide by an award on condition that it is given by a specified person cannot become due at a time when no dispute has yet been submitted to that person.[125] Similarly, an f.o.b. seller's promise to deliver the goods alongside the ship cannot become due at a time when no ship has yet been nominated.[126] For these reasons, the first method, by way of an acceleration of a future obligation, is now obsolete.

It was the second method, known as the 'implied promise' theory, that took central stage for a considerable period after *Hochster*. As argued in the previous Chapter, the theory originated in the principle in *Elderton v Emmens*,[127] namely, that in a contract of personal service there was prima facie an implied promise by both parties to maintain the contractual relationship during the contract term. In modern employment cases, this implied promise was usually stated to be one to maintain confidence and trust between the parties.[128] In *Hochster*, however, Lord Campbell took the bold step of extending what was a special principle in employment cases into a general doctrine by introducing into every type of contract an implied promise not to act inconsistently with the contractual relationship. *Hochster* was decided at a time when the law relating to the implication of promises was undergoing a profound change. The legal technique of implying promises was employed in the 17th and 18th centuries mainly to create a contract where there was none.[129] There was little said about when and how a promise could be implied. The technique was thus characterised by a strong instrumentalism and was used without proper restraint. In the 19th century, even though the courts retained a role of 'gap-filling',[130] they were increasingly subject to an objective

[125] *Vynior's Case* (n 32).

[126] *Peter Turnbull* (n 5) 260, 266 (Taylor J).

[127] n 68.

[128] *British Aircraft Corp v Austin* [1978] IRLR 332 (EAT); *Post Office v Roberts* [1980] IRLR 347 (EAT); *Woods v WM Car Services (Peterborough) Ltd* [1982] ICR 693 (CA) 698 (Lord Denning MR), aff'g [1981] ICR 666 (EAT) 670 (Browne-Wilkinson J); *Lewis v Motorworld Garages Ltd* [1986] ICR 157 (CA); *Imperial Group Pension Trust Ltd v Imperial Tobacco Ltd* [1991] 1 WLR 589 (Ch); *Mahmud v Bank of Credit and Commerce International SA* [1998] AC 20 (HL) 45 (Lord Steyn); *Morrow v Safeway Stores Ltd* [2002] IRLR 9 (EAT).

[129] For multiple purposes: eg to facilitate the payment of a pre-existing debt, *Slade's Case* (1602) 4 Co Rep 91a, 94a, 76 ER 1072, 1077; to protect a reliance interest, *Coggs v Barnard* (1703) 2 Ld Ray 909, 92 ER 107; *Hammersely v De Biel* (1845) 12 Cl & Fin 45, 8 ER 1312; *Denton v Great Northern Rly Co* (1856) 5 El & Bl 860, 119 ER 701; *Warlow v Harrison* (1859) 1 El & El 309, 120 ER 925; to enforce statutory duties, *City of London v Goree* (1677) 2 Lev 174, 83 ER 505; *Shuttleworth v Garnet* (1688) 3 Mod 239, 87 ER 156; to restore ill-gotten or gratuitous gains, *Bradshaw v Porter*, cited in (1680) 2 Lev 245, 83 ER 540. Also, SJ Stoljar, *A History of Contract at Common Law* (Canberra, Australian National University Press, 1975) 80; Atiyah (n 7) 460; Baker (n 14) 47 *et seq.*

[130] EA Farnsworth, 'Disputes over Omission in Contracts' (1968) 68 *Columbia Law Review* 860.

test of intention that aimed to prevent an erroneous application or abuse of that technique.[131] In time it would become commonplace that the courts had no power to rewrite a contract even if they thought it fair, just or reasonable to do so. Modern implication rules were still in embryonic form when *Hochster* was decided. Exactly 10 years after *Hochster*, a theory was still advanced to explain the doctrine of frustration on the ground of an implied condition in the contract,[132] only to be denounced in the next century.[133] The law had to wait until the end of the 19th century for the 'business efficacy' test to emerge.[134] As for a demarcation between implication 'in fact' and implication 'in law', that was to take almost a further century to be acknowledged.[135] In *Hochster* Lord Campbell's failure to, and his ignorance of the need to, spell out the legal basis for the implication of the promise to maintain the contractual relationship seemed to reflect the instrumentalism of earlier days. With the implication of promises becoming modernised in the 20th century, the influence of the 'implied promise' theory quickly waned. Although still occasionally adverted to,[136] it seems generally to have lost its enamour. However, it has not been subject to any formal denunciation and continues to represent the mainstream of the 'actual breach' analysis. It has also been accepted by some leading scholars.[137] Should the theory be endorsed, the courts would be expected to take three steps in approaching an anticipatory breach case. First, they must find out whether an implied obligation not to act inconsistently with the contractual relationship is present at the time when the alleged 'anticipatory breach' is committed. Secondly, if the answer is yes, they must then decide whether such an implied obligation is breached. Thirdly, if the obligation is breached, they must further assess whether the breach justifies a wholesale termination of the contract at common law. Only when all the above three questions are answered in the affirmative can the alleged 'anticipatory breach' be established.

The Inferential Breach Analysis

The alternative way of conceptualising an anticipatory breach is premised on a distinction between an anticipatory breach and an actual breach. The distinction is discernible from the courts' reasoning in many anticipatory breach cases, yet the

[131] Atiyah (n 7) 459; A Phang, 'Implied Terms, Business Efficacy and the Officious Bystander—A Modern History' [1998] *Journal of Business Law* 1, 3.

[132] *Taylor v Caldwell* (1863) 3 B & S 826, 122 ER 826.

[133] *Davis Contractors Ltd v Fareham Urban DC* [1956] AC 696 (HL).

[134] *The Moorcock* (1889) 14 PD 64 (CA).

[135] Implication 'in law' was not adopted until *Liverpool CC v Irwin* [1977] AC 239 (HL). Also, Atiyah (n 7) 150.

[136] *Bradley v Newsom* [1919] AC 16 (HL) 53–4 (Lord Wrenbury); *Maredelanto Compania Naviera SA v Bergbauhandel GmbH (The 'Mihalis Angelos')* [1971] 1 QB 164 (CA) 196 (Lord Denning MR). Also, *Tramways Advertising Pty Ltd v Luna Park (NSW) Ltd* (1938) 38 SR (NSW) 632 (NSWSC Full Ct) 646 (Jordan CJ), rev'd on other grounds (1938) 61 CLR 286 (HCA).

[137] Eg *Corbin on Contracts* (n 5) § 961; EA Farnsworth, *Farnsworth on Contracts*, 3rd edn (New York, ASPEN, 2004) vol II, 552.

law has not as yet laid down a solid theoretical foundation for it. The distinction seems, originally, to have been alluded to in *Frost v Knight*, a renunciation case where Cockburn CJ stated that the 'eventual non-performance' might, 'by anticipation, be treated as a cause of action' for damages.[138] An anticipatory breach was, accordingly, ineluctably linked to a future breach. His Lordship, however, did not explain why the future breach should constitute a present cause of action. The statement was, admittedly, somewhat inconsistent with his Lordship's earlier characterisation in the same judgment of the renunciation as an interference with an 'inchoate right'.[139] This, in fact, reflected a feature of the earlier law of anticipatory breach. An anticipatory breach was alternatively analysed as either an actual breach of a present, implied obligation or a non-actual breach of a future obligation. This alternative analysis can be seen from *Guy-Pell v Foster*.[140] The claimant, on the defendant's advice, invested in some company debentures, redeemable at par on 1 July 1930, at a price less than the par value. The claimant promised to give the defendant one-fourth of the profit he might receive on the investment at the date of redemption and the defendant in return promised to indemnify the claimant against any loss thereon. In 1925, the claimant, in the face of the defendant's protests, resold the debentures to his son for a nominal price. The claimant sued twice to enforce the indemnity. The legal question of interest to us was whether the resale constituted a breach of the contract and thus a good defence. In the first action,[141] it seems to be implicit in the judgments of a majority of the House of Lords that the resale constituted an actual breach of an implied obligation to retain the debentures up to the date of redemption.[142] In the second action, a majority of the Court of Appeal ruled that, as an alternative to that characterisation, the resale might also be viewed as an anticipatory breach by way of renunciation.[143] On either view, it was the deprivation of the defendant's right to receive the profit at the date of redemption that was unanimously held to form the basis of that breach.[144]

Further, there has been a general trend that either asserted or assumed the distinction between anticipatory and actual breach. That an anticipatory breach was better seen as a breach of a future obligation was first reflected in a rule of law that damages for an anticipatory breach should generally be assessed by reference to the time of contractual performance rather than any earlier time.[145] The distinction became

[138] *Frost v Knight* (n 87) 114. Also, *Roehm v Horst* (n 5) 19–20.

[139] *Ibid.* Text to n 106 above.

[140] *Guy-Pell v Foster* [1930] 2 Ch 169 (CA).

[141] *Guy-Pell v Foster* (HL 1925 G 1888). Unlike the second action, this first action was brought in 1925 before the claimant repurchased the debentures from his son and the company wound up in 1928.

[142] Lord Cave LC, Lord Dunedin and Lord Shaw.

[143] *Guy-Pell v Foster* (n 140) 180 (Lord Hanworth MR); 187–8 (Lawrence LJ); *cf* 189 (Romer LJ).

[144] Especially *ibid* 180 (Lord Hanworth MR); 187–8 (Lawrence LJ).

[145] *Roper v Johnson* (1873) LR 8 CP 167; *Michael v Hart & Co* [1902] 1 KB 482 (CA); *Millett v Van Heek and Co* [1921] 2 KB 369 (CA); *Tai Hing Cotton Mill Ltd v Kamsing Knitting Factory (A Firm)* [1979] AC 91 (PC Hong Kong).

clearer in a number of further cases. For example, a party had *locus poenitentiae* to withdraw an anticipatory, but not an actual, breach.[146] In the case of an anticipatory breach, no cause of action arose and the statutory limitation period would not run until it was 'accepted', whilst a cause of action arose and the statutory limitation period started to run from the moment an actual breach was committed.[147] Where a debtor committed a breach of contract with its creditor which entitled the latter to terminate the contract, whether the breach was actual or anticipatory might sometimes affect a guarantor's liability. To be specific, where the guarantor undertook to perform the debtor's obligations if the debtor failed to perform, the guarantor was liable to the creditor only for those obligations of the debtor that had not been performed when due.[148] By construction, the guarantor was liable only for the debtor's actual breach. An anticipatory breach by the debtor did not entitle the creditor to sue the guarantor. In contrast, where the guarantor undertook to see to it that the debtor performed its obligations, the guarantor would be liable to pay damages to the creditor to the same extent as the debtor, whether the debtor was in actual or anticipatory breach of its contract with the creditor.[149] The reason was said to be that, whenever the creditor terminated its contract with the debtor for the latter's actual or anticipatory breach, the guarantor would immediately be put in breach of its express obligation to the creditor.[150] In all these cases, however, the courts stopped short of spelling out clearly what an anticipatory breach was if it was not an actual breach and, in particular, by what means a future obligation could be breached presently.

It is thus necessary to see if it is theoretically sound to endorse the possibility of a breach of a future obligation. The answer can be presented in four steps. First, there is nothing in either principle or reason that compels the conclusion that a breach of contract must be an actual breach. The question whether there might be a breach of a contractual obligation yet to fall due for performance is thus entirely open. Secondly, the concept of 'anticipatory breach' was once criticised as conveying the misconception that a future breach could trigger present legal remedies.[151] Yet an anticipatory breach is a present breach, a breach committed presently, because it is embodied in a party's 'present' words or conduct. An anticipatory breach is not a breach committed in the future. It is a present breach of a

[146] *North-Western Cachar Tea Co Ltd v British & Beningtons Ltd* (1922) 10 Ll L Rep 381 (CA) 387 (Scrutton LJ), aff'd on other grounds [1923] AC 48 (HL); *Norwest Holst Group Administration Ltd v Harrison* [1985] ICR 668 (CA); *Buckland v Bournemouth University Higher Education Corp* [2010] EWCA Civ 121, [39]–[43] (Sedley LJ).

[147] *Bell v Peter Browne & Co* [1990] 2 QB 495 (CA) 511–12 (Mustill LJ). Also, *Wright Prospecting Pty Ltd v Hancock Prospecting Pty Ltd (1)* [2007] WASC 78, [36]–[37], [49] (Murray J).

[148] *Hyundai Heavy Industries Co Ltd v Papadopoulos* [1980] 1 WLR 1129 (HL).

[149] *Moschi v Lep Air Services Ltd* [1973] AC 331 (HL); *Sunbird Plaza Pty Ltd v Maloney* [1988] HCA 11, (1988) 166 CLR 245, 256 (Mason CJ), 270 (Gaudron J).

[150] *Moschi v Lep Air ibid* 350–51 (Lord Diplock). Also, *Photo Production* (n 109) 848 (Lord Diplock).

[151] *Frost v Knight* (n 87) 326–27 (Kelly CB); *Bradley v Newsom* (n 136) 53–54 (Lord Wrenbury); *The Mihalis Angelos* (n 136) 196 (Lord Denning). Also, M Furmston, *Cheshire, Fifoot & Furmston's Law of Contract*, 15th edn (Oxford, OUP, 2007) 682–3.

future obligation. The cause of action in anticipatory breach cases thus resides in what one has done, rather than what one will do. Thirdly, an anticipatory breach is innately linked to a future obligation and thus to a future, actual breach of that obligation. A party's present words or conduct are recognised as a contractual wrong precisely because they give rise to an inference that the future obligation will not be duly performed when due. It is submitted, accordingly, that a contractual obligation can, before its due time arrives, become the subject of a present breach via a legal inference. An anticipatory breach is thus best characterised as an inferential breach, a breach established by way of inference. A legal inference transforms the inferred, future breach into a present breach capable by itself of eliciting immediate legal responses. An anticipatory breach must, therefore, be distinguished from the inferred future breach (or anticipated breach).[152] The latter breach is 'future' in the sense that it occurs later in time than the anticipatory breach. It does not necessarily post-date the commencement of an action or the conduct of a trial. It may well be a 'hypothetical' breach that would have occurred, whether prior or subsequent to the action or trial, had the contract gone ahead. The anticipated breach, if it eventuates, constitutes a distinct cause of action from that constituted by the anticipatory breach and may produce different remedial consequences, such as, for example, a different quantum of damages and a different commencement time for the purpose of the Statute of Limitations. The two breaches might be relied upon as alternative, but not as joint, grounds.[153] This is due to the principle of res judicata and the 'once-for-all' nature of common law actions.[154] The two breaches are, in effect, variants of not performing the same contractual obligation. Hence the anticipatory breach exists only while the anticipated breach is still anticipated. The anticipatory breach is automatically translated into the anticipated breach once the obligation 'anticipatorily' breached falls due to be performed and is not performed.[155] Conversely, the victim's cause of action remains in the anticipatory breach before performance of that obligation is due.[156] Fourthly, in order for an inference of a future breach to constitute a breach and trigger present remedies, there must be some good justificatory reason for an acceleration of the legal remedies for the inferred breach, which remedies would otherwise be available only if and when that breach is committed. These remedies refer principally to a termination of the contract and loss of bargain damages. The

[152] *Cf Hutchison v Graham's Executrix* 2006 SCLR 587, 2006 GWD 14–259 (CSOH). One of the Key Words in the case note was 'anticipatory breach'. But the breach in the case was in fact a breach anticipated (and provided for) by the contract.

[153] *Stocznia Gdanska SA v Latvian Shipping Co, Latreefer Inc* [1998] 1 WLR 574 (HL) 593 (Lord Goff).

[154] *Henderson v Henderson* (1843) 3 Hare 100, 114–15, 67 ER 313, 319 (Wigram V-C); *Greenhalgh v Mallard* [1947] 2 All ER 255 (CA); *Brisbane CC v A-G of Queensland* [1979] AC 411, 425, (1978) 19 ALR 681 (PC Australia); *Talbot v Berkshire CC* [1994] QB 290 (CA) 296–7 (Stuart-Smith LJ). Also, B Coote, 'Chance and the Burden of Proof in Contract and Tort' (1988) 62 *Australian Law Journal* 761, 766.

[155] *Foran v Wight* [1989] 168 CLR 385 (HCA) 394–5 (Mason CJ); 416–17 (Brennan J); 433 (Deane J); 441–2 (Dawson J).

[156] *Peter Turnbull* (n 5) 260, 266 (Taylor J); *cf* 252 (Kitto J); 249 (Webb J).

good justificatory reason consists in the need to avoid waste, to free resources from fruitless or inefficient use, and to encourage early mitigation of loss. These reasons are present only when the inferred breach is so serious as to deprive the victim of substantially all the benefit intended to be acquired by it under the contract. In such a case, considerable waste and gross injustice would result if the victim were required to be bound by the contract, to continue to perform its part and to wait for the breach to materialise. It is thus necessary to recognise that the inference creates a present, 'anticipatory' breach that entitles the victim immediately to treat itself as discharged from the contract and to take steps to minimise any loss that may accrue to it. As will be shown in Chapter 4, the seriousness required for the inferred breach must be pitched at the level of a 'fundamental' breach. Only then can future remedies be accelerated and the inferred breach be converted into an anticipatory breach.

The 'inferential breach' analysis necessitates an entirely different approach to determining the existence of an anticipatory breach from that envisaged by the 'actual breach' analysis. It requires two steps to be taken. First, the party alleging an anticipatory breach must satisfy the court that a legal inference may be drawn that a future breach is likely to occur. Secondly, the party must also satisfy the court that the inferred breach is sufficiently serious to compel an acceleration of the legal remedies for it. For this purpose the inferred breach must be shown to be a 'fundamental' breach. Both of these tests must be met in order for an anticipatory breach to eventuate.

Making the Choice

The choice between the 'actual breach' analysis (which is largely nothing but another name for the 'implied promise' theory) and the 'inferential breach' analysis is not a hard one to make. For three main reasons it is submitted that the 'inferential breach' analysis represents the better view and the 'implied promise' theory should be allowed to pass into oblivion.

First, whilst the 'inferential breach' analysis offers a genuine explanation as to why a right of termination (and the ensuing right to claim expectation damages) should immediately be granted following an anticipatory breach, to base the entire law of anticipatory breach on the 'implied promise' theory is artificial, sidesteps the real issue in contention, and is out of fashion with more recent developments in other areas of contract law.[157] There is realistic concern that, if the 'actual breach' analysis is followed, the doctrine of anticipatory breach may be downgraded to a mere means of sanctioning the termination of a contract in whatever circumstances the courts think fit. On the other hand, the 'inferential

[157] Eg the theory has largely been discredited in the context of the doctrines of frustration (*Davis Contractors v Fareham* (n 133) 720–1 (Lord Reid)) and common mistake (*Great Peace Shipping Ltd v Tsavliris Salvage (International) Ltd (The 'Great Peace')* [2002] EWCA Civ 1407, [2003] QB 679, [73] (Lord Phillips MR)).

breach' analysis explicitly recognises that the reason why an anticipatory breach is regarded as a wrong lies precisely in the fact that it foreshadows a prospective breach which is serious enough to entitle the victim to terminate the contract. By illuminating the substantial reasons upon which decisions in anticipatory breach cases either openly or tacitly rest, the 'inferential breach' analysis, far from introducing perplexity and subtlety into the law, renders the law more rational, transparent and consistent.

Secondly, the practical effectiveness of the 'actual breach' analysis must be doubted. The theory is founded on the false premise that an implied obligation not to act inconsistently with the contractual relationship can be extracted from every contract. In fact, the courts are reluctant to imply one identical term indiscriminately into all types of contract.[158] Above all, such a term may not be capable of clear expression.[159] In many cases the implication of an obligation not to act inconsistently with the contractual relationship cannot be justified either by reference to the contracting parties' intention or to the nature of the contract, whether adopting a 'business efficacy',[160] 'officious bystander'[161] or '(reasonable) necessity' criterion.[162] It is demonstrably inconsistent with the general test enunciated in the latest case *A-G of Belize v Belize Telecom Ltd*,[163] where Lord Hoffmann, giving the advice of the Privy Council, stressed that in implying a term the court should not go beyond 'what the instrument, read as a whole against the relevant background, would reasonably be understood to mean'.[164] The implication of the above obligation might also contradict a party's statutory duty.[165] In addition, it is far from clear what kind of words or conduct would be held to be inconsistent with the contractual relationship. Little assistance can be found in the case law. Nor is it straightforward that every breach of the aforesaid implied obligation will necessarily give rise to a right to terminate the contract. The adoption of the 'implied promise' theory would, therefore, run the risk of using, inappropriately, rules concerning the implication of contract terms as a check on granting a right of termination. In contrast, the application of the 'inferential breach' analysis does not seem to cause as many problems. One key ingredient of this analysis is that the inferred breach must be a 'fundamental' or a repudiatory breach. Not only is there plenty of useful guidance in the case law with respect to what constitutes such a

[158] E Peden, 'Policy Concerns Behind Implication of Terms in Law' (2001) 117 *LQR* 459.

[159] *Shell UK Ltd v Lostock Garage Ltd* [1976] 1 WLR 1187 (CA) 1197 (Lord Denning MR); 1201 (Ormrod LJ); *cf* 1204 (Bridge LJ); *BP Refinery (Westernport) Pty Ltd v Shire of Hastings* (1977) 180 CLR 266 (PC Australia) 282–3 (Lord Simon).

[160] *The Moorcock* (n 134). In *Concord Trust v The Law Debenture Trust Corp* [2005] UKHL 27, [2005] 1 WLR 1591 [37] (Lord Scott of Foscode), the House of Lords refused, on the basis of the test in *The Moorcock*, to imply into a trust deed a promise not to give an invalid notice of acceleration or a promise not to assert unjustifiably the occurrence of an event of default. For a fuller analysis, ch 3, text to n 324 below.

[161] *Shirlaw v Southern Foundries (1926) Ltd* [1939] 2 KB 206 (CA) 227 (McKinnon LJ).

[162] *Liverpool CC v Irwin* (n 135).

[163] *A-G of Belize v Belize Telecom Ltd* [2009] UKPC 11, [2009] 2 All ER 1127 (PC Belize).

[164] *Ibid* [21].

[165] *William Cory & Son Ltd v City of London Corp* [1951] 2 KB 476 (CA).

breach, but it also supplies a test widely accepted, both in civilian and common law jurisdictions, as more appropriate for the grant of a right of termination for breach of contract.

Last but not least, it is the 'inferential breach' analysis or some parts of it, rather than the 'actual breach' analysis (including the 'implied promise' theory), that has so far received the vast majority of support in decided cases. The 'actual breach' analysis, notwithstanding its appearance in earlier cases, has seldom featured subsequently. On the other hand, the 'inferential breach' analysis has effectively been constantly applied in English courts since the concept of 'anticipatory breach' was created. It is hard to find a case where an anticipatory breach was established which did not involve an inferred future breach that was serious enough to trigger a right of termination. For the above reasons, the 'inferential breach' analysis must be accepted as the best theoretical basis of the doctrine of anticipatory breach.

B. Nomenclature

The conceptualisation of an anticipatory breach has a direct bearing on the terminology used in association with it. The term 'anticipatory breach' itself has been subject to vigorous attack. The criticism is mainly two-fold. First, as mentioned earlier, the word 'anticipatory' is said to convey, misleadingly, a sense of futurity which led to an anticipatory breach being mistaken for a future breach. However, 'anticipatory' should not be read as 'anticipated', but as 'of an anticipatory nature'. As has been seen, an 'anticipatory' breach is a present breach that anticipates a future actual breach. Secondly, the word 'breach' might be said to cast the net too widely by implying that *every* future actual breach might be translated into an anticipatory breach. This is clearly not so. The anticipated, or inferred, breach must be a serious breach. It must at least be a breach that justifiably gives rise to a right to terminate the contract. Consequently, it seems preferable to rename 'anticipatory breach' in a way that properly addresses this requirement of seriousness. This second criticism needs closer examination.

English law uses the standard of 'repudiation' to measure what amounts to an anticipatory breach. The latter is thus defined as a 'repudiation of [an] obligation not yet ripe for performance'.[166] A 'repudiation' of the contract always vests in the repudiatee a right to terminate the contract. It was said that a repudiation could be either actual or anticipatory[167] and the doctrine of anticipatory breach was 'but a species of the genus repudiation'.[168] Frequently, a repudiation precedes the

[166] Furmston (n 151) 682, citing Dawson (n 61); JW Carter, 'The Embiricos Principle and the Law of Anticipatory Breach' (1984) 47 *MLR* 422.

[167] *Cehave NV v Bremer Handelsgesellschaft mbH (The 'Hansa Nord')* [1976] QB 44 (CA) 59 (Lord Denning MR).

[168] *Afovos Shipping Co SA v Romano Pagnan and Pietro Pagnan (Trading As R Pagnan & F.lli) (The 'Afovos')* [1983] 1 WLR 195 (HL) 203 (Lord Diplock).

time for performance and constitutes an anticipatory breach.[169] In this context, it is usually called 'renunciation'.[170] Therefore 'anticipatory repudiation'[171] or 'renunciation' becomes a natural replacement for 'anticipatory breach'. In the USA the term 'anticipatory repudiation' is actually preferred. As Farnsworth noted, the English term 'anticipatory breach' is 'elliptical' and, if rewritten in full, should read 'breach by anticipatory repudiation'.[172] Repudiation is a synonym for 'repudiatory breach'. For this reason the courts in some recent cases have felt tempted to adopt the somewhat clumsy term 'anticipatory repudiatory breach'.[173]

There are two distinct, albeit connected, problems with the above terms proposed as substitutes for 'anticipatory breach'. The first problem relates to the clarity of the meaning of the terms 'repudiation' and 'repudiatory'. 'Repudiation' is not an easy word. It has been used in quite different contexts and carries several different senses.[174] The multiplicity of its senses has caused some confusion. It is thus necessary to identify the sense with which that word is used in every particular context. We must first exclude the use of 'repudiation' in a non-contractual context. For example, a 'repudiation' may simply mean a rejection by an academic commentator of a proposition or argument made by another.[175] This usage is of no concern to us. However, even if it is a contract or contractual obligation that is 'repudiated', the word 'repudiation' may still have three distinct senses. The first sense is now largely obsolete. In this sense, 'repudiation' means a legitimate denial of the existence or validity of a contract,[176] or a lawful putting of a contract to an end both retrospectively and prospectively. Historically, this sense has been regarded as the common law equivalent of equitable 'rescission'.[177] In this sense, 'repudiation' is a remedy arising out of some vitiating factors, such as misrepresentation. We can frequently find the word 'repudiate' used in 19th-century cases as a synonym for 'rescind', 'avoid', 'wipe out', or 'set aside for all purposes'.[178] In the 20th century, however, English courts were more inclined to use 'repudiation' in a

[169] *Heyman v Darwins* (n 93) 379 (Lord Wright), 397 (Lord Porter).

[170] *Chilean Nitrate Sales Corp v Marine Transportation Co Ltd & Pansuiza Compania de Navègacion SA; Marine Transportation Co Ltd v Pansuiza Compania de Navègacion SA (The 'Hermosa')* [1982] 1 Lloyd's Rep 570 (CA) 572 (Donaldson LJ).

[171] Eg *Ms E A Nelson v Kingston Cables Distributors Ltd*, Independent, 12 June 2000 (EAT) [16] (Mr Comr Howell QC).

[172] *Farnsworth on Contracts* (n 137) 550 fn 2.

[173] *Nelson v Kingston* (n 171) [20] (Howell QC); *HSS Hire Services Group plc v BMB Builders Merchants Ltd, Grafton Group (UK) plc* [2004] EWHC 2013 (QB) [4] (Simon Brown QC), rev'd on the issue of costs [2005] EWCA Civ 626, [2005] 1 WLR 3158, damages determined [2006] EWHC 3677 (QB).

[174] *Heyman v Darwins* (n 93) 378 (Lord Wright), 397 (Lord Porter).

[175] Eg *First National Bank v Thompson* [1996] Ch 231 (CA) 236 (Millett LJ).

[176] *Heyman v Darwin* (n 93) 378 (Lord Wright); *Toller v Law Accident Insurance Society Ltd* (1936) 55 Ll L Rep 258 (CA) 260 (Scott LJ).

[177] PS Atiyah, *An Introduction to the Law of Contract*, 5th edn (Oxford, Clarendon, 1995) 398. The relevant discussion was removed from the latest edition: SA Smith, *Atiyah's Introduction to the Law of Contract*, 6th edn (Oxford, Clarendon, 2006).

[178] Eg *Clarke v Dickson* (1858) El Bl & El 148, 153, 120 ER 463, 466 (Erle J), 155, 466 (Crompton J); *Erlanger v New Sombrero Phosphate Co* (1877–78) LR 3 App Cas 1218 (HL) 1278 (Lord Blackburn).

second sense, which refers to lawfully putting a contract to an end prospectively only. 'Repudiation' in this second sense is thus equated with 'termination' or 'discharge' as a remedy for breach of contract. This usage is complicated by an historical confusion between 'rescission' and 'termination'.[179] For a considerable period of time, English courts have used 'rescission' to convey the same meaning as 'termination'. But clearly the better practice is that 'rescission' should be used only when a contract is put to an end *ab initio*, or retrospectively.[180] Since then, the second sense of 'repudiation', referring to 'termination', has prevailed over its first sense, referring to 'rescission', in the modern law. For example, throughout the Sale of Goods Act (SGA) 1979, the word 'repudiation' is used as an equivalent to 'termination'. Thus, a party to a contract for the sale of goods is entitled to treat the contract as 'repudiated' for the other party's breach.[181] Notwithstanding their obvious differences, the above two senses of 'repudiation' share a common feature—they both concern a lawful bringing to an end of a contract and thus belong in the category of legal remedy, which clearly separates them from the third sense of 'repudiation'. In this third sense, 'repudiation' is a serious contractual wrong. It is often referred to as 'repudiatory breach'. The latter, however, has two slightly different meanings. The first meaning identifies it with a 'discharging breach'[182] and embraces all breaches that give rise to a right to terminate the contract.[183] The second meaning, by contrast, is narrower and comprises only those breaches that are serious enough to give rise to such a right.[184] The third sense of 'repudiation' coincides, for the most part, with the second meaning of 'repudiatory breach'. It does not, therefore, cover a mere breach of 'condition' (used in its strict, technical sense). Nevertheless, the contrast between this third sense and the first two senses is stark. Yet the second and the third senses have frequently been muddled. Nowhere is this seen more clearly than in section 31(2) of the SGA 1979, which states:

> [I]t is a question in each case depending on the terms of the contract and the circumstances of the case whether *the breach of contract is a repudiation of the whole contract* or it is a severable breach giving rise to a claim for compensation but not to *a right to treat the whole contract as repudiated*. (Emphasis added.)

In a way, the line between the second and third senses may not be absolute. Where a party to a contract purports to 'repudiate' the contract in the second sense but

[179] AM Shea, 'Discharge from Performance of Contracts by Failure of Condition' (1979) 42 *MLR* 623, 626.

[180] *Johnson v Agnew* [1980] AC 367 (HL) 392–3 (Lord Wilberforce).

[181] SGA 1979 ss 11, 61(1).

[182] JW Carter, *Breach of Contract*, 2nd edn (Sydney, Law Book, 1991) [705]. Of course, the breach does not discharge the contract; it entitles the victim to discharge it.

[183] Eg *Bremer Vulkan Schiffbau und Maschinenfabrik v South India Shipping Corp Ltd* [1981] AC 909 (HL) 980–1 (Lord Diplock); *Koompahtoo Local Aboriginal Land Council v Sanpine Pty Ltd* [2007] HCA 61, (2007) 233 CLR 115 [44] (Gleeson CJ, Gummow, Heydon and Crennan JJ). Also, JM Thomson, 'The Effect of A Repudiatory Breach' (1978) 41 *MLR* 137, 137–8.

[184] *Lombard North Central plc v Butterworth* [1987] QB 527 (CA) 535 (Mustill LJ); 541, 542–3 (Nicholls LJ).

it turns out to have no legal right to do so, its conduct constitutes a 'repudiation' in the third sense.[185] Its conduct would then constitute a wrong. In this situation, it is necessary for clarity to use 'repudiation' in one sense only. 'Repudiation' will be reserved in this book for its third sense, namely, a serious contractual wrong. The first and the second senses of 'repudiation' will respectively be replaced by 'rescission' and 'termination'.

The second problem with the terms 'anticipatory repudiation', 'anticipatory repudiatory breach' or 'renunciation' is the appropriateness of any of them as a label for the type of wrong customarily dubbed 'anticipatory breach'. This is not merely an issue of nomenclature, and it cannot be definitely dealt with until the proper legal test for an anticipatory breach is devised. It is the task of the bulk of Part II, not of this Chapter, to assess the desirability of the courts' common practice of employing 'repudiation' to determine the existence of an anticipatory breach. The current discussion is therefore confined to the terminological aspect of the problem. According to the *Oxford English Dictionary*, the basic meaning of 'repudiation' is 'the action of rejecting a debt'.[186] In our context the word 'debt' must be substituted by 'contractual obligation', as it is the latter that has become the epitome of modern contract law. In this sense, 'repudiation' is interchangeable with 'renunciation', an outright refusal to honour one's contractual obligations. When used to measure 'anticipatory breach', however, 'repudiation' suffers from a notable restriction. Originally, 'repudiation' was not only a serious wrong but also an *intentional* wrong.[187] Even though 'repudiation' is at times employed in a sense that exceeds this original meaning, it is still haunted by the latter. It was thus said that neither 'repudiation' nor 'repudiatory breach' was 'always an entirely satisfactory label', because for a right of termination to arise it was 'not an invariable requirement' that a party had to 'demonstrate an intention to abandon contractual obligations'.[188] The use of 'repudiation' to embrace all areas covered by 'anticipatory breach' has led the English courts to look to the *intention* of the party allegedly in breach, rather than the *nature* or *consequences* of its words or conduct, in search for an anticipatory breach. Whether this was a false step is a question to be addressed in the next Part of this book. At this point, it is sufficient to say that the restrictiveness of 'repudiation' or 'repudiatory' counts significantly against its installation as a replacement for 'anticipatory breach'. Despite the shortcomings of both 'anticipatory breach' and 'repudiation', they can be retained provided that it is kept in mind that an 'anticipatory breach' does not arise from every inferred future breach and a 'repudiation' is not necessarily intentional. One final note

[185] Eg *Smith v Butler* [1900] 1 QB 694 (CA).

[186] JA Simpson and ESC Weiner (comps), *The Oxford English Dictionary*, 2nd edn (Oxford, Clarendon, 1989) vol XIII, 674: 'Repudiation has not been the course of those who could not, but of those who, having the means, would not pay.'

[187] Smith (n 111) 198.

[188] *Rice (t/a Garden Guardian) v Great Yarmouth BC* [2003] TCLR 1, (2001) 3 LGLR 4 (CA) [35] (Hale LJ). Perhaps for similar reasons, Knox CJ preferred 'a breach by anticipation' to 'repudiation': *Bowes v Chaleyer* (1923) 32 CLR 159 (HCA) 169.

must be added. A repudiation as understood above can only be an anticipatory breach. The term 'actual repudiation'[189] is thus misleading. For, even if a repudiation occurs at or after the time set for performance under the contract, it must be distinguished from an actual non-performance of the already matured obligation and there is only one way of making that distinction, namely, to characterise the repudiation as a breach of a future obligation. A failure to deliver goods on time must therefore be distinguished from a simultaneous repudiation of the contract. The former is an actual breach of a 'temporal' obligation to deliver goods at the fixed time, whilst the latter is an anticipatory breach of a 'substantive' obligation to deliver goods at any future time.[190] There is no such a thing as 'actual repudiation'. In this book, therefore, 'repudiation' will be used interchangeably with 'anticipatory breach'.

[189] Eg NC Seddon and MP Ellinghaus, *Cheshire and Fifoot's Law of Contract*, 9th Australian edn (LexisNexis, 2008) [21.14]. Cf *Roehm v Horst* (n 5) 19 ('there can be no controlling distinction ... between [a renunciation before the time for performance and a renunciation in course of performance]').

[190] *Foran v Wight* (n 155) 420 (Brennan J).

Part II

Establishing Anticipatory Breach

This Part is concerned with the constitution of an anticipatory breach. It is centred on the question: what ought to be the proper legal test? Chapter 3 attempts to demolish the legal test dominating the existing law. Chapter 4 then proposes a new unifying test. Chapter 5 discusses a related issue, namely, whether and how a party might exonerate itself from liability for breach of contract on the ground of the other party's future, anticipated breach(es).

3

A Critique of the Prevailing Test

A. The Dichotomy of English Law

Since its inception, the doctrine of anticipatory breach has been widely employed by counsel in numerous legal battles as a vehicle to justify a premature termination of a contract. It was perhaps with confidence in such frequent exposure of the doctrine to judicial examination that Lord Wilberforce once declared that the rules determining the existence of an anticipatory breach constituted 'one of the more perspicuous branches of the law of contract'.[191] With due respect, his Lordship seemed to be too optimistic. When one takes a closer look at decided cases, it is hard to resist the conclusion that this area of law is still plagued by inconsistency, uncertainty and incoherence. Where the existence of an anticipatory breach of contract is in dispute, the courts have been applying two distinct approaches to fact patterns of the same nature. A major cause of this disparity is the courts' failure to realise in some cases that what they are dealing with are anticipatory breach cases and they should be subject to a uniform test. This cognitive failure is largely attributable to the fact that, although the term 'anticipatory breach' has been severely criticised, little has been done to illuminate the very nature of an anticipatory breach and what distinguishes it from an actual breach. Another cause of the disparity of the courts' approaches is perhaps English law's case-to-case, piecemeal methodology.[192] Pragmatic though this methodology may be, it is sometimes necessary to amass the fragmented pieces and fit them into a clear and stable conceptual structure, thereby articulating the law at a higher level of generalisation.[193] It is the purpose of this Chapter to expose the problems with which the prevailing test under the current law has been afflicted. Only when these problems are diagnosed can we proceed to offer a cure for them by proposing a general legal test for all types of anticipatory breach and then bring order, rationality and unity to this presently chaotic area of law.

[191] *Federal Commerce & Navigation Ltd v Molena Alpha Inc* [1979] AC 757 (HL) 778.

[192] Generally, T Weir (tr), K Zweigert and H Kötz, *An Introduction to Comparative Law*, 3rd edn (Oxford, OUP, 1998) 69–70, 259.

[193] The value of such a conceptual structure, a feature of Romanist legal traditions, has been increasingly appreciated by English jurists, eg Birks (n 14); P Birks, *Unjust Enrichment*, 2nd edn (Oxford, OUP, 2005).

Many of these problems originate in two contradictory approaches the courts have taken to determining the existence of an anticipatory breach. English law hence exhibits a patent dichotomy in this regard. The orthodox, and predominant, approach adopted by English courts focuses on the intention of the party who is alleged to have committed an anticipatory breach,[194] while a more recent, but apparently less influential, approach turns to the potential consequences of that party's words or conduct on the performance of the contract as a whole. The courts have, however, so far refrained from saying anything about the precise relationship between these two approaches. Consequently, this dichotomy has introduced a considerable degree of instability into the law. This is well illustrated by two leading decisions of the House of Lords, which have long been considered to be among the most difficult to reconcile.[195] They are now examined respectively.

1. *Federal Commerce & Navigation Ltd v Molena Alpha Inc*[196]

The dispute in this case arose between two parties to a time charterparty. The source of the dispute was that, due to a world recession in shipping, the charter became disadvantageous to the charterers. The charterers began to make a series of deductions from the hire, to which the owners strongly objected. To force the charterers to pay the deducted hire, the owners instructed the master of the ship not to sign bills of lading marked 'freight pre-paid'. Meanwhile they submitted the dispute over the hire to arbitration. Before the owners' instruction was carried out, the charterers promptly terminated the charter. The owners brought an action for wrongful termination and claimed damages. Since the owners' instruction was never carried out, there was no actual breach by them of their contractual obligation to sign bills of lading marked 'freight pre-paid'. The key question thus turned upon whether the giving of the instruction itself constituted an 'anticipatory breach' by the owners.[197] The House of Lords, affirming the decision of the Court of Appeal,[198] unanimously answered that question in the affirmative. To reach that conclusion, Lord Wilberforce and Lord Fraser,[199] with whom

[194] Similarly, in Canada, *McCallum v Zivojinovic* (1977) 79 DLR (3d) 133, 16 OR (2d) 721 (CA); *Sanko Steamship Co v Eacom Timber Sales Ltd (The 'Sanko Iris' and 'Sanko Venus')* (1986) 32 DLR (4th) 269, 8 BCLR (2d) 69 (SC), [1987] 1 Lloyd's Rep 487; *Pompeani v Bonik Inc* (1997) 35 OR (3d) 417 (Ontario CA); *United Food & Commercial Workers International Union v Finnamore* 2005 BCSC 1454, (2005) 143 ACWS (3d) 669 [61]. In Australia, *Carr v JA Berriman Pty Ltd* (1953) 89 CLR 327 (HCA) 349–50, 351 (Fullagar J); *DTR Nominees Pty Ltd v Mona Homes Pty Ltd* (1978) 138 CLR 423 (HCA) 431 (Stephen, Mason and Jacobs JJ); *Laurinda Pty Ltd v Capalaba Park Shopping Centre Pty Ltd* (1989) 166 CLR 623 (HCA) 634 (Mason CJ), 657–8 (Deane and Dawson JJ), *cf* 647 (Brennan J).

[195] *Cf Gulf Agri Trade Fzco v Aston Agro Industrial AG* [2008] EWHC 1252 (Comm), [2008] 2 Lloyd's Rep 376 [44] (Aikens J).

[196] n 191.

[197] *Ibid* 778 (Lord Wilberforce).

[198] *Federal Commerce & Navigation Co Ltd v Molena Alpha Inc* [1978] QB 927 (CA).

[199] *Federal Commerce v Molena* (n 191) 779 (Lord Wilberforce); 783 (Lord Fraser).

the other Law Lords concurred,[200] cited with approval the approach adopted by Buckley LJ in *Decro-Wall International SA v Practitioners in Marketing Ltd*.[201] In Lord Wilberforce's words, the correct question was whether the owners' conduct 'went to the root of the contract as depriving the charterers of substantially the whole benefit of the contract'.[202] This approach, focusing on the *consequences* of the owners' prospective conduct, shall henceforth be called the 'fundamental breach' approach because it was in essence based on the concept of 'fundamental breach' as defined by Lord Diplock on two previous occasions.[203] The Law Lords were convinced by the umpire's finding that the consequences of the owners' instruction, had it been carried out, would have been 'extremely serious' because it would have resulted in the charterers being blacklisted by grain shippers and incurring substantial liability to third parties.[204] Under this approach, the owners' intention or good faith was held to be wholly immaterial. The Law Lords thus dismissed the owners' arguments that they honestly believed that they had the right under the charter to issue the instruction, that they intended to perform the charter, and that their conduct was only a tactical move that was conditional on a favourable verdict of the arbitrators. Arguments of this kind, however, became highly relevant in a subsequent case where the House of Lords adopted a different approach.

2. *Woodar Investment Development Ltd v Wimpey Construction UK Ltd*[205]

In this case, two parties concluded a contract for the sale of a piece of land, which sale was to be completed within two months from the grant by the relevant authorities of planning permission. The contract also contained a 'condition E', which conferred on the purchasers a right to terminate the contract in certain circumstances. After the conclusion of the contract, land prices fell drastically and the purchasers decided to extricate themselves from the contract. Under the impression that planning permission would soon be granted by the authorities (and thus that the date of completion would soon arrive), the purchasers, after taking legal advice from their solicitors and consequently in the belief that they were entitled to do so, served a notice under condition E to terminate the contract. The vendors refused to accept the validity of the notice and brought an action seeking a declaration that it was unlawful. Shortly after the vendors brought the first action, they purported to treat the purchasers as

200 Viscount Dilhorne, Lord Russell and Lord Scarman.

201 *Decro-Wall International SA v Practitioners in Marketing Ltd* [1971] 1 WLR 361 (CA) 380.

202 *Federal Commerce v Molena* (n 191) 779. Also, 785 (Lord Russell).

203 *Hongkong Fir Shipping Co Ltd v Kawasaki Kisen Kaisha Ltd* [1962] 2 QB 26 (CA) 66; *Photo Production* (n 109) 849.

204 *Federal Commerce v Molena* (n 191) 780 (Lord Wilberforce); 783–4 (Lord Fraser); 785–6 (Lord Russell).

205 *Woodar Investment Development Ltd v Wimpey Construction UK Ltd* [1980] 1 WLR 277 (HL).

having 'repudiated' the contract, resold the land to a third party at a loss, and then brought a second action claiming damages upon the alleged repudiation. In the first action, Fox J held that the purchasers were not entitled to terminate the contract pursuant to condition E, a decision not challenged by the purchasers. In the second action, both Fox J and the Court of Appeal held that the purchasers' notice of termination constituted a repudiation of the contract. The House of Lords, by a bare majority (Lord Salmon and Lord Russell dissenting), reversed the decision of the Court of Appeal.

In deciding the appeal, both the majority and the minority in *Woodar* were unified in their approach. The approach adopted was to ascertain whether the purchasers had evinced an intention not to perform the contract.[206] The focus of this approach was thus upon a party's *intention* at the time when the other party treated the former's conduct as a repudiation of the contract, not on the potential *consequences* that might flow thereafter from this conduct. As Lord Sumner had remarked in a much-cited decision, 'anticipatory breach' is 'a matter of intention'.[207] We shall henceforth call this approach the 'renunciation approach', because the term 'renunciation' has naturally been associated with an intention not to perform the contract.[208] Surprisingly enough, despite the fact that three of the Law Lords in *Woodar* also sat in *Federal Commerce* (Lord Wilberforce, Lord Scarman and Lord Russell), the fundamental breach approach applied one year earlier in *Federal Commerce* was not even mentioned in *Woodar*. The majority in *Woodar* came to the conclusion that the purchasers did not evince an intention not to perform the contract on three major grounds. First, the purchasers, by serving the notice, acted *bona fide* on their solicitors' advice.[209] Secondly, although it was clear that the purchasers subjectively intended to get out of the contract, their conduct, objectively assessed, did not evince an intention to 'abandon' or 'repudiate' the contract because the notice of termination was a 'neutral document' and, by serving the notice, they were merely relying on the contract and 'invoking one of its provisions'.[210] Thirdly, the purchasers' intention should be judged not from the notice alone but from all the surrounding circumstances, and, since the vendor disputed the lawfulness of the notice in court, the purchasers' intention to bring the contract to an end was not *absolute* but was *conditional* on the court's decision.[211] We shall return to the issue of the correctness of the majority's

206 *Ibid* 282 (Lord Wilberforce); 287–8 (Lord Salmon); 292 (Lord Russell); 294–5 (Lord Keith); 298 (Lord Scarman).

207 *British & Beningtons Ltd v North West Cachar Tea Co* [1923] AC 48 (HL) 69 (Lord Sumner). Also, *Sentinel International Ltd v Cordes (The 'Bahamas')* [2008] UKPC 60 (Bahamas) [41], [2008] All ER (D) 141 (Dec); *Connaught Laboratories Ltd v R* [1978] FCJ No 605 (FCC) [27] (Cattanach J).

208 *Mersey Steel and Iron Co v Naylor Benzon & Co* (1884) 9 App Cas 434 (HL) 438–9 (Earl of Selborne LC), aff'g (1882) 9 QBD 648 (CA).

209 *Woodar v Wimpey* (n 205) 283 (Lord Wilberforce); 295 (Lord Keith): 'a genuinely held but erroneous view as to the validity or effect of a contract does not constitute a repudiation'.

210 *Ibid* 280–1 (Lord Wilberforce).

211 *Ibid* 294–6 (Lord Keith); 299 (Lord Scarman); 280, 282 (Lord Wilberforce).

application of the renunciation approach shortly; our current concern is the difference in approach revealed by these two decisions.

3. *Some Reflections*

The fact patterns of *Federal Commerce* and *Woodar* are of the same nature and raise the same legal question. Both the giving of the instruction and the serving of the notice pointed to a future breach of contract (a failure to sign 'freight pre-paid' bills of lading and a failure to complete the contract respectively). The legal question in both cases was whether the anticipated future breach might justify a present right of termination. Although a conveyancing contract is in many respects different from a commercial charterparty, it does not seem to be convincing to assert that the vendors in *Woodar* had more room than the owners in *Federal Commerce* to test the other party's honesty.[212] In fact, both of the parties in *Woodar* were under a false impression as to the imminence of completion and consequently acted with some urgency. The most unusual feature of the two cases is, therefore, the inexplicable divergence in the approaches adopted by the Law Lords to answer the same question. English law thus fails patently here to treat like cases alike. The fundamental breach approach in *Federal Commerce* and the renunciation approach in *Woodar* may produce wholly different results. Had the renunciation approach been applied to *Federal Commerce*, the arguments advanced by the owners in that case would likely have been fatal to the allegation of anticipatory breach. Clearly, the owners had no intention to abandon or repudiate the charter, which was lucrative and beneficial to them. It was the charterers who were desperate to get out of the contract. It would be preposterous for the charterers to claim that they reasonably believed that the owners, by making the instruction, intended not to perform the contract. Even if there was such an intention, it was probably not absolute and unconditional because presumably the owners were prepared to withdraw their instruction if the arbitrators reached a decision contrary to their interpretation of the contract. Furthermore, the owners seemed to be no less a *bona fide* party than the purchasers in *Woodar*, as the owners also honestly believed that they were entitled to give the instruction under the contract. On the whole, the owners' conduct, under the renunciation approach applied in *Woodar*, would probably not constitute an anticipatory breach of the contract. On the other hand, if we apply the fundamental breach approach to *Woodar*, it seems that the minority's view would prevail. Whether the purchasers were in good faith or not, their wrongful termination of the contract simply meant that they would not complete the contract, thereby in effect depriving the vendors of the whole bargain. Although the purchasers relied on a termination provision in the contract, their reliance had been conclusively adjudged as misplaced. Their conduct would therefore amount to an anticipatory breach.

212 *Cf* Carter (n 182) 257; Furmston (n 151) 684.

This area of English law is thus extremely uncertain, unpredictable and plagued by inconsistent authority. The courts adopt two different approaches that may well lead to opposite results when applied to the same set of facts. We receive little guidance from the courts as to when they will apply one approach in favour of the other, nor is it clear that the courts realise that they are applying two very different approaches. It is thus of some urgent importance to resolve the relationship between those two approaches and to devise a universal and consistent test capable of application to all types of anticipatory breach. The next two sections conduct a critical review of the orthodox renunciation approach and assess its suitability for the role of a general test for anticipatory breach.

B. The Decline of the Renunciation Approach

This section attempts to illustrate, by a survey of some typical cases to which the renunciation approach has been applied, the necessity and inevitability of its downfall. It consists of three subsections. Subsection (1) examines instalment contract cases, the provenance of the approach but now increasingly a graveyard for it. Subsection (2) deals with wrongful termination, which seemingly constitutes a straightforward form of renunciation but in fact has caused enormous problems in practice. Subsection (3) turns to disablement, the antonym of renunciation yet mysteriously regarded as a form of anticipatory breach governed by the approach.

2. Impure Anticipatory Breach in Instalment Contracts

Just as they witnessed the rise of the renunciation approach, instalment cases are now betokening its downfall. The classic statement of the renunciation approach can be found in *Freeth v Burr*, where Lord Coleridge CJ defined it as finding 'an intention to abandon and altogether to refuse performance of the contract' or 'an intention no longer to be bound by the contract'.[213] These seemed to be two distinct statements, with only the former embracing an element of deliberateness or recklessness. Without distinguishing them, however, the House of Lords approved the former statement and adopted a test of 'renunciation' or 'absolute refusal' in *Mersey Steel v Naylor*.[214] By contrast, Lord Coleridge's second statement cited above seemed to be favoured in the following summarisation by Atkin LJ of the approach:

> A repudiation has been defined in different terms—by Lord Selborne as an absolute refusal to perform a contract; by Lord Esher as a total refusal to perform it; by Bowen LJ

[213] *Freeth v Burr* (1874) LR 9 CP 208, 213.

[214] *Mersey Steel* (n 208) 439 (Lord Selborne LC).

> in *Johnstone v Milling* as a declaration of an intention not to carry out a contract when the time arrives, and by Lord Haldane in *Bradley v H Newsom, Sons & Co Ld* as an intention to treat the obligation as altogether at an end. They all come to the same thing, and they all amount at any rate to this, that it must be shown that the party to the contract made quite plain his own intention not to perform the contract.[215]

Under an instalment contract, the renunciation approach was frequently applied to determine the existence of an 'impure'[216] or 'hybrid'[217] anticipatory breach, namely, one that was embodied in, yet was conceptually separate from, an actual breach in respect of one or more (usually earlier) instalments.[218] The application of the approach to those cases, including *Freeth* and *Mersey Steel*, exposed an acute problem derived from Lord Coleridge's two variant statements of the approach.

The courts in *Freeth* and *Mersey Steel* faced similar factual scenarios. In both cases there was a sales contract under which goods were to be delivered in instalments and paid for upon each delivery. Due to an unexpected rise in the market, the seller(s) made the first delivery late. The buyer(s) refused to pay for that delivery. The seller(s) treated this refusal as a repudiation of the whole contract and commenced an action. Both cases raised the same issue, namely whether the buyer(s)' refusal to pay amounted to a repudiation. In *Freeth*, the buyer refused to pay the full amount for the first delivery and insisted upon setting off its loss resulting from the delay against that amount. It was held that the buyer, who was evidently anxious to have the contract performed, did not evince an intention to 'abandon' the contract.[219] Similarly, in *Mersey Steel*, the buyers, in bona fide reliance on their solicitor's erroneous advice, refused to pay on the ground that, since a petition for winding up the sellers' company had been lodged, the sellers should obtain a court order before payment could be made. A majority of the House of Lords applied the renunciation approach to reach the conclusion that the buyers' refusal did not amount to a repudiation.[220] Two main grounds were given. The first was that the buyers were 'desirous of fulfilling the contract'.[221] The second was that they acted bona fide and in reliance on legal advice.[222] Thus, clearly, the renunciation approach, as applied in both cases, was characterised by a subjective test. A renouncing party was required to act deliberately or recklessly.

215 *Spettabile Consorzio Veneziano di Armamento e Navigazione v Northumberland Shipbuilding Co Ltd* [1918–19] All ER Rep 963 (CA) 968 (citations omitted).

216 Mustill (n 4) 54.

217 *Norwest Holst v Harrison* (n 146) 678E (Cumming-Bruce LJ).

218 *Millar's Karri and Jarrah Co (1902) v Weddel, Turner & Co* [1908–10] All ER Rep Ext 1274 (KB) 1276 (Bigham J), 1277 (Walton J); *Maple Flock Co Ltd v Universal Furniture Products (Wembley) Ltd* [1934] 1 KB 148 (CA) 154 (Lord Hewart CJ); *J Rosenthal & Sons Ltd v Esmail* [1965] 1 WLR 1117 (HL) 1131 (Lord Pearson), aff'g [1964] 2 Lloyd's Rep 447 (CA); *Gunton v Richmond-upon-Thames LBC* [1981] Ch 448 (CA) 467–8 (Buckley LJ); *Bell v Peter Browne* (n 147) 512 (Mustill LJ).

219 *Freeth v Burr* (n 213) 215 (Keating J). Also, 213 (Lord Coleridge).

220 *Mersey Steel* (n 208) 443 (Lord Selborne); 445 (Lord Watson); 446 (Lord Bramwell). Lord FitzGerald concurred. Lord Blackburn came to the same conclusion via a different approach.

221 *Ibid* 441 (Lord Selborne). Also, 445 (Lord Watson); 446 (Lord Bramwell).

222 *Ibid* 440 (Lord Selborne).

Although in some later cases it was insisted that the requisite 'intention' be assessed objectively,[223] this subjective application of the renunciation approach, as *Woodar v Wimpey* signally demonstrated, has somehow persisted. The subjective interpretation is evidently problematic. It is overly rigid in that it excludes non-deliberate refusal to perform from the domain of renunciation. Its coexistence with the objective test indicates that there are severe interpretative difficulties with the requisite 'intention', which makes the renunciation approach obscure, unpredicatable and hence hard to apply.

The renunciation approach, however, even in those earlier days, was by no means the only available approach. In *Mersey Steel*, therefore, Lord Blackburn took a completely different line. According to his Lordship, the legal test extractable from both *Hochster* and *Freeth* was whether a party's conduct 'goes to the root of the contract, goes to the foundation of the whole'.[224] The buyers' conduct in that case was clearly not of such a kind. A material fact shared by *Mersey Steel* and *Freeth* was that the buyer(s)' punctual payment was not a condition precedent to the seller(s)' next delivery.[225] The delay in making the payment was thus insubstantial. Furthermore, it could not be inferred from the buyers' conduct that they would persist in their refusal to pay should the sellers continue to make the next delivery. In this respect Lord Blackburn distinguished *Mersey Steel* from *Withers v Reynolds*,[226] where a buyer was held to have repudiated the contract by insisting upon deferring payment due upon the delivery of an instalment until the next delivery. The latter was analogous to a case where a bank's refusal to make an instalment payment under an irrevocable letter of credit it issued was held to constitute a repudiation of the contract embodied in the letter of credit.[227] Just as the bank's repudiation was regarded as having the effect of undermining the independence of the documentary credit and thus going to the root of the contract, the buyer's deferral constituted a repudiation in that it turned a cash transaction into a credit transaction.[228] Lord Blackburn's approach in *Mersey Steel* was thus completely in line with the fundamental breach approach. That approach was also reflected in the rule that the more instalments a party has delivered, the less likely its conduct in relation to one of them would constitute a repudiation of the contract.[229]

Before long, in instalment cases, the renunciation approach began to be overshadowed by the fundamental breach approach. The transition gathered momentum at the turn of the 20th century. This could be seen from the development of

[223] *Johnstone v Milling* (n 88) 474 (Bowen LJ); *Forslind v Bechely-Crundall* (n 5) 179 (Viscount Haldane).

[224] *Mersey Steel* (n 208) 443–4. Also, 447 (Lord Bramwell).

[225] *Ibid* 439 (Lord Selborne). Similarly, *Payzu Ltd v Saunders* [1919] 2 KB 581 (CA).

[226] n 63.

[227] *Urquhart Lindsay & Co Ltd v Eastern Bank Ltd* [1922] 1 KB 318.

[228] *Mersey Steel* (n 208) 443 (Lord Blackburn); 446 (Lord Bramwell).

[229] *Hoare v Rennie* (1859) 5 H & N 19, 157 ER 1083; *Honck v Muller* (1881) 7 QBD 92 (CA); *Cornwall v Henson* [1900] 2 Ch 298 (CA) 304 (Collins LJ). Also, *Smith's Leading Cases* (n 14) 46.

case law under the SGA 1893 section 31(2).[230] The test in the subsection was held to be one of 'repetition', namely, 'if the breach is of such a kind, or takes place in such circumstances as reasonably to lead to the inference that similar breaches will be committed in relation to subsequent deliveries'.[231] It was specifically dismissed as 'a fallacy' that an 'intention to repudiate' the contract should be regarded as a necessary ingredient of a repudiation.[232] The test was confirmed in *Maple Flock v Universal Furniture*,[233] where the issue was whether, out of some 67 instalments of rag flock, nonconformity with the guaranteed standard of contamination shown by a sample drawn from the 16th instalment constituted a repudiation of the whole contract according to section 31(2). Lord Hewart CJ, delivering the judgment of the Court of Appeal, stated that the subsection was a codification of previous cases such as *Freeth* and *Mersey Steel* and in essence required the court to determine 'what effect, if any, the breach or breaches should have on the contract as a whole'.[234] Taking special notice of Lord Selborne's omission of the word 'intention' in his judgment in *Mersey Steel* and Lord Coleridge's analogy between renunciation and frustration in *Freeth*,[235] the Chief Justice stated that 'the true test will generally be, not the subjective mental state of the defaulting party, but the objective test of the relation in fact of the default to the whole purpose of the contract'.[236] After reviewing several post-1893 cases,[237] he concluded that the test hinged on, 'first, the ratio quantitatively which the breach bears to the contract as a whole, and secondly the degree of probability or improbability that such a breach will be repeated'.[238] On the facts, it was held that the sellers conducted their business prudently and the chance of the nonconformity being repeated was 'practically negligible'.[239] It was therefore held that a case of repudiation was not made out.

The increasing role of the fundamental breach approach was also affirmed in *Decro-Wall*.[240] The defendants, an English marketing company, contracted to act exclusively for the claimants, a French manufacturing company, to develop a market for the latter's goods in the UK. The goods were to be supplied in instalments and paid for upon each delivery. Due to a shortage of working capital, the defendants regularly made late payments. The claimants accepted them without objection until three years into the contract, when they promptly terminated the

[230] Now SGA 1979 s 31(2). See ch 2, quotation after n 184.

[231] *Millar's Karri v Weddel* (n 218) 1276 (Bigham J). Also, *Luna Park (NSW) Ltd v Tramways Advertising Proprietary Ltd* (1938) 61 CLR 286 (HCA) 304–5 (Latham CJ).

[232] *Millar's Karri ibid* 1277 (Walton J).

[233] n 218.

[234] *Ibid* 155.

[235] *Freeth* (n 213) 214.

[236] *Maple Flock* (n 218) 156.

[237] *Robert A Munro & Co v Meyer* [1930] 2 KB 312; *Taylor v Oakes Roncoroni & Co* [1922] All ER Rep Ext 866, (1922) 27 Com Cas 261 (CA).

[238] *Maple Flock* (n 218) 157.

[239] *Ibid.*

[240] n 201.

contract upon a failure by the defendants once again to pay on time. One major issue arising from the case was whether the defendants' regular delay in making payment, coupled with the inference that they would probably commit similar breaches in the future, constituted a repudiation of the whole contract. The defendants had been successful in developing the UK market and plainly could not have intended to withdraw from the contract. The Court of Appeal, unanimously, adopted the fundamental breach approach as the correct test. According to Salmon LJ, the 'repudiation' question depended on the 'legal consequence' of the breach and the courts should 'look at the practical results of the breach in order to decide whether or not it does go to the root of the contract'.[241] Since the delays had caused only minor losses recoverable from the defendants and the claimants never doubted the defendants' ability to pay eventually, no repudiation was established. In a later case, Potter LJ, delivering the judgment of the Court of Appeal, laid down the test more lucidly:

> [I]n any given case, where a party is alleged to be in repudiatory breach by reason of a failure or delay in payment of an instalment or interim sum due under a contract, the 'potency' and legal effect of such breach falls to be judged in the light of *the seriousness of the breach and its effect upon the continuing performance of the contract*. This involves an examination of the circumstances of the breach itself as well as *its implications for the future of the contract and any likelihood of repetition*.[242] (Emphasis added.)

This formulation of Potter LJ and that of Lord Hewart in *Maple Flock* represent two outstanding efforts of the courts in the quest for a better, more rational approach to determining a repudiation. However, the transition has gone largely unnoticed. Despite the problems with its interpretation and application, the renunciation approach became entrenched into a general test that dominated the entire doctrine of anticipatory breach. In the next two subsections, we shall continue to demonstrate that this unusual development was none the less more apparent than real.

2. Wrongful Termination

An outright refusal to perform the contract was the earliest form of anticipatory breach recognised by the courts. It appeared to be relatively common by the early 20th century.[243] In such cases a subjective test was often applied. Thus, in *British & Beningtons v Cachar*, it was held that no repudiation could be established if the repudiator evinced no intention to 'repudiate' and its 'real intention … was

[241] *Ibid* 368.

[242] *Shyam Jewellers Ltd v Cheeseman* [2001] EWCA Civ 1818 [57], [2001] All ER (D) 423 (Nov). Also, *M & J Polymers Ltd v Imerys Minerals Ltd* [2008] EWHC 344 (Comm), [2008] 1 All ER (Comm) 893 [13]–[15] (Burton J).

[243] Eg *Rubel Bronze & Metal Co Ltd v Vos, re an Arbitration* [1918] 1 KB 315.

to perform [its] legal obligations, whatever they might be'.[244] An outright refusal, however, soon became uncharacteristic because it was 'too clear to litigate'.[245] Its modern equivalent is 'wrongful termination'. For our purposes, 'wrongful termination' comprises all cases where a contracting party purports, without lawful ground, to rescind[246] or terminate[247] the contract or declare it void. A wrongful termination invariably requires a clear and final intention to bring the contract to an end.[248] The renunciation approach, however, has great difficulties in answering the question whether a wrongful termination constitutes an anticipatory breach. A major problem is that a wrongful termination does not usually possess a character of deliberateness. A party, not infrequently, terminates with the honest belief that it is entitled to do so and is genuinely minded to mitigate its loss consequent upon a breach of the other party, rather than to escape from a bad bargain.

The difficulties with the renunciation approach are amply demonstrated by the House of Lords' reasoning in *Woodar v Wimpey*.[249] As discussed above in section A, the majority's decision in favour of the purchasers was based on three major grounds: (1) they acted bona fide upon their solicitors' advice; (2) they did not intimate an intention to 'abandon' or 'repudiate' the contract; and, (3) their intention was 'qualified' by or 'conditional' upon the outcome of ongoing court proceedings. This decision has attracted almost unanimous criticism from commentators.[250] All the above three grounds are controversial and constitute sources of uncertainty.[251] First, an influential factor lurking behind the majority's decision was the purchasers' good faith in serving the notice, yet it is debatable what role good faith should assume in determining the existence of an anticipatory breach.[252] An enquiry into good faith is likely to result in 'longer trials and greater uncertainty' in the law.[253] As the minority in *Woodar* pointed out, if the purchasers were exonerated for their good faith, this would in effect impose upon

244 *British & Beningtons* (n 207) 69 (Lord Sumner). Similarly, *Johnstone v Milling* (n 88) 468 (Lord Esher MR).

245 Carter, *Breach of Contract* (n 182) [809].

246 Eg *Garnac Grain Co Inc v HMF Faure & Fairclough Ltd* [1968] AC 1130 (HL).

247 Eg *James McKelvie & Co v Murray & Co Ltd* (1928) 31 Ll L Rep 80 (CSOH); *Scandinavian Trading Co A/B v Zodiac Petroleum SA & William Hudson Ltd (The 'Al Hofuf')* [1981] 1 Lloyd's Rep 81 (QB); *Huntington v Imagine Group Holdings Ltd* [2008] EWCA Civ 159, [2008] All ER (D) 40 (Feb).

248 *Spettabile v Northumberland* (n 215); *Essex Line Ltd v Société Charbonnière de Reception en Commun* [1939] 64 Ll L Rep 295 (KB); *Jaks (UK) Ltd v Cera Investment Bank SA* [1998] 2 Lloyd's Rep 89 (QB).

249 n 205.

250 A Nicol and R Rawlings, 'Changing Attitudes to Anticipatory Breach and Third Party Beneficiaries' [1980] 43 *MLR* 696; '*Woodar v Wimpey*' (case note) [1980] 96 *LQR* 321; JW Carter, 'Regrettable Developments in the Law of Contract?' [1980] *CLJ* 256; Furmston, *Law of Contract* (n 151) 598.

251 Eg *Dalkia Utilities Services plc v Celtech International Ltd* [2006] EWHC 63 (Comm), [2006] 1 Lloyd's Rep 599 [148] (Christopher Clarke J). Whilst Clarke J accepted the majority's recognition of the role of good faith in *Woodar*, it was held that a bona fide yet invalid notice to exercise a contractual right of termination in *Dalkia*, unlike the one in *Woodar*, was unconditional and thus constituted a repudiation ([149]–[150]).

252 Eg JE Murray, *Murray on Contracts*, 4th edn (Matthew Bender, 2001) § 109 [C].

253 '*Woodar v Wimpey*' (case note) (n 250) 322.

the vendors a duty to prove the purchasers' dishonesty and would open the door to using honesty as an excuse for escaping from a bad bargain.[254] The majority's approach also seemed to be trumped by Lord Denning MR's observation in the Court of Appeal in *Federal Commerce v Molena* when he stated:

> I have yet to learn that a party who breaks a contract can excuse himself by saying that he did it on the advice of his lawyers; or that he was under an honest misapprehension. Nor can he excuse himself on those grounds from the consequences of a repudiation.[255]

On appeal, Lord Wilberforce approved this observation and stated that a party's 'subjective desire to maintain the contract cannot prevent the other party from drawing the consequences of his actions'.[256] In a number of subsequent cases,[257] it seems that the courts have swung towards the majority's view in *Woodar* and maintained that an honest but erroneous construction of a contract does not by itself amount to a repudiation. There is, however, a vital distinction between *Woodar* and those later cases. Whilst the notice of termination in *Woodar* involved the bringing of the whole contract to an end, the same cannot be said of the conduct complained of in the later cases. Indeed, that conduct (erroneous construction of a contract) was invariably found not to go to the root of the contract. Although the courts relied upon the misinterpreting party's good faith, it seems that this was not essential to their final conclusion. In *Vaswani v Italian Motors*, for instance, Lord Woolf confined the role of good faith to non-repudiatory breaches. Hence, if the conduct under examination was repudiatory, viz 'inconsistent with the continuance of the contract', 'the *bona fide* motives of the party responsible' would be immaterial.[258] Accordingly, the better view appears to be that the question of repudiation depends on the consequences of the conduct and the misinterpreting party's *bona fide* would *not* necessarily 'prevent repudiation'.[259] This is

[254] *Woodar v Wimpey* (n 205) 288 (Lord Salmond); 292 (Lord Russell).

[255] *Molena* (n 198) 979. In *Woodar*, however, Lord Keith suggested that Lord Denning's observation was intended for an actual breach and might not be applied to anticipatory breach cases, (n 205) 296–7. Similarly, *Blyth v Scottish Liberal Club* 1982 SC 140 (SD) 143 (Wheatley LJC); 149 (Lord Dunpark); 154–5 (Lord Wylie), [1983] IRLR 245, [1983] SLT 260. It is extremely doubtful whether such a distinction could be read out of Lord Denning's observation.

[256] *Federal Commerce v Molena* (n 191) 780.

[257] *James Schaffer LD v Findlay Durham & Brodie* [1953] 1 WLR 106 (CA); *Cargo Ships El Yam Ltd v Invoeren Transport Onderneming Invotra NV* [1958] 1 Lloyd's Rep 39 (Com Ct); *Sweet & Maxwell v Universal News* [1964] 3 All ER 30 (CA); *Vaswani v Italian Motors (Sales and Services) Ltd* [1996] 1 WLR 270 (PC Hong Kong); *Stocznia v Latvian Shipping* [2001] 1 Lloyd's Rep 537 (Com Ct) [181] (Thomas J).

[258] *Vaswani ibid* 276–7. Also, *Woodar* was applied in *Jim Ennis Construction Ltd v Combined Stabilisation Ltd* [2010] CILL 2820 (QB) where it was held that an employer under a construction contract did not repudiate the contract by withholding in good faith merely 5 per cent of the agreed sum payable to a contractor.

[259] *Financial Techniques (Planning Services) Ltd v Hughes* [1981] IRLR 32 (CA) [27]–[29] (Templeman LJ). Also, *Hvalfangerselskapet Polaris A/S v Unilever Ltd, Lever Bros Ltd* (1932) 42 Ll L Rep 215 (CA) 221–2 (Scrutton LJ), rev'd on other grounds (1933) 46 Ll L Rep 29 (HL); *Ross T Smyth & Co Ltd v TD Bailey Son & Co* [1940] 3 All ER 60 (HL) 72 (Lord Wright); *Alfred C Toepfer v Peter Cremer* [1975] 2 Lloyd's Rep 118 (CA) 125 (Lord Denning MR); 129 (Scarman LJ). *cf Bliss v South East Thames Regional Health Authority* [1987] ICR 700 (CA) 715 (Dillon LJ), criticised in B Perrins

consistent only with the consequence-based fundamental breach approach, not with the intention-based renunciation approach.

Secondly, the majority in *Woodar* held that the purchasers' notice of termination did not in itself intimate an intention to 'abandon' or 'repudiate' the contract. Their Lordships thus adopted the narrow, subjective interpretation of the renunciation approach. This was in stark contrast to the minority's view that the approach required 'an intention to bring the contract to an end'.[260] The minority's view was vividly depicted by Devlin J in another case:

> Anticipatory breach was not devised as a whip to be used for the chastisement of deliberate contract-breakers, but from which the shiftless, the dilatory, or the unfortunate are to be spared. It is not confined to any particular class of breach, deliberate or blameworthy or otherwise; it covers all breaches that are bound to happen.[261]

However, it might be going too far to assert, as a dissenting judge, Lord Russell, did, that a wrongful termination could not 'by any circumstances be watered down or deprived of its repudiatory quality'.[262] In *Woodar*, had there been no slump in the value of land and thus no question of the purchasers attempting to get out of a bad bargain, the circumstances might have been such that it would be unjust to allow the vendors to take advantage of a minor technical fault in the notice and to 'accept' it as a repudiation and hold the purchasers solely and wholly responsible. In short, not only is the renunciation approach subject to two different interpretations, but these two interpretations are also both problematic. The application of the renunciation approach thus tends to cause uncertainty and unpredictability.

Thirdly, in *Woodar*, could the notice be said to be, as the majority asserted, 'conditional' on the outcome of the court proceedings in progress and intended to be withdrawn in the event that it should be adjudged to be unjustified? Undoubtedly, the requisite intention under the renunciation approach must be determined from all the surrounding circumstances.[263] It must be unequivocal and unqualified.[264] But it can be argued that the majority's view was inconsistent with an objective assessment of the purchasers' intention. It is not necessary that the purchasers should evince an 'absolute' intention to refuse performance irrespective of a judicial determination contrary to their interpretation of condition E.[265]

(ed), *Harvey on Industrial Relations and Employment Law* (London, LexisNexis, 1996) [504]; *David Eady v Treklogic Technologies Inc, TrekLogic Inct & Advanced Solutions Group, Inc* 2009 ONCA 710, aff'g (unreported, Ontario SC, 30 August 2008) [67] (Herman J), citing with approval JD McCamus, *The Law of Contracts* (Toronto, Irwin Law, 2005) 655–6.

260 *Woodar* (n 205) 285–6 (Lord Salmon). Also, *Heyman v Darwins* (n 93) 378–9 (Lord Wright).

261 *Citati* (n 2) 438.

262 *Woodar* (n 205) 292.

263 *Ibid* 299 (Lord Scarman); *Mersey Steel* (n 208) 438–9 (Lord Selborne).

264 *Rees v Lines* (1837) 8 Carr & P 126, 173 ER 427; *Ehrensperger v Anderson* (1848) 3 Exch 148, 158, 154 ER 793, 797 (Parke B); *Barrick v Buba* (n 83) 579–80, 543 (Cockburn CJ); *Ross v Bailey* (n 259) 71 (Lord Wright); *Peter Dumenil & Co Ltd v James Ruddin Ltd* [1953] 1 WLR 815 (CA) 823 (Jenkins LJ); *The Hermosa* (n 170) 572 (Donaldson LJ).

265 *Cf Woodar* (n 205) 296 (Lord Keith).

Clearly, they intended the notice to bring the contract to an end immediately[266] so as to prevent the date of completion from arriving and this intention was known to the vendors. In fact, it was the purchasers who had made the wrong move, by immediately serving the notice without seeking a court declaration as to their right to do so.[267] Consequently, they ran 'the risk of catching a severe cold'.[268] Furthermore, there seemed to be little evidence for the suggestion that, had the vendors not accepted the notice as a repudiation, the purchasers would not have appealed against the decision of both Fox J and the Court of Appeal that their notice constituted a repudiation but would have withdrawn that notice. Should the majority's view be adopted, the question of repudiation might be made dependent on whether the victim happens to bring an action to dispute the lawfulness of the notice. The absoluteness of the requisite intention under the renunciation approach might, therefore, have been overstated.

In summary, although it might be said that some of the above difficulties are attributable to the court's incorrect application of the renunciation approach, our analysis indicates that the approach itself is unsatisfactory. Above all, the fact that *Woodar* was decided by a bare majority and that the Law Lords' disagreement on so many important aspects of the approach has yet to be resolved shows that there must be something wrong with the approach and appropriate reform is needed.

3. Disablement

Whilst a 'renunciation' negates a contracting party's 'willingness', or disposition, to perform the contract, an act of 'disablement' removes its 'readiness', or ability, to do the same.[269] Despite this conceptual distinction, however, 'disablement' has long been characterised as an intention-based rather than an ability-based wrong. The root of this characterisation can be found in a time-honoured principle in Year Book cases that a disablement was 'irreparable'.[270] According to this principle, a disablement, once constituted, was a complete and irreversible wrong. As was once observed by Mustill: 'it was the act of self-disablement, not the fact of inability, which discharged the promisor and … gave him a remedy in damages'.[271] In a 19th-century American case, a disablement was defined as a 'voluntary act inconsistent with an intention to perform' the contract and 'equivalent to a refusal to perform the contract'.[272] It mattered not whether the party who disabled itself from performing the contract might have regained its ability in

[266] *Ibid* 292 (Lord Russell).

[267] Carter (n 182) 258.

[268] *Woodar* (n 205) 293 (Lord Russell).

[269] *De Medina v Norman* (1842) 9 M & W 820, 827, 152 ER 347, 350 (Lord Abinger CB).

[270] Temp E 1 Covenant 29; 1 Roll Abr 248 pl 1 (8 Vin 225); Co Litt 221b, cited 21 Edw 4 (CB) 55 (Lord Coke); *Main's Case* (n 30) 21a, 81; *Ford v Tiley* (n 44) 328, 473.

[271] Mustill (n 4) 25.

[272] *John Heard v Charles E Bowers* 40 Mass 455 (1839) 460 (Wilde J).

time for performance.[273] Earlier disablement cases could all be explained on this ground. In *Robson & Sharpe v Drummond*, for instance, a coachmaker's transfer of his stock-in-trade to a third party before a five-year contract for the hire of a chariot to a customer ran out, a clear act of disablement, was held to constitute a renunciation of the hire contract.[274] According to the above principle, this was so even though the coachmaker might purchase the stock back and be in a position to perform the hire contract again.[275] Even today, although 'renunciation' and 'disablement' are recognised as two different types of anticipatory breach,[276] the renunciation approach continues to govern them both.

Nevertheless, it seems to be a mistake to regard a disablement as 'irreparable'. Even a renunciation is by no means 'irreparable'. Although a renunciation cannot be undone, it can be retracted. A party reverses a disablement not by retrieving an evinced intention, but by regaining an impaired ability. The renunciation approach has to be stretched to accommodate a disablement. This can clearly be seen from Devlin J's statement: 'inability often lies at the root of unwillingness to perform. Willingness in this context does not mean cheerfulness; it means simply an intent to perform. To say: "I would like to but I cannot" negatives intent just as much as "I will not."'[277] Despite this extension of the requisite intention under that approach, a group of 'impossibility' cases were from the beginning severed from renunciation cases.[278] 'Impossibility' occurred when a party became 'wholly and finally disabled' from performing the contract.[279] Indisputably, 'impossibility' rested upon inability rather than intention. It was endorsed and applied by some members of the House of Lords in *Continental Contractors Ltd and Ernest Beck & Co Ltd v Medway Oil & Storage Co Ltd*,[280] where their Lordships held that the sellers, who encountered difficulties in procuring the kerosene necessary for performing the sales contract, did not repudiate the contract because they were not 'wholly and finally disabled'[281] and their performance was not, 'as an anticipatory result', rendered 'impossible'.[282] In so holding they rejected (wrongly in the author's view) the decision of Mackinnon J at first instance that the sellers' inability could be reasonably inferred from the circumstances.[283] Despite the differences between these two tests, they were evidently both ability-based. It

[273] *Smith's Leading Cases* (n 14) 39.

[274] *Robson & Sharpe v Drummond* (1831) 2 B & Ad 303, 109 ER 1156. Similarly, *Omnium D'Enterprises v Sutherland* [1919] 1 KB 618 (CA).

[275] *Smith's Leading Cases* (n 14) 39.

[276] E Peel, *Treitel: The Law of Contract*, 12th edn (London, Sweet & Maxwell, 2007) [17–073].

[277] *Citati* (n 2) 437.

[278] *Ibid* 436. Alternatively, 'inevitable breach': *Cargo Ships v Invoeren* (n 257) 52 (Devlin J). Also, *Gulf Agri v Aston* (n 195) [14] (Aikens J); *SK Shipping (S) PTE Ltd v Petroexport Ltd (The 'Pro Victor')* [2009] EWHC 2974 (Comm) [84] (Flaux J).

[279] *British & Beningtons* (n 207) 72 (Lord Sumner).

[280] *Continental Contractors Ltd and Ernest Beck & Co Ltd v Medway Oil & Storage Co Ltd* (1926) 25 Ll L Rep 288 (HL), rev'g (1925) 23 Ll L Rep 124 (CA), rev'g (1925) 22 Ll L Rep 260 (KB).

[281] *Ibid* 295–6 (Lord Sumner); 302 (Lord Blanesburgh).

[282] *Ibid* 300–1 (Lord Parmoor).

[283] *Continental Contractors v Medway* (1925) 22 Ll L Rep 260, 266–7.

was immaterial that the sellers were eager to perform the contract and that their suppliers expressed a willingness to supply.

The notion of 'impossibility' was, however, too crude and rigid. It was inevitable that it would eventually give way, as it did, to a more refined, flexible test. This coincided with a transition from the renunciation approach to the fundamental breach approach. A Scottish case, *Forslind v Bechely-Crundall*,[284] which embraced the English doctrine of anticipatory breach, best illustrates this transition. The defender contracted with the pursuer on 4 May 1918 to start felling a certain lot of timber and delivering it on to a train immediately after making the contract. Due to both a legal prohibition not disclosed by the defender and bad weather, the felling and delivery of the timber was seriously retarded. The defender continuously put forward unreasonable demands until the pursuer finally purported to terminate the contract in April 1919. The House of Lords, by a three to one majority, held that the defender was liable for repudiating the contract.[285] Although most judges adopted, ostensibly, the renunciation approach,[286] the reality could not be more different.

The dissenting judge, Viscount Finlay, in agreement with the Second Division of the Court of Session, was faithful to the narrow, subjective interpretation of the renunciation approach and required the pursuer to show an intention to repudiate or abandon the contract on the defender's part.[287] As Lord Dundas in the Second Division put it, the *onus probandi* of establishing such an intention was 'obviously an exceedingly heavy one' and he could not 'recollect any Scots case in which such an *onus* has been successfully discharged'.[288] On the other hand, two majority judges in the House, Viscount Haldane and Lord Dunedin, together with the Lord Ordinary (Sands), paid lip service to the renunciation approach and transformed it into an attitude-based test of 'lack of commitment'.[289] The test did not hinge on 'any express or even conscious intention' of the defender, but enquired into whether he 'had adopted and was following a course of conduct which would, as its natural result, put it out of his power to fulfil his contract when the time came for doing so'.[290] Their Lordships found against the defender because he 'was not seriously setting himself to comply with his obligations',[291] showed a 'shilly-shallying attitude',[292] treated the pursuer 'with some levity' and 'pooh-poohed his justifiable complaints'.[293] This attitude-based test came very close to the fundamental breach approach. It revolved around the

[284] n 5.

[285] Viscount Haldane, Lord Dunedin and Lord Shaw. Viscount Finlay dissented.

[286] Viscount Haldane and Viscount Finlay, Lord Dunedin.

[287] *Forslind* (n 5) 184 (Viscount Finlay). The Scots Law Times Report contains the decision of the Second Division: 1922 SLT 496, 500 (Scott Dickson LJC); 501 (Lord Dundas); 502 (Lord Salvesen).

[288] 1922 SLT 496, 501.

[289] *Forslind* (n 5) 177 (Lord Sands); 182 (Viscount Haldane); 190 (Lord Dunedin).

[290] *Ibid* 181 (Viscount Haldane).

[291] *Ibid.*

[292] *Ibid* 190 (Lord Dunedin).

[293] *Ibid* 177 (Lord Sands).

magnitude of the defender's prospective non-performance. Lord Shaw, unlike his brethren, was more open and direct. He explicitly said that he was only dissuaded from rejecting the renunciation approach because it was 'too late to do so'.[294] According to his Lordship, that approach might lead to impracticability and undesirability as

> the psychological operations within the mind of a party to a contract may be very difficult to analyse into an intention one way or another. The party may lack decision or clearness of purpose, he may have no gift whatsoever of what may be called business faculty, and he may really have no intention one way or another except to go on procrastinating in the hope that something may turn up which would enable all puzzles to be smoothed out.[295]

The 'proper and more workable' solution, stated his Lordship, was to strip the renunciation approach of its 'intention' element and focus on the 'effect' the contract-breaker's words or conduct 'would be reasonably calculated to have upon a reasonable person' in the victim's position.[296] The test was whether the defender's words or conduct would 'fundamentally affect the fair carrying out of the bargain as a whole', namely, whether his 'procrastination is so persistently practised as to make a most serious inroad into the rights of' the pursuer.[297] In line with earlier cases where a shipowner was held to be liable for anticipatory breach for turning a commercial voyage into a war-like expedition,[298] this proposal of Lord Shaw was later developed into an important part of the fundamental breach approach, which centred on a reasonable inference of a self-induced frustrating delay.[299]

The transition from an intention-based test to an ability-based test, and hence from the renunciation approach to the fundamental breach approach, is evident in many other modern disablement cases. A disablement often takes the form of an unauthorised reallocation of essential resources designated to the contract in question to other uses. In a case discussed above, *Robson v Drummond*,[300] the coachmaker simply could not be said to have, solely by making a general business decision to transfer his stock-in-trade, evinced an intention not to perform the particular hire contract. Rather, the case should have been decided on the basis that the transfer constituted a breach striking at the heart of that contract because the customer had bought the 'judgment and taste' of the coachmaker as

[294] *Ibid* 191.

[295] *Ibid.*

[296] *Ibid*, citing *Carswell v Collard (The 'Victoria')* [1893] AC 635 (HL), 20 R (HL) 47 (Lord Herschell).

[297] *Ibid* 190, 192.

[298] *Burton v Pinkerton* (1866–67) LR 2 Ex 340 (CE); *O'Neil v Armstrong, Mitchell & Co* [1895] 2 QB 418 (CA). Also, *Smith's Leading Cases* (n 14) 41.

[299] *Citati* (n 2) 435 (Devlin J), citing *Stanton v Richardson* (1871–72) LR 7 CP 421, aff'd (1873–74) LR 9 CP 390 (EC); *Hongkong Fir v Kawasaki* (n 203) 66–9 (Diplock LJ); *Trade and Transport Inc v Iino Kaiun Kaisha Ltd (The 'Angelia')* [1973] 1 WLR 210 (QB) 221 (Kerr J); *The Pro Victor* (n 278) [123] (Flaux J).

[300] n 274.

a central part of his contractual benefits.[301] Conversely, if personal performance is not essential to the contract, the question of repudiation is determined largely depending on whether the transferee (and sometimes also the transferor) is willing and able to perform that contract.[302] In other words, the enquiry is focused on the overall effect of the transfer on the performance of the contract. By analogy, where a contracting party goes into insolvency or bankruptcy, unless that party's personal performance is of the essence of the contract[303] or unless the contract makes provision for that event,[304] mere insolvency or bankruptcy does not by itself amount to either a disablement[305] or a renunciation.[306] The reason is said to be that the solvent party's right to treat it as a repudiation hinges on its impact on the particular contract.[307] It is suggested that the solvent party has a better chance to succeed if the fact of insolvency or bankruptcy is relied upon to establish a renunciation because a disablement implies impossibility and has a narrower scope.[308] Yet it is clear that the constitution of a renunciation does not depend solely on the insolvent party's intention, but, more importantly, on the decision of the person in charge of the insolvency process.[309] The test has thus transformed from an intention-based one to a consequence-based one. Further, as explained earlier, disablement should be interpreted more broadly than impossibility. Thus, where the insolvency or bankruptcy is accompanied by a declaration of the inability of the person in charge (such as a liquidator) to secure goods necessary for the performance of the contract,[310] a disablement may be established on the ground of a prospective inability of both the insolvent party and the liquidator to perform the contract.[311]

The above survey of three main groups of 'renunciation' cases delineates the drift of judicial opinions that has since the beginning of the 20th century begun to move away from the renunciation approach in favour of the fundamental breach approach. Although the renunciation approach is still frequently pronounced by

[301] *Smith's Leading Cases* (n 14) 39. *cf British Waggon Co v Lea & Co* (1879–80) LR 5 QBD 149.

[302] *Ross v MacFarlane* (1893) 1 SLT 175 (CSOH), aff'd (1894) 1 SLT 463 (SD); *Fratelli Sorrentino v Buerger* [1915] 3 KB 367 (CA); *HSS v BMB* (n 173).

[303] Eg an employer went insolvent: *Reid v Explosives Co Ltd* (1887) LR 19 QBD 264 (CA); *Brace v Calder* [1895] 2 QB 253 (CA); *Measures Bros Ltd v Measures* [1910] 2 Ch 248 (CA); *Holt & Anor v Faulks & Anor* [2001] BCC 50 (Ch).

[304] *Perar BV v General Surety & Guarantee Co Ltd* [1994] 43 Con LR 110 (CA).

[305] *Re Agra Bank ex p Tondeur* (1867–68) LR 5 Eq 160; *Re Barber & Co ex p Agra Bank* (1869–70) LR 9 Eq 725; *Winterton Constructions Pty Ltd v Hambros Australia Ltd* (1992) 39 FCR 97 (FCA) 667 (Hill J).

[306] *Re Edwards* (n 63); *Morgan v Bain* (1874) LR 10 CP 15; *In re Phoenix Bessemer Steel Co* (1876) 4 Ch D 108 (CA); *Mess v Duffus* (1901) 6 Com Cas 165.

[307] MS Wee, 'Insolvency and the Survival of Contracts' [2005] *Journal of Business Law* 494, 501, 502.

[308] *Ibid* 499, 504; F Oditah, 'Assets and the Treatment of Claims in Insolvency' (1992) 108 *LQR* 459, 496.

[309] *Morgan v Bain* (n 306) 22–3 (Lord Coleridge CJ), 24–5 (Keating J), 27 (Brett J); *Sale Continuation Ltd v Austin Taylor & Co Ltd* [1968] 2 QB 849, 860. Also, Oditah *ibid* 496.

[310] *Edinburgh Grain Ltd (in liquidation) v Marshall Food Group Ltd* 1999 SLT 15 (CSOH).

[311] *Ibid* 23 (Lord Hamilton).

the courts as the dominating test, much of its territory has been encroached upon by the fundamental breach approach. The downfall of the renunciation approach is predestined.

C. The Defects of the Renunciation Approach

The exploration of case law in the previous section showed that the renunciation approach suffered from three main defects. These defects must be summarised, highlighted and dissected.

1. Restrictiveness in Scope

The renunciation approach operates in an extremely cramped space. It was historically developed from and tailored for an 'outright refusal' to perform the contract. In some sense a stringent approach is justified, as 'repudiation of a contract is a serious matter, not to be lightly found or inferred',[312] and is 'a drastic conclusion which should only be held to arise in clear cases of a refusal, in a matter going to the root of the contract, to perform contractual obligations'.[313] Indeed, it might be argued that the renunciation approach is useful in defending the sanctity of contract and in controlling the accrual of a right of termination. But restraint must not be divorced from rationality. With modern forms of anticipatory breach of contract extending far beyond a 'renunciation' properly so called, it seems more and more artificial to maintain that the approach should have a rational claim on the whole territory of the law of anticipatory breach.[314] The approach often had to be over-stretched and distorted in order to embrace new forms of anticipatory breach.

The renunciation approach is rooted in parochialism. To take a declaration of inability as an example, an intention-based test tends to confine the courts' attention to exterior expressions alone. While exterior expressions are important, they are by no means the only ground for granting a right of termination. If, for instance, a declaration is adjudged not to be clear enough to evince an intention not to perform, a right to terminate should nevertheless be justified on the basis of an actual prospective inability to perform the contract.[315] Whether or not a party has committed an anticipatory breach should not 'depend simply on whether his adversary is artful enough to conceal his state of mind or obstinate enough not to admit his inability'.[316] It is thus imprudent to focus exclusively on a party's

[312] *Ross v Bailey* (n 259) 71 (Lord Wright).

[313] *Woodar* (n 205) 283 (Lord Wilberforce). Note, the word 'refusal' again testifies the influence of the renunciation approach.

[314] *Thomas Marshall (Exports) Ltd v Guinle* [1979] Ch 227, 239 (Sir Robert Megarry V-C).

[315] *Citati* (n 2) 446 (Devlin J).

[316] *Ibid.*

willingness or intention in search for an anticipatory breach, neglecting entirely its inability to perform the contract.[317] Instead of looking at expressions alone, we ought also to see what those expressions reveal. Instead of lingering over the form, we ought to go further and explore the substance. The case for a right of termination is as strong where a party is unable to perform the contract as where it is unwilling to do so. The renunciation approach overlooks an important dimension by subjecting disablement to an intention-based rather than ability-based test.

In fact, the courts' insistence on searching for an outright refusal based on the elusive business of exploring the defendant's 'intention' is not justified either by logic or policy. To rest a finding of breach on a party's intention is itself an anomaly. It is not what one intends, but what one does, that makes a breach of contract. A renunciation, however interpreted, is not a properly devised check on the accrual of a right of termination. Not infrequently, the exercise of discovering a party's intention is either unnecessary or futile. More importantly, the renunciation approach is a closed rather than an open system. It does not have the elasticity required to accommodate newly arising forms of anticipatory breach. The consequence is that the victim may be denied a legitimate entitlement to terminate the contract in cases where an 'outright refusal' or its equivalent cannot be found. It might be argued that the restrictiveness of the renunciation approach could be cured by adopting a broader interpretation of 'intention' capable of being extended to non-refusal cases; but it is strongly believed that as long as an intention-based test remains in place, the austerity of the approach will survive and considerable uncertainty may ensue. The latter point must be explained in more detail.

2. Uncertainty in Application

At first glance the renunciation approach may look simple and straightforward. But the appearance can be deceptive. The difficult part is always its application to the particular circumstances of individual cases.[318] A closer look at the approach in action reveals that there is considerable uncertainty over the way it should be applied. This has been amply demonstrated by a number of the cases reviewed above, especially the majority's approach in *Woodar v Wimpey*. Uncertainty arises from inconsistency and vacillation. The concomitance of two distinct interpretations of the requisite intention under the approach constitutes the main source of uncertainty. These two interpretations were derived from Lord Coleridge's somewhat lax statements of the approach in *Freeth v Burr*. The requisite intention was described as both an intention to abandon or repudiate the contract and an intention not to perform the contract. Although the distinction dictates whether an

[317] Eg *Thorpe v Fasey* [1949] Ch 649; *Anchor Line Ltd v Keith Rowell Ltd (The 'Hazelmoor')* [1980] 2 Lloyd's Rep 351 (CA).

[318] *James Schaffer* (n 257) 117 (Singleton LJ).

element of deliberateness is required,[319] it has never been openly acknowledged. The consequence is that inconsistent results follow. For example, when Lord Coleridge applied the same approach in *Freeth* to similar facts in *Mersey Steel*, he reached an opposite conclusion that was subsequently overturned by the Court of Appeal.[320] What is more, the difference in interpretation has enabled the courts to manipulate the application of the approach to achieve an outcome they desire. Lord Wilberforce's adherence to the narrow, subjective interpretation in *Woodar*, for example, not only contradicted some of his earlier statements in *Federal Commerce*, but seemed also to be but a means to achieve his preferred end, namely, that it was the vendors, not the purchasers, who should shoulder the loss. The uncertainty of the renunciation approach thus first and foremost stems from the courts' treatment of the element of deliberateness. There is a blatant failure to clarify whether the requisite intention under that approach must carry a degree of deliberateness. As the law stands, it appears to insist upon deliberateness when it facilitates a desirable outcome and ignore it at other times.

Furthermore, even if the element of deliberateness is severed from the renunciation approach and the requisite intention is simply interpreted as an intention not to perform the contract, the uncertainty caused by the approach is not eliminated. The entanglement of an anticipatory breach with 'intention' gives rise to the delicate issue of good faith. The assimilation of good faith into the renunciation approach adds significantly to its uncertainty. Indeed, it undermines much of the purpose for which the doctrine of anticipatory breach was invented, namely, to enable a party, in anticipation of a future breach, to act swiftly and extricate itself from a sinking project. Similarly, the emphasis on the absoluteness of the requisite intention, defeasible by a whole range of indefinite surrounding circumstances, increases unnecessarily the complexity of the exercise. For all of these reasons, the renunciation approach does not sit easily with the principle that a contractual liability is usually a strict one. By tying itself to a party's intention, it seems to have inadvertently brought some degree of 'fault' into the constitution of an anticipatory breach. There is thus much to be said for assessing the requisite intention *objectively*. Even so, however, to fix one's attention exclusively on 'intention' may cause problems. As evidenced by wrongful termination cases, an objective intention not to perform the contract is present wherever a party serves a termination notice, yet such conduct does not always constitute an anticipatory breach. In addition, the uncertainty caused by the renunciation approach arises also from its obscure relationship with the fundamental breach approach. The renunciation approach creates rather than solves problems. In this sense, the doctrine of anticipatory breach can be said to be better off without 'intention' being adopted as the essential benchmark.

319 *Cf Gulf Agri v Aston* (n 195) [46]–[48] (Aikens J). Aikens J, endorsing the reasoning of the GAFTA Board of Appeal, equated an intention to terminate the contract with an intention to abandon it.

320 *Mersey Steel* (n 208) 665 (Lindley LJ).

3. Superficiality in Nature

The superficiality of the renunciation approach derives from its restrictiveness. Due to the historical origin of the approach, it has the tendency to put form above substance and to overlook the fundamental issue why a manifestation of an intention not to perform the contract should give rise to a right immediately to terminate the contract and claim damages. Attributes peculiar to an outright refusal, such as unequivocal declaration and deliberateness, have constantly crept in and claimed application to dissimilar types of anticipatory breach. If a contracting party tears the contract apart on the same day that it is signed, and denies any future obligation under it, this is clearly a renunciation and an anticipatory breach.[321] However, it is the prospect of a future total non-performance this conduct implies, not the way that prospect is unveiled, that justifies an immediate termination of the contract and a claim for damages. The other party is not entitled to terminate simply because of the contract-breaker's malice, indifference to the contract, or the exorbitant manner of its conduct. If the contract-breaker, instead of abandoning the whole contract, merely deletes an auxiliary clause with the same intent and in the same manner, can we still say that this would give rise to a right to terminate the whole contract? The answer is indisputably in the negative because the intention of the contract-breaker does not go to 'the whole consideration'.[322] But this highlights the danger of retaining the renunciation approach. A party's desire or good will does not exclude repudiation. Its insistence that the contract will be duly performed counts for nothing when controverted by its inability to do so. An outright refusal justifies termination by its totality, not by its forthrightness. Similarly, when the notion of renunciation is extended to the conduct of a party who intends to fulfil a contract but only in a way which is inconsistent with the terms of the contract, this obscures the fact that the extent of the inconsistency plays a vital role in justifying the other party's right of termination. It has been held that 'a suspension of performance until the terms of the contract are changed is capable of being a repudiation'.[323] But this is only because the suspension of performance is considered to be serious enough to give rise to a right of termination. Therefore, even though the application of the renunciation approach in pure outright refusal cases leads to the accrual of a right of termination, it conceals the true ground on which such a right rests, namely, the prospective non-performance foreshadowed by the contract-breaker's conduct. This true ground must be recognised overtly; the courts' failure to do so has led the law astray.

[321] *Hasham v Zenab* (n 116).

[322] *Johnstone v Milling* (n 88) 468 (Lord Esher MR).

[323] *Dymocks Franchise Systems (NSW) Pty Ltd v Todd* [2002] UKPC 50, [2002] 2 All ER (Comm) 849 (PC New Zealand) 870 (Lord Browne-Wilkinson), applied *Miller Fabrications Ltd v J & D Pierce (Contracts) Ltd* [2010] CSIH 27, 2010 GWD 15–283, [15] (Lord Kingarth).

The superficiality of the renunciation approach can also be gleaned from the revelation that a manifestation of an intention not to be bound by the contract does not necessarily constitute an anticipatory breach. In the recent case of *Concord Trust v The Law Debenture Trust Corp*,[324] where the trustee of bondholders gave an invalid notice of acceleration to the bond issuer to render the bonds immediately due and payable, a question arose as to whether 'the giving of an invalid notice of acceleration' would confer upon the issuer a cause of action for substantial damages against the trustee.[325] The House of Lords agreed with the Court of Appeal that such conduct was an act devoid of legal significance and could not give rise to a right of action for damages on the ground of either breach of contract or tort. However, an objective application of the renunciation approach to the case seems inevitably to lead to the conclusion that by giving such a notice the trustee has clearly evinced an intention no longer to be bound by the contract and thus committed an anticipatory breach. Yet since the bondholders had already executed their side of the contract, their intention not to be bound by it did not entail any future non-performance. For this reason the giving of the notice could not constitute an anticipatory breach. There was no further obligation to be breached. The renunciation approach fails to recognise that the manifestation of an intention is not sufficient for the constitution of an anticipatory breach and the existence (and breach) of a future obligation is indispensable.

In conclusion, the renunciation approach is demonstrably unsuitable for the role of a general test of anticipatory breach. It is unduly restrictive, obsolete and inflexible. Its application tends to cause uncertainty. Even in respect of outright refusal cases, it has prevented the courts from pursuing the true basis of this form of anticipatory breach. To be sure, the argument put forward is that the courts should cease to apply the renunciation approach in determining the existence of an anticipatory breach. This is not to dismiss the relevance of 'intention' altogether. As will be seen, there continues to be a role, albeit a much more limited one, for 'intention'. In the next Chapter, we will explain how a unifying test can be formulated on the basis of the fundamental breach approach.

[324] n 160.

[325] *Ibid* [36] (Lord Scott).

4

The Making of a Unifying Test

A. The Rise of the Fundamental Breach Approach

Our overview of decided cases in the previous Chapter suggests that the fundamental breach approach, despite the lack of the kind of express credentials the courts have given to the renunciation approach, has emerged as a more promising candidate for the role of a general test for all forms of anticipatory breach. In its earlier days, the fundamental breach approach was interlaced with the renunciation approach and did not acquire an independent status.[326] At this stage, the fundamental breach approach was mainly employed to thwart the establishment of a renunciation on the ground that the intention was directed only at an insubstantial part of the renouncing party's outstanding performance. An indication by a lessor of its inability to perform an obligation to repair the premises was for this reason held not to go to 'the whole consideration' and thus not to constitute an anticipatory breach.[327] Nor was an unauthorised, premature disposition by a stockbroker of a small portion of readily marketable securities deposited with it.[328] This requirement of 'fundamentality' was at the time only supplementary to the renunciation approach. It was not until the concept of 'fundamental breach' was firmly and widely acknowledged with respect to breach of contract in general that the two approaches began to be seen as aiming at 'two classes' of anticipatory breach of contract.[329] As evidenced by many of the cases discussed in the previous Chapter, the fundamental breach approach gradually gained the upper hand in anticipatory breach cases which did not involve an outright refusal. It is now sometimes applied either alternatively to or jointly with the renunciation approach.[330] Unfortunately, in many cases where it alone was applied, the courts did not seem to realise that the case at hand

[326] *Davidson v Gwynne* (1810) 12 East 381, 389, 104 ER 149, 152 (Lord Ellenborough CJ); *Mersey Steel* (n 208) 443–4 (Lord Blackburn); *Rhymney Rail Co v Brecon & Merthyr Tydfil Rail Co* [1900–03] All ER Rep 582 (CA), (1900) 69 LJ Ch 813; *Rubel Bronze v Vos* (n 243) 321–2 (Mccardie J). Also, *Smith's Leading Cases* (n 14) 35.

[327] *Johnstone v Milling* (n 88).

[328] *Ellis & Co's Trustee v Dixon-Johnson* [1924] 2 Ch 451 (CA) 467 (Pollock MR), aff'd on other grounds [1925] AC 491 (HL); *cf* [1924] 1 Ch 342, 355 (Lawrence J).

[329] *Hongkong Fir* (n 203) 64 (Upjohn LJ); 66 (Diplock LJ).

[330] Eg *South West Water Services Ltd v International Computers Ltd* [1999] BLR 420, [2001] Lloyd's Rep PN 353 (TCC).

involved an anticipatory breach. *Federal Commerce v Molena* is a good example which shows that the court, while applying the approach to vindicate the existence of an anticipatory breach, failed to see or explicitly recognise what it was really doing. Lord Wilberforce, particularly, although he employed the term 'anticipatory breach' in that case, did not seem to realise that the approach he applied should also govern a case like *Woodar v Wimpey*. Today, the fundamental breach approach is still encumbered by the renunciation approach. Two examples suffice. In *Torvald Klaveness A/S v Arni Maritime Corp (The 'Gregos')*,[331] the dispute arose out of an order given by the charterers as to the last voyage under a time charter. The order, if complied with, would result in the vessel being redelivered late. Nevertheless, the charterers refused to give a new, more reasonable, order. Lord Mustill applied the fundamental breach approach and the renunciation approach respectively to the charterers' giving of the order and their refusal to replace it without revealing the slightest discomfort.[332] Clearly, since the issue was whether either conduct constituted an anticipatory breach, the same approach, rather than two different approaches, should be applied. In a recent Canadian case, *Spirent Communications of Ottawa Ltd v Quake Technologies (Canada) Inc*,[333] Gillese JA, on behalf of the Court of Appeal for Ontario, while relying principally upon the fundamental breach approach, opined that in order for a repudiation of the contract to arise, an intention to 'repudiate' the contract should be shown in addition to a prospective fundamental breach.[334] The consequence of applying both approaches to the same conduct was that an enquiry into 'intention' was deemed to be essential in every anticipatory breach case and the victim might thus be denied a right of termination where the other party's words or conduct was adjudged not to evince the requisite intention due to, for instance, an absence of deliberateness on its part.

The requirement of fundamentality was openly acknowledged by Lord Diplock when he forcibly stated that 'it is to fundamental breaches alone that the doctrine of anticipatory breach is applicable'.[335] A 'fundamental breach' was defined by his Lordship as a breach which 'has the effect of depriving the other party of substantially the whole benefit which it was the intention of the parties that he should obtain from the contract'.[336] The concept of 'fundamental breach' has been used in two completely different contexts. In the first context it refers to any breach that is so serious as to justify the termination of a contract. In the second context, the concept is used to determine the effectiveness of an exemption clause.

331 *Torvald Klaveness A/S v Arni Maritime Corp (The 'Gregos')* [1994] 1 WLR 1465 (HL).

332 *Ibid* 1474–5.

333 *Spirent Communications of Ottawa Ltd v Quake Technologies (Canada) Inc* (2008) 291 DLR (4th) 163, 88 OR (3d) 721.

334 *Ibid* [37], [46]–[48]. Also, HG Beale (ed), *Chitty on Contracts*, 30th edn (London, Sweet & Maxwell, 2008) vol 1 'General Principles' [24–018], approved *Dalkia v Celtech* (n 251) [133], [134] (Christopher Clarke J).

335 *The Afovos* (n 168) 203.

336 *Photo Production* (n 109) 849. Also, *Hongkong Fir* (n 203) 66.

Its use in the second context, as far as it conveys the rule of law that liability for a fundamental breach cannot effectively be excluded by the contract, has now conclusively been rejected by the courts.[337] Our reference to 'fundamental breach' is thus confined to its use in the first context only. Thus, to constitute an anticipatory breach, whether by way of renunciation or disablement or anything else, stated Lord Diplock, 'the resulting non-performance' or '[t]he non-performance threatened must itself satisfy the criteria of a fundamental breach'.[338] Although the fundamental breach approach is by no means immune from criticism, there can be no doubt that it has obvious advantages over the renunciation approach and has set the all-important tone for a general test for anticipatory breach. The notion of fundamental breach unlocks the door to a genuine rationalisation of the doctrine of anticipatory breach. It is open and flexible. It has also been well litigated in the past. Lord Diplock's statement is not only supported by numerous decisions by the English courts, but it has also received widespread concurrence from international conventions and *lex mercatoria*.[339] Although there is still some uncertainty as to what breach is 'fundamental', at least the definition given by Lord Diplock does not give rise to such interpretative problems as those associated with the meaning of 'intention' under the renunciation approach. Furthermore, the installation of the fundamental breach approach as a general test for anticipatory breach is unlikely to cause upheaval over the settled case law. The only upshot is that all cases decided on the renunciation approach would have to be seen in a different, but clearer, light—it is not a party's intention, but the consequences of its words or conduct, that defines what an anticipatory breach truly is.

This does not mean, however, that the defendant's intention is wholly irrelevant to the constitution of an anticipatory breach. The intention still has a role. This actually reveals the inadequacy of the fundamental breach approach. Whilst the fundamental breach approach successfully captures a single common core of all forms of anticipatory breach, namely, the fundamentality of the anticipated breach, it cannot be said to encompass all components essential to an anticipatory breach. Although it was said that, whether a repudiation consisted in an actual or an anticipatory breach, 'the nature of the repudiation which is required' was the same,[340] an anticipatory breach should not be too readily likened to an actual fundamental breach. Thus, in *Federal Commerce v Molena*,[341] the House of Lords based its decision on the consequences of a prospective breach, namely, the implementation of the owners' instruction, rather than the giving of the instruction itself. However, a prospective fundamental breach is not sufficient by itself to constitute an anticipatory breach; it must also be 'anticipated', namely, reasonably

[337] *Photo Production* (n 109). However, very clear, in the sense of strong, language is required to exempt liability for a 'deliberate personal repudiation': *Internet Broadcasting Corp v MAR LLC* [2009] EWHC 844 (Ch), [2009] All ER (D) 177 (Apr).

[338] *The Afovos* (n 168) 203.

[339] CISG art 25; PECL arts 8:103, 9:304; PICC art 7.3.3.

[340] *Thorpe v Fasey* (n 317) 661 (Wynn-Parry J).

[341] n 191.

inferred. The residual role of the defendant's intention lies in recognising that that intention, assessed objectively, is but one of the ways in which a prospective fundamental breach could reasonably be inferred. So viewed, intention has little to do with the fundamentality of the anticipated breach and must indeed be severed from it. Unfortunately, the distinctive presence of 'inference' has not been explicitly recognised by the courts either in *Federal Commerce* itself or in many other cases where the fundamental breach approach was applied, thereby preventing the complete development of an appropriate general test for anticipatory breach. To a large degree this is attributable to a lack of exposition of the distinction between an anticipatory breach and an actual breach—the former is *not* an actual breach of an implied promise of an indefinable scope but a breach, by way of legal inference, of a future obligation. It is thus clear that a general test for anticipatory breach must comprise two constituent ingredients: a reasonable inference of a prospective breach and the fundamentality of that breach. It is to these two ingredients that we must now turn.

B. The Principle of Inferred Fundamental Breach: The Dual Tests

The existence of an anticipatory breach is determined by applying both a test of reasonable inference and a test of fundamentality. The two tests are inextricably linked to each other and must be applied simultaneously. The fundamentality of a future breach, as well as its occurrence, can only be inferred. Conversely, the only subject of the inference is the future breach. The unity of these two tests leads therefore to a principle of inferred fundamental breach. According to this principle, in order to establish an anticipatory breach, it must be shown that a reasonable person in the victim's position could have drawn, at the time when the breach is alleged to take place, an inference that the other party is likely, on the balance of probabilities, to commit a fundamental breach when the time for its performance arrives. The replacement by the dual tests of the renunciation approach means that, contrary to what has been suggested,[342] the constitution of an anticipatory breach should be regarded as a mixed question of fact and law.

1. The Test of Reasonable Inference

The test of reasonable inference prescribes how a future breach may be inferred and measures the likelihood of the inferred breach. The victim must show that

[342] *Cf Forslind* (n 5) 179 (Viscount Haldane); *Woods v WM Car Services (Peterborough) Ltd* (1982) ICR 693 (CA) 699 (Lord Denning MR). The fundamentality of the future breach was said to be a question of fact in *Citati* (n 2) 435 (Devlin J) but a question of law in *The Angelia* (n 299) 220–1 (Kerr J).

it can be reasonably inferred from the circumstances existing at the time of the alleged anticipatory breach that a future breach is likely, on the balance of probabilities, to occur. The leading case for this test is *The Hermosa*.[343] In October 1974, M, the charterer, sub-chartered the vessel *Hermosa* to N for a period of two years starting from 24 October 1979. In early 1975, *Hermosa* was put off hire for substantial repairs. The owners and M, as disponent owners, displayed wholly different attitudes towards this event. The owners, fully aware of the true condition of the vessel, failed to perform the necessary repairs timeously, tried to conceal the true condition by evicting N's surveyors from the vessel, and neglected to reply promptly and appropriately to N's enquiries and lawful demands. In contrast, M, who was in no better position than N to assess the true condition of the vessel, pressed the owners for repairs and replies, agreed to have N's surveyors on board to conduct examinations, and acted reasonably thereafter. On 10 August 1975, N sent an ultimatum to M demanding that the owners give an undertaking within 10 days to perform repairs and to admit its surveyors. Upon receipt of a strongly worded letter from M's lawyers, threatening to hold N responsible for breach of contract, N terminated the sub-charter on 26 August 1975. Unknown to both M and N, the owners had already commenced substantial repairs to the vessel on that date. The key question in the case was whether N's termination was justifiable on the ground of an anticipatory breach by M. Donaldson LJ, delivering the judgment of the Court of Appeal, held that N's termination was unlawful because M had not evinced an intention not to repair the vessel properly. At first sight, this seemed to be a routine application of the renunciation approach. However, Donaldson LJ's analysis was actually more refined. Much of his effort was directed towards determining the implications of the owners' conduct for M's future performance of the sub-charter. It was held that N's termination was unjustified, 'not because the breach which [N] anticipated was insubstantial, but because the conduct of [M] and the owners did not justify *a firm inference* that there would be a further breach'.[344] A mere suspicion was said to be insufficient. The distinction between a mere suspicion and a firm inference (or 'conclusion') was, in Donaldson LJ's words, analogous to that between 'a possibility of breach and a reasonable probability'.[345] Such an inference is essential to the establishment of an anticipatory breach. Although it is not usually presented as a distinctive element, some references to it can be found in decided cases. In some instalment contract cases, for example, the court adopted a test entailing the 'degree of probability or improbability'[346] or 'likelihood of repetition'.[347] This was in effect a test of reasonable inference. In *Universal Cargo v Citati*, Devlin J also admitted that a broadly interpreted renunciation hinged on

[343] n 170.
[344] *Ibid* 580 (emphasis added).
[345] *Ibid*.
[346] *Maple Flock* (n 218) 157 (Lord Hewart).
[347] *Shyam v Cheeseman* (n 242) [57] (Potter LJ).

the 'likelihood and a forecast of future events'.[348] *The Hermosa*, as well as these supporting cases, indicates that before a future breach can be appraised it must be anticipated. The requirement of anticipation concretises into a test of reasonable inference. This test is necessitated by the characterisation of an anticipatory breach as a present breach of a future obligation. It is sometimes suggested that there is a category of anticipatory breach based on actual inability or 'inability in fact'.[349] This is misleading. An 'actual' inability does not give rise to an anticipatory breach. A prospective inability does. The latter cannot be proved in fact. It can only be inferred. An anticipatory breach is thus inferential in nature. The requirement of a reasonable inference, it is submitted, is the most distinctive feature of an anticipatory breach. It defines the latter. A failure to recognise that a future breach may, via a reasonable inference, be converted into a basis for present liability is to shut one's eyes to the entire facility of the doctrine of anticipatory breach.

Four points can be made in respect of the test of reasonable inference. First, the test must be applied objectively—hence there must be a *reasonable* inference. An inference must be drawn by reference to 'the reasonable perceptions and reactions of the party asserting a repudiatory breach',[350] rather than the views taken by any specific bystander.[351] The reasonableness must be adjudged by reference to the time when an anticipatory breach is alleged to occur, which, by and large in practice, coincides with the time when the victim purports to accept that breach. Given the universal recognition given by the courts to this objective approach, it came as something of a surprise to find that in the recent case of *The Pro Victor*,[352] the Commercial Court ventured into a dangerous zone by suggesting that for a renunciation of contract to arise it was essential that the party alleging such a renunciation should subjectively believe its existence. In that case Flaux J endorsed in full a proposition that even if a party's words and conduct, assessed objectively, were renunciatory, they were insufficient to constitute a renunciation where the other party subjectively did not consider those words and conduct as evincing a clear and absolute intention not to perform the contract.[353] Of course, the judge did not go so far as to suggest that a party wishing to establish an anticipatory breach should bear the burden of proving its own subjective belief in the existence of that breach. Yet even the proposition adopted by him must be considered as inconsistent with established authorities. None of the judicial statements

[348] *Citati* (n 2) 440.

[349] *Ibid* 425, 454 (Devlin J). Also, *Finlayson v Finlayson* (2002) 29 Fam LR 460 (FAMCA) [199]; JLR Davies, NC Seddon and G Masel (eds), *The Laws of Australia: Contract* (Lawbook, 2003) [104], [105], [107]; Carter, *Breach of Contract* (n 182) [912].

[350] *Shyam v Cheeseman* (n 242) [58] (Potter LJ); *Spiricor of Saint Lucia Ltd v AG of St Lucia* (unreported, PC St Lucia, 1 December 1999).

[351] *Littlehampton Book Services Ltd v Dorling Kindersley Ltd* (unreported, Com Ct, 17 May 2001), [2001] All ER (D) 224 (May).

[352] n 278.

[353] *Ibid* [89], [98].

cited by Flaux J supports that proposition.[354] In fact, they all went the opposite way. Notably, in *Forslind*, Lord Shaw, as has been shown earlier, was critical of the renunciation approach for its tendency to implicate the alleged contract-breaker's subjective status.[355] Similarly, in *The Victoria*, although Lord Herschell used the expression that the defender 'thought' that the pursuer was unwilling to perform the contract, this was irrelevant, and the pursuer's conduct, objectively viewed, was held not to be sufficient to justify the defender's termination of the contract.[356] Further, Flaux J's decision is based on a misconceived analogy between renunciation and non-fraudulent misrepresentation.[357] Whilst misrepresentation must be a cause for the representee's entry into contract and thus requires both actual reliance or inducement as well as that such reliance or inducement is objectively reasonable, there does not, as will be shown shortly, have to be a causal link between an anticipatory breach and its acceptance.[358] Perhaps most significantly, Flaux J's decision is likely to cause great harm to commercial certainty, which is of paramount importance to the parties to a charterparty. Given its obvious departure from the commercial reality, the proposition that the victim's subjective belief should enter into the equation when determining the existence of an anticipatory breach must be firmly rejected.

Secondly, the source of a reasonable inference can be any existing circumstance indicative of a future breach. A prior actual breach, for example, irrespective of whether it gives rise to a right to terminate the contract and, if so, whether that right has been lost, forms part of a factual matrix from which a reasonable inference may be drawn.[359] An inference does not have to be drawn from the alleged contract-breaker's words or conduct. The latter's inability to perform the contract, for example, may be inferred from the words or conduct of a third party, such as a bank, a supplier or a sub-contractor. The inability may even be inferred from a general deterioration of the party's business. In this last situation, admittedly, it might take more to establish a reasonable inference.

Thirdly, there is an issue as to the degree of likelihood required to establish a reasonable inference. In *Maple Flock*, the court found in favour of the sellers on the ground that the chance of their actual breach (nonconformity with the contamination standard) being repeated in future instalments was 'practically negligible'.[360] In *The Hermosa*, Donaldson LJ stated that the requisite likelihood should be 'a reasonable probability'.[361] The point was picked up subsequently in

[354] The judge cited *Forslind* (n 5) 184 (Viscount Finlay); 191 (Lord Shaw) and *The Victoria* (n 296) 20 R (HL) 47, 48 (Lord Herschell).

[355] Text to n 295 above.

[356] *The Victoria* (n 296) 20 R (HL) 47, 48–9.

[357] *The Pro Victor* (n 278) [96].

[358] Text to n 440 and n 595 below.

[359] *Forslind* (n 5) 177 (Lord Sands); *Lewis v Motorworld Garages Ltd* (1985) ICR 157 (CA) 165 (Ackner LJ), 168 (Neil LJ), 170 (Glidewell LJ). Also, *Carr v Berriman* (n 194) 351 (Fullagar J).

[360] *Maple Flock* (n 218) 157 (Lord Hewart).

[361] *The Hermosa* (n 170) 580.

Alfred C Toepfer International GmbH v Itex Itagrani Export SA.[362] The defendants contracted to buy 22,000 tons of goods and undertook to load them on a nominated ship. The ship was nominated by the sub-buyers to whom the defendants had agreed to sell the goods. The sub-buyers, however, contracted to load other goods on the ship, with the consequence that the remaining space of the ship would accommodate only some 15,400 tons of the goods the defendants were bound to load. One of the main issues was whether the defendants were in anticipatory breach by reason of their prospective inability to load all the goods on the ship. The court answered in the negative. The test formulated by Saville J was whether the defendants had, 'on the balance of probabilities', 'put it out of [their] power' to perform the contract.[363] It was held that the claimants (sellers) had failed to establish that the defendants *could not* perform, and at most had only established that they *might not* be able to perform. Since the arbitrators found that, had the claimants not 'accepted' the alleged anticipatory breach, the sub-buyers would have allowed the defendants to load all the goods, there was 'only a chance' that the defendants would break their obligation to load.[364] In the recent case of *Polymers v Imerys*, the test was stated to be one that it was 'more likely than not' that future serious breaches would arise.[365] From these three cases it can be seen that the requisite likelihood does not seem to differ from the 'balance of probabilities', the latter being the standard of proof in civil actions and meaning 'more probably than not'.[366] It must be noted that in the majority of anticipatory breach cases, since the courts have not openly recognised the need to establish a reasonable inference, there is scarcely any discussion of the degree of likelihood required. Nevertheless, when determining the likely occurrence and fundamentality of a future breach, the courts, undoubtedly, have consistently applied the default 'balance of probabilities' test. Therefore, it can be safely concluded that a future breach is reasonably inferred only when it has a 51 per cent or more chance of occurring.

Fourthly, whether a reasonable inference can be drawn in a given case must, naturally, depend on the particular circumstances of the case. Some guidelines can, however, be extrapolated from the case law. The chance of drawing a reasonable inference increases with the weight of available supporting evidence. For example, a reasonable inference is less likely to be drawn where a party, instead of persisting in a failure to pay 'despite receipt of demands and/or protests', merely commits a single actual breach, such as a non-payment simpliciter.[367] Mere 'vibes'

362 *Alfred C Toepfer International GmbH v Itex Itagrani Export SA* [1993] 1 Lloyd's Rep 360 (Com Ct).
363 *Ibid* 362.
364 *Ibid.*
365 *Polymers v Imerys* (n 242) [15].
366 *Miller v Minister of Pensions* [1947] 2 All ER 372 (KB) 374 (Denning J). In New Zealand, the Contractual Remedies Act s 7(3)(c) provides that 'a party to a contract may cancel it if … [i]t is *clear* that a [term] in the contract will be broken by another party to that contract.' The preferred interpretation for the word 'clear' has been stated to be a 'sensible probability' rather than an 'inevitability': *Ken & Ken Corp Ltd v Kenji Umezaki* [2005] NZHC 479 [28]–[29] (Baragwanath J), citing with approval *Brooklands v Bridge* (n 5) 260, 461 (Blanchard J).
367 *Fenton v Gothaer* (n 94) 180 (Potter J).

are hardly sufficient.[368] Similarly, while a mere threat to terminate the contract may not be sufficient to give rise to a reasonable inference,[369] it may be different if it is made with a view to procuring a fundamental alternation to the contract.[370] On the other hand, an intimation, however anti-contractual it is, may not be treated as irretrievably foretelling a future breach if there is still room for renegotiation or rectification.[371] This point is relevant to a determination whether a wrongful termination constitutes an anticipatory breach. Generally, a wrongful termination leads to a reasonable inference that further performance will not be rendered and is thus prima facie an anticipatory breach.[372] This general rule should have been applied in *Woodar v Wimpey*.[373] However, the rule must not be regarded as an absolute one. To hold otherwise might undermine the general function of contract termination as an effective, albeit drastic, remedy. Besides, English law does not recognise 'middle house' remedies (such as a suspension of performance or a demand for adequate assurance) for the less serious case of 'insecurity of performance'.[374] This has sometimes caused an over-reliance by contracting parties upon termination as a means of resolving disputes arising before the time for performance. Consequently, if the wrongfulness of a termination lies solely in a technical error that is, to the knowledge of the recipient, easily rectifiable, it may not be possible for the recipient to draw a reasonable inference of a future fundamental breach. For example, where an employer invokes a dismissal provision under the contract but fails to follow the procedures prescribed by it in a minor aspect, it may not be appropriate for the employee to infer that s/he is to be excluded unlawfully from employment.[375] Conversely, if a party jumps at the step of termination without first exhausting a less drastic remedy, such as, if appropriate, seeking a declaratory order as to its entitlement to terminate,[376] it should be held liable for anticipatorily breaching the contract. The reason is that, if the party acts unreasonably in terminating the contract, it is more likely to

[368] *Texaco Ltd v The Eurogulf Shipping Co Ltd* [1987] 2 Lloyd's Rep 541 (Com Ct).

[369] *Haseltine Lake & Co v Dowler* [1981] ICR 222 (EAT).

[370] *Greenaway Harrison Ltd v Wiles* [1994] IRLR 380 (EAT). Also, *Nelson v Kingston* (n 171) [15] (Comr Howell QC).

[371] *The Gregos* (n 331) 1476 (Lord Mustill).

[372] *Never-Stop Railway (Wembley) Ltd v British Empire Exhibition (1924) Inc* [1926] Ch 877; *Sinason-Teicher Inter-American Grain Corp v Oilcakes & Oilseeds Trading Co Ltd* [1954] 1 WLR 1394 (CA); *Bremer Handelsgesellschaft mbH v JH Rayner & Co Ltd* [1979] 2 Ll Rep 216 (CA); *The Mihalis Angelos* (n 136); *Applied Computer Expertise Ltd v Parallellweb Ltd* (unreported, Com Ct, 18 September 2001).

[373] n 205.

[374] *Cf* UCC § 2–609; *Restatement (Second) of Contracts* § 251; CISG art 71; PECL art 8:105; PICC art 7.3.4. But English courts did recognise that in appropriate circumstances a contracting party might be justified in making a request for confirmation of performance and the other party's failure to provide it would constitute an anticipatory breach: eg *Portaga Comercio Internacional SA v Federative Republic of Brazil* (unreported, Com Ct, 5 February 1998); *The Pro Victor* (n 278). To some extent, perhaps, this has brought English law closer to the US position.

[375] *Gunton v Richmond* (n 218) 469 (Buckley LJ).

[376] *Société Maritime et Commerciale v Venus Steam Shipping Co Ltd* (1904) 9 Com Cas 289; *Spettabile v Northumberland* (n 215) 969 (Atkin LJ); *James Schaffer* (n 257) 118 (Singleton LJ).

draw the inference that a future fundamental breach is forthcoming. The test of reasonable inference also means that the matter in issue is not one of the alleged contract-breaker's contractual right, but one of probability. Thus, simply because the charterer under a voyage charter was 'technically … not obliged to load any cargo at all', it does not follow that its potential inability to find cargo to load the vessel in full was not liable to give rise to an anticipatory breach.[377] To the contrary, as shipping without the vessel being fully loaded would not be economically attractive to the charterer,[378] this seems to indicate that the charterer would, on the balance of probabilities, not perform the contract. For this reason, the charterer's entitlement to order the vessel to sail with a half load or even in ballast is irrelevant.

2. The Test of Fundamentality

The test of fundamentality measures the seriousness of an inferred future breach. As noted earlier in this Chapter, a fundamental breach is a breach that deprives the victim of substantially the whole benefit intended to be acquired by it under the contract. There are two matters that require closer attention. First, it is necessary to explain why the seriousness of the inferred breach must be pitched at the level of 'fundamentality'. Secondly, special issues arising from the application of the test in the context of anticipatory breach must be considered. Regarding the first matter, there has been much controversy as to the relationship between 'anticipatory breach' and 'fundamental breach'. In Canada, for example, text writers exhibit two contradictory views. On the one hand, it is said that an anticipatory breach is not necessarily a fundamental breach.[379] On the other hand, anticipatory breach is also sometimes viewed as a variant on the generic concept of fundamental breach.[380] This controversy can be dealt with in two steps. First, there is a question whether the inferred breach must be a breach that gives rise to a right of termination at all. Secondly, even if the inferred breach is such a breach, it must be asked whether more is required for it to be transformed into an anticipatory breach.

With respect to the first question, there are suggestions that the inferred breach might be a breach sounding in damages only and that there might even be an anticipatory breach of a warranty.[381] This argument is based on a lack of proper understanding of the nature of anticipatory breach. If the inferred breach does not entitle the victim to terminate the contract, there would be no good reason to accelerate the right to claim damages for that breach. The victim

[377] *Cf The Pro Victor* (n 278) [123] (Flaux J).

[378] *Ibid* [119].

[379] Fridman (n 5) 607–10; DM McRae, 'Repudiation of Contracts in Canadian Law' (1978) 56 *Can Bar Rev* 233, 240. Also, in Australia, *Wood Factory Pty Ltd v Kiritos Pty Ltd* (1985) 2 NSWLR 105 (NSWCA) 144–5 (McHugh JA).

[380] SM Waddams, *The Law of Contracts*, 5th edn (Toronto, Canada Law Book, 2005) [587].

[381] *Citati* (n 2) 430 (Devlin J). Also, H McGregor, *Contract Code Drawn up on Behalf of the English Law Commission* (Milano, Dott A Giufferè Editore, 1993) 74.

is not prejudiced by being precluded from bringing a claim until the inferred breach actually materialises. On the contrary, if the victim is awarded damages for a future breach while the contract subsists, this would not only subject the other party to a unilateral enlargement of its obligations under the contract, but would also rest that party's liability upon an assumption that the future breach is certain to occur when it might still be put right.[382] Let us take a hypothetical case instanced by McGregor. A decorator who promises to come back 12 months after painting a house to do necessary touching-up renounces that promise immediately after painting the house. McGregor argued that it would be unjust to force the householder to see out the 12-month period in order to maintain a claim for damages against the decorator.[383] However, it would be an anomaly to hold the decorator immediately liable in damages while his obligation to do touching-up remains intact. A claim for damages should be allowed only on the footing that the contract is forthwith terminated. The hypothesis, therefore, instead of attesting an anticipatory breach which sounds in damages only, actually lends support to the proposition that the inferred breach must be a breach that entitles the victim to terminate the contract. For example, if the householder is yet to pay any contract price, it would be ludicrous to suggest that the decorator's renunciation would entitle the householder to discharge himself from the obligation to pay. In such a situation the householder must not be allowed to bring an immediate claim for damages.

Even if the inferred breach is a breach that gives rise to a right of termination, it is debatable whether that is sufficient to give rise to an anticipatory breach. At the centre of the controversy is an enquiry whether a future actual breach of a 'condition', which does not produce 'fundamental' consequences, might, via a reasonable inference, be converted into an anticipatory breach. A 'condition' in its strict, technical sense, as a contrast to both a 'warranty' and an 'intermediate term', refers to a contract term which, once actually breached, invariably confers upon the victim a common law right of termination, however trivial the consequences of the breach might be. An actual breach of 'condition' also entitles the victim to claim damages for the loss of bargain, namely, the loss of the benefit of the contract-breaker's future performance.[384] As regards the question whether there might be an anticipatory breach of a 'condition', Australian

[382] *Cf* McGregor *ibid* 75.

[383] McGregor *ibid.*

[384] This distinguishes a condition from an express term which confers on one or both parties a right to terminate the contract in the event of a breach of that term, which breach does not trigger a common law right to claim loss of bargain damages: *Financings Ltd v Baldock* [1963] 2 QB 104 (CA); *Lombard v Butterworth* (n 184); *Stocznia v Latvian Shipping* [2002] EWCA Civ 889, [2002] 2 All ER (Comm) 768 [75]–[76] (Rix LJ); *State Securities plc v Initial Industry Ltd* (unreported, Ch, 29 January 2004), [2004] All ER (D) 317 (Jan). In Australia, *Shevill v Builders Licensing Board* (1982) 149 CLR 620 (HCA); *Foran v Wight* (n 155) 395 (Mason CJ). *cf* GH Treitel, 'Damages on Rescission for Breach of Contract' [1987] *Lloyd's Maritime and Commercial Law Quarterly* 143; BR Opeskin, 'Damages for Breach of Contract Terminated under Express Terms' [1990] 106 *LQR* 293; P Dobson, 'Late Payment of Instalments by Hirers' (1987) *Journal of Business Law* 147.

courts seem to answer affirmatively.[385] In England, the picture is more intricate. A distinction is drawn between a condition arising from an express provision (an express condition) and a condition arising by reason of an implication of law (an implied condition). While there seems to be a general consensus that a termination of a contract on the sole basis of an inferred future breach of an express condition is deemed to be premature,[386] an implied condition is widely considered to be capable of being anticipatorily breached.[387] They need to be looked at separately.

The view on express condition is best illustrated by *The Afovos*. By Clauses 5 and 31 of a time charter, the owners were given a power to serve a 48-hour notice to withdraw the vessel whenever the charterers failed to pay any instalment of hire punctually into the owners' designated account. The case concerned a particular instalment of hire due on 14 June 1979. The charterers instructed their bank on 13 June to transfer the money but, as a consequence of a mistake by the bank, the money went astray. At 16.40 hours on 14 June, the owners served a 48-hour notice. The charterers disputed the effectiveness of the notice but kept the vessel at their service on a without prejudice basis. The House of Lords, unanimously, held that since the instalment did not become due until midnight on 14 June, the owners' notice was premature and therefore they were only entitled to hire calculated by the contract rate, rather than the higher market rate.[388] The owners' main argument was that the charterers, even if they had been notified of the transfer problem at the time of the notice, would not have been able to make another payment on time. This was therefore an anticipatory breach by way of disablement, which entitled the owners immediately to terminate the contract. Lord Diplock roundly rejected this argument on the ground that the anticipated breach, namely, the charterers' failure to pay by midnight on 14 June, being merely an actual breach of an express condition rather than an actual fundamental breach, could not give rise to an anticipatory breach.[389]

The aversion to an anticipatory breach of an express condition, despite its tendency to cause commercial inconvenience and uncertainty,[390] is said to have a firm basis in the parties' intention to oust an 'anticipatory right' to terminate the

[385] *Foran v Wight* (n 155) 395 (Mason CJ); 416 (Brennan J); 432 (Deane J); 441 (Dawson J).

[386] *British & Beningtons* (n 207) 70, 72 (Lord Sumner); *Christie & Vesey Ltd v Maatschappij Tot Exploitatie Van Schepen en Andere Zaken, Helvetia NV (The 'Helvetia-S')* [1960] 1 Lloyd's Rep 540 (Com Ct) 551–2 (Pearson J); *Cheikh Boutros Selim El-Khoury v Ceylon Shipping Lines Ltd (The 'Madeleine')* [1967] 2 Lloyd's Rep 224 (Com Ct) 244 (Roskill J); *The Mihalis Angelos* (n 136) 200–1 (Edmund Davies LJ), 207–8 (Megaw LJ), *cf* 195 (Lord Denning MR); *Fercometal Sarl v MSC Mediterranean Shipping Co SA (The 'Simona')* [1989] AC 788 (HL) 796 (Lord Ackner). Also, *Treitel's Law of Contract* (n 276) [17–083]; Carter, *Breach of Contract* (n 182) [744B]. *cf* WVH Rogers, 'The Late Ship and the Non-Existent Cargo' (1971) 34 *MLR* 190, 193 fn 14; G Marston, 'The Cancelling Clause in Charterparties' [1969] *Journal of Business Law* 187.

[387] *Treitel's Law of Contract ibid*; Carter *ibid*.

[388] *The Afovos* (n 168) 201–2 (Lord Hailsham LC); 203 (Lord Diplock). Lord Keith, Lord Roskill and Lord Brightman concurred.

[389] *Ibid* 203.

[390] *The Helvetia-S* (n 386) 552 (Pearson J); *The Madeleine* (n 386) 244 (Roskill J).

contract.[391] This, however, suggests that what is in contention is no more than a matter of contract construction. The mere classification of a term as a condition does not necessitate the conclusion that a right of termination arising under it accrues only when it is actually breached. Equally, such a classification cannot be said to evince an intention to grant the victim an 'anticipatory right' to terminate the contract. The main difficulty in this constructionist approach is thus that a contract seldom evidences an unequivocal intention either to grant or to exclude such an 'anticipatory right'. It is submitted that the solution lies in something different from contract construction. The victim of a future breach of condition should not generally be allowed to terminate the contract before that breach materialises, unless it is unequivocally authorised by the contract to do so. The reason is that only when an inferred future breach satisfies the test of fundamentality does there arise a good justificatory reason for accelerating the legal remedies for it and converting it into an anticipatory breach. The fundamentality of the inferred breach, as will be explained herein, must be assessed by reference to the time when the alleged anticipatory breach occurs. This necessarily entails that, judged by reference to that time, the victim will be deprived of substantially the whole benefit intended to be acquired by it under the contract. A present need thus arises upon the victim to avoid waste, to free resources from fruitless or inefficient use, and to engage in early mitigation of loss. The test of fundamentality thus furnishes a compelling justification for an acceleration of legal remedies, including primarily a right of termination and a right to claim loss of bargain damages. A future breach of condition, by contrast, unless it also constitutes a fundamental breach, does not constitute a good justificatory reason for an acceleration of such legal remedies. Even if the victim shows that it would exercise its right to terminate the contract when the future breach of condition occurs, there is some difficulty in saying that it is that breach that deprives it of its contract benefit. The victim is not deprived of the benefit. It chooses to substitute a right to claim damages for a right to that benefit. At any rate, the victim loses only the benefit that accrues after the future breach of condition occurs. Since that breach does not amount to a fundamental breach, this suggests that, judged by reference to the time of the alleged anticipatory breach, the victim may still reap a substantial part of the benefit intended to be acquired by it under the contract. There is, consequently, no wastefulness or inefficiency that justifies an immediate release of the victim from that performance. A fortiori, if the inferred breach is of an express term rather than a condition—it entitles the victim only to recover for losses sustained up to the time of its occurrence and no loss of bargain damages is available—there is even less ground for asserting an acceleration of the victim's remedies.

This argument is equally applicable to a breach of an implied condition. A snapshot of some of the main cases that endorsed an anticipatory breach of an implied

[391] *The Madeleine ibid.* Also, *Treitel's Law of Contract* (n 276) [17–083], especially the previous edition: GH Treitel, *The Law of Contract*, 11th edn (London, Sweet & Maxwell, 2003) 861; Carter (n 182) [744].

condition shows that the inferred breach in those cases could all be alternatively analysed as a fundamental breach. In *Metro Meat Ltd v Fares Rural Co Pty Ltd*, for example, Lord Diplock apparently contradicted his own position in *The Afovos* by recognising 'an anticipatory breach of a fundamental term'.[392] The concept of 'fundamental term' was normally regarded as a synonym of 'condition'.[393] Indeed, Lord Diplock used it in the case to refer to an implied condition that a seller should arrange a loading and shipping schedule for two remaining instalments under the contract. In reaching the conclusion that the term was 'fundamental', however, his Lordship relied principally on the fact that the buyer would incur hefty potential liabilities under a contract with the sub-buyer.[394] A breach of that 'fundamental term' would, therefore, amount to a fundamental breach. In *The Gregos*, Lord Mustill also seemed to have implicitly accepted that in an anticipatory breach case the 'threatened breach' might embrace a breach of condition.[395] The case itself, however, bore no witness to this suggestion. His Lordship relied upon *Federal Commerce v Molena* as clear authority and formulated the legal question as one of 'whether the threatened breach is not of a fundamental character'.[396] In the latest case, *PT Berlian Laju Tanker Tbk v Nuse Shipping Ltd (The 'Aktor')*,[397] the buyers of a ship insisted, instead of paying as agreed the full contract price through a Greek bank nominated by the sellers on the date for delivery, on having 10 per cent of the price paid out of a deposit held in a Singaporean bank. It was held by Clarke J that the sellers were 'entitled to anticipate' a future breach of an implied condition on the buyers' part and to terminate the contract immediately.[398] This conclusion was, however, according to the learned judge, substantially based on the finding that the anticipated breach by the buyers would be likely to prevent 'redemption at the time of payment and out of the payment of any mortgage on the vessel' and expose 'the sellers to the risk involved in transferring the monies'.[399] All these cases, therefore, are testimony to the test of fundamentality. Devlin J, however, in a case to be discussed in some detail shortly, once stated that a future breach of an implied condition would, 'ipso facto', entitle the victim to terminate at present.[400] This appeared to be an unreasoned assertion. It was also not supported by the facts of the case, which indicated that the future obligation in question was a 'warranty' rather than an implied condition.

392 *Metro Meat Ltd v Fares Rural Co Pty Ltd* [1985] 2 Lloyd's Rep 13 (PC Australia) 15.

393 *Suisse Atlantique Société d'Armement Maritime SA v NV Rotterdamsche Kolen Centrale* [1967] 1 AC 361 (HL) 421–2 (Lord Upjohn); *Thomas Marshall v Guinle* (n 314) 239 (Sir Robert Megarry V-C).

394 *Metro Meat* (n 392) 15.

395 *The Gregos* (n 331) 1476.

396 *Ibid*.

397 *PT Berlian Laju Tanker Tbk v Nuse Shipping Ltd (The 'Aktor')* [2008] EWHC 1330 (Comm), [2008] 2 All ER (Comm) 784, [2008] 2 Lloyd's Rep 246.

398 *Ibid* [69].

399 *Ibid* [68].

400 *Citati* (n 2) 429.

We now turn to the application of the test of fundamentality. A fundamental breach, as noted earlier, is simply a breach so serious as to entitle the victim to terminate the contract. The term 'fundamental breach' is not distinct from other terms used in the same sense, such as 'material breach'[401] or 'substantial non-performance'.[402] The real question is how serious a breach must be in order to give rise to a right of termination. This question has to be answered according to the circumstances of each case. Generally speaking, the standard of seriousness/fundamentality does not vary according to whether the breach under scrutiny is actual or anticipatory. The courts are frequently called upon to assess the potential consequences of an actual breach. In many respects, therefore, the application of the test of fundamentality in our context can be assisted by decided actual fundamental breach cases.[403] The test, however, acquires two distinctive features when it is applied to anticipatory breach cases. First, the test must be applied by reference to the time when an anticipatory breach is alleged to occur, rather than the time when an inferred future breach is about to occur (which is also the time for performance). It may thus be insufficient for the purpose of establishing an anticipatory breach to show that, had the victim waited until the time for performance, the contract-breaker would have committed an actual fundamental breach. The inferred breach must be adjudged to be fundamental as at the time of the alleged anticipatory breach. It must be so serious as to justify a discharge of the part of the contract which is still executory at that time. A future actual breach may be adjudged to be fundamental by reference to the time when it materialises (namely the time for performance), yet it may not be sufficiently serious to warrant a release of the victim not only from its obligations due after the time for performance, but also from its obligations due between the time of the alleged anticipatory breach and the time for performance. To determine whether the inferred breach is sufficiently serious, the court must consider its effect on either the contract-breaker's outstanding performance at the time of the alleged anticipatory breach or (assuming that a reciprocal relationship can be established between individual parts of each party's performance) the part of its performance, both past and future, which is reciprocal to the victim's outstanding performance at that time, whichever is greater in magnitude. Secondly, in *The Hermosa*, the court raised but left unanswered a question as to whether 'actual and anticipated breaches can be treated as cumulative' to 'yield a state of affairs amounting to a repudiation', 'even if the individual elements were

[401] *Cf Spirent v Quake* (n 333) [39] (Gillese JA).

[402] Eg Waddams (n 380) [587].

[403] *Ibid* [591]. Waddams summarised five 'obvious indicators' of an actual fundamental breach: (1) the quantitative ratio of the party's obligation affected by the non-performance to the obligation as a whole; (2) the seriousness of the breach to the innocent party; (3) the probability of repetition; (4) the seriousness of the consequences of breach in the particular case; (5) the relationship of the part of the obligation performed to the whole obligation. In the case of anticipatory breach, clearly indicator (3) relates not to the test of fundamentality but to the test of reasonable inference.

not in themselves repudiatory'.[404] An affirmative answer was given in a number of cases.[405] This answer is consistent with our earlier revelation that past actual breaches may form part of a factual matrix from which a reasonable inference can be extracted. What is anticipated is thus effectively a future moment when the consequences of all those breaches accumulate to a degree of fundamentality. Nevertheless, the process is by no means a simple matter of mathematical aggregation. It is possible to envisage a situation where the benefit deprived by one actual breach may be of so different a type from that deprived by another actual breach that the two benefits cannot simply be added together. For instance, it seems hard to conceive how the gravity of an anticipated delay in delivering occupancy to a lessee could be increased by an actual breach by the lessor of an obligation to deliver a draft lease.[406] In short, the test of fundamentality determines whether the seriousness, assessed by reference to the time of the alleged anticipatory breach, of an inferred future breach is sufficient to entitle the victim immediately to terminate the contract.

C. Two Evidential Modes of Establishing Anticipatory Breach

An anticipatory breach is conventionally divided into two categories: renunciation and disablement. The former is based on unwillingness whilst the latter on inability or unreadiness. It was suggested by Devlin J in the *Citati* case that the distinction might also be attributable to the evidential mode in which an anticipatory breach was established. This has created a new, perhaps more significant, categorisation of anticipatory breach. If a party terminates the contract and then attempts to justify it on the basis of an anticipatory breach, it may establish the breach in two distinct modes. A reasonable inference of a prospective fundamental breach must be drawn from circumstances existing by or at the time of the termination. However, not all such circumstances may be transparent to the party at that time. The anticipatory breach may be established on the basis of evidence available by or at the time of the termination (hereinafter 'pre-acceptance evidence'). Alternatively, it may be established on the basis of evidence that does not become available until after that time (hereinafter 'post-acceptance evidence'). In both cases, we are looking at evidence adduced to satisfy both the test of reasonable inference and the test of fundamentality.

[404] *The Hermosa* (n 170) 580 (Donaldson LJ).

[405] *Lewis v Motorworld Garages Ltd* (1985) ICR 157 (CA) 169 (Glidewell LJ); *Omilaju v Waltham Forest LBC (No 2)* [2004] EWCA Civ 1493, [2005] ICR 481; *The Pro Victor* (n 278) [88], [100]–[101] (Flaux J).

[406] *Cf Spirent v Quake* (n 333) [49], [50], [52] (Gillese JA). The delay and the actual breach might, of course, together show that a reasonable inference could be drawn.

1. Establishing Anticipatory Breach on the Basis of Pre-Acceptance Evidence

This is by far the more common of the two evidential modes. But it has its own downside. A reasonable inference drawn on pre-acceptance evidence can be based on limited and incomplete information. Although reasonable at the time of the termination, it may subsequently prove to be incorrect. The main question posed in this connection is how far a reasonable, yet incorrect, inference may still trigger the remedies that common law has accorded to an anticipatory breach. The question consists of two different aspects. The first aspect asks whether a termination of a contract based on such an inference ought to be reversed. The second aspect asks whether a claim for damages based on such an inference must be disallowed.

Regarding the first aspect of the question, it naturally follows from the nature of anticipatory breach as a breach 'by inference' that a termination of contract based on a reasonable inference must be conclusive and not susceptible to attack grounded on actual facts. An anticipatory breach does not depend on concrete proof that a contractual obligation has fallen due and not been performed or on the absolute certainty that such an obligation will not be performed when due. A termination of the contract is justified solely by the reasonableness of an inference of a prospective fundamental breach. It is immaterial whether the inference is in fact correct or not. It hardly makes any sense to sanction a termination of contract for an inferential breach if the inference can subsequently be countermanded and the termination reversed. The conclusiveness of a reasonable inference seemed to be visible in the Court of Appeal's decision in *The Hermosa*. In that case, when N terminated the sub-charter on 26 August 1975, a reasonable person in its position was unable to infer that M would not perform its side of the contract. Donaldson LJ indicated in his judgment that, had it been otherwise, N's termination would have been justified irrespective of the fact that the owners had in fact commenced repairing the ship, which would certainly put M in a position to perform.[407] In other words, the incorrectness of the inference drawn would be irrelevant to the lawfulness of N's termination. The reasonableness alone would be sufficient to justify N's right to terminate. Accordingly, an anticipatory breach is constituted and completed at the moment a 'reasonable inference' is drawn. Nothing more is required. The underlying rationale seems to be that a businessman 'must be entitled to act on reasonable commercial probabilities at the time when they are called upon to make up their minds'[408] and 'be protected even if [information which he has and upon which he acts] turns out to be unreliable or untrue'.[409] Lord Sumner put it this way: '[r]ights ought not to be left in suspense or to hang on the chances of subsequent events. The contract binds or it does not bind, and the law ought

[407] *The Hermosa* (n 170) 573.
[408] *Embiricos v Sydney Reid & Co* [1914] 3 KB 45, 54 (Scrutton J). Also, Carter (n 166) 434.
[409] *Citati* (n 2) 440 (Devlin J).

to be that the parties can gather their fate then and there'.[410] In essence, the need for commercial certainty dictates that a termination of a contract on the ground of a reasonable inference should not be disturbed simply because certain evidence that becomes available afterwards renders that inference incorrect.

The above reasoning was echoed in *Cargo Ships v Invoeren*,[411] where Devlin J held that the charterers under a time charter were entitled to draw from the owners' overstatement of the total capacity of the deep tanks an inference that the capacity of the holds was reduced accordingly so as to be 'fundamentally different' from that described in the charter.[412] Since only the holds could be put to the intended use of carriage of coal, the charterers were entitled to accept the owners' overstatement as an anticipatory breach despite the fact that the actual capacity of the holds remained in conformity with the description. Similarly, in the Canadian case of *Sanko Steamship Co Ltd v Eacom Timber Sales Ltd*,[413] a termination of a charterparty by the cargo-owner, Eacom, was held to be justified by a declaration by the carrier, Sanko, of its intention to commence insolvency proceedings, which led to a reasonable inference of the latter's prospective non-performance of the contract, even though that inference was later shown to be incorrect.[414] In Macdonald J's words, Eacom had 'the right in law to be wrong about Sanko's future ability to perform the [contract], provided its decision was reasonable at the time'.[415]

The second aspect of the question as to the conclusiveness of a reasonable inference arises from a statement of Devlin J in the *Citati* case where, speaking of a disablement, he said that '[a]n anticipatory breach must be proved in fact and not in supposition'.[416] In the learned judge's view, only a renunciation, but not a disablement, could be established by way of a reasonable inference.[417] Treitel attempted to justify this statement on the ground that to recognise a reasonable inference of a party's prospective actual inability would be to subject that party to a claim for damages even where its actual ability was not impaired.[418] It plainly makes sense not to allow a claim for damages on the basis of a reasonable, yet incorrect, inference. Unlike the case of termination of contract, commercial certainty does not

[410] *Bank Line Ltd v Arthur Capel & Co* [1919] AC 435 (HL) 454–5. Also, *Hirji Mulji v Cheong Yue Steamship Co Ltd* [1926] AC 497 (PC Hong Kong) 508 (Lord Sumner), citing *Geipel v Smith* (1871–72) LR 7 QB 404, 414 (Blackburn J). All three cases concerned a situation of anticipatory or prospective frustration. The legal test as to whether an event justifies the termination of a contract, according to Diplock LJ, is the same irrespective of whether or not the event is caused by a breach by a party to the contract: *Hongkong Fir* (n 203) 66.

[411] n 257.

[412] *Ibid* 53. The learned judge held otherwise only because the owners' overstatement did not relate to all the three deep tanks, but merely two of them.

[413] (n 194) 492 (Macdonald J).

[414] *Ibid* 493.

[415] *Ibid* 491.

[416] *Citati* (n 2) 450.

[417] *Ibid* 439.

[418] *Treitel's Law of Contract* (n 276) [17–086]. Also, Carter, *Breach of Contract* (n 182) [936]–[937].

require or support such a claim. Nevertheless, it does not seem that the availability of a claim for damages should depend on whether the anticipatory breach in question takes the form of a renunciation or a disablement. Both forms of anticipatory breach must succumb to the same test, namely, the principle of inferred fundamental breach. A disablement is centred on a prospective inability, which can only be inferred. Perhaps, disablement does differ from renunciation in that the correctness of a reasonable inference in relation to a prospective inability, as opposed to unwillingness, is more prone to dispute. This is, however, not a difference in principle. As a matter of principle, it must be recognised that a reasonable inference, whether embodied in a renunciation or a disablement, if proved wrong, would cease to be a ground for claiming damages.

2. Establishing Anticipatory Breach on the Basis of Post-Acceptance Evidence

An anticipatory breach, if it cannot be established solely on pre-acceptance evidence, may alternatively be founded on post-acceptance evidence, namely, evidence that becomes available only after the purported acceptance is made. The admissibility of such evidence in establishing an anticipatory breach was first explicitly endorsed by Lord Sumner in *British & Beningtons v Cachar*, where he stated obiter:

> I do not see how the fact that the buyers have wrongly said "we treat this contract as being at an end, owing to your unreasonable delay in the performance of it" obliges them, when that reason fails, to pay in full, if, at the very time of this repudiation, the sellers had become *wholly and finally disabled from performing essential terms of the contract altogether.*[419] (Emphasis added.)

This dictum was affirmed in a later decision of the House of Lords.[420] It was, however, not until *Universal Cargo v Citati*[421] that the dictum was first applied. By a voyage charterparty dated 30 June 1951, a vessel was engaged to load at Basrah a cargo of scrap iron for Buenos Aires. The vessel duly arrived at Basrah on 12 July 1951. But the charterer failed to nominate either a loading berth or a shipper, as the party from whom the charterer contracted to buy the scrap iron desired to get out of the sales contract on a rising market. The vessel remained at the port until 18 July 1951, three days before the agreed lay-days were set to expire, when the owners re-chartered the vessel to a third party. The legal question was whether this termination of the contract by the owners could be justified by an anticipatory breach on the charterer's part.[422] A major issue concerned whether

419 *British & Beningtons* (n 207) 72.

420 *Continental Contractors v Medway* (n 280) 292 (Viscount Cave).

421 n 2.

422 The charterer had committed several actual breaches by the date of the termination in failing to nominate a berth, to provide a cargo and possibly to nominate a shipper. None of them entitled the owners to terminate the contract, *ibid* 428, 429.

such an anticipatory breach might be established by relying upon evidence that became available after 18 July 1951, the date of the termination. Devlin J, in his first judgment, held that the arbitrator answered this issue incorrectly and thus ordered the case to be remitted for a further finding of fact.[423] The learned judge agreed with the arbitrator that the only way to establish a renunciation was by relying upon pre-acceptance evidence and the owners failed to prove on that basis that the charterer had evinced an intention not to complete loading before the delay lasted so long as to frustrate the contract.[424] However, it was held that the arbitrator applied the wrong legal test in determining the issue of disablement, namely, whether 'the charterer had on July 18 "become wholly and finally disabled" from finding a cargo and loading it before delay frustrated the venture'.[425] This issue, according to Devlin J, should be considered 'in the light of all the events—whether occurring before or after the critical date—put in evidence at the trial'.[426] Subsequently the arbitrator gave his second award in accordance with this direction and this award, which answered the above issue of disablement in the affirmative, was upheld by Devlin J.[427] Devlin J's reasoning was later approved.[428] This mode of establishing an anticipatory breach, however, has not received as much judicial or scholarly attention as it probably deserves. The reason may be that, with the exception of the *Citati* case, there seem to be few cases where the facts necessitate resort to post-acceptance evidence.

Nevertheless, this mode is firmly supported by a long-established principle of law that a termination of contract can be justified by a valid reason unknown or undisclosed at the time of the termination, provided that the reason exists at that time. This principle of law is critical to a proper understanding of establishing an anticipatory breach on post-acceptance evidence. Therefore some further exposition is called for. The principle took shape in some early employment cases. Originally, it was formulated such that, where an employer had knowledge of a good ground for dismissing an employee but did not disclose it or gave a bad reason when dismissing the employee, the dismissal was not wrongful.[429] Several reasons were given. For one thing, it was said that the employer's motives were difficult to ascertain and thus immaterial.[430] Furthermore, 'it is not what he declares, but the authority which he has is his justification'.[431] And, 'if good ground of dismissal existed, the [employee] suffered no wrong from the dismissal from not

[423] The decision of remission aff'd [1957] 1 WLR 979 (CA).

[424] *Citati* (n 2) 439.

[425] *Ibid* 446.

[426] *Ibid* 446–7.

[427] *Universal Cargo Carriers Corp v Pedro Citati (No 2)* [1957] 2 Lloyd's Rep 311 (Com Ct), rev'd on the issue of costs [1958] 2 QB 254 (CA).

[428] *The Angelia* (n 299) 219 (Kerr J).

[429] *Ridgway v The Hungerford Market Co* (1835) 3 Ad & E 171, 111 ER 378; *Baillie v Kell & Hogg* (1838) 4 Bing NC 638, 132 ER 934; *Cussons v Skinner* (1843) 11 M & W 161, 152 ER 758.

[430] *Ridgway ibid* 177, 380 (Lord Denman CJ); 178–9, 381 (Patteson J); 180, 381 (Coleridge J).

[431] *Doctor Grenville v The College of Physicians* (1796) 12 Mod 386, 387, 88 ER 1398, 1398 (Holt CJ).

having been accused of it'.[432] The essence of these reasons was that the existence of a legal right should be determined by objective facts rather than by the relevant party's subjective conception of the right. Initially it was thought that, in order for the employer to rely upon the valid ground, it was necessary for it to know at the time of the dismissal of that ground.[433] But it became clear later that the requirement of knowledge was imposed in certain cases solely because of the existence of a pleading rule that, in modern terms, if the employer had incorporated the ground into a statement of case and had served it, it could only be amended either with the written consent of all the parties or with the court's permission.[434] The requirement of knowledge was eventually removed by the Court of Appeal.[435] The modified principle, which originated in employment contracts, was also applied to other types of contract, for example, contracts for the sale of goods,[436] agency contracts,[437] charterparties,[438] and construction contracts.[439] In *Taylor v Oakes*, Greer J elevated the principle to the status of a general principle of contract law:

> It is a long established rule of law that a contracting party, who, after he has become entitled to refuse performance of his contractual obligations, gives a wrong reason for his refusal, does not thereby deprive himself of a justification which in fact existed, whether he was aware of it or not.[440]

Thus the terminating party's knowledge or conception of the reason is irrelevant. A fortiori it is also immaterial whether the reason actually induces the termination. The existence of a legal right should not be determined by how it is understood by its possessor. The law should sanction a termination as long as it is *in fact* justified by an existing reason. To provide otherwise is equivalent to requiring every terminating person to be a detective or a qualified lawyer. This principle has since been entrenched in numerous cases.[441] We shall henceforth call it 'the *Taylor v Oakes* principle'.

[432] *Mercer v Whall* (1845) 5 QB 447, 466, 114 ER 1318, 1325 (Lord Denman CJ).

[433] *Cussons v Skinner* (n 429) 172–3, 763 (Parke B).

[434] *Mercer v Whall* (n 432) 466, 1325 (Lord Denman CJ). Now CPR 17.1(2).

[435] *Boston Deep Sea Fishing & Ice Co v Ansell* (1888) 39 Ch D 339 (CA) 357 (Cotton LJ), 364 (Bowen LJ), 370 (Fry LJ); *Cyril Leonard & Co v Simo Securities Trust Ltd* [1972] 1 WLR 80 (CA) 85–6 (Russell LJ), 88 (Sachs LJ), 89 (Stamp LJ); *Denmark Productions Ltd v Boscobel Productions Ltd* [1969] 1 QB 699 (CA) 722, 724 (Salmon LJ).

[436] *Taylor v Oakes* (n 237) 869 (Greer J); *Henry Dean & Sons (Sydney) Ltd v P O'Day Pty Ltd* (1927) 39 CLR 330 (HCA) 359 (Starke J). *cf Braithwaite v Foreign Hardware Co* [1905] 2 KB 543 (CA) 552 (Collins MR); JW Carter, 'The Higher Altitudes of Contract Law' [1989] *Lloyd's Maritime and Commercial Law Quarterly* 81, 85.

[437] *Shepherd v Felt and Textiles of Australia Ltd* (1931) 45 CLR 359 (HCA) 378 (Dixon J).

[438] *Citati* (n 2) 443 (Devlin J).

[439] *Sheffield v Conrad* (1987) 22 Con LR 108 (CA).

[440] *Taylor v Oakes* (n 237) 869. Also, *Shepherd v Felt* (n 437) 378 (Dixon J): 'the rule is of general application in the discharge of contract by breach'.

[441] Eg *The Mihalis Angelos* (n 136) 193 (Lord Denning MR); *Albion Sugar Co Ltd v William Tankers Ltd and Davies (The 'John S Darbyshire')* [1977] 2 Lloyd's Rep 457 (Com Ct) 467 (Mocatta J); *The Al Hofuf* (n 247) 90 (Mocatta J). Also, *Sunbird v Maloney* (n 149), noted J Harris, 'Anticipatory Breach—Innocent Party's Right to Terminate' (1988) 1 *Journal of Contract Law* 177.

The principle applies equally to a case where the unknown or undisclosed reason is an anticipatory breach. The principle is said to be subject to several qualifications,[442] such as where the reason is one which if disclosed 'could have been put right'[443] or where the terminating party is estopped from relying upon the reason.[444] The application of the principle to anticipatory breach cases is, however, not seriously hindered by these qualifications. The first qualification, for example, is largely irrelevant as an anticipatory breach is rarely committed by a slip of the tongue and is thus not usually expected to be retracted once disclosed. Therefore, a termination of a contract is justifiable by an anticipatory breach of which the terminating party is ignorant or makes no mention. This is easily transformable to a rule of evidence. It should not matter that the terminating party fails, or is unable, to adduce sufficient evidence at the time of the termination in proof of the anticipatory breach. All evidence made available at the trial must be admissible. The *Taylor v Oakes* principle is thus a strong justification for establishing an anticipatory breach on post-acceptance evidence. It also answers an argument that to recognise the latter might open the door too widely, particularly by allowing a post-acceptance change of circumstances to be relied upon in establishing an anticipatory breach. The principle is premised on an existing valid reason for the termination of the contract. There must be an anticipatory breach existing at the time of termination. A reasonable inference must be supported by existing rather than future circumstances. It cannot be drawn retrospectively. As Donaldson LJ stated in *The Hermosa*:

> [T]he conduct relied upon is to be considered as at the time when it is treated as terminating the contract, in the light of the then existing circumstances. These circumstances will include the history of the transaction or relationship. Later events are irrelevant, save to the extent that they may point to matters which the parties should have considered as hypothetical possibilities at the relevant time.[445]

What those existing circumstances are can of course be determined in accordance with all the evidence available at the trial, regardless of whether the evidence becomes available before or after the termination. The terminating party is not entitled to draw an inference that no one at the time of the termination was capable of drawing. For instance, it cannot be said that since, as things turn out, a party would have disabled itself from performing the contract had the other party not terminated it earlier, there should necessarily be an anticipatory breach existing at the time of the termination.[446] This is a point which is not apparently consistent with Devlin J's above-cited statement in the *Citati* case[447] but which must

[442] *Glencore Grain Rotterdam BV v Lebanese Organisation for International Commerce (The 'Lorico')* [1997] 2 Lloyd's Rep 386 (CA) 395–7 (Evans LJ).

[443] *Heisler v Anglo-Dal Ltd* [1954] 1 WLR 1273 (CA) 1278 (Somervell LJ).

[444] *Panchaud Frères SA v Etablissements General Grain Co* [1970] 1 Lloyd's Rep 53 (CA) 57 (Lord Denning MR). Also, SGA 1979 s 35(1).

[445] *The Hermosa* (n 170) 573.

[446] *Sheffield v Conrad* (n 439) 112 (Russell LJ).

[447] n 426.

be recognised as a corollary of the inferential nature of an anticipatory breach. The requirement that a reasonable inference can only be drawn from existing circumstances, coupled with the stringent test of fundamentality, helps to curtail opportunistic withdrawal from the contract.

As a final note, the argument that only a disablement, not a renunciation, can be established on post-acceptance evidence must be dealt with. As Devlin J suggested in the *Citati* case, a party's words or conduct, as opposed to actual inability, 'can only be interpreted in the light of the events that are known to the interpreter at the time'.[448] In *Nottingham Building Society v Eurodynamics Systems plc*,[449] the Court of Appeal refused to allow a supplier of some computer software to rely upon its buyer's internal communications to prove the latter's intention not to perform the contract. The reason was said to be that a reasonable person in the supplier's position would not have had access to those internal communications at the time when the supplier purported to terminate the contract.[450] However, just as in the case of the conclusiveness of a reasonable inference, there can be no rational divide between renunciation and disablement with respect to the admissibility of post-acceptance evidence. If a reasonable but incorrect inference gives rise to a renunciation, it would be very odd not to give effect to a reasonable inference which is supported by evidence, even though the evidence comes to light only after the acceptance. With both renunciation and disablement being now united into a reasonable inference of a prospective fundamental breach, the ruling in the above cases must be rejected.

To conclude this Chapter, the fundamental breach approach has been shown to be a more suitable basis on which a single unified test can be constructed. The unified test requires not only that some future breach must be reasonably inferred, but also that the inferred breach must be fundamental, namely, so serious as to entitle the victim presently to terminate the contract. To establish the reasonable inference, it is usually sufficient, but by no means necessary, for the victim to show that the contract-breaker has evinced an intention not to perform the contract. When attempting to show that circumstances existing at the time when it purports to accept the alleged anticipatory breach support a reasonable inference of a prospective fundamental breach, the victim may rely upon all evidence available at the trial, whether it comes to light before or after the time of the purported acceptance.

448 *Citati* (n 2) 440.
449 *Nottingham Building Society v Eurodynamics Systems plc* [1995] FSR 605.
450 *Ibid* 612 (Gibson LJ).

5

Anticipated Breach as Defence

Where a party brings a claim for the other party's breach of contract, the latter may raise a defence that the claimant itself is likely to be in breach of the contract when its performance falls due. We are concerned in this Chapter only with a complete defence of this sort, one which exonerates the defendant from liability for its breach (whether actual or anticipatory) entirely.[451] The issue whether some minor future breach(es) by the claimant might serve as a partial defence, thereby reducing damages payable by the defendant, will be left to a later Chapter.[452] A complete defence based on the claimant's future breach(es) bears some resemblance to a claim of anticipatory breach, both being centred on future, anticipated breach(es) of a fundamental character. Yet there are also important distinctions between the two. Above all, a claim aims to establish liability whilst a defence aims to dismantle it. The principle of inferred fundamental breach applies where an anticipatory breach is sought to be established as a liability basis. This is so even where it is the defendant who seeks to establish an anticipatory breach in a counter-claim.[453] The key question to be addressed in this Chapter is, however, whether the principle of inferred fundamental breach or any other principle should govern the situation where one party's future, anticipated breach(es) is (are) relied upon not to establish its liability, but solely for the purpose of exonerating the other party from liability. Section A puts the question in context by examining a much-criticised decision of the English courts. Section B attempts to ascertain the true basis of a theory under which the claimant's future, anticipated breach(es) is (are) said to be 'waived' by a prior (most likely anticipatory) breach by the defendant. Section C then investigates the issue of how the claimant's unwillingness or unreadiness to perform the contract might be brought to bear on the defendant's liability.

A. The *Braithwaite* Conundrum

In order to give a principled answer to the question posed above, we must start from the Court of Appeal's decision in *Braithwaite v Foreign Hardware Co*,[454]

[451] Eg *British & Beningtons* (n 207) 71 (Lord Sumner).
[452] Ch 8 s B 2) d).
[453] Eg *Guy-Pell v Foster* (n 140); *Littlehampton v Dorling* (n 351).
[454] n 436.

which has long been considered notoriously hard to rationalise. A contract for the sale of rosewood provided that the goods were to be shipped in two consignments. While the first consignment was on the sea, the buyers purported to terminate the contract. The buyers relied upon a force majeure clause under the contract. This was an invalid ground as the alleged clause was found to be in fact non-existent. Subsequently the buyers refused to accept bills of lading for both consignments when the goods arrived and the seller had to resell them at a loss. It was later revealed that, while the second consignment was in accordance with the contract, a portion of the first consignment did not answer the contract description. The seller sued the buyers for damages on the ground of wrongful termination. At the trial the two consignments were regarded as 'severable' and treated like two separate contracts.[455] The only dispute between the parties arose out of the contract embodied in the first consignment and this alone will be the subject of our discussion. Counsel for the buyers sought a total exoneration from liability by arguing that, had they not terminated the contract, the seller would have committed an actual breach of its obligation to deliver corresponding goods. It was nevertheless held by Kennedy J at first instance that, first, the buyers had wrongfully terminated the contract and were thus liable in damages, and secondly, the damages should be reduced in proportion to the decrease in value of the goods for inferiority. The Court of Appeal unanimously affirmed the first part of this decision,[456] whilst Collins MR, with whom Cozens-Hardy LJ concurred, reserved his opinion on the second part. The decision has since been subject to severe criticism in both England and other commonwealth countries.[457]

As regards the buyers' legal position in the case, there appeared to be two different routes by which a complete defence might be raised on the ground of the seller's prospective failure to deliver corresponding goods. First, it might be argued that that future breach by the seller somehow constituted a justificatory ground for the buyers' termination and the seller's claim for wrongful termination should be dismissed as a result. If this argument was accepted, not only would the buyers be exonerated from liability, they would also be entitled to hold the seller fully liable for their loss of bargain. The argument thus operated offensively as well as defensively. Secondly, a less ambitious tactic might be adopted. To legitimatise the buyers' termination might be considered too intricate a route to pursue. Consequently, the buyers might want to confine themselves to a submission that the seller's future breach precluded it from claiming for the buyers' wrongful termination. The effect of this submission was purely defensive. It could not enable the buyers to make a claim against the seller for its future breach. The

[455] *Ibid* 554 (Mathew LJ).

[456] Collins MR, Cozens-Hardy and Mathew LJJ.

[457] *Cooper Ewing & Co Ltd v Hamel Horley Ltd* (1922) 13 Ll L Rep 590 (KB) 593 (Sankey J); *Barley v Robertson* (n 5) 209 (McArthur J); *British & Beningtons* (n 207) 70 (Lord Sumner); *Esmail v J Rosenthal & Sons Ltd* [1964] 2 Lloyd's Rep 447 (CA) 463 (Davies LJ); *The Al Hofuf* (n 247) 90 (Mocatta J). Also, Carter (n 436).

first route hinges on the doctrine of anticipatory breach. It must be dealt with first. Two related observations can be made in this regard. The first observation is that the court in *Braithwaite's* case seemed to assume that the buyers' termination, being a termination on a wrong reason, should automatically be wrongful. It was thus held to be 'incompetent' for the buyers to 'hark back' and rely on their 'after-acquired knowledge' as a defence.[458] In the case, the buyers committed two acts of purported termination. The first act occurred while the goods were still at sea. The second act was the buyers' rejection of the bill of lading when the goods arrived.[459] Neither termination could be justified by an actual breach on the seller's part. As regards the first termination, the seller committed no actual breach as it was under no obligation to ship goods that were in conformity with the contract.[460] As regards the second termination, there was also no actual breach. As noted in a series of subsequent cases,[461] the seller merely offered to tender the bill of lading and, when that offer was rejected, resold the goods. Therefore, its obligation to deliver corresponding goods, which would not come due until the bill was tendered, was never 'actually' breached. On this basis the court concluded that both attempts of the buyers to terminate the contract were 'unlawful'. Yet, the court omitted to consider the possibility that a termination for a wrong reason might still be justified by an alternative ground and would thus not be wrongful. Carter sought to justify the court's reasoning on the ground that 'the wrongful conduct itself precludes reliance on the alternative ground' for termination.[462] This suggestion, however, stems from a logical fallacy. A termination on a wrong reason is not 'wrongful conduct' unless the terminating party is prevented from relying upon alternative grounds. But it cannot be said that the reason the terminating party is so prevented is that the termination is 'wrongful conduct'. Instead, according to the *Taylor v Oakes* principle discussed in the last Chapter, given that the buyers were not estopped from relying upon the seller's future breach as an alternative ground, that breach should have at least been considered as a possible justificatory ground for the buyers' termination even though it was unknown until the goods were tendered.

The second observation thus concerns the role of the doctrine of anticipatory breach in exonerating a party from its liability in a factual situation like that in

[458] *Braithwaite* (n 436) 552 (Collins MR).

[459] Rejection of shipping documents as well as goods might be regarded as merely withholding one's performance where the defects were disclosed and a cure was expected: R Bradgate and F White, 'Rejection and Termination in Contract for the Sale of Goods' in J Birds, R Bradgate and C Villiers (eds), *Termination of Contracts* (Wiley Chancery, 1995) 53. This was evidently not the case in *Braithwaite*. The seller's rejection was also not an actual breach as no documentary transaction was involved: GH Treitel, 'Rights of Rejection under C.I.F. Sales' [1984] *Lloyd's Maritime and Commercial Law Quarterly* 565; F Reynolds, 'Rejection of Documents' [1984] *Lloyd's Maritime and Commercial Law Quarterly* 191.

[460] Eg *Kwei Tek Chao (t/a Zung Fu Co) v British Traders and Shippers LD* [1954] 2 QB 459, 480–1 (Dvelin J); *Berger & Co Inc v Gill & Duffus SA* [1984] AC 382 (HL) 390 (Lord Diplock).

[461] *Taylor v Oakes* (n 237) 869–70 (Greer J); *Esmail v Rosenthal* (n 457) 466 (Salmon LJ); *The Simona* (n 386) 803–5 (Lord Ackner).

[462] Carter (n 436) 85.

Braithwaite's case. The court in that case clearly overlooked the possibility that the seller's prospective failure to deliver corresponding goods might, by virtue of the doctrine of anticipatory breach, be transformed into a present justificatory ground for the buyers' purported termination.[463] To be sure, the issue was never raised by counsel for the buyers. At a time still dominated by the renunciation approach, a submission to that effect, even if made, would have had little chance of success. It is obvious that the seller could not possibly be said to have evinced an intention not to perform the contract by the time when the buyers purported to terminate it. Nevertheless, the question must be asked whether, according to the principle of inferred fundamental breach, the prospective defective delivery was such that the seller might be considered to have committed an anticipatory breach by the time of the buyers' purported termination. Since this option was not conjured up by the lawyers at the time, the material facts were not fully debated in *Braithwaite's* case. Some clues could nevertheless be gathered from the law report. The actual decision of the court recognised the seller's future breach as a partial, rather than complete, defence against the claim. This did not, however, result from a conscious reasoning that the future breach was not serious enough to constitute a complete defence. Kennedy J found that the inferiority of the goods 'was such as would have entitled' the buyers to terminate the contract 'had they not previously wrongfully [terminated]'.[464] It was not made clear whether this was based on the seriousness of the inferiority or the fact that the contract description departed from amounted to an express or an implied condition. In the Court of Appeal, Mathew LJ, the only judge who chose to express an opinion on the matter, reached a contrary decision that the inferiority was negligible.[465] This was later criticised by Lord Sumner as having been made 'under some misapprehension as to the percentage of the cargo which was inferior to the contract quality'.[466] Thus, it seems likely that the buyers might have been able to establish, by relying upon post-acceptance evidence, an anticipatory breach by the seller. Subsequently, in *Taylor v Oakes*, a case indistinguishable from *Braithwaite's* case, while Greer J openly stated that the decision in *Braithwaite's* case was 'not inconsistent with' the *Taylor v Oakes* principle,[467] the route of establishing an anticipatory breach on the non-terminating sellers' part was again not pursued. In *Taylor v Oakes*, the buyers under a contract for the sale of goods by instalments purported to terminate the contract after having accepted and paid for the first delivery. It was found that they 'neither knew of nor suggested any ground which could be alleged as a justification for' the termination.[468] The sellers accepted the termination as a repudiation of the contract and claimed damages. A major defence

[463] *Foran v Wight* (n 155) 428–9 (Brennan J).
[464] *Braithwaite* (n 436) 546.
[465] *Ibid* 553. *cf* 553 (Collins MR).
[466] *British & Beningtons* (n 207) 71.
[467] *Taylor v Oakes* (n 237) 870.
[468] *Ibid* 866.

raised on behalf of the buyers was that the goods delivered did not comply with the contract description. It was held by Greer J at first instance, affirmed by the Court of Appeal, that the defence neither provided the buyers with an excuse from their liability for wrongful termination nor served as a significant set-off against the damages they were liable to pay, since the first delivery was found to deviate from the contract description only 'in a slight but appreciable degree'.[469] Clearly, the buyers' termination could not be justified by the sellers' actual breach in respect of the first delivery, which breach, albeit of an implied condition,[470] should be treated as a 'severable breach' as the buyers failed to take the opportunity to reject the goods.[471] Despite the finding that, had the buyers not terminated the contract, the sellers would, 'in all probability, indeed as a practical certainty', have tendered the same goods as those already delivered,[472] the court felt bound by *Braithwaite's* case and held that the buyers' termination was 'wrongful'. Bankes LJ, specifically, made the point that 'the breach of contract complained of' under the SGA 1893 section 31(2) referred to an actual breach only.[473] This was an unwarranted interpretation. In Chapter 3 above, we saw that in a great number of cases the phrase was interpreted to embrace an anticipatory breach.[474] Given that the sellers' breach would have been repeated in future instalments, the question should have been asked whether the sellers' breaches, both present and future, might indeed cumulatively produce the same effect as a fundamental breach and thus give rise to an anticipatory breach. *Taylor v Oakes*, therefore, again attested a general failure by the courts at the time to visualise an inference of one or more future breaches as a present justificatory ground for terminating the contract. A cautionary note must be added at this juncture. On the facts of both *Braithwaite's* case and *Taylor v Oakes* the doctrine of anticipatory breach might have been employed to justify an otherwise wrongful termination. The application of that doctrine is, however, not confined to 'wrongful' termination cases. The defendant may exonerate itself from liability by establishing an anticipatory breach on the claimant's part even in cases where no wrongful termination is involved. For example, the defendant may have committed an actual breach and an anticipatory breach by the claimant will wipe off its liability. All of those cases where the doctrine of anticipatory breach is in play, however, possess a common feature. The defendant is entitled to bring a counter-claim against the claimant for its anticipatory breach, subject to a set-off based on the defendant's own breach. The doctrine of anticipatory breach is in its nature a weapon to be used offensively, eliciting a full liability on the party in breach, with the incidental defensive consequence that the victim

469 *Ibid* 868.

470 SGA 1893 s 13. Now SGA 1979 s 13.

471 *Taylor v Oakes* (n 237) 868 (Greer J), 870 (Bankes LJ), applying SGA 1893 s 31(2). Now SGA 1979 s 31(2), also, ss 11(4), 35(4).

472 *Taylor v Oakes* (n 237) 868 (Greer J).

473 *Ibid* 871. Now SGA 1979 s 31(2) but the words 'complained of' were deleted.

474 Ch 3, text after n 230 above.

(defendant)'s liability is thus exonerated. The establishment of an anticipatory breach has been covered in the last Chapter and requires no further discussion here. With the recognition of the principle of inferred fundamental breach, this route is certainly made more available to litigants.

Let us turn to the second route. There is in the first place an issue as to whether there is such an alternative route at all. It may be asked whether the defendant must establish an anticipatory breach on the claimant's part when attempting to use the latter's future breach(es) as a basis for raising a complete defence. Clearly, an affirmative answer would cause two sorts of difficulty. First, the onus of proof in relation to the existence of an anticipatory breach lies in the defendant and is not a light burden to discharge. Without dispute, there must inevitably be cases where a party cannot or fails to prove the existence of an anticipatory breach even though the other party's future breach(es) would have been likely to deprive it of substantially all of its benefits under the contract had the contract gone ahead. In such cases it might be too harsh to deny the former party the possibility of raising a complete defence on the basis of the latter party's future breach(es). Secondly, it is unnecessary and inappropriate to require a party to establish an anticipatory breach when that party seeks only to exonerate itself from liability. The reason why the onus of establishing an anticipatory breach is a heavy one is that such an endeavour, if successful, has drastic consequences. It entitles the victim immediately to terminate the contract and claim loss of bargain damages. In *Braithwaite's* case, for example, if the buyers successfully established an anticipatory breach on the seller's part and the prior termination thus constituted an acceptance of it, they would not only be relieved from any liability for wrongful termination, but would also be entitled to make a counter-claim for the entire loss of bargain under the contract. Yet the buyers did not ask for damages in that case; they simply asked for the seller's claim to be rejected. Logic compels the conclusion that the buyers should not be saddled with the heavy burden of establishing an anticipatory breach where they sought merely to raise a complete defence, rather than making a counter-claim, on the basis of the seller's future breach. Due to these two difficulties, therefore, the doctrine of anticipatory breach should not be adopted as the governing principle over the question whether a complete defence based on future breach(es) is made out. The existing law in fact opts for a far less demanding legal test. The claimant is required to satisfy the court that it is willing and ready to perform the contract once the defendant puts it in issue. The onus is thus shifted to the claimant. The claimant's unwillingness or unreadiness denotes future, anticipated breach. Yet the doctrine of anticipatory breach is not invoked. This process can thus be called the 'defence of anticipated breach'.

Whether the buyers had pursued the route of establishing an anticipatory breach or raising the defence of anticipated breach in *Braithwaite's* case, a theory put forward by Collins MR would have put it to rest. Unsurprisingly, Collins MR dismissed entirely the relevance of the inferiority of the seller's goods to the buyers' liability. His Lordship's reasoning was, however, adventurous. In his words, the buyers' 'wrongful' termination, even upon the footing that it was not 'accepted', was by itself 'a waiver by them of the performance by the [seller] of the conditions precedent which would otherwise have been necessary to the enforcement by him of the contract'.[475] Thus, the buyers' purported termination 'waived' the seller's future obligation to deliver corresponding goods. We henceforth call this the 'waiver theory'. It eliminates any future breach on the claimant's part and thus undermines any defence formed on that basis. Most strikingly, Collins MR even expressed the view that such a 'waiver' would lead to an assessment of the seller's damages as if the goods had answered the contract description[476] and would thus, as a matter of 'strict law', exclude the seller's future breach from that assessment.[477] This last view, which effectively closed the door for recognising the seller's future breach even as a partial defence in reduction of its damages, was first doubted[478] and then rejected by both the Court of Appeal and the House of Lords.[479] Our current interest is confined to the effect of the waiver theory on a complete defence and thus on the entirety of the buyers' liability. In that respect an interesting development occurred shortly after *Braithwaite's* case. First in *British Beningtons v Cachar*, one of the unsuccessful counsel in *Braithwaite's* case, Lord Sumner, as he had become, openly questioned the waiver theory and stated obiter that a claimant's disablement from its future performance might serve as a 'defence either as to the whole or as to part' of the contract.[480] It was said that the theory was 'wrong' as the terminating party should not be precluded from relying upon (particularly) the other party's unwillingness or unreadiness to perform the contract as a justificatory ground for the termination.[481] Then in a later case, *Continental Contractors v Medway*, Scrutton and Atkin LJJ, who were the successful counsel in *Braithwaite's* case, stated, in spite of Lord Sumner's earlier unequivocal dictum, that they would 'continue to follow' and 'adhere to' Collins MR's reasoning.[482]

In summary, the central fallacy of the Court of Appeal's decision in *Braithwaite's* case lies in its failure to recognise that the defendant in an action for breach of contract may rely upon the claimant's future breach(es) as a complete defence either by way of establishing an anticipatory breach on the claimant's part or through the vehicle of the defence of anticipated breach. In fact, the waiver theory advanced by Collins MR in that case has the potential to defeat any defence of such a kind. That theory is critically evaluated in section B. Section C then looks into the defence of anticipated breach and explores how the claimant's unwillingness or unreadiness to perform the contract may give rise to that defence.

475 *Braithwaite* (n 436) 551. Also, 554 (Mathew LJ).
476 *Ibid.*
477 *Ibid* 552 (Collins MR).
478 *Continental Contractors v Medway* (1925) 23 Ll L Rep 124, 133 (Scrutton LJ).
479 *Esmail v Rosenthal* (n 457) 466 (Salmon LJ); *The Simona* (n 386) 803–5 (Lord Ackner).
480 *British & Beningtons* (n 207) 71.
481 *Ibid* 70.
482 *Continental Contractors v Medway* (n 478) 132, 133 (Scrutton LJ); 135 (Atkin LJ).

B. The Waiver Theory

The waiver theory advanced by Collins MR in *Braithwaite's* case asserted that a termination of contract by a party for a wrong reason would automatically relieve the other party from its future obligations. Collins MR made it clear that such a termination would not only preclude the other party's future breach from being relied upon as a ground for the termination, but would also exclude that future breach from the assessment of the damages payable by the terminating party. As mentioned earlier, the latter aspect, which is concerned with a partial defence only, has been firmly rejected in later cases. The waiver theory to be discussed here is confined to the former aspect. It can be more generally stated to be that an anticipatory breach (or more narrowly, a particular form of anticipatory breach, viz wrongful termination), even unaccepted, may sometimes trigger a 'waiver' and thereby relieve the victim from its primary obligations under the contract. Accordingly, the victim's future conduct, even in contradiction of the terms of the contract, does not constitute a breach at all. It is thus impossible for the party in breach (or the terminating party) to rely upon the victim's future 'breach' to raise a complete defence. The waiver contemplated by Collins MR was distinct from a similar proposition that arose later. It was suggested that a 'waiver' might arise only if and when the wrongful termination was accepted as an anticipatory breach.[483] This is not a 'waiver'. This is a discharge of the contract caused by the acceptance. Clearly, a discharge of contract, although capable of relieving the victim from further performance, including its willingness and readiness to perform at the time for performance,[484] cannot possibly dispense with the necessity that the victim would have been willing and ready to perform had the contract continued.[485] It is necessary to analyse the legal foundation of the waiver theory in the context of anticipatory breach.

'Waiver' is an elusive word.[486] Literally, it means 'an act or instance of refraining from insisting on or from demanding a right or claim'.[487] When used in the law of obligations, it has long been criticised as denoting no more than the 'end-result' of election or estoppel.[488] It could thus be said that 'waiver' has no substance of

[483] *Cachar* (n 146) 387 (Scrutton LJ), aff'd *British & Beningtons* (n 207) 63 (Lord Atkinson); *Taylor v Oakes* (n 237) 869 (Greer J), 872 (Bankes LJ), 873 (Scrutton LJ), 873 (Atkin LJ). Also, AG Guest, *Benjamin's Sale of Goods*, 6th edn (London, Sweet & Maxwell, 2002) [9–016]–[9–018].

[484] *North Sea Energy Holdings NV v Petroleum Authority of Thailand* [1999] 1 Lloyd's Rep 483 (CA), aff'g [1997] 2 Lloyd's Rep 418 (QB) 432 (Thomas J); *State Trading Corp of India v M Golodetz* [1989] 2 Lloyd's Rep 277 (CA).

[485] F Dawson, 'Waiver of Conditions Precedent on A Repudiation' (1980) 96 *LQR* 239, 243; MG Lloyd, 'Ready and Willing to Perform: The Problem of Prospective Inability in the Law of Contract' (1974) 37 *MLR* 121, 125.

[486] *Oliver Ashworth (Holdings) Ltd v Ballard (Kent) Ltd* [2000] Ch 12 (CA) 28 (Robert Walker LJ): a waiver was not 'a precise term of art'.

[487] *Concise Oxford English Dictionary*, 11th edn rev (Oxford, OUP, 2008).

[488] *China National Foreign Trade Transportation Corp v Evlogia Shipping Co SA of Panama, (The 'Mihalios Xilas')* [1979] 1 WLR 1018 (HL) 1034 (Lord Scarman); *Oliver Ashworth v Ballard* (n 486)

its own, tends to obscure the process by which an abandonment of a right or benefit is effected, and should consequently be abolished.[489] Although the term 'unilateral waiver' appears to be recognised in some quarters,[490] 'waiver' is said to be best viewed as either 'waiver by estoppel' or 'waiver by election'.[491] In the current context, a 'waiver' operates where an alleged anticipatory breach, in particular a wrongful termination, is said to be capable by itself of relieving the victim from obligations or burdens under the contract. In the following paragraphs it will be shown that the loss or suspension of a contractual right or benefit accruing to the party allegedly in anticipatory breach requires reliance by the victim and is not caused by a mere unilateral declaration by that party that the right or benefit is abandoned. Consequently, 'waiver' is best seen as a convenient expression of what is truly in operation—estoppel.

This type of 'waiver' can be traced back to a long line of earlier cases discussed in Chapter 1, where the courts, applying the reasoning in *Main's Case*, brought a renouncing or disabled party's future obligation into immediate maturity by 'exempting' or 'dispensing with' a condition precedent to that obligation.[492] This is sometimes explained on the ground that fulfilment of the condition precedent is 'prevented' by the disablement or renunciation, such as where a party is released from making delivery or payment if the other party refuses to take it.[493] The notion of 'prevention' centres on the resulting inability and is thus not an appropriate basis for 'waiver'. A more telling explanation of 'waiver' is an assertion that 'the law will not enforce any one to do a thing which will be vain and fruitless'.[494] In other words, a performance is 'waived' because an anticipatory breach renders it pointless. Two different lines of argument have been advanced on the basis of the above assertion. One maintains that in order for the said 'waiver' to take effect,

29A–B (Robert Walker LJ); *Kammins Ballrooms Co Ltd v Zenith Investments (Torquay) Ltd* [1971] AC 850 (HL) 882–3 (Lord Diplock). Also, *Agricultural & Rural Finance Pty Ltd v Bruce Walter Gardiner & Anor* [2008] HCA 57, [51] *et seq* (Gummow, Hayne and Kiefel JJ), *cf* [143]–[145] (Kirby J); P Feltham, D Hochberg and T Leech, *Spencer Bower: The Law Relating to Estoppel by Representation*, 4th edn (Tottel, 2004) paras XIII.1.4, XIII.1.20–21; T Dugdale and D Yates, 'Variation, Waiver and Estoppel—A Re-Appraisal' (1976) 39 *MLR* 680; JW Carter, 'Waiver (of Contractual Rights) Distributed' (1991) 4 *Journal of Contract Law* 59.

489 *The Commonwealth of Australia v Verwayen* (1990) 170 CLR 394 (HCA) 406–7 (Mason CJ), 451–2 (Dawson J), *cf* 467–8, 472–5 (Toohey J), 481–2, 485 (Gaudron J), 491, 497 (McHugh J), 423–4, 428 (Brennan J). Also, J Ewart, *Waiver Distributed* (Harvard University Press, 1917); GS Bower and AK Turner, *The Law Relating to Estoppel by Representation*, 3rd edn (London, Butterworths, 1977) 320; AM Sheppard, 'Demystifying the Right of Election in Contract Law' [2007] *Journal of Business Law* 442. *cf* K Arjunan, 'Waiver and Estoppel—A Distinction Without a Difference?' (1993) 21 *Australian Business Law Review* 86.

490 *Glencore Grain Ltd v Flacker Shipping Ltd (The 'Happy Day')* [2002] 2 Lloyd's Rep 487 (CA) [64] (Potter LJ); *Verwayen ibid* 467–8, 472–5 (Toohey J), 496–7 (McHugh J).

491 *Panchaud* (n 444) 57 (Lord Denning MR). *cf* Feltham et al (n 488) paras XIII.1.25, XIII.1.28.

492 Eg *Ripley v M'Clure* (n 11) 359–60, 1251 (Parke B). Further, Ch 1, text to n 31 above.

493 *Cort v Ambergate* (n 62) 142, 145, 1235, 1236 (Lord Campbell CJ). Also, Dawson (n 61) 95.

494 *Lex neminem cogit ad vana seu inutilia peragenda, Main's Case* (n 30) 21a, 81, citing 2 Roll Rep 408, Hard 387b, Co Lit 127b, 197b. Also, *Sinason-Teicher v Oilcakes* (n 372) 944 (Devlin J); *Etablissements Chainbaux SARL v Harbormaster Ltd* [1955] 1 Lloyd's Rep 303 (QB) 310 (Devlin J).

the declaration of pointlessness must be relied upon so as to create an estoppel. The other, by contrast, insists that the declaration is self-operative as it induces or causes a failure to render the 'waived' performance.

Both arguments were raised in an Australian case, *Peter Turnbull v Mundus*.[495] The seller under an f.o.b. contract was bound to deliver goods alongside ship at the port of Sydney during the months of January and February 1951. This obligation was subject to a condition precedent that the buyer should fulfil its obligations to nominate a ship and to give the seller 14 days' notice of its shipping date. On 31 January the seller informed the buyer that it could supply the goods only from Melbourne. During the month of February the buyer made every effort to change the port of loading from Sydney to Melbourne but failed. The buyer did not nominate a ship for loading in Sydney, nor did the seller attempt to supply the goods from there, when the last day of February passed. The buyer bought at a higher price elsewhere at the beginning of March and claimed damages for the difference. The seller's main defence was that the buyer had no cause of action to bring the claim as the seller's anticipatory breach on 31 January was not accepted and no actual breach accrued to the seller due to the buyer's failure to nominate a February ship and to give due notice of its shipping date. The High Court of Australia, by a three to one majority,[496] held that the buyer was entitled to recover damages on the ground of the seller's actual non-delivery. The majority's reasoning was that the seller was in actual breach of its obligation to deliver the goods as the condition precedent to that obligation, namely, the buyer's nomination of a ship and service of a notice, was 'waived' and that obligation became unconditional and fell due at the end of February. No matter on what basis such a 'waiver' was explained, this reasoning, as noted by the dissenting judge, Taylor J, had a conceptual difficulty.[497] How could a seller actually breach an obligation to deliver goods alongside ship when no ship was nominated and no notice was given? The majority's response was that the buyer's nomination and notice was dispensed with for the purpose of recovering damages only and the dispensation could not be alleged for specific enforcement of the seller's obligation to deliver.[498] This was hardly convincing, for the real issue was not which remedy was available to the buyer but whether the seller was in breach in the first place. The better approach, it is submitted, is to hold that the buyer's cause of action lay in the seller's anticipatory breach on 31 January, which breach, although still unaccepted, did not develop into an actual breach at the end of February as the seller's obligation to deliver did not fall due to be performed then.[499] That anticipatory breach hence survived the end of February, the time for performance, and was accepted by the buyer in early March when it bought elsewhere, as its earlier

[495] n 5.

[496] Dixon CJ, Webb and Kitto JJ (Taylor J dissenting).

[497] *Peter Turnbull* (n 5) 260, 266.

[498] *Ibid* 252 (Kitto J); 249 (Webb J).

[499] *Foran v Wight* (n 155) 433 (Deane J); 441 (Dawson J).

attempts to arrange shipping from Melbourne did not constitute an affirmation of the contract.[500]

This leads us to the issue whether the buyer's nomination of a ship and service of a notice could be said to be 'waived' by the seller's anticipatory breach. The buyer's right to accept that breach and claim damages would be open to question if those obligations were not 'waived' and the buyer was not itself willing or ready to perform them. The court was divided as to the basis on which such a 'waiver' should operate. On the one hand, Dixon CJ resorted to the notion of 'estoppel'. The seller's communication on 31 January was held to amount not merely to an anticipatory breach, but also 'something more', namely, an intimation that it was pointless for the buyer to nominate a ship and to serve a notice for loading in Sydney.[501] This intimation was then relied upon by the buyer to its detriment, who refrained from finding a suitable ship when there was still time and was thus excused from doing so.[502] On the other hand, Kitto J simply stated that 'the non-completion of the contract proceeded from' the seller's anticipatory breach rather than the buyer's omission to nominate a ship and to serve a notice.[503] The underlying reasoning seemed to be that it was the seller's breach that induced or caused the buyer's omission, not the other way around.

The latter 'inducement' view must be rejected. It was adopted in some earlier cases where the issue was stated to be whether it was a party's anticipatory breach or the other party's subsequent failure of performance that caused the non-completion of the contract.[504] This is, however, an extremely vague, overly simplistic and misleadingly confounding test. It does not provide an operable means by which the existence and extent of inducement or causation can be ascertained. It naively assumes that the non-completion of the contract must be attributable to one rather than both of the parties. By invoking the concept of 'causation', it runs into the danger of confusing the issue of liability with that of damages. In fact, inducement or causation is but an obscure reference to the 'reliance' ingredient of an estoppel, a more accurate legal concept that has come to be favoured by courts of modern times. Nevertheless, it might be argued that a party can 'waive' the other party's contractual obligation or burden independently of contract, election or estoppel. Such a 'waiver' is a unilateral declaration of intention that by itself releases the other party without any need to prove consideration, conscious choice or reliance. In particular, it is often said to operate where the 'waived' obligation or burden is solely for the benefit of the 'waiving' party, such as 'the essentiality of the requirement as to time of performance'.[505] For example, where the 'essentiality' of a contract term is waived, late performance would elicit a liability in damages only

[500] *Peter Turnbull* (n 5) 249 (Webb J).

[501] *Ibid* 245–6 (Dixon CJ).

[502] *Ibid* 248. Also, 249 (Webb J).

[503] *Ibid* 254.

[504] *Pontifex v Wilkinson* (1845) 1 CB 75, 90–1, 135 ER 464, 470 (Tindal CJ); *Cort v Ambergate* (n 62) 144, 1236 (Lord Campbell); *Cooper Ewing v Hamel* (n 457) 593 (Sankey J).

[505] *Foran v Wight* (n 155) 458 (Gaudron J).

and no right of termination would arise. Certainly, if such a 'waiver' exists at all, the only thing that one party can 'waive' without injuring the other is a benefit that is exclusively his/hers. There is, however, a vital difference between what one can do and what, if done, binds one. That something is solely for the benefit of a party does not make a unilateral disposition of it binding. In particular, it is hard to see why, if a unilateral declaration of intention to 'waive' is not relied upon, it should by itself prevent the 'waiving' party from reverting to its previous position. Reversion ought to be permissible as long as it causes no harm to the opposite party. Instead of resorting to the irrational concept of 'waiver', it is evidently more congruous to make the enforceability of such a declaration dependent on the equitable doctrine of estoppel.

For this reason, it is submitted that Dixon CJ's estoppel view must be preferred. The earlier cases sanctioning the dispensation of a condition precedent, for example, are also better seen as founded on estoppel.[506] An anticipatory breach must first contain an 'additional element', namely, an unequivocal intimation that it is pointless for the victim to fulfil a condition precedent.[507] Not every anticipatory breach meets this threshold.[508] The intimation constitutes a representation as to a future fact. So what is later brought into operation is a promissory estoppel.[509] The representation is extracted from the anticipatory breach. Compared to an actual breach, an anticipatory breach can be said to be more likely to contain such a representation. The representation has to be relied upon. Whether the law requires reliance to be detrimental or not, there must be a change of position on the victim's part as a result of the representation.[510] The act of reliance might simply be a failure to commit the very act that was said to be 'waived', namely, the fulfilment of a condition precedent. The party in anticipatory breach is estopped from alleging only those breaches that are or will be committed in reliance on the representation. The estoppel does not necessarily excuse every future breach by the victim. There must be a linkage by reliance. Reliance is a key factor in determining whether it would be inequitable for the party in anticipatory breach to regress and insist that the victim fulfil the condition precedent. But whether that party is estopped is ultimately subject to the court's discretionary power. The leading authority adopting the estoppel view is *The Simona*.[511] Clause 10 of a voyage charter gave the charterers the option of cancelling the charter should the vessel not be ready to load on or before 9 July 1982. The charterers cancelled the contract on 2 July when the owners requested an extension of the ready-to-load date. The owners' request did not entitle the charterers to so act. They thus committed an anticipatory breach by wrongfully terminating the contract. The owners, despite the fact that the nominated vessel, *The Simona*, could not have been ready to load

[506] *Ibid* 420 (Brennan J); 434 (Deane J); 442 (Dawson J); *cf* 457–8 (Gaudron J).
[507] *Peter Turnbull* (n 5) 245 (Dixon CJ).
[508] *Foran v Wight* (n 155) 410 (Mason CJ).
[509] *Ibid* 411.
[510] *Ibid* 412–13.
[511] n 386.

until after 9 July, persisted in the performance of the contract. The charterers sent out a further cancellation notice on 12 July. The House of Lords unanimously held that the charterers had not lost their right of cancellation under Clause 10 as a result of their prior unaccepted anticipatory breach. Lord Ackner, with whom all other Law Lords concurred, rejected the waiver theory enunciated by Collins MR and concluded that if the owners were to be relieved from any of their obligations under the contract, they should accept the charterers' anticipatory breach; the owners might not keep the contract alive and in the same breath deny liability for a failure to tender a ready-to-load ship on time.[512] The only way by which the owners might so escape from their liability was to establish an estoppel. This route was closed to the owners as they did not, and could not, adduce any evidence substantiating either that the charterers' 2 July notice amounted to a representation that the ship was no longer required to be ready on time or that the owners' failure to meet the appointed date was 'induced' by—namely, resulting from their reliance on—that notice.[513] This dictum of Lord Ackner indicated strongly and unmistakably that a 'waiver' in the current context was a misnomer and what was truly in operation was a promissory estoppel.

Therefore, an anticipatory breach does not 'waive' a contractual right or benefit; the party in breach is 'estopped' from insisting upon that right or benefit. The same can be said of an actual breach which carries with it an intimation that it is pointless to render future performance. In such cases any allegation of the victim's future breach is precluded. The victim is relieved, to the extent of the estoppel, from its further obligations. It is thus impossible for the party in breach to raise a defence, either complete or partial, on the basis of the victim's future breach. On the facts of *Braithwaite's* case an estoppel was out of the question.[514] The seller would have delivered inferior goods anyway even if the buyers had not purported to terminate the contract or reject the bill of lading earlier.[515] Where an estoppel cannot be established, the key question is whether the claimant's future breach, short of an anticipatory breach, may none the less be raised as a complete defence against the claim. This requires discussion in a separate section.

C. The Averment of Willingness and Readiness

The answer to the question raised at the end of the previous section is of course in the affirmative. The defence of anticipated breach provides that a complete defence arises where the claimant fails to satisfy the court that it would have been willing and ready to perform the contract had it not been for the breach

512 *Ibid* 805.
513 *Ibid.*
514 *Cf Cooper Ewing v Hamel* (n 457) 593 (Sankey J).
515 *Braithwaite* (n 436) 551 (Collins MR); 554 (Mathew LJ).

by the defendant. The term 'willingness and readiness' was perhaps first adopted in cases where the reasoning in *Main's Case* was brought to play. A contracting party renounced or disabled its performance before a condition precedent to that performance was fulfilled by the other party. Actual fulfilment of the condition was regarded as pointless and dispensed with. Yet the contract-breaker's performance did not thus become unconditional. Instead of showing that the condition had been fulfilled, it was necessary, as well as sufficient, for the victim to show its 'readiness' to fulfil the condition.[516] Proof of 'readiness' to perform rather than actual performance has gradually become prevalent since the early 18th century as contracts tended increasingly to contain mutually dependent performances.[517] While in *Kingston v Preston*, Lord Mansfield still insisted that both a tender of performance and readiness to perform should be shown,[518] his Lordship shifted his position eight years later and treated readiness as the only necessary 'averment'.[519] His Lordship's remarks on the latter occasion have become the classical statement in this field: '[t]he party must shew he was ready; but, if the other stops him on the ground of an intention not to perform his part, it is not necessary for the first to go farther, and do a nugatory act'.[520] Although the word 'willingness' was omitted, for years 'willingness and readiness' has been established vocabulary for contract lawyers. Concurrently with its recognition by the courts the term developed a special tie with renunciation and disablement cases.[521] The majority of the cases in which the term was invoked involved some form of anticipatory breach. This is fairly understandable. It is precisely in cases where a contract has to be brought to a premature end that the claimant's willingness and readiness to perform is likely to be raised as an issue. A successful 'traverse' (denial) of the victim's willingness or readiness has thus long been regarded as a good defence for not performing the contract.[522] With the inauguration of the doctrine of anticipatory breach in the mid-19th century, 'willingness and readiness' rose in status. It was no longer a mere substitute for actual fulfilment of a condition precedent, the latter having been rendered wholly irrelevant in anticipatory breach cases. Instead, 'willingness and readiness' became the only condition that ought to be satisfied in order to succeed in an action for anticipatory breach.[523] Then in 1883 a change of pleading rules made 'willingness and readiness' an implied averment in all cases—hence no proof was required unless the defendant put it in issue—and thereby further

516 *Peeters v Opie* (n 55).

517 *Turnor v Goodwin* (1748) Fort 145, 92 ER 796.

518 Cited in (1773) 2 Doug 689, 691, 99 ER 437, 438, *sub nom Anon* (1773) Lofft 194, 98 ER 606.

519 *Jones v Barklay* (1781) 2 Doug 685, 694, 99 ER 434, 440. An 'averment' is a solemn declaration. In the present context it refers to demonstrating one's case on evidence.

520 *Jones v Barklay ibid.*

521 *Withers v Reynolds* (n 63); *Cort v Ambergate* (n 62); *Ellen v Topp* (1851) 6 Exch 424, 155 ER 609.

522 *Lawrence and Another Assignees of W Okill, a Bankrupt v Knowles* (1839) 5 Bing NC 399, 132 ER 1152; *Griffith v Selby* (1854) 9 Ex 393, 156 ER 167.

523 Eg *Inchbald v Western Neilgherry* (n 63); *Re Edwards Ex p Chalmers* (n 63).

alleviated the burden of a claimant, including the victim of an anticipatory breach, in establishing its cause of action.[524]

In anticipatory breach cases particularly, the victim's willingness and readiness gives rise to a number of intriguing issues. To what extent must the victim satisfy the court that it is willing and ready to perform the contract? By reference to what point of time must the victim be willing and ready? Does it make any difference where the victim does not accept the anticipatory breach and brings an action after the time for performance for actual breach? If the victim fails to show willingness or readiness, does this go to the effectiveness of the victim's acceptance, its right of action for damages or the assessment of damages? All these issues were dealt with, in an enlightening fashion, by the High Court of Australia in *Foran v Wight*.[525] There was a contract for the sale of land due to be completed on 22 June 1983, time being of the essence of the contract. On 20 June, the vendors informed the purchasers that they would be unable to complete on time due to a delay in registering a right of way necessary for the completion. No action was taken and no attempt made to complete the contract by either party on 22 June. Two days later, the purchasers purported to terminate the contract. The whole dispute between the parties revolved around the issue whether a deposit prepaid by the purchasers was recoverable. The purchasers sought a declaration that they validly terminated the contract on 24 June and were thus entitled to recover the deposit. The vendors contended that the purchasers' termination was invalid because they would not have raised sufficient finance to complete on 22 June had the vendors registered the right of way on time; accordingly it was the vendors who had validly terminated the contract on 28 September 1984 when they resold the land for a smaller sum, thereby resulting in a forfeiture of the deposit. The High Court of Australia, by a four to one majority (Mason CJ dissenting), endorsed the purchasers' argument and allowed their appeal from the decision of the Court of Appeal of New South Wales.[526]

The vendors' 20 June intimation, according to the judges, constituted an anticipatory breach of an essential term.[527] Being unaccepted and unretracted, that breach would naturally develop into an actual breach if all conditions precedent to the vendors' conveyance of the land were fulfilled by 22 June. If so, the purchasers' termination on 24 June would be justified by the actual breach by the vendors on 22 June. The key issue was, however, whether the purchasers' willingness and readiness to complete the contract on 22 June, being one of the conditions precedent to the vendors' conveyance, was satisfied on the facts of the case.

[524] RSC 1883 Ord 19 r 14, now RSC Ord 18 r 7(4). Also, *Foran v Wight* (n 155) 393 (Mason CJ); 451–2 (Dawson J).

[525] n 155.

[526] *Wight v Foran* (1987) 11 NSWLR 470.

[527] *Foran v Wight* (n 155) 395 (Mason CJ); 416 (Brennan J); 432 (Deane J); 440–1 (Dawson J). According to the principle of inferred fundamental breach enunciated in ch 4 earlier, this might not constitute an anticipatory breach at all if the prospective failure to complete the sale on time was not a fundamental breach.

If the purchasers were themselves unwilling or unready to complete, the vendors' conveyance of land could not be said to have fallen due and there would not be an actual breach on the vendors' part, which justified the purchasers' termination. The purchasers' willingness and readiness was thus essential to their claim. Three separate points can be extracted from five distinctive judgments. First, given that the vendors' anticipatory breach embodied an implied intimation that it would be pointless for the purchasers to complete the contract, a majority of the court expressed the view that that intimation could not relieve, either by way of 'waiver'[528]—if there were such a thing—or estoppel,[529] the purchasers from the burden of showing their willingness and readiness to perform. As for the two judges who decided differently on this point, their reasoning was hardly commendable. Resort to 'waiver' was problematic for reasons stated earlier.[530] Estoppel was also unhelpful.[531] If the purchasers had relied upon the intimation to their detriment and were as a result not in a position to complete the contract on 22 June,[532] the vendors would have undoubtedly been estopped from alleging the purchasers' resulting inability. However, the vendors were not estopped from alleging that the purchasers would have been unable to complete the contract anyway, even if the vendors had not committed the anticipatory breach. In other words, the doctrine of estoppel is powerless to preclude the defendant from raising the claimant's future breach as a defence if that breach is not committed in reliance on the intimation embodied in the defendant's breach. On the facts of *Foran v Wight*, it seems that the vendors had at least an arguable case that the purchasers would still have been unable to raise sufficient finance to complete the contract on 22 June in the absence of the anticipatory breach. The purchasers' willingness and readiness thus remained an issue that should be addressed by the court. The next two points concern the court's legal approach to addressing that issue.

Secondly, it was unanimously agreed that the onus was on the purchasers to satisfy the court that they were willing and ready to complete the contract on 22 June and all the judges except Gaudron J endorsed a distinction between two types of willingness and readiness. The first type of willingness and readiness required that the purchasers were not on the date of the anticipatory breach substantially disabled from completing the contract.[533] In other words, 'nothing but a substantial incapacity or definitive resolve or decision against doing in the future what the contract requires is counted as an absence of readiness and willingness'.[534] 'Substantial incapacity' was held to be 'a test of degree' less 'demanding'[535]

[528] *Ibid* 398, 403 (Mason CJ). *cf* 458 (Gaudron J).

[529] *Ibid* 412–13 (Mason CJ); 427 (Brennan J); 452 (Dawson J). *cf* 436–7 (Deane J).

[530] *Cf ibid* 458 (Gaudron J).

[531] *Cf ibid* 436 (Deane J).

[532] *Ibid* 436 (Deane J). *cf ibid* 412–13 (Mason CJ).

[533] *Ibid* 408–9 (Mason CJ); 425, 427 (Brennan J); 454 (Dawson J).

[534] *Rawson v Hobbs* (1961) 107 CLR 466, 481 (Dixon CJ). Also, *Psaltis v Schultz* (1948) 76 CLR 547, 560 (Dixon J).

[535] *Foran v Wight* (n 155) 425 (Brennan J).

than the 'wholly and finally disabled' test formulated by Lord Sumner,[536] which, as can be recalled, concerned the establishment of an anticipatory breach by way of disablement as a legal ground for an otherwise wrongful termination. This, at least partly, reflects the difference adverted to earlier between a defence and a claim. Since it was not the purchasers' liability that was in issue, whether they were 'wholly and finally disabled' was irrelevant. They were required only to show that they were not 'substantially disabled'. On the other hand, the difference in wording also seems to denote that from the purchasers' point of view the test in *Foran v Wight* is more demanding than a test requiring a mere demonstration that they were not 'wholly and finally disabled'. The second type of willingness and readiness required that the purchasers would have been willing and ready to complete the contract had it not been for the vendors' anticipatory breach.[537] This did not refer to the purchasers' willingness and readiness on the date of the anticipatory breach. The purchasers were not obliged to be willing or ready to complete earlier than the date of completion. They were required to show willingness and readiness on the date of completion on the hypothesis that the anticipatory breach had not occurred. The court in *Foran v Wight* also distinguished these two types of willingness and readiness in that the first type could be satisfied by merely demonstrating 'a real chance' to complete the contract,[538] whilst the second type required proof that the contract would 'on the balance of probabilities' have been completed.[539] Evidently, it is more difficult to show the second type of willingness and readiness than the first. This means that the vendors' chance of succeeding in their defence would be improved if the second type of willingness and readiness was required from the purchasers. It was found on the facts that the purchasers succeeded in showing only the first, less stringent, type of willingness and readiness.

Thirdly and lastly, the court dealt with the issue which of the two types of willingness and readiness should be adopted. There were two conflicting views. On the one hand, Mason CJ suggested that the first type of willingness and readiness should only be required in the case of an accepted anticipatory breach (in which case 'the date of breach' should be substituted by 'the date of acceptance'). In the present case, since the purchasers had not accepted the anticipatory breach by 22 June, they were required (and failed) to show the second type of willingness and readiness.[540] Consequently, the Chief Justice concluded that the vendors' defence was successful and the purchasers were not entitled to terminate the contract on 24 June on the ground of a breach (either anticipatory or actual) on the vendors' part. The deposit was thus forfeited. On the other hand, three other judges were agreed that the type of willingness and readiness to be applied hinged on the

[536] *British & Beningtons* (n 207) 72.

[537] *Foran v Wight* (n 155) 393, 398, 405 (Mason CJ); 424–5, 427 (Brennan J); 437 (Deane J); 451–2, 454 (Dawson J).

[538] *Ibid* 436 (Deane J).

[539] *Ibid* 408–9 (Mason CJ); 430 (Brennan J).

[540] *Ibid* 408–9 (Mason CJ).

remedies sought, rather than whether the anticipatory breach was accepted. All three judges recognised that in order to recover substantial damages, the second type of willingness and readiness should be shown.[541] Brennan and Dawson JJ shared the view that the first type of willingness and readiness was sufficient for a right of termination and a cause of action to arise.[542] Deane J, by contrast, held that a right of termination required no proof of willingness and readiness at all and the second type of willingness and readiness (assuming that it was not excused by estoppel) was also required for the accrual of a cause of action.[543]

It is submitted that Deane J's analysis provides the most sensible approach. First, Mason CJ's distinction between accepted and unaccepted anticipatory breach is not at all convincing. It does not seem that different standards of willingness and readiness ought to be imposed on the victim of an anticipatory breach according to whether it has accepted that breach or not. Either way it is the victim's willingness and readiness by reference to the time for performance, not the time of breach or acceptance, that constitutes the basis for a complete defence. Such a defence must not be rejected simply because the victim is not 'substantially incapacitated' prior to the time for performance—as much where the anticipatory breach is accepted as where it is not accepted. Secondly, a heavier onus on the victim to show willingness and readiness is supported by the fact that once the onus is successfully discharged, the victim is inevitably put in a position to terminate the contract and claim loss of bargain damages on the ground of either the anticipatory breach (if that breach is accepted) or an actual breach that the anticipatory breach develops into (if no acceptance is made). As a majority of the court openly recognised, the first type of willingness and readiness was not a sufficient reason for the purchasers to recover such damages. In order for the purchasers either to prove substantial loss or to seek specific performance,[544] they were required to show positively that they would have, on the balance of probabilities, been willing and ready to complete the contract on 22 June had it not been for the vendors' anticipatory breach. A lighter onus would be dissonant with the remedies available.

Thirdly, there is much to be said for the view that a party's willingness and readiness must be severed from the question whether a right of termination accrues to it. As Deane J observed, the conditionality of a right of termination on a demonstration of either type of willingness and readiness is blatantly unsatisfactory. He regarded it as 'unjustified by either principle or common sense' that a party should be put to expense to show its willingness and readiness in order to terminate the contract.[545] This was an unorthodox, minority view. The rest of the court held that the purchasers were entitled to terminate the contract only if

[541] *Ibid* 430–1 (Brennan J); 438–9 (Deane J); 454–5 (Dawson J). *cf* 402, 406–7 (Mason CJ).

[542] *Ibid* 427 (Brennan J); 454 (Dawson J).

[543] *Ibid* 437.

[544] *Ibid.*

[545] *Ibid.*

they were themselves willing and ready to perform the contract. This has indeed been the orthodox view in the common law tradition. The reason seems to be that a party must be classified as either an innocent party or a guilty party and only when it is classified as an innocent party is it entitled to resort to such remedies as termination of contract and damages. This orthodox view is, however, overly rigid and detached from the reality. In a case like *Foran v Wight*, where 'the failure of the contract was as much due to the purchasers' incapacity as that of the vendors',[546] neither party should be classified as the innocent party. There is no 'primary rule' that neither party might terminate if neither could show its willingness and readiness,[547] for the contract should not be left to 'hang like an albatross around their necks'.[548] The correct approach is to allow either party to terminate the contract provided a valid ground for termination is established. It does not matter which party terminates first. The truth is that a party's willingness or readiness to perform the contract has no bearing on its right to terminate the contract at all. The latter right should be determined solely on the basis of the nature or quality of the other party's breach. Even if the purchasers failed to show its willingness and readiness, their termination on 24 June would still be justified by the vendors' anticipatory breach on 20 June, which breach, for the same reason given earlier in respect of the seller's anticipatory breach in *Peter Turnbull v Mundus*,[549] did not develop into an actual breach on 22 June and thus survived that date.[550] By the same token, the vendors might equally have lawfully terminated the contract before the purchasers did if an anticipatory breach was established on the purchasers' part. The fallacy of the orthodox view was rooted in an erroneous assumption that a lawful termination by a party of the contract should necessarily shift all responsibilities to the opposite party. In fact, the issue of liability is best considered to be separate from the issue of termination. A claim for restitution, such as that in *Foran v Wight*, must be dealt with by exploring whether it is 'unjust' for the vendors to retain the deposit as an enrichment at the expense of the purchasers. This cannot be answered solely by a determination of which party had lawfully terminated the contract. Similarly, that the purchasers lawfully terminated the contract on 24 June did not necessarily make the vendors liable in damages. The vendors might be exonerated from liability if the purchasers failed to show their willingness and readiness to perform the contract.

In conclusion, in an action for breach of contract, the claimant's future breach(es) can be raised as a complete defence even if no anticipatory breach is established on its part. Once the defendant puts it in issue, the onus is shifted to the claimant to show that it would have been willing and ready to perform the contract had it not been for the breach complained of. The defence of

[546] *Ibid* 413 (Mason CJ). Also, 452 (Dawson J).
[547] *Ibid* 417 (Brennan J).
[548] *Ibid* 438 (Deane J).
[549] n 5.
[550] Text to n 500 above.

anticipated breach, as it is so called, operates to deny the claimant a right of action for damages but has no bearing on its right of termination. The claimant's future breach would be rendered irrelevant if the defendant is estopped from alleging it. The word 'waiver' used by Collins MR in *Braithwaite's* case is a misnomer of such an estoppel. But the real deficiency of the decision in that case lies in the fact that it did not realise the legal significance of the claimant's future breach at all. The decision must be criticised for its ignorance of both the doctrine of anticipatory breach and the defence of anticipated breach.

Part III

'Election' Following Anticipatory Breach

Once an anticipatory breach is established, the issue of remedy arises. The doctrine of anticipatory breach, however, insists that the type and scope of remedies available to the victim depends on the course of action it adopts consequent on the breach. The victim's reactions to the breach are accommodated under a principle of 'election'. In short, the victim must 'elect' between 'accepting' the breach, thereby terminating the contract, and 'affirming' the contract, thereby keeping the contract alive and relinquishing the right to 'accept' the breach. Such an 'election' determines not only whether the contract subsists but also what remedies the victim might seek. For instance, no right of action for expectation damages or restitution arises unless and until an effective 'acceptance' occurs, whilst specific performance is available only while the contract is 'affirmed'. In the following two Chapters, 'acceptance' and 'affirmation' will be examined respectively, in order to see how they are constituted and whether either of them fits in with the legal characterisation of 'election'.

6

Unlocking the Enigma of Acceptance

'Acceptance' is a mysterious word. It certainly does not mean 'consent' or 'approval'. 'Acceptance' of an anticipatory breach has variously been described by the courts as treating the contract as 'repudiated', 'rescinded' or 'abrogated',[551] or treating the conduct complained of as 'a wrongful repudiation of' or 'a wrongful putting an end to' the contract[552] or 'a breach going to the root of the contract'.[553] Restoring words like 'repudiate' and 'rescind' to their intended meanings, these descriptions all come down to the same thing: an acceptance brings the contract to an end and releases both parties from further performance. There are two issues that must be attended to. The first issue is what constitutes an effective acceptance. The second issue concerns the legal nature of acceptance—in particular, whether an acceptance is distinct from a termination of the contract and whether it may be characterised as an act of 'election'.

A. The Constitution of Acceptance

This section deals with the first issue. In respect of the constituent ingredients of an effective acceptance, there are three main points to be made. First and foremost, the legal test for acceptance is whether an unequivocal intention to bring the contract to an end is manifested. Secondly, we must explore the forms in which that intention may be manifested. Thirdly, there is a question whether an acceptance must be made with the knowledge of and in response to an anticipatory breach.

As regards the first point, the test for acceptance is in essence a test of intention. The victim must manifest an intention to bring the contract to an end. The requisite intention has two distinct elements. The first is unequivocality. The second is immediacy. The requisite intention must contain both elements. This is best

[551] Eg *Johnstone v Milling* (n 88) 469 (Lord Esher MR); *Ellis & Co's Trustee v Dixon-Johnson* (n 328) 355 (Lawrence J); *Norwest Holst v Harrison* (n 146) 683 (Sir Denys Buckley).

[552] Eg *Johnstone v Milling ibid* 468 (Lord Esher MR); *Frost v Knight* (n 87) 113 (Cockburn CJ).

[553] Eg *Hvalfangerselskapet v Unilever* (n 259) 221–2 (Scrutton LJ); *The Alma Shipping Corp of Monrovia v Mantovani (The 'Dione')* [1975] 1 Lloyd's Rep 115 (CA) 118 (Lord Denning MR); *Peter Turnbull* (n 5) 205–6 (Dixon CJ).

illustrated by the decision in *Norwest Holst v Harrison*.[554] The claimant was employed by the defendant company as a chief engineer and director. By a letter dated 14 June 1982, the company informed the claimant that he was to be removed from the post of director and relocated to a remote office as from 1 July 1982. The claimant replied on 17 June, treating the 14 June letter as 'a determination of my employment with effect from 30 June 1982' and at the same time claiming '12 months' salary and benefits in lieu of notice, together with redundancy payment under relevant statutes'. There followed an exchange of correspondence and a meeting between the two parties, culminating in a formal withdrawal on 24 or 25 June by the company of its 14 June letter. The claimant, however, insisted that the employment contract had been effectively terminated and that the defendant was liable in damages for wrongful dismissal. Having concluded that the company's 14 June letter constituted an anticipatory breach, which the company had *locus poenitentiae* to retract, the court concentrated on the issue whether the claimant's 17 June letter constituted an acceptance of that breach, thereby rendering the 24/25 June retraction ineffective. It was unanimously held that the 17 June letter did not amount to an 'unequivocal communication of acceptance'.[555] All three judges in the Court of Appeal relied upon the fact that the letter started with the words 'Without Prejudice' and its penultimate paragraph read:

> With respect your letter was indefinite on a number of points, and I would ask you to contact me immediately if you feel I have misunderstood what has been said or if further discussion would assist an amicable resolution of the matter.[556]

These two parts of the letter were held to have 'altered to a decisive extent … the prima facie effect' of the rest of the letter and thus were fatal to the claimant's action.[557] As a result the letter amounted merely to a proposal to commence 'a process of negotiation or compromise' or to 'enter into discussions'.[558] The defendant did not manifest an unequivocal intention to bring the parties' contractual relationship to a final conclusion.

The question whether the victim of an anticipatory breach manifests an unequivocal intention to bring the contract to an end depends on 'the particular contractual relationship and the particular circumstances' of each case.[559] The standard of unequivocality is objectively applied and does not hinge on the victim's subjective state of mind. As usual, what the victim does generally speaks louder than what it says. In many cases the enquiry is thus focused on whether the victim's conduct is consistent with the continuance of the contract.[560] A party cannot, in one and the same breath, assert rights which are consistent with the

[554] n 146.
[555] *Ibid* 679 (Cumming-Bruce LJ); 682 (Neill LJ); 683 (Sir Denys Buckley).
[556] *Ibid* 679 (Cumming-Bruce LJ).
[557] *Ibid* 682 (Neill LJ).
[558] *Ibid* 679, 680 (Cumming-Bruce LJ); 683 (Sir Denys Buckley).
[559] *Vitol SA v Norelf Ltd (The 'Santa Clara')* [1996] AC 800 (HL) 811 (Lord Steyn).
[560] *Boyo v Lambeth LBC* [1994] ICR 727 (CA) 743 (Ralph Gibson LJ).

continuance of the contract, and yet claim that it has accepted the anticipatory breach.[561] Hence, remaining in a tenancy and continuing to pay rent following a landlord's anticipatory breach thus precludes an acceptance being formed.[562] The same can be said where an application is made to a court for a declaration that the contract is valid and subsisting.[563] Conversely, to constitute an acceptance, the conduct in question must be consistent *only* with the discontinuance of the contract. A resale of specific or unique goods or real property, for instance, must be taken to manifest an unequivocal intention to discontinue the contract.[564] Similarly, negotiating with a third party with a view to obtaining substitute performance may be strong evidence of an acceptance.[565]

Interestingly, in *Norwest Holst v Harrison*, aside from the equivocality of the claimant's 17 June letter, Sir Denys Buckley gave an additional reason for the conclusion that it did not constitute an acceptance. In that letter, the claimant proposed that the contract be brought to an end with effect from 30 June. This, according to the learned judge, did not constitute an acceptance as the claimant's intention was not to bring the contract to an *immediate* end.[566] This seems to be a sensible proposition. A notice of a prospective termination of a contract is of dubious legal significance. It may be retracted at any time before the date appointed for termination arrives, provided the victim is not estopped from so doing. Even if the notice is not retracted, it is the time when the contract is terminated, rather than the time when the termination is foretold, that decides the legal consequences of the anticipatory breach, such as the accrual of a right to claim damages and a duty to mitigate losses. Indeed, the very idea that an acceptance might precede a termination of the contract is a strikingly odd one. Whilst any attempt of the victim, following the notice, to reap benefits from the contract would not be considered as an affirmation, the contract-breaker would be denied a right to retract the anticipatory breach. To suggest that an anticipatory breach gives rise to a power to set a future time of termination at will tends overly to favour the victim at the expense of the contract-breaker. Therefore, the immediacy of termination must be recognised as an indispensable element for an acceptance.

An acceptance requires the manifestation of an unequivocal intention to bring the contract to an immediate end. The second point concerns the forms in which such an intention may be manifested. The general principle is that an acceptance requires 'no particular form' and need not be 'couched in the language of acceptance'.[567] No express reference to 'acceptance' or 'termination' is necessary.

561 *Ivory v Palmer* [1975] ICR 340 (CA) 346 (Cairns LJ), 352 (Roskill LJ), 355 (Browne LJ); *Dietman v Brent LBC* [1987] ICR 737 (QB).

562 *Johnstone v Milling* (n 88).

563 *Garnac Grain v Faure* (n 246) 1139 (Lord Pearson).

564 *Holland v Wiltshire* (1954) 90 CLR 409 (HCA) 416 (Dixon CJ); 422 (Kitto J).

565 *Danube v Xenos* (n 84) 175–7, 762–3 (Erle CJ), 178–9, 764 (Williams J), 180–1, 764 (Byles J), 181, 765 (Keating J); *Peter Turnbull* (n 5) 243 (Dixon CJ). *cf Domb v Isoz* [1980] Ch 548 (CA).

566 *Norwest Holst v Harrison* (n 146) 683.

567 *The Santa Clara* (n 559) 810–11 (Lord Steyn).

Thus, a notice that inadvertently describes itself as a notice to 'rescind' the contract may very well amount to an effective acceptance.[568] By the same token, given that an unequivocal intention to bring the contract to an immediate end is manifested, a purported exercise of a contractual right of termination may also constitute an 'acceptance' of an existing anticipatory breach, irrespective of whether the contractual right 'corresponds to' the common law right of termination arising from such a breach or is exercised in accordance with contract provisions.[569] Although the point has yet to be authoritatively settled, it seems that not only the service of a writ for damages, but also a mere issue of it, might in appropriate cases constitute an acceptance.[570] An acceptance may even be made after the commencement of legal proceedings,[571] such as in the form of a defence.[572] A question arising in this connection is whether silence and inaction following an anticipatory breach might constitute an acceptance. For the most part, the answer must be in the negative, for silence and inaction are usually equivocal.[573] As Robert Goff LJ opined:

> In the absence of special circumstances, silence and inaction by a party ... are, objectively considered, just as consistent with his having inadvertently forgotten about the matter; or with his simply hoping that the matter will die a natural death if he does not stir up the other party; or with his office staff, or his agents, or his insurers, or his solicitors, being appallingly slow.[574]

However, this is by no means an absolute rule. Robert Goff LJ himself acknowledged that there might be 'special circumstances' which justified an exception to the rule. The House of Lords subsequently carved out such an exception in *The Santa Clara*.[575] The buyers under a c.i.f. contract, facing a falling market, sent out a telex renouncing the contract on 8 March 1991. By the time the telex came to the notice of the sellers on 11 March, the ship had already sailed away with loaded goods two days earlier, which fact became apparent to the buyers several days later. Thereafter, the sellers failed to take any step to perform or confirm the contract. The date of delivery under the contract was 19–20 March, but the sellers resold the cargo on 15 March and sent the buyers a notice of termination. The sellers

[568] Eg *The Mihalis Angelos* (n 136); *Stocznia v Latvian Shipping* [1997] 2 Lloyd's Rep 228, 237 (Colman J); *Stocznia v Latvian Shipping* [2001] 1 Lloyd's Rep 537 [179] (Thomas J); *Rawson v Hobbs* [1961] 107 CLR 466 (HCA).

[569] An acceptance was found on the ground that a contractual right of termination 'corresponded to' the common law right of termination as an exercise of the contractual right did not give rise to remedies inconsistent with a claim for the loss of bargain damages: *Stocznia Gdynia SA v Gearbulk Holdings Ltd* [2009] EWCA Civ 75, [2009] 1 Lloyd's Rep 461 [44]–[45] (Moore-Bick LJ). *cf Dalkia v Celtech* (n 251) [143] (Christopher Clarke J). The converse may not be true. A purported 'acceptance' may not be an effective exercise of a contractual right of termination: *Decro-Wall* (n 201) 371 (Salmon LJ); 378 (Sachs LJ); 382 (Buckley LJ).

[570] *Garnac Grain v Faure* (n 246) 1140.

[571] *Tilcon v Land & Real Estate* (n 112).

[572] *Guy-Pell v Foster* (n 140).

[573] Eg *Farrow Mortgage Services Pty Ltd v Edgar* (1993) 114 ALR 1 (FCA) 9.

[574] *Allied Marine Transport Ltd v Vale do Rio Doce Navegacao SA* [1985] 1 WLR 925 (CA) 937.

[575] n 559.

claimed damages on the ground that they had 'accepted' the buyers' anticipatory breach, not by reselling the goods or sending the notice of termination,[576] but by their mere failure to perform the contract following the breach and before the resale. The arbitrator allowed their claim, holding that their failure to perform amounted to an effective acceptance. Since this was a finding of fact, the buyers challenged the award by raising 'a question of law of impossible breadth',[577] namely, whether a failure to perform the contract, being mere inactivity, could *ever* in law constitute an acceptance.

The House of Lords allowed an appeal from the decision of the Court of Appeal[578] and restored the affirmative answer given by Phillips J at first instance to the above question.[579] Lord Steyn gave the leading speech, in which the other Law Lords concurred. The speech can be analysed from three different angles. First, as a matter of principle, it would be impossible to say that a failure to perform the contract could never constitute an acceptance. Much will depend on the particular context of the non-performance.[580] Whilst a failure to perform that commences before the anticipatory breach and continues thereafter would 'necessarily be equivocal', in appropriate circumstances 'an omission to act may be as pregnant with meaning as a positive declaration'.[581] Secondly, the particular facts of *The Santa Clara* supported an affirmative answer. The buyers' payment was conditional on the prompt tender by the sellers of a bill of lading. Without the bill of lading the contract could not proceed. To the knowledge of the buyers, sufficient time had elapsed following the completion of the loading, but no bill of lading was tendered. *The Santa Clara* was thus characterised by the fact that a performance essential to the continuance of the contract had fallen due and was not rendered.[582] In such circumstances, the non-performance might be incapable of any other interpretation than as being an acceptance. Lord Steyn gave another illustration in his speech: where the victim complied with a request contained in a wrongful termination that it should not perform a particular act, this act of compliance would clearly evince an intention to have the contract terminated and would thus constitute an acceptance.[583] Special facts of this kind might thus drive a case away from the normal course where silence was 'inertia'.[584] Thirdly, an analogy could be drawn between acceptance of an anticipatory breach and acceptance of an offer. The analogy probably originated in the 'offer to rescind' theory that

[576] The sellers might have argued, but chose not to, that these were two acts of 'acceptance': *ibid* 813 (Lord Steyn).

[577] S Hedley, 'Eloquent Silences and Reasonable People' [1996] *CLJ* 430, 431.

[578] *The Santa Clara* [1996] QB 108.

[579] *The Santa Clara* [1994] 1 WLR 1390 (Com Ct).

[580] *The Santa Clara* (n 559) 811.

[581] *Ibid* 812.

[582] *Ibid* 811.

[583] *Ibid.*

[584] *The Santa Clara* [1994] 1 WLR 1390, 1395 (Phillips J).

thrived by the time *Hochster v De la Tour* was decided.[585] As a result, acceptance of an anticipatory breach has been seen as 'the converse of that of making the same contract'.[586] The former would succumb to the same general requirement of communication as the latter.[587] As a rule, the victim should take reasonable steps to bring its intention to terminate specifically to the contract-breaker's attention.[588] A cessation of work, for instance, would not be treated as an acceptance unless and until so communicated.[589] On the other hand, just as silence and inaction might in exceptional cases constitute an acceptance of an offer,[590] an anticipatory breach might also be accepted where the victim's intention was not specifically communicated but merely made overt.[591] This seems to be the case where the parties' conduct shows a common understanding or assumption that the contract is at an end.[592] Certainly, there would be no acceptance if the victim's intention to terminate is neither specifically communicated nor made overt.[593]

The analogy between acceptance of an anticipatory breach and acceptance of an offer must not, however, be pushed too far. Indeed, it was even once said to be 'quite erroneous' to draw such an analogy.[594] This leads to our third point, namely, that acceptance of an anticipatory breach, unlike acceptance of an offer, need not be made with the knowledge of or in response to the anticipatory breach.[595] The foundation of this assertion resides in the *Taylor v Oakes* principle.[596] According to that principle, the termination of a contract can be justified by an existing

[585] *Ehrensperger v Anderson* (n 264) 158, 797 (Parke B); *De Bernardy v Harding* (n 14); *Hochster* (n 1) 685, 924 (Crompton J).

[586] *Denmark Productions v Boscobel* (n 435) 731–2 (Winn LJ). Also, *Lefevre v White* [1990] 1 Lloyd's Rep 569 (QB) 574 (Popplewell J). This analogy was said to give rise to the rule that if two joint contracting parties fell victim to an anticipatory breach, the assent of both was required to make an effective acceptance: *Lion White Lead Ltd v Rogers* (1918) 25 CLR 533 (HCA) 551 (Isaacs and Rich JJ), followed *Net Parts International Pty Ltd v Kenoss Pty Ltd* [2008] NSWCA 324 (unreported, 4 December 2008) [18], [28] (MacFarlan JA). Injustice may, however, arise if a victim is precluded from exercising a right of termination which arises by operation of law simply because the other victim does not assent to the exercise of that right.

[587] *Entores v Miles Far East Corp* [1955] 2 QB 327 (CA); *Tenax Steamship Co v Owners of the Motor Vessel Brimnes (The 'Brimnes')* [1975] QB 929 (CA).

[588] *The Santa Clara* (n 559) 811 (Lord Steyn), citing *Wood Factory v Kiritos* (n 379) 146 (McHugh JA); *Majik Markets Pty Ltd v S & M Motor Repairs Pty Ltd (No 1)* (1987) 10 NSWLR 49 (NSWSC) 54 (Young J). Also, *The Santa Clara* [1994] 1 WLR 1390, 1394–5 (Phillips J); *Holland v Wiltshire* (n 564). *cf Gator Shipping Corp v Trans-Asiatic Oil Ltd SA and Occidental Shipping Establishment (The 'Odenfeld')* [1978] 2 Lloyd's Rep 357 (Com Ct) 379 (Kerr J).

[589] *Stocznia v Latvian Shipping* [1997] 2 Lloyd's Rep 228, 237 (Colman J).

[590] Eg *Rust v Abbey Life Assurance Co Ltd* [1979] 2 Lloyd's Rep 334 (CA).

[591] *The Santa Clara* (n 559) 812 (Lord Steyn). Also, *American National Red Cross v Geddes Bros* (1920) 61 SCR 143 (SCC); *Chatfield v Jones* [1990] 3 NZLR 285 (CA).

[592] *MSC Mediterranean Shipping Co SA v BRE-Metro Ltd* [1985] 2 Lloyd's Rep 239 (Com Ct).

[593] *RV Ward Ltd v Bignall* [1967] 1 QB 534 (CA) 548 (Diplock LJ); *State Trading v Golodetz* (n 484) 286 (Kerr LJ).

[594] *Moschi v Lep Air* (n 149) 349–50 (Lord Diplock). Also, JW Carter, 'Failure to Perform as "Acceptance" of a Repudiation' (1997) 11 *Journal of Contract Law* 255.

[595] *Cf* the case of accepting an offer: *Williams v Carwardine* (1833) 5 Car & P 566, 172 ER 1101; *R v Clarke* (1927) 40 CLR 227 (HCA).

[596] Ch 4, text to n 440 above.

undisclosed or unknown ground. Therefore, as a corollary of applying the *Taylor v Oakes* principle, if the undisclosed or unknown ground is an anticipatory breach, the purported termination then becomes an acceptance of that breach.[597] The term 'acceptance' thus accommodates a termination without knowledge. This exposes, to some extent, the inaccuracy of the term 'acceptance'. In spite of what that term seems to suggest, the law is not looking for 'acceptance' as such. No knowledge of the anticipatory breach, the right of termination or the consequences of termination is required. An acceptance does not have to be an informed or conscious choice. The victim does not 'accept' (in the sense of 'condoning') the anticipatory breach; in fact, it acts strongly against it. The fact that there is, objectively assessed, an intention to terminate the contract does not imply any knowledge on the victim's part. Neither does the lawfulness of that termination require such knowledge. The lawfulness of the termination depends solely upon the existence of an anticipatory breach at the time of the termination; the victim's motive is immaterial. The victim might attempt a termination of the contract, not knowing, still less 'accepting', the breach. It might terminate for an entirely different reason. The coincidence of the breach and the termination might be accidental. Yet none of these points matters. It is not necessary that an acceptance must have a mental or causal linkage with the anticipatory breach accepted. What is required for an acceptance to occur is simply a termination of the contract, which is justified by an anticipatory breach existing at the time of the termination.[598]

B. The Nature of Acceptance

An exploration of the nature of acceptance calls for discussion of two separate issues. First, since, as shown above, acceptance of an anticipatory breach is built upon an intention to terminate the contract, a question may be asked whether acceptance and termination are but two names for the same thing. Secondly, the orthodox view that characterises an acceptance as an act of 'election' must be appraised.

1. Acceptance as Termination

In respect of the first issue, two different arguments have been advanced in an attempt to distinguish acceptance from termination. The first argument asserts that an anticipatory breach entitles the victim, as an alternative to terminating the contract, to 'rescind' it.[599] An acceptance may accordingly take the form of either a

[597] *Cyril v Simo* (n 435) 86 (Russell LJ). eg *Citati* (n 2).

[598] Carter, *Breach of Contract* (n 182) [750], [754].

[599] *Hulle v Heightman* (1802) 2 East 145, 102 ER 324; *Hochster* (n 1) 685, 924 (Crompton J in colloquy); *Goodman v Pocock* (n 14) 581–2, 579 (Patteson J), 583, 580 (Erle J). Also, *Smith's Leading Cases* (n 14) 23, 35.

termination or a rescission of the contract. This assertion is profoundly mistaken and has long been dead and buried in case law. The distinction between termination and rescission of a contract is well established. While a termination operates prospectively only and does not affect accrued rights under the contract, a rescission wipes out both the future and the past, demolishing the contract and with it any claim that could possibly arise under it.[600] Rescission is an equitable remedy commonly triggered by defects in the making of a contract, such as misrepresentation, duress, undue influence and mistake, which vitiate or deflect the true consent given by one or both parties. By contrast, a breach of contract, whether actual or anticipatory, does not vitiate or deflect the parties' consent to the act of contracting. It concerns defects in contract performance, not contract formation. Instead of treating the contract as if it has never existed at all, the suitable redress is to excuse the victim from its future performance only. The prospective effect of an acceptance is evident. For example, although it is capable of relieving the victim from further performance, including its being willing and ready to perform at the time for performance,[601] an acceptance could not possibly dispense with the condition that the victim should be in a position at the time of acceptance to render further performance.[602] The option to rescind the contract was recognised in the early days of the doctrine of anticipatory breach, when the courts were still under a misconception that in order to be able to bring a restitutionary claim the victim of an anticipatory breach should rescind, rather than terminate, the contract. In modern times, the relevant question is no longer whether the victim rescinds or terminates the contract, but whether, in the event that the contract is terminated, the victim elects for contractual damages or restitution. The first argument must thus be dismissed. An anticipatory breach endows its victim with no right of rescission. The only way to accept it is to terminate the contract.

The second argument is that an acceptance converts an anticipatory breach into a fully fledged breach of contract and is thus distinct from a termination of the contract. Acceptance is thus defined as 'simply an election to treat an anticipatory breach as a breach with a view to claiming damages which necessarily terminates the contract'.[603] It precedes and causes a termination of the contract.[604] This argument is deeply rooted in the breach-conversion rule, under which an anticipatory breach is not regarded as a breach of contract unless and until accepted. In Chapter 2, it was demonstrated that the breach-conversion rule is logically fallacious. An anticipatory breach is in itself a wrong and no further conduct of the victim is required to complete that wrong. Even assuming

[600] *Heyman v Darwins* (n 93) 399 (Lord Porter); *Johnson v Agnew* (n 180) 392–3 (Lord Wilberforce); *Photo Production* (n 109) 844 (Lord Wilberforce). Also, *McDonald v Dennys Lascelles Ltd* (1933) 48 CLR 457 (HCA) 476–7 (Dixon J).

[601] *North Sea Energy* (n 484); *State Trading v Golodetz* (n 484).

[602] Ch 5, text to n 485 above.

[603] JC Smith, *Smith & Thomas: A Casebook on Contract*, 11th edn (London, Sweet & Maxwell, 2000) 568.

[604] Thomson (n 183) 143; *Anson's Law of Contract* (n 14) 565.

that the breach-conversion rule is tenable, however, what the victim is required to do to complete the breach is nothing but a termination of the contract. As shown in the previous section, an acceptance of an anticipatory breach is simply a termination of the contract on the ground of that breach. Any suggestion that two distinct legal concepts (acceptance and termination) should be used to describe the same conduct would be unmeritorious. If acceptance is not distinct from termination, its adoption can be said to be not only unnecessary but also problematic. It gives rise to the false impression that the victim is required to do something different from evincing an intention to terminate before the contract is in fact terminated. However, a change of terminology is not considered to be wholly necessary. The term 'acceptance' is too entrenched in case law to be abandoned at once. The point has been made that there is no difference between acceptance and termination. Acceptance is henceforth used herein interchangeably with termination.

A note must be added in this juncture. The word 'termination' must not be misunderstood. Although it gives the misconception that a contract is brought to an end in its entirety, what is actually meant is only the release of both parties from their obligation further to perform the contract.[605] What is gone is not the contract itself, but the parties' primary obligations under it. If an anticipatory breach is seen as a failure of a condition, it is a failure of a condition precedent to the victim's outstanding performance. It does not undermine the validity of the entire contract. The contract as a whole may be defunct, yet life still lingers over certain parts of it, such as dispute settlement clauses. The surviving parts are intended or expected to survive, mostly for the purpose of ascertaining or quantifying a secondary obligation to pay damages.[606] It is thus said that the 'termination' of a contract for breach 'only moves the contract into a new sphere, the sphere of remedies'.[607] The same applies to an acceptance of an anticipatory breach. It does not destroy the contract in its entirety, but merely releases the parties from their obligations further to perform the contract.

2. Is an Acceptance an Act of Election?

The second issue is of a distinct nature from the first one. It concerns the conventional characterisation of an acceptance as an act of 'election'. This characterisation seems to have a strong connection with an important feature of the termination of a contract for breach. As a rule, a breach of contract does not automatically terminate the contract. With the exception of a case where it provides otherwise,[608] the contract subsists unless and until the victim effectively

605 Shea (n 179); J Swanton, 'Discharge of Contracts for Breach' (1981) 13 *Melbourne University Law Review* 69.

606 *Photo Production* (n 109) 844 (Lord Wilberforce); 850 (Lord Diplock).

607 McGregor (n 381) 71.

608 *Artpower Ltd v Bespoke Couture Ltd* [2006] EWCA Civ 1696, 150 Sol Jo LB 1463.

terminates it.[609] This is in sharp contrast to a frustrating event, which automatically terminates a contract so that neither party can profit from the event by holding the other to a fundamentally different undertaking.[610] The justifications for denying a breach of contract, however serious it might be, the effect of automatically bringing the contract to an end lie in the need to protect the victim by putting the matter into his hands, to prevent the contract-breaker from taking advantage of its own wrong, and a preference for upholding a deal over destroying it.[611] In this respect, an anticipatory breach is not to be treated differently from an actual breach. It does not terminate the contract but merely renders it terminable by the victim. This is reinforced by the fact that an anticipatory breach is a retractable wrong. It would deny the contract-breaker an opportunity of undoing the wrong if the breach is treated automatically as terminating the contract. From this it has generally been assumed that what follows is a matter of 'election' for the victim. The victim is required to 'elect' between acceptance and affirmation. Yet the logic is disjointed. That the victim may decide whether to exercise its right of termination does not in itself create a situation of 'election'. In order to assess the appropriateness of the use of the term 'election' in the current context we must first state summarily what an 'election' is.

An 'election' in the context of contract law is a common law, as distinguished from equitable, choice between inconsistent substantive rights.[612] A party (the 'elector') makes an 'election' by communicating to the other party (the 'electee') an unequivocal intention to exercise one of the options. Whether an 'election' is effectively made is a question of fact.[613] Generally speaking, the intention to 'elect' is assessed objectively;[614] subjective intention is immaterial.[615] However, there has been a lasting debate over whether, and to what extent, an 'election' requires knowledge on the part of the putative elector. The consensus seems to be that the putative elector must 'at least know of the facts which give rise to those legal rights, as between which an election must be made'.[616] The onus of proof rests upon the

609 *Leigh v Paterson* (1818) 8 Taunt 540, 541, 129 ER 493, 494 (Dallas CJ); *Hirji Mulji v Cheong Yue* (n 410) 509 (Lord Sumner); *Heyman v Darwins* (n 93) 361–2, 365 (Viscount Simon LC), 373–4 (Lord Macmillan), 376 (Lord Wright). *cf* Thomson (n 183).

610 *Hirji Mulji ibid* 507 (Lord Sumner). For the test of fundamental/essential difference, *Davis Contractors v Fareham* (n 133).

611 *New Zealand Shipping Co Ltd v Société des Ateliers et Chantiers de France* [1919] AC 1 (HL) 9 (Lord Atkinson). Also, *Heyman v Darwins* (n 93) 361 (Viscount Simon).

612 *Oliver Ashworth v Ballard* (n 486) 32 (Laws LJ). Also, *Agricultural & Rural Finance v Gardiner* (n 488) [58]–[59] (Gummow, Hayne and Kiefel JJ).

613 *Clarkson Booker Ltd v Andjel* [1964] 2 QB 775 (CA) 792 (Willmer LJ).

614 *Benjamin Scarf v Alfred George Jardine* (1881–1882) LR 7 App Cas 345 (HL) 361 (Lord Blackburn); *Abram Steamship Co Ltd v Westville Shipping Co Ltd* [1923] AC 773 (HL) 779 (Lord Dunedin); *The Mihalios Xilas* (n 488) 1024 (Lord Diplock); *Motor Oil Hellas (Corinth) Refineries SA v Shipping Corp of India (The 'Kanchenjunga')* [1990] 1 Lloyd's Rep 391 (HL) 398 (Lord Goff).

615 *Kammins v Zenith* (n 488) 883 (Lord Diplock); *The Kanchenjunga ibid* 398 (Lord Goff).

616 *Sargent v ASL Developments Ltd* (1974) 131 CLR 634 (HCA) 642 (Stephen J). Also, *Matthews v Smallwood* [1910] 1 Ch 777, 786–7 (Parker J); *Kammins v Zenith ibid* 883 (Lord Diplock); *The Kanchenjunga* (n 614) 398 (Lord Goff); *GEC Marconi Systems Pty Ltd v BHP Information Technology Pty Ltd* [2003] FCA 50, (2003) 128 FCR 1 [357] (Finn J).

party who alleges that an election has been made.[617] The putative elector is not required to be aware of the legal consequences of the election.[618] As regards the issue of the putative elector's knowledge of its legal right to elect, the decided cases are divided. The prevailing view, stated several times by the Court of Appeal, is that such knowledge is required for an effective acceptance to occur.[619] This seems, however, to contradict previous dicta of the House of Lords.[620] The prevailing view was criticised in that to require such knowledge would 'encourage perjury and reward those who do not seek advice'[621] and contravene 'objective standards' favoured by the common law.[622] Nevertheless, it is often said that an election must be an informed[623] or conscious[624] choice. A choice made without knowing that there is a right to choose can hardly be described as informed or conscious.[625] An election is an exercise of an option which simultaneously excludes all other options. It is absurd to suggest that one might make an election without knowing the existence of all options or one's right to choose between them. There is thus much to be said for the view that an election requires knowledge of both the underlying facts and the putative elector's legal rights. In this respect, an election can be contrasted with an estoppel. The party setting up an estoppel is generally not required to establish that the party alleged to be estopped has knowledge of either the underlying facts or its legal rights.[626] An acceptance of an anticipatory breach, according to the *Taylor v Oakes* principle, does not require the victim to have any knowledge of either aspect. It is true that in most anticipatory breach cases the victim accepts the breach with knowledge of both the breach and its right of termination. Yet such knowledge is not regarded at law as something necessary in order for an acceptance to be established. Therefore, an acceptance does not have to be an informed or conscious choice. It must thus be distinguished from an act of election.

An election, once made, is said to be final, binding and irrevocable, without the need to show consideration, deed or reliance.[627] The customary explanation for

[617] *Matthews v Smallwood ibid* 787 (Parker J).

[618] *Kammins v Zenith* (n 488) 883 (Lord Diplock). Also, Sheppard (n 489) 448.

[619] *Peyman v Lanjani* [1985] Ch 457 (CA) 486–7 (Stephenson LJ), 494 (May LJ), 500 (Slade LJ); *Stevens & Cutting Ltd v Anderson* [1990] 1 EGLR 95, [1990] 11 EG 70 (CA); *HB Property Developments Ltd v Secretary of State for the Environment* (1998) 78 P & CR 108 (CA). Also, *Coastal Estates Pty Ltd v Melevende* [1965] VR 433 (SCV Full Ct); Feltham et al (n 488) 431–2.

[620] *Kammins v Zenith* (n 488) 866 (Lord Morris); 877–8 (Lord Pearson); 883 (Lord Diplock).

[621] *Ibid* 878 (Lord Pearson).

[622] KR Handley, 'Exploring Election' (2006) 122 *LQR* 82, 96–7.

[623] *Oliver Ashworth v Ballard* (n 486) 27 (Walker LJ).

[624] *Boyo v Lambeth* (n 560) 743 (Gibson LJ); *HB Property v Secretary of State* (n 619) 114 (Sir Christopher Staughton).

[625] Feltham et al (n 488) 430.

[626] *Oliver Ashworth v Ballard* (n 486) 27 (Walker LJ); *The Kanchenjunga* (n 614) 399 (Lord Goff). Also, Feltham et al (n 488) 462.

[627] *The Kanchenjunga* (n 614) 398, 399 (Lord Goff), approving *Scarf v Jardine* (n 614) 360 (Lord Blackburn). Also, *Clough v London & North Western Railway Co* (1871) LR 7 Ex 26 (EC) 34; *Turner v Labafox International Pty Ltd* (1974) 131 CLR 660 (HCA) 663 (Stephen J); *Peyman v Lanjani* (n 619) 501 (Slade LJ); *Yukong Line Ltd of Korea v Rendsburg Investments Corp of Liberia* [1996] 2 Lloyd's Rep 604 (Com Ct) 608 (Moore-Bick J).

the irrevocability of an election is inconsistency. It is important to acknowledge that not every choice made between inconsistent options constitutes an election and is thus legally binding. It has been suggested that an election occurs only when the elector is 'confronted' with inconsistent options,[628] or, in other words, when 'the stage has been reached' where a choice must be made 'once and for all'.[629] No satisfactory guideline has, however, been offered as to how to decide whether or not a party is 'confronted' with inconsistent options. Sometimes, the argument is simply locked into a logical conundrum, in the form of an assertion that an election is not due when, if made, it would not be irrevocable.[630] Sometimes, 'confrontation' seems to be tied to the expiry of a 'reasonable time' within which a right of termination must be exercised.[631] Sometimes, the underlying rationale is broadly stated to be 'to do justice to the other party'.[632] Apparently, the requirement of 'confrontation' constitutes a potential source of confusion and uncertainty and is thus not a satisfactory explanation for the irrevocability of an election. Nevertheless, it does send a vital message that an election requires something more than a mere choice between inconsistent options. In light of this, it seems questionable to hold, as English courts usually did, that a party's decision whether or not to exercise a right that becomes available to it, 'being a matter of choice', must be 'called in law an election'.[633] The fallacy of this assertion lies in two points. First, it is wrong to equate an election with a choice between inconsistent options. In order to determine whether such a choice constitutes an election, it is of the utmost importance to enquire whether there is any good reason for it to be held irrevocable. An example of such good reason is the need to avoid double recovery and to preserve the finality of court judgments where a party makes an election between remedies during legal proceedings,[634] such as one made by a victim who has accepted the anticipatory breach between a claim for expectation damages and a restitutionary claim.[635] If an acceptance is looked at separately, it is indisputably irrevocable. A party who accepts an anticipatory breach cannot then affirm the contract.[636] The main reason for this is the destructive effect of the

[628] *Immer (No 145) Pty Ltd v The United Church in Australia Property Trust (NSW)* [1992–1993] 182 CLR 26 (HCA) 41 (Deane, Toohey, Gaudron and McHugh JJ), citing with approval Bower and Turner (n 489) 313. The requirement of 'confrontation' was seemingly kept intact in the latest edition: Feltham et al (n 488) 360.

[629] *Immer v United Church ibid* 42.

[630] *Verwayen* (n 489) 408–9 (Mason CJ).

[631] *Ibid* 427 (Brennan J).

[632] *O'Connor v SP Bray Ltd* (1936) 36 SR (NSW) 248 (NSWSC) 262 (Jordan CJ), rev'd on other grounds (1937) 56 CLR 464 (HCA). Also, *Immer v United Church* (n 628) 31–2 (Brennan J).

[633] *The Kanchenjunga* (n 614) 398 (Lord Goff).

[634] *United Australia Ltd v Barclays Bank Ltd* [1941] AC 1 (HL) 30 (Lord Atkin); *PR of Tang Man Sit v Capacious Investments Ltd* [1996] 1 AC 514 (PC Hong Kong) 521–2; *Oliver Ashworth v Ballard* (n 486) 28, 31 (Robert Walker LJ).

[635] *Goodman v Pocock* (n 14).

[636] *Hitchin v Campbell* (1746–1779) 2 Black W 827, 96 ER 487; *Pearl Mill Co Ltd v Ivy Tannery Co Ltd* [1919] 1 KB 78, 84 (McCardie J); *Anderson v Equitable Life Assurance Society* (1926) 134 LT 557 (CA) 563 (Bankes LJ); *A-G v Pritchard* (1928) 97 LJKB 561, 44 TLR 490.

termination of a contract. A contract, once terminated, cannot be re-established without the consent of both parties.[637] What is dead is dead.[638] To enable a party who terminates a contract to revive it unilaterally would undermine profoundly the bilateral character of the contract. The irrevocability of an acceptance, however, does not make it an act of election. So secondly, if the label of 'election' is appropriate at all, it must be attached to *either* choice made between the options. Acts of election must come in pairs. A decision to adopt one of the options cannot be characterised as an act of election if a decision to adopt the other option is not. It is a matter of both or neither. For this reason, an acceptance constitutes an act of election only if an affirmation is equally held to be irrevocable and to constitute an act of election. As will be further explained in the next Chapter, an affirmation, if it is understood to be an alternative to an acceptance, namely, a decision not to exercise a right of termination, is not irrevocable as it does not by itself extinguish that right. In fact, a general distinction can be drawn between a choice between option A and option B and a choice as to whether or not to adopt option A.[639] An election usually takes the former form. In contrast, the latter may not constitute an election as the putative elector is given two options which are inconsistent with each other but which 'are such that the adoption of one of them does not necessarily indicate a final intention to abandon the other'.[640] In the current context, this occurs where the victim adopts the option to affirm the contract. It disqualifies not only an affirmation, but also an acceptance, from constituting an act of election.

To recapitulate, there are two main reasons why it is impossible to view an acceptance as an act of election. First, according to the *Taylor v Oakes* principle, an acceptance does not require any knowledge on the victim's part of either the anticipatory breach or the right of termination arising from it. An acceptance does not have to be an informed or conscious choice. It is perhaps for this reason that Stephen J in his oft-cited judgment in the Australian case of *Sargent v ASL Developments* explicitly denied election a role 'in the common case of avoidance of a contract for breach'.[641] Secondly, an acceptance alone does not make an election. Although an acceptance is incontrovertibly irrevocable, this does not mean that it may constitute an act of election on its own. An election does not arise unless both an acceptance and an affirmation can be held to be irrevocable. Consequently, the critical question in relation to the issue of acceptance is whether the victim has effectively terminated the contract and whether that termination is justifiable by the anticipatory breach. If the answer is yes, the contract discontinues and the victim may sue for expectation damages. If the answer is no, the contract subsists

[637] Ewart (n 489) 83–4.

[638] *Johnson v Agnew* (n 180) 398 (Lord Wilberforce).

[639] *Cf* KR Handley, *Estoppel by Conduct and Election* (London, Sweet & Maxwell, 2006) [14–002], [14-003].

[640] Feltham et al (n 488) 426, *cf* 427.

[641] *Sargent* (n 616) 641.

and the victim may not sue for expectation damages. There is no need to resort to the notion of 'election'.

To conclude this Chapter, when the termination of a contract is justified by an existing anticipatory breach, it is an acceptance of that breach. The victim when accepting the breach must manifest an unequivocal intention to bring the contract to an immediate end, yet no knowledge of or reference to that breach is required. The irrevocability of an acceptance is derived from the destructive effect of a termination of the contract. This does not, however, warrant the characterisation of an acceptance as an act of election. We next turn to what turns out to be a completely distinct type of act, affirmation.

7

The Use and Misuse of 'Affirmation'

Despite the undeniable advantages of terminating a contract *in toto*, the victim of an anticipatory breach may find that an unattractive option in certain circumstances. Substitute performance may not be readily available. The contract-breaker may be a supplier or client whom the victim cannot afford to lose. Consequently, instead of accepting the anticipatory breach, the victim may prefer to continue with the contract in the hope that the contract-breaker might repent and perform it. In doing so the victim is said to have 'affirmed' the contract. In this Chapter, we explore the legal basis and constitution of an affirmation. Section A reveals the existing approach to a judicial determination of an affirmation and examines several major attempts made by the courts to solve the problems associated with it. Section B rejects the characterisation of an affirmation as an act of 'election' and seeks to build a new and more rational basis for it.

A. The Orthodox Test and Its Attempted Salvation

Just like acceptance, affirmation has been described in decided cases in varying terms: to 'wait till the time [for performance], still holding [the contract] as prospectively binding',[642] to '[keep] the contract alive for the benefit of [both parties]',[643] to 'proceed with' the contract 'on the footing that it exists',[644] etc. All these expressions seem to liken an affirmation to the continuance of, or a failure to terminate, the contract. In other words, affirmation is viewed simply as that which is not acceptance. The orthodox test for affirmation thus maintains that if the victim does not accept the breach, it must have affirmed the contract, and vice versa. It is submitted that this test is deeply flawed and has caused grave problems in determining the existence of an affirmation.

The above expressions, consistently employed by the courts, show a distinct inclination to find an affirmation when an anticipatory breach is not accepted. Yet this remarkable feature of the orthodox test does not sit easily with the irrevocability of an affirmation. It is trite that the victim of an anticipatory breach who

[642] *Hochster* (n 1) 691, 927 (Lord Campbell).
[643] *Frost v Knight* (n 87) 112 (Cockburn CJ).
[644] *Johnstone v Milling* (n 88) 467 (Lord Esher).

affirms cannot later revert to its right of termination arising out of that breach.[645] Put simply, an affirmation leads to the loss by the victim of its right to accept the anticipatory breach. This causes two sequential difficulties. First, the orthodox test is badly targeted. It does not address the issue whether and why the right to accept the anticipatory breach is lost. The focus of enquiry under that test is upon whether a contract subsists or ceases to subsist. The courts are only interested in the question whether the victim, either expressly or impliedly, evinces an intention either to uphold or to end the contract. An 'election' between acceptance and affirmation is seen as tantamount to a choice between termination and non-termination. It is difficult, however, to see why the relinquishment of a right of termination should depend on the subsistence of the contract. Secondly and consequently, the notion of affirmation under the orthodox test tends to acquire a scope broader than necessary. Affirmation is not clearly distinguished from, and is even equated with, mere non-acceptance or non-termination. To be sure, in some cases the courts have begun to temper the vigour of the orthodox test and confine an affirmation to the victim's words or conduct consistent *only* with the continuance of the contract. Sometimes the courts depicted it in an even more promising way, such as, 'treat[ing] [the anticipatory breach] as inoperative'.[646] Nevertheless, the implication remains that to keep the contract alive, or simply not to terminate it, would prima facie constitute an affirmation. Hence, continuous pressing for performance, failure to set a deadline for repentance, and dealing with a sub-contractor in preparation for performance are all regarded as instances of affirmation.[647] The practical consequence of adopting such a blunt approach is that the victim is often unduly penalised for its reasonable efforts to rescue the contract. The courts are not wholly ignorant of or indifferent to the overstretching of the meaning of 'affirmation' and the harshness caused by it. In the following paragraphs we shall examine three major judicial attempts to avoid or rectify this problem. First, the courts have endeavoured to narrow down the scope of affirmation by adopting a more restrictive interpretation of it. Secondly, a 'third option' has been created for the victim in addition to acceptance and affirmation. Thirdly, the courts have formulated a 'continuing repudiation' theory, which asserts that an anticipatory breach continuing after an affirmation may still be accepted. It will be shown that none of these attempts are successful and that the correct response is to discard rather than to seek to rectify the orthodox test.

1. Restrictive Interpretation

The most obvious solution to the problem of an overly broad notion of affirmation is to interpret it restrictively, thereby turning it into something narrower

645 *Richardson v Dunn* (1841) 2 QB 218, 114 ER 85.
646 *Frost v Knight* (n 87) 112 (Cockburn CJ).
647 *Carr v Berriman* (n 194) 348 (Fullagar J).

than non-termination. A prominent illustration is *Yukong v Rendsburg*.[648] The charterers under a three-year time charter refused on 23 January 1996 to perform the contract, before the ship was due to be delivered. The next day the owners sent a telex, along with the service of a notice of delivery of the ship pursuant to the contract, stating that the charterers were 'strongly requested to honour their contractual obligations' and would be held responsible for all losses '[i]n case of non-performance'. On 29 January, the owners gave another notice of delivery by telex. When their request and pressure produced no effect, the owners on 1 February 1996 purported to 'accept' the charterers' previous repudiation of 23 January. The key issue in the case was whether the owners' telex on either 24 or 29 January respectively, upon proper construction, amounted to an affirmation and whether it precluded them from accepting the charterers' repudiation. It was held that neither did. In reaching that conclusion Moore-Bick J endorsed and applied the orthodox test that bound affirmation with the subsistence of the contract. Nevertheless, the judge was anxious to qualify the way such a test should be applied. He warned against taking 'an unduly technical approach' and stated that 'the Court should generally be slow to accept that the injured party has committed himself irrevocably to continuing with the contract' even though there was 'an unequivocal statement of some kind' to keep it in being, which if relied upon could have worked an estoppel.[649] The judge therefore drew an important distinction between an election to affirm and a representation capable of triggering an estoppel, opining that the former entailed an irrevocable commitment without the necessity of reliance and thus required 'very clear evidence'.[650] He further stressed that to make an affirmation the victim should communicate an intention to 'go on with the contract notwithstanding the other party's repudiation'[651] or 'regardless of the position adopted by' it.[652] Accordingly, the owners' 24 January telex, 'as a whole', could 'only be read as a cry of protest'.[653] The same could be said of the owners' 29 January telex.[654]

These conclusions are not to be questioned. What causes discontent is the approach adopted by the judge. The distinction drawn between an irrevocable commitment and an unequivocal statement is particularly problematic. Little has been suggested as to what the victim must do, if a mere unequivocal statement is insufficient, to commit itself irrevocably to continuing with the contract. Clearly, Moore-Bick J tried to restrict the scope of affirmation without disturbing the orthodox test. The main difficulty with this approach is that it fails to spell out where to draw the line and thus tends to give rise to uncertainty. To say that an

[648] n 627.

[649] *Ibid* 608. Also, *Carillion JM Ltd v Bath & North East Somerset Council* [2009] EWHC 166 (TCC) [17]–[18] (Coulson J), [2009] All ER (D) 62 (Feb).

[650] *Yukong* (n 627) 607, 608.

[651] *Ibid* 608.

[652] *Ibid* 609.

[653] *Ibid.*

[654] *Ibid.*

affirmation needs 'very clear evidence' and carries a sense of absoluteness does not seem to go much further from an 'unequivocal representation' required for an estoppel. Even if the line could be drawn somewhere, a restrictive interpretation may still give rise to another difficulty. The orthodox test, however restrictively it is applied, seems to be inapt to explain some cases adequately. In *Danube v Xenos*,[655] for example, the victim of a renunciation continuously pressed for performance and embarked on negotiation with a third party only on the date for performance. It was nevertheless held that the commencement of negotiation on that date was an effective acceptance. Yet in terms of legal principle it is hard to see why, under the orthodox test, the victim had not affirmed the contract by continuously pressing for performance until the date for performance. These difficulties originate in the fact that the orthodox test is poorly formulated and misdirected. Its focus is upon the subsistence of the contract alone. But this plainly misses the point. Indeed, it could be deduced from Moore-Bick J's following statement that the real issue was otherwise:

> The law does not require an injured party to snatch at a repudiation and he does not automatically lose his right to treat the contract as discharged merely by calling on the other to reconsider his position and recognize his obligations.[656]

So, quite clearly, what is central to the constitution of an affirmation is the abandonment of a right to accept the anticipatory breach. The orthodox test loses grip of this central issue and inevitably runs into problems. As a result, it is incapable of answering, and in fact evades, the fundamental question whether and why an affirmation should be held to be irrevocable.

2. A 'Third Option'

In an attempt to narrow down the scope of affirmation, the courts also invented a 'third option' outside the traditional duality of acceptance and affirmation. The 'third option' so created would occupy some of the territory that belonged to affirmation. Thus, even if an anticipatory breach is not accepted, the victim may be held to have adopted the 'third option' rather than affirming the contract and have thereby retained its right to accept the breach. The leading case is *Stocznia v Latvian Shipping*,[657] which involved six almost identical shipbuilding contracts dated 11 September 1992. Under each of these contracts, in consideration of the yard building a vessel for them, the buyers agreed to pay the price in instalments, including a second instalment (20 per cent of the price) following the service by the yard of a notice of keel-laying. All six contracts contained a Clause 5.05 which entitled the yard to 'rescind' (read 'terminate') the contract if the second instalment was not paid within 21 days after the date when it fell due and to retain and apply

[655] n 84.
[656] *Yukong* (n 627) 608.
[657] [2002] EWCA Civ 889.

instalments already paid to the recovery of its losses. The buyers then committed an anticipatory breach under each of the six contracts as their conduct between November 1993 and April 1994 clearly indicated that they would not perform the contracts on their existing terms.[658] Nevertheless, the yard duly served a notice of keel-laying under contracts 1 and 2 respectively on 3 December 1993 and 9 March 1994 but in each case the buyers failed to pay the second instalment. The yard notified the buyers of the 'rescission' of both contracts respectively in March and April 1994 and served a notice of keel-laying respectively under contracts 3 and 4, then under contracts 5 and 6, using the keels laid under contracts 1 and 2.[659] When the buyers again failed to pay the second instalments under these four contracts, the yard served a notice of 'rescission' respectively under each of them.

The legal proceedings that followed were complex. In the earlier part of the proceedings, it was conclusively held by the House of Lords that Clause 5.05 did not exclude common law claims for debt or damages (including a damages claim for anticipatory breach) and the yard was therefore entitled to claim the second instalments under contracts 1 and 2 as debt but not under contracts 3 to 6, because the notices of keel-laying served under the latter four contracts were all invalid.[660] The differentiation between contracts 1 and 2 on the one hand, and contracts 3 to 6 on the other, meant that they gave rise to different issues in relation to anticipatory breach. As for contracts 1 and 2, there was no dispute that they had been lawfully terminated by the yard and the buyers were liable in damages for breach of contract. The main dispute was over the quantum of damages. This hinged on whether the buyers committed a 'repudiatory' breach, which would support a claim for the loss of bargain damages, before the service of the notice of 'rescission' under either contract. In the subsequent consolidated proceedings,[661] it was held that the yard was entitled to recover for the loss of bargain as the buyers had committed an anticipatory breach under either contract before the yard served the notice of 'rescission' or, in any event, their non-payment of the second instalment constituted an 'actual repudiatory breach'.[662] In the former case, the notice of 'rescission' would constitute an effective acceptance of the anticipatory breach in accordance with the *Taylor & Oakes* principle.

658 The buyers indicated between September and December 1993 that they were unable to pay, withdrew all their technicians from the yard's site between the end of January and the beginning of February 1994, and then made it clear around March and early April 1994 that they would not perform any of the contracts unless the price payable was substantially reduced. The anticipatory breach could thus be committed at the earliest in September 1993 and at the latest in early April 1994.

659 The notice was served under contracts 3 and 4 in mid-April 1994 and under contracts 5 and 6 in mid-June 1994.

660 *Stocznia v Latvian Shipping* [1998] 1 WLR 574, rev'g [1996] 2 Lloyd's Rep 132 (CA), rev'g [1995] 2 Lloyd's Rep 592 (Clarke J) (an action for debt under contracts 1 and 2), aff'g (unreported, Com Ct, 23 Nov 1995) (Waller J) (an action for debt under contracts 3 to 6 and for damages under all the contracts).

661 The yard's pleadings in these proceedings included, inter alia, a claim for damages for anticipatory breach, a claim to have the buyers wound up and a claim against a third party, the buyers' parent company, for a tort of inducing the buyers' breach of contract.

662 *Stocznia v Latvian Shipping* [2002] EWCA Civ 889 [75]–[76] (Rix LJ).

The principal issue on anticipatory breach in the case, however, arose in connection with contracts 3 to 6. There being no actual breach by non-payment, the buyers' prior anticipatory breach became the only possible ground for their liability. The main contention on behalf of the buyers was that the yard's attempts to invoke the contractual machinery under Clause 5.05 (by serving the notice of keel-laying) following the anticipatory breach constituted an affirmation of those contracts and thus precluded it from subsequently accepting that breach. In the earlier part of the proceedings, Colman J rejected an application by the yard to amend its claim to include anticipatory breach as a basis for claiming damages. The learned judge held that the yard's conduct constituted an affirmation and thus disentitled it to accept the breach.[663] Colman J's decision was subsequently set aside in toto by the House of Lords, which left substantive issues on anticipatory breach to further trials.[664] In the ensuing consolidated proceedings, Rix LJ, with whom Aldous and Tuckey LJJ concurred, affirming the decision of Thomas J,[665] held that the yard's serving of the keel-laying notice did not constitute an affirmation of the contract.[666] Rix LJ based this decision on a theory that, aside from acceptance and affirmation, a third option, a 'middle ground', was available to the victim of an anticipatory breach, which would give the victim a period of time to '[make] up his mind what to do'.[667] The yard's service of the keel-laying notice was considered to fall within this third category and not to have a conclusory force. In this regard his Lordship purported to derogate from Lord Ackner's earlier remarks in *The Simona*, which were believed to indicate that acceptance and affirmation were the only two options available to the victim.[668] Lord Ackner said in that case:

> There is no third choice, as a sort of via media, to affirm the contract and yet to be absolved from tendering further performance unless and until [the contract-breaker] gives reasonable notice that he is once again able and willing to perform.[669]

On a proper reading, this passage means no more than that an anticipatory breach, unaccepted, does not relieve the victim from further performance of the contract. Lord Ackner did not, therefore, reject the 'third option' later relied upon by Rix LJ, namely, the possibility that the victim might keep the contract in being while retaining the right to accept the anticipatory breach. The merit of introducing such a 'third option' is that it demonstrates the disparity between

[663] *Stocznia v Latvian Shipping* [1997] 2 Lloyd's Rep 228. The learned judge (at 237) held that the yard might even have affirmed before the notice of keel-laying was served, when it commenced a legal action in January 1994 claiming, inter alia, injunctive relief restraining the buyers' parent company from inducing them to breach the contract. This decision is unsustainable and is inconsistent with established case law. See text to n 720 below.

[664] *Stocznia v Latvian Shipping* [1998] 1 WLR 574, 594 (Lord Goff).

[665] *Stocznia v Latvian Shipping* [2001] 1 Lloyd's Rep 537.

[666] *Stocznia v Latvian Shipping* [2002] EWCA Civ 889 [92].

[667] *Ibid* [87].

[668] *Ibid* [84].

[669] *The Simona* (n 386) 805.

non-acceptance and affirmation. In particular, the utmost caution must be exercised when the victim's mere inaction following the anticipatory breach is to be held as either an acceptance or an affirmation. The 'third option' is closely associated with the principle that a right of termination arising out of a breach of contract must generally be exercised 'with every reasonable dispatch'.[670] It follows from this that the victim has a reasonable time following the anticipatory breach to decide how to react.[671] The victim's inaction, if it is extended beyond that time, may be held to constitute an affirmation.[672] Nevertheless, this 'third option' has a dubious status in law. It is in fact an ephemeral, undefined and thus unreal option. The victim has to either accept or affirm eventually.[673] Even if we recognise the temporary existence of the 'third option', its duration is left to be measured by a 'reasonable time' of which there appears to be no clearly discernable criterion. Moreover, the 'third option' seems to come alive only where the victim remains silent and inactive following the anticipatory breach. It is thus incapable of solving the problem that the victim tends to be unduly penalised under the orthodox test for its efforts to rescue the contract.

Having said that, some parts of Rix LJ's judgment did point in a more promising direction. His Lordship was of the view that the yard's conduct was not 'inconsistent with reliance on repudiatory conduct for effecting a common law acceptance of an anticipatory breach'.[674] Although there was no 'express reservation of rights', the yard's conduct should be held to be 'tantamount or analogous to the classic means by which time is remade of the essence of a contract', rather than an 'unconditional affirmation'.[675] It is common ground that conduct of such a nature, far from divesting the victim of a right of termination, would reinstate that right to the victim in the event of a further breach.[676] Rix LJ's above statements should compare favourably with earlier remarks of both Colman J and Thomas J. Colman J applied the orthodox test and simply stated that the yard's conduct was 'an unequivocal assertion of the continuing operation of the contract'.[677] On the other hand, Thomas J vaguely stated that the yard when serving the notices still had 'some hope' that the buyers might perform.[678] Rix LJ's

[670] *Halkett v Earl of Dudley* [1907] 1 Ch 590, 597 (Parker J); *Berners v Fleming* [1925] 1 Ch 264 (CA) 275 (Sargant LJ), 269–270 (Pollock MR).

[671] *Clough v London & North Western Railway* (n 627).

[672] *Smethurst v Mitchell* (1859) 1 El & El 622, 120 ER 1043; *Scarf v Jardine* (n 614) 360 (Lord Blackburn). *cf Allen v Robles* [1969] 1 WLR 1193 (CA).

[673] *The Kanchenjunga* (n 614) 398 (Lord Goff): 'In all cases, [the elector] has in the end to make his election, not as a matter of obligation, but in the sense that, if he does not do so, the time may come when the law takes the decision out of his hands, either by holding him to have elected not to exercise the right which has become available to him, or sometimes by holding him to have elected to exercise it.'

[674] *Stocznia v Latvian Shipping* [2002] EWCA Civ 889 [88].

[675] *Ibid* [89]–[90].

[676] *Ibid* [89], citing *Charles Rickards Ltd v Oppenhaim* [1950] 1 KB 616 (CA). Also, *Tropical Traders Ltd v Goonan* (1964) 111 CLR 41 (HCA) 55 (Kitto J).

[677] *Stocznia v Latvian Shipping* [1997] 2 Lloyd's Rep 228, 234.

[678] *Stocznia v Latvian Shipping* [2001] 1 Lloyd's Rep 537 [162]–[163].

statements, in contrast, suggested that the orthodox test was superficial and ineffective. It is irrelevant that the contract is subsisting or not subsisting. The real issue is whether or not the victim has lost its entitlement to rely upon the anticipatory breach as a ground to terminate the contract. An affirmation is not a mere failure to exercise the option of acceptance; it is the abandonment of that option. On the facts of *Stocznia v Latvian Shipping*, the yard's service of the notice of keel-laying plainly could not be said to constitute an affirmation. The reason was, however, not that it amounted to an exercise of the 'third option', but that it did not suggest that the yard's common law right of termination should cease to be exercisable.[679]

3. The 'Continuing Repudiation' Theory

The third major attempt to rectify the orthodox test is not to narrow down the scope of affirmation, but, effectively, to make a significant dent in its irrevocability. An illustrative case is *Safehaven Investments Inc v Springbok Ltd*.[680] The case involved a contract for the sale of property concluded on 22 February 1994. Before the contract was due to be completed, by a letter dated 16 March 1994, the purchaser purported, wrongfully, to rescind the contract for an alleged misrepresentation of the vendor. Apparently, the purchaser desired to pull out of the contract as it turned out to be unprofitable. This amounted indisputably to an anticipatory breach. The vendor refuted the allegation of misrepresentation and urged the purchaser to supply information necessary for the completion of the contract. On 20 April 1994, when all efforts to press for performance had been to no avail, the vendor purported to treat the contract as at an end on account of the purchaser's 16 March repudiation. The purchaser's reply was that having previously affirmed the contract, the vendor was not entitled to terminate the contract and was thus liable itself for repudiating the contract. This argument failed. It was held that the vendor's 20 April letter constituted an effective acceptance of the anticipatory breach. In considering whether the vendor had previously affirmed the contract, Mr Jonathan Sumption QC (sitting as a Deputy High Court Judge) took a novel and unnecessarily complicated approach.

His reasoning consisted of two separate, whilst conflicting, steps. First, it was held that the vendor's conduct subsequent to 16 March and prior to 20 April 'unequivocally treated the contract as continuing' and thus amounted to an affirmation.[681] Surprisingly, the learned judge then opined that this affirmation did not have an irrevocable effect and could not prevent the vendor from accepting the purchaser's anticipatory breach.[682] Neither point can be supported.

[679] Also, *McRae & Anor v Bolaro Pty Ltd* [2000] VSCA 72 (unreported, 5 May 2000) [31] (Ormiston JA).

[680] *Safehaven Investments Inc v Springbok Ltd* (1996) 71 P & CR 59 (Ch).

[681] *Ibid* 67.

[682] *Ibid* 68.

The decision on the constitution of an affirmation demonstrates patently the looseness of the orthodox test. The vendor was found to have affirmed simply because its conduct amounted to an unequivocal assertion of the continuance of the contract. Yet as a rule such an assertion does not necessarily carry an implication that an antecedent anticipatory breach will not be relied upon as a ground for terminating the contract in the future. The vendor's conduct in the case certainly could not be construed as carrying such an implication. The decision on the revocability of the affirmation was equally problematic and wholly unnecessary. The learned judge relied upon an earlier observation of Lord Wilberforce which stated that an action for specific performance did not constitute an 'eternal and unconditional affirmation'.[683] The reliance was evidently misplaced. Lord Wilberforce was not saying that a temporary and conditional affirmation might exist; instead, what he meant was that an affirmation, if characterised as an act of election, should always be 'eternal and unconditional'. In fact, every enquiry into the existence of an affirmation is premised on its irrevocability. It is self-contradictory to assert that a party makes a *revocable* affirmation. The phrase 'revocable affirmation' is by itself an offence to logic: if an act is revocable, it will be no affirmation at all. Without irrevocability, an affirmation is devoid of legal meaning. Mr Sumption QC was probably trying to evade the undesirability caused by the orthodox test, as it was demonstrably inappropriate to deprive the vendor of its right to accept the anticipatory breach by reason of its efforts to press for performance. The learned judge was nevertheless reacting in a rather instinctive and unprincipled way. The more rational approach should be to address directly what is wrong with the orthodox test and to hold that in such a case there is simply no affirmation.

In the second step of his reasoning, Mr Sumption QC proceeded to state that the vendor's 20 April letter should be regarded as a lawful acceptance, not of the original anticipatory breach residing in the purchaser's 16 March letter, but of 'the continuing repudiation reflected in the [purchaser]'s behaviour after the affirmation'.[684] Yet for the purpose of establishing such a continuing repudiation it was unnecessary for post-affirmation acts 'in themselves [to] have been repudiatory'.[685] According to the learned judge, it was sufficient that by 20 April a reasonable person in the position of the vendor would have inferred from the overt acts of the purchaser that it was 'persisting in' and 'adhering to' the original anticipatory breach.[686] This extraordinary approach was adopted

[683] *Johnson v Agnew* (n 180) 398.

[684] *Safehaven* (n 680) 68.

[685] *Ibid* 70.

[686] *Ibid* 68–9. The learned judge identified four specific supporting facts: (1) the immediate response of the purchaser to the vendor's pressing for performance on 17 March was to reassert its right to rescind and call for the return of the deposit; (2) the purchaser invited the vendor to renegotiate the contract at a lower price on 23 March; (3) the fact that the purchaser's bankers appeared to have commissioned a valuation for loan purposes on 23 March was equally consistent with its proposing to raise funds for a renegotiated contract; (4) notwithstanding several requests, the purchaser failed

in full by Rix LJ in *Stocznia*, where, while admitting that it was unnecessary to do so, he expressed the view that even if the yard had affirmed the contract, this would not have prevented it from accepting the buyers' anticipatory breach as 'a continuing repudiation after affirmation'.[687] The continuance of the repudiation was held to be inferred from the buyers' 'speaking silence', which, 'overlaid with all that had gone before', infringed their 'obligation to clarify [their] new intentions', if any, to retract the repudiation.[688] Hence the 'continuing repudiation' theory.

This theory can be criticised in a number of ways. First, it is far from clear what amounts to a 'continuing' repudiation. Unlike the case of actual breach, this cannot depend on whether the obligation breached is of a continuing nature,[689] because, as we have seen, an anticipatory breach is linked to a future, unmatured obligation. Whether such an obligation is of a continuing nature has no direct bearing on the continuity of the breach. The courts generally tend to view an anticipatory breach as 'continuing'. In *Safehaven*, for example, Mr Sumption QC expressed the opinion that an anticipatory breach, unretracted, was prima facie 'continuing'.[690] Similarly it was suggested by Colman J that a breach was 'continuing' if and when it was curable.[691] An anticipatory breach is generally retractable and thus 'continuing'. Rix LJ also seemed to take the view that as a rule every anticipatory breach was 'continuing' because it invariably looked to the future.[692] The difference between these two analyses can be seen from a situation where a party who agrees to sell a specific item destroys it before the date of delivery arrives. This act of disablement would not be 'continuing' according to Mr Sumption's analysis because it is not retractable.[693] Yet if Rix LJ's analysis is applied, it would still be 'continuing', because the inability to deliver the item would persist. It is not easy to say which analysis represents the better view for it is far from clear why either the curability/retractability or the prospective nature of an anticipatory breach should dictate the victim's entitlement to accept the breach after having affirmed the contract. What precludes acceptance is actual retraction, not mere retractability. At any rate, if it is accepted that an anticipatory breach, as opposed to a non-continuing 'actual repudiatory breach',[694] is generally

to co-operate with the vendor in getting the contract completed by answering some straightforward questions raised by the vendor.

[687] *Stocznia v Latvian Shipping* [2002] EWCA Civ 889 [96], aff'g [2001] 1 Lloyd's Rep 537 [169]–[170], [175] (Thomas J).

[688] *Ibid.*

[689] *Cf Larking v Great Western (Nepean) Gravel Ltd* (1940) 64 CLR 221 (HCA) 236 (Dixon J).

[690] *Safehaven* (n 680) 68.

[691] *Stocznia v Latvian Shipping* [1997] 2 Lloyd's Rep 228, 236.

[692] *Stocznia v Latvian Shipping* [2002] EWCA Civ 889 [99].

[693] Also, *Stocznia v Latvian Shipping* [2001] 1 Lloyd's Rep 537 [174] (Thomas J); GH Treitel, 'Affirmation after Repudiatory Breach' (1998) 114 *LQR* 22, 25.

[694] A continuing actual breach, 'such as a failure to pay or to deliver', was treated in the same way as an anticipatory breach: *Stocznia v Latvian Shipping* [2002] EWCA Civ 889 [100] (Rix LJ). *cf Stocznia v Latvian Shipping* [1997] 2 Lloyd's Rep 228, 236 (Colman J); Treitel (n 693) 24–5.

'continuing', this would effectively render the notion of affirmation completely irrelevant in anticipatory breach cases. The orthodox test would be marginalised instead of being ameliorated. This could not be what the courts intended to do.

Secondly, it is questionable why the continuity of an anticipatory breach should be relevant at all. It is, in fact, both odd and unjustifiable to hold that when a right of termination arising out of an anticipatory breach is spent on an affirmation, the mere continuance of that breach should give rise to a new right of termination. Understandably, an affirmation following an anticipatory breach does not preclude an acceptance of a subsequent separate anticipatory breach.[695] But the acceptance is directed at an independent breach constituted by either a 'positive statement' or a 'fresh repudiation'.[696] Similarly, a failure to remedy an actual repudiatory breach may constitute an anticipatory breach, thus entitling the victim to terminate the contract, even though it has previously affirmed the contract following the actual breach.[697] There are two breaches that give rise to two rights of termination and only one of them is lost by affirmation. By contrast, a mere repetition of a previous breach is not a fresh breach. It should not be acknowledged as a ground for terminating the contract. Otherwise 'the accidents of negotiation' would be allowed to supersede 'considerations of substance or policy'.[698] The abnormality of the 'continuing repudiation' theory lies in the fact that for a new right of termination to arise no fresh breach or further act is required. Rix LJ seemingly went even further than that. Not only is a fresh 'repudiation' unnecessary, but there also need not be any 'qualitative difference' in the contract-breaker's conduct following the affirmation.[699] Mere silence or recalcitrance, or failure to retract, 'against the background of an earlier anticipatory breach', is regarded as sufficient to give rise to a right of termination.[700] This brings about a striking phenomenon. What is effectively a single anticipatory breach is according to this theory capable of giving rise to two separate rights of termination. Having given up one by affirming the contract, the victim acquires the other automatically. It means that the victim of a 'continuing' anticipatory breach is powerless to relinquish its right to terminate the contract. There can be no justification for such a bizarre rule.

Thirdly, even if the 'continuing repudiation' theory is justified, it is certainly not the best way to determine whether the victim might rely upon the anticipatory breach as a ground for terminating the contract. The theory aims to remedy a major defect of the orthodox test, namely, that the victim of an anticipatory breach tends to be unduly penalised for pressing for performance and consequently compelled to 'engage in performance that is entirely pointless

[695] *Yukong* (n 627) 607 (Moore-Bick J).

[696] *Ibid* 609. Also, *Ogle v Comboyuro Investments Pty Ltd* [1976] 136 CLR 444 (HCA) 459 (Gibbs, Mason and Jacobs JJ).

[697] *Carr v Berriman* (n 194) 349–50 (Fullagar J).

[698] Treitel (n 693) 26.

[699] *Stocznia v Latvian Shipping* [2002] EWCA Civ 889 [99].

[700] *Ibid.*

and wasteful'.[701] Yet it operates in an artificial, perplexed and disproportionate manner. The courts first recognise the pressing for performance as an affirmation and then empty it of all substance. They never question the correctness of the orthodox test or explore on what basis the victim's pressing for performance might be held to be an affirmation. Instead of resorting to a loosely defined notion of 'affirmation' and an indiscriminate theory of 'continuing repudiation', it is a more direct, simpler and more rational solution to the above problem that the constitution of an affirmation is refocused and properly restrained. For example, Treitel postulated a scenario where the claimant in *Frost v Knight* begged the defendant to keep faith with her following the defendant's renunciation of his promise to marry her and the defendant simply remained silent in the face of her request.[702] Would this request prevent the claimant from terminating the contract and claiming damages? The answer must be in the negative. The real reason for this is not that the repudiation was 'continuing' or that the claimant made a revocable affirmation, but that the request, as many other forms of pressing for performance, did not constitute an affirmation at all. The claimant, by making the request, did not unequivocally intimate that the defendant's repudiation would not be relied upon as a ground for terminating the contract. Similarly, in *Stocznia v Latvian Shipping*, Thomas J adopted an alternative reasoning to the 'continuing repudiation' theory, namely, that an affirmation following an anticipatory breach should not be regarded as irrevocable unless relied upon by the contract-breaker.[703] There is much force in this alternative reasoning, except that the issue ought to be put as one of the constitution, rather than the revocability, of an affirmation.

Therefore, none of the above three attempts to salvage the orthodox test from its predicament is satisfactory. By sticking to the orthodox test, the courts have shown a remarkable obsession with the equation between affirmation and non-acceptance. The correctness of that test is assumed without question. This tends to encourage a general inclination to infer an affirmation from a mere failure to accept, especially when the latter is coupled with efforts to press for performance. Neither a restrictive interpretation nor the creation of a 'third option' brings about a substantial improvement. The 'continuing repudiation' theory introduces unnecessary complications and exacerbates the existing problems. All these endeavours fail to recognise that the fundamental issue in the current context is whether the victim relinquishes its right to treat the anticipatory breach as a ground for terminating the contract. Only when this issue is restored to the central stage can an appropriate test for affirmation be formulated.

701 *Stocznia v Latvian Shipping* [2001] 1 Lloyd's Rep 537 [172] (Thomas J).

702 Treitel (n 693) 26.

703 *Stocznia v Latvian Shipping* [2001] 1 Lloyd's Rep 537 [176], citing with approval Treitel (n 693).

B. Revitalising Affirmation: An Estoppel View

1. Unequivocal Representation

It follows from the foregoing discussion that the victim's relinquishment of its right to accept the anticipatory breach lies at the heart of the notion of affirmation. The victim does not 'affirm' the contract. It disposes of its right. An enquiry into the constitution of an affirmation thus consists of two steps. First, it must be ascertained whether the victim intends to relinquish its right to accept the anticipatory breach. Secondly, there is a question whether the victim is bound by a mere manifestation of that intention. The current subsection deals with the first step. The victim's intention has to be ascertained from its words or conduct. The task of the courts is thus to determine whether the victim makes an unequivocal representation that the anticipatory breach is not to be relied upon as a ground for terminating the contract.

Such an unequivocal representation may be made in an expressed or implied form. When it is made impliedly, although some 'distinct' or 'positive' act is usually present,[704] there is no reason why it could not in appropriate cases be constituted by silence or mere inaction. Either way, it must be communicated to the contract-breaker in 'clear and unequivocal terms'; 'a qualified or conditional decision' does not make an affirmation.[705] Whether there is an unequivocal representation must be assessed objectively from the perspective of the contract-breaker. In this exercise the courts may take the contract-breaker's knowledge into account. Thus, if it is established that the contract-breaker does not understand that the victim has made such a representation, then no affirmation can be upheld.[706] Similarly, although the victim's mistake in affirming is generally irrelevant, it should preclude an effective affirmation if known to the contract-breaker.[707] With the installation of the test of representation, a clear line can be drawn between affirmation and non-acceptance. Mere delay does not in itself amount to an unequivocal representation to relinquish the right to accept the anticipatory breach.[708] Nor does negotiation with the contract-breaker with a view to persuading it to resume performance.[709] Similarly, where the victim brings an action seeking a declaration of its entitlement to terminate the contract, this should not be held to be an affirmation.[710] Of course, an unequivocal representation may be debarred by an express

[704] *Craine v The Colonial Mutual Fire Insurance Co Ltd* [1920] 28 CLR 305 (HCA) 326, 327 (Isaacs J).

[705] *Yukong* (n 627) 607 (Moore-Bick J).

[706] *Stocznia v Latvian Shipping* [2002] EWCA Civ 889 [90] (Rix LJ).

[707] *Immer v United Church* (n 628). *cf Central Estates (Belgravia) Ltd v Woolgar (No 2)* [1972] 1 WLR 1048 (CA) 1052–3 (Lord Denning MR); 1054–5 (Buckley LJ); 1056–7 (Cairns LJ).

[708] *WE Cox Toner (International) Ltd v Crook* [1981] IRLR 443 (EAT) 446 (Browne-Wilkinson J); *Cantor Fitzgerald International v Callaghan* [1999] ICR 639 (CA) 652–3 (Judge LJ).

[709] *Sudan Import & Export Co (Khartoum) Ltd v Société Générale de Compensation* [1958] 1 Lloyd's Rep 310 (CA).

[710] Eg RSC Ord 25 r 5. *cf Howard v Pickford Tool* (n 94).

reservation of the right to accept the anticipatory breach.[711] The use of the words 'without prejudice' may not be sufficient to constitute a reservation.[712] The act of the victim to invoke an arbitration clause may also involve a retention of such a right and is thus sometimes said to defer the constitution of an affirmation.[713]

In practice, a question frequently arises as to whether the victim's acts in an attempt to enforce or perform the contract constitute an affirmation. It is sometimes said to be advisable generally to distinguish the 'exercise of a right conferred by or under a contract' from a mere 'recognition of the contract'.[714] The former is normally taken to constitute an unequivocal representation whilst the latter is not. Such a distinction should not be sustained, since a search for an unequivocal representation necessarily involves asking far more specific questions, such as what contractual right is exercised and to what extent the contract is recognised. For instance, where the victim exercises a contractual right of termination and seeks consensual remedies under the contract, this conduct may not be viewed as an affirmation since, having evinced an intention to terminate the contract, the victim cannot be said to have made a representation not to treat it as discharged.[715] Thus, whether an unequivocal representation is made is 'a decision of fact based upon all the evidentiary data' and '[t]here is no overriding principle of law that an act done under the contract will always communicate the decision to affirm, regardless of the surrounding circumstances'.[716] In fact, an act is usually done under a contract on condition of or with a reasonable expectation of the contract-breaker's performance or willingness and readiness to perform. Such an act may be no more than 'an election sub modo' and may be consistent with the retention of the right of termination which is exercisable in case of a further breach.[717] By contrast, where the victim freely accepts a substantial performance rendered by the contract-breaker, this is most likely to constitute an unequivocal representation to forgo the right of termination.[718] In all circumstances, it must be remembered that the issue is not the enforcement or maintenance of the contract per se, but the disposition of the right of termination. Therefore, it cannot be said that, for example, the yard's service of the notice of keel-laying under contracts 3 to 6 in *Stocznia v Latvian Shipping* did not constitute an affirmation solely because it was not entitled to act in the way

711 *Champtaloup v Thomas* [1976] 2 NSWLR 264 (NSWCA).

712 *GEC Marconi v BHP* (n 616) [361] (Finn J). *cf* UCC § 1–207.

713 *Larratt v Bankers & Traders' Insurance Co Ltd* (1941) 41 SR (NSW) 215 (NSWSC) 229 (Jordan CJ).

714 *Sargent* (n 616) 656 (Manson J). Also, *GEC Marconi v BHP* (n 616) [360] (Finn J).

715 *Cf Stocznia Gdynia v Gearbulk* (n 569) [33]–[37] (Moore-Bick LJ). While recognising the inconsistency between terminating and affirming a contract and criticising *United Dominions Trust (Commercial) Ltd v Ennis* [1968] 1 QB 54 (CA) 65–6 (Lord Denning MR); 68 (Harman LJ), Moore-Bick LJ regarded the issue as dependent on 'the intention of the parties in each case' ([35]). Also, *cf* E Peel, 'Affirmation by Termination' (2009) 125 *LQR* 378, 383.

716 *Champtaloup v Thomas* (n 711) 269 (Glass JA).

717 *Immer v United Church* (n 628) 30 (Brennan J).

718 *Hunt v Silk* (1804) 5 East 449, 102 ER 1142; *Blackburn v Smith* (1848) 2 Exch 783, 154 ER 707; *Harnor v Groves* (1855) 15 CB 667, 139 ER 587.

it did and the buyers disputed the lawfulness of its act.[719] According to the test of representation, even the commencement of an action for specific performance might not be seen as an affirmation. The victim may discontinue the action and terminate the contract even after an order of specific performance has been given, as long as it has not been complied with.[720] Where such an order has been given, an application for leave to terminate the contract may be necessary.[721] It is then at the court's discretion whether or not to allow the action for specific performance to be discontinued and the contract terminated. Therefore, an action for specific performance is said to be 'but a continuance of the contract under control of the court which control involves the power, in certain events, to terminate it'.[722] Such an act does not normally carry with it an intimation that the right of termination is henceforth given up, irrespective of whether or not the contract-breaker's actual performance is successfully obtained.

An unequivocal representation of the above description is required whether an affirmation is characterised as an act of election or as an estoppel. As acknowledged by Lord Goff, an 'important similarity' between election and estoppel was that 'each requires an unequivocal representation'.[723] The only question is whether the test applied varies according to the characterisation. Lord Goff, for example, took the view that the representation required for an act of election was 'different in nature' from that required for an estoppel, in that an elector 'is communicating his choice whether or not to exercise a right which has become available to him', whilst a party alleged to be estopped 'is representing that he will not in future enforce his legal rights'.[724] This seems to be a distinction without difference. A choice not to exercise a right invariably relates to the future, whilst a representation not to enforce that right can equally be seen as a choice. In *Yukong v Rendsburg*, Moore-Bick J attempted to draw the line by insisting that an election to affirm required an 'irrevocable commitment'.[725] Yet that term clearly adds little to 'unequivocal representation'. It fails to explain why the label of 'election' should render the representation irrevocable. Nevertheless, it is generally accepted that an election differs from an estoppel in that the former must be an informed choice,[726] whilst the latter requires no knowledge

719 *Cf Stocznia v Latvian Shipping* [2002] EWCA Civ 889 [90] (Rix LJ). Also, *Stocznia v Latvian Shipping* [1997] 2 Lloyd's Rep 228, 237 (Colman J).

720 *Johnson v Agnew* (n 180). Also, *Chatfield v Jones* (n 591).

721 *Sunbird v Maloney* (n 149) 260 (Mason CJ). No leave is required where the contract-breaker commits a fresh breach that entitles the victim to terminate the contract: *Ogle v Comboyuro* (n 696) 460–2 (Gibbs, Mason and Jacobs JJ).

722 *Johnson v Agnew* (n 180) 398 (Lord Wilberforce). Also, *Stocznia v Latvian Shipping* [1997] 2 Lloyd's Rep 228, 236 (Colman J): it was 'by the very nature of the remedy an expedient which, if unsuccessful, might have to be abandoned in favour of termination'.

723 *The Kanchenjunga* (n 614) 399.

724 *Ibid.*

725 *Yukong* (n 627) 608.

726 *Oliver Ashworth v Ballard* (n 486) 27 (Robert Walker LJ); *Insurance Corp of the Channel Islands, Royal Insurance (UK) Ltd v Royal Hotel Ltd* [1998] Lloyd's Rep IR 151 (Com Ct) 161 (Mance J), leave to appeal refused (unreported, CA, 14 February 1997). Also, *Hughes v Huppert* [1991] 1 NZLR 474 (HC).

on the representor's part.[727] However, if the victim is found to have made an unequivocal representation to relinquish its right to accept the anticipatory breach, it is a necessary inference from this that the victim must at least have some 'apparent awareness' of both the breach and its right to accept.[728] Whether it is by way of election or estoppel, the victim cannot give up something of which it is ignorant. The distinction between election and estoppel lies in whether an affirmation can be disproved by showing the want of knowledge. The point was raised and briefly dealt with in *Yukong v Rendsburg*, where Moore-Bick J, clearly viewing an affirmation as an act of election, held that the victim should be aware not only of the facts (anticipatory breach) but also of 'his right to choose between affirming the contract and treating it as discharged'.[729] An argument was put forward in that case on behalf of the victim owners that the charterers, who alleged that the owners had affirmed the contract, had failed to prove the owners' 'actual knowledge' of their right to terminate the contract. The learned judge rejected this argument. It was held that the owners had the burden of showing the want of such knowledge, which knowledge could be inferred from their telex, and that they failed to discharge this burden.[730] It appears that it is possible to disprove an affirmation in this way only because it is viewed as an act of election. If an affirmation works an estoppel, the victim's want of actual knowledge would be irrelevant as its unequivocal representation has been relied upon by the contract-breaker.[731] Indeed, there is much to be said for the view that, given the victim's constructive knowledge apparent from its representation, an allegation of affirmation should not be defeated solely by contrary evidence that shows its absence of actual knowledge. At any rate, since it is argued in the following subsections that an affirmation is best viewed as estoppel-based, the victim's actual knowledge should not be regarded as one of its constituent ingredients.

2. The Elective View

In the second step of our enquiry, we ask whether and why the victim should be held legally bound by a mere representation that it foregoes its right to accept the anticipatory breach. The current law views an affirmation as an act of election. Accordingly, the victim's representation is said to be by itself final, binding and

[727] *Bremer Handelsgesellschaft v Vanden Avenne-Izegem* [1978] 2 Lloyd's Rep 109 (HL) 126 (Lord Salmon).

[728] *HIH Casualty & General Insurance Ltd v Axa Corporate Solutions* [2002] 2 All ER (Comm) 1053 (CA) [21]–[23] (Tuckey LJ). Also, *James v Heim Gallery Ltd* (1980) 41 P & CR 269 (CA) 271 (Oliver LJ); *Youell v Bland Welch & Co Ltd (the 'Superhulls Cover' Case) (No 2)* [1990] 2 Lloyd's Rep 431 (Com Ct) 450 (Phillips J); *North Down Hotels Ltd v Province-Wide Filling Stations Ltd* [1993] NI 261 (Ch) 267 (Carswell J).

[729] *Yukong v Rendsburg* (n 627) 607.

[730] *Ibid* 609.

[731] *Sarat Chunder Dey v Gopal Chunder Laha* (1892) LR 19 Ind App 203 (PC Bengal) 215 (Lord Shand).

irrevocable, without the presence of consideration, deed or reliance. An affirmation is thus seen to be a purely unilateral process. The victim is precluded from accepting the anticipatory breach solely by reason of its representation. This gives rise to a critical question: what gives an 'election' to affirm such conclusory power?

There are a number of possible explanations. First, it could be argued that an 'election' to affirm is irrevocable simply because the victim is put to an election between inconsistent rights. 'Inconsistency' is, however, an ambiguous word. It is usually taken to mean that the rights are mutually exclusive. Yet mutual exclusivity does not necessarily mean mutual destruction.[732] True, the victim cannot both enjoy the benefits of the contract and be released from its obligations.[733] To put it bluntly, one cannot have one's cake and eat it too, or blow both 'hot and cold'.[734] This does not, however, necessarily preclude the victim from retreating from one option and switching to the other. Inconsistency in conduct is not by itself a bar to a change of mind. In fact, 'inconsistency' arises in almost all cases where a party is called upon to make a choice. A party agrees to make a gift. This is 'inconsistent' with a decision not to make the gift. Yet the promise to make the gift is not binding without consideration. A landlord gratuitously agrees to reduce the rent. This is 'inconsistent' with a claim for full rent. Yet the representation that the rent will be reduced is not binding without being relied on by the tenant.[735] In this respect, a representation to give up a right of termination is not distinguishable from a representation to give up a right to performance.[736] It cannot be said that whilst the latter right can be relinquished only by way of contract, deed or estoppel, the former right, being a 'procedural' one, is additionally vulnerable to an 'election' to affirm.[737]

Secondly, it could be said that an 'election' to affirm, being an informed choice, should necessarily be irrevocable.[738] The victim's knowledge, either of the anticipatory breach or of its right to terminate, is, however, not decisive. If a promise is unenforceable for lack of consideration, it is not rendered enforceable by the mere fact that it is made with full knowledge. Equally, a representation may well be made with full knowledge, yet cannot work an estoppel without reliance. Knowledge, as shown earlier, is usually imputed to the victim in the process of ascertaining an unequivocal representation. Beyond that it should barely matter. Contrary to what is commonly assumed, an informed choice is not always irrevocable. The presence of knowledge does not necessitate

732 *Cf Sargent* (n 616) 641 (Stephen J): neither option 'may be enjoyed without the extinction of the other'. Also, Handley (n 622) 82.

733 *Tropical Traders v Goonan* (n 676) 55 (Kitto J). *cf* CJ Rossiter, 'The Doctrine of Election and Contracts for the Sale of Land' (1986) *Auatralian Law Journal* 563, 564.

734 *Smith v Hodson* (1790) 4 TR 211, 217, 100 ER 979, 982 (Lord Kenyon CJ); *Sudan v Société Générale* (n 709) 315 (Lord Evershed MR). Also, *Smith's Leading Cases* (n 14) 147.

735 *Central London Property Trust v High Trees House* [1947] KB 130.

736 *Cf* Seddon and Ellinghaus (n 189) 90.

737 *Cf ibid* [21.28]. The authors did, however, propose that 'in the interest of simplicity and uniformity', estoppel should be adopted as 'the ruling criterion in all such cases'.

738 *Sargent* (n 616) 642 (Stephen J).

irrevocability. As stated in the previous Chapter, a real election hinges on the existence of a good reason for its irrevocability. Knowledge is not as such a good reason. The fact that an election must be made with full knowledge does not mean that every choice made with full knowledge constitutes an election.

The third possible justification for the elective view of affirmation is certainty and justice to the contract-breaker. It was said that the contract-breaker was 'entitled to assume that the innocent party will not change his mind' as it 'needs to know with certainty whether the contract ... has been terminated or kept alive, for, if it is still alive, he will yet have the opportunity of performance'.[739] Clearly, according to this analysis, what the contract-breaker 'needs to know with certainty' is whether the victim's right to accept the anticipatory breach has been exercised, not whether it still retains that right. It seems that, although certainty for the contract-breaker requires an acceptance to be final and binding, it does not necessitate the adoption of the elective view. After all, the more appropriate way of making certain of the 'opportunity of performance' is for the contract-breaker to retract its anticipatory breach, rather than by holding a mere representation of the victim to be irrevocable. In addition, the above argument was criticised in that it was based on 'hypothetical hardship' and its force was thus 'reduced, one is tempted to say to vanishing point, where the facts appear to negative the possibility that such hardship will be suffered'.[740] Indeed, the rejection of 'hypothetical hardship' naturally calls for a doctrine based on 'actual hardship'. This generally means that the contract-breaker must at least have relied upon the victim's representation. The difficulty in proving reliance is often cited in support of its dispensation,[741] yet this is outweighed by the fact that in the absence of 'actual hardship' the contract-breaker cannot be said to have suffered any injustice.

Fourthly, in other contexts involving an 'election', there were suggestions that the victim, having reaped benefits or advantages from the continuance of the contract, cannot be allowed to terminate it again.[742] It seems to be essential to this argument that the victim must have actually received some benefit. Mere assertion of a right to benefit is insufficient. The rationale seems to be to prevent the victim from obtaining a windfall by acting inconsistently. However, in most cases, active co-operation, or at least acquiescence, of the contract-breaker is required for the victim to reap any benefit from the contract. Such conduct of the contract-breaker is likely to constitute either a retraction of the anticipatory breach or reliance on the victim's unequivocal representation. Even if a retraction or reliance cannot be established,

[739] *Stocznia v Latvian Shipping* [1997] 2 Lloyd's Rep 228, 235–6 (Colman J). Similarly, *Sargent* (n 616) 656 (Manson J). Also, EA Farnsworth, *Changing Your Mind: The Law of Regretted Decisions* (New Haven, Yale University Press, 1998) 184–5; DB Dobbs, 'Pressing Problems for the Plaintiff's Lawyer in Rescission: Election of Remedies and Restoration of Consideration' (1972) 26 *Arkansas Law Review* 322, 340; Feltham et al (n 488) 359, 375.

[740] Treitel (n 693) 27. *cf Stocznia v Latvian Shipping* [2002] EWCA Civ 889 [91] (Rix LJ).

[741] Dobbs (n 739) 340: allowing the victim to terminate again 'would be very likely to prejudice [the contract-breaker] in unproveable ways'. For a similar argument in the context of abandoning a claim for specific performance, Waddams (n 380) [611].

[742] *Craine v Colonial Mutual Fire* (n 704) 326 (Isaacs J); *Sargent* (n 616) 641 (Stephen J).

it is hard to see why the mere fact that the victim has reaped some benefit from the contract, however small the benefit might be, should invariably kill off its right to accept the anticipatory breach. It makes better sense to allow the victim to terminate the contract, and then either let it retain the benefit to offset damages or, if appropriate, order a restitution of the benefit on the ground of a total failure of consideration.

The fifth argument for the elective view of affirmation is what was dubbed by the late Professor Farnsworth as the 'anti-speculation principle'.[743] The principle is based on a perception of a contract as a vehicle to shift market risks[744] and a 'pronounced judicial distaste for allowing one party to speculate at the other's risk'.[745] This principle is bound up with the rule that a party in which a power of termination is vested must exercise it with reasonable promptitude, for procrastination in exercising it would prolong 'the time during which the other party is at [the terminating party's] mercy'.[746] It is thus supposedly inappropriate to allow the victim of an anticipatory breach to uphold the contract when the market is in favour of contract performance, and then terminate it when the market turns against it. This 'anti-speculation' principle thus dictates that the victim must be given only one opportunity to choose between accepting the breach and affirming the contract. The difficulty with this principle is the definition of 'speculation'. If 'speculation' is intended to entail opportunism and hence low motives or bad faith, clearly those elements are neither necessary nor material to the constitution of an affirmation. The victim's unequivocal representation is objectively assessed. Its motives are largely irrelevant. So understood, 'speculation' is fairly narrow and is irrelevant in the majority of anticipatory breach cases. If, more probably, an act of 'speculation' is intended to arise wherever the contract-breaker is said to be at the victim's mercy and 'vulnerable' to a right of termination, then it is too readily assumed. It seems to be somehow ironical to suggest that, just because the contract-breaker's anticipatory breach confers upon the victim a right to terminate the contract, the contract-breaker should be viewed as a weaker party in need of special protection. Still less can it be assumed that, since the contract-breaker is at the receiving end of a possible termination, the victim must necessarily be 'speculating' when it withholds the termination. To be sure, the victim must exercise its right of termination within a reasonable time after the anticipatory breach is communicated to it. A failure to do so would give rise to an affirmation. Yet that affirmation is not constituted by the mere fact that the victim fails to exercise its right of termination, which meanwhile keeps the contract-breaker 'vulnerable'. Instead, the 'reasonable time' is imposed to prevent injury to the contract-breaker and must therefore depend on the latter's reliance upon the victim's delay in

[743] Farnsworth (n 739) 184–5.

[744] Also, R Kreitner, 'Speculations of Contract, or How Contract Law Stopped Worrying and Learned to Love Risk' (2000) 100 *Columbia Law Review* 1096, 1097 fns 2, 3.

[745] Farnsworth (n 739) 184–5.

[746] *Ibid.*

terminating the contract. To put it another way, without being relied upon, the victim's delay cannot be said to cause injury to the contract-breaker and the 'reasonable time' cannot be said to have expired. More importantly, the 'anti-speculation' principle seems to have entirely overlooked cases where the victim makes a genuine endeavour to persuade the contract-breaker to repent and by doing so is held to have unequivocally represented that its right to accept the anticipatory breach will not be exercised. An application of the principle to those cases tends to discourage reasonable efforts to rescue the contract. Therefore, the principle is founded on an assumed rather than established act of 'speculation' and is heavily biased in favour of the contract-breaker.

Consequently, none of the above arguments constitutes a convincing justification for the elective view. On the contrary, as suggested in the previous Chapter, in order for a choice between inconsistent options to constitute an election, a good reason for its irrevocability must be identified. There is no good reason that a mere representation not to accept an anticipatory breach should be held to be irrevocable. It is thus unfounded to characterise an affirmation as an act of election. We must seek an alternative basis on which the irrevocability of an affirmation can be satisfactorily explained.

3. The Estoppel View

Once it is realised that the notion of affirmation centres upon and proceeds from a representation that the anticipatory breach in question will not be accepted, it is natural to suggest that an affirmation is not constituted and does not acquire the force of irrevocability unless and until the representation is relied upon by the contract-breaker. The representation relates to a future fact. The reliance must be placed in such a way as to make it unconscionable for the victim to accept the breach. This falls within the category of promissory estoppel.[747]

Obviously, this estoppel view faces overwhelmingly one-sided judicial statements in favour of the elective view. Nevertheless, it is not something entirely foreign to the law. Besides the fact that its inception is a logical corollary of the rejection of the elective view, the estoppel view has in fact long been recognised as an alternative to the elective view. Support for it can be found in both case law and academic works. With regard to case law, there are three points to be noted. First, it is well settled that where the contract-breaker fails to establish an 'election' to affirm, it might invoke promissory estoppel as an alternative ground to challenge the victim's right to accept the anticipatory breach.[748] Secondly, although

[747] *Woodhouse AC Israel Cocoa SA v Nigerian Produce Marketing Co Ltd* [1972] AC 741 (HL); *Legione v Hateley* (1983) 152 CLR 406 (HCA). Also, Handley (n 639) [13–009], [13–015]; E Cooke, *The Modern Law of Estoppel* (Oxford, OUP, 2000) chs 3–4.

[748] *Peyman v Lanjani* (n 619) 488 (Stephenson LJ), 500–1 (Salde LJ); *Yukong* (n 627) 608 (Moore-Bick J); *MSC v BRE-Metro* (n 592); *Stocznia v Latvian Shipping* [2001] 1 Lloyd's Rep 537 [176], citing with approval Treitel (n 693). Also, *Foran v Wight* (n 155) 458–9 (Gaudron J).

the elective view has been widely espoused, it is very difficult, if not impossible, to find an anticipatory breach case where a mere representation not to accept the breach, without being relied upon, was held to be binding. Indeed, two cases most frequently cited in support of that view, *Bentsen v Taylor, Sons & Co (No 2)*[749] and *The 'Kanchenjunga'*,[750] both of which concerned actual rather than anticipatory breach, were on their facts testament to the necessity of reliance.[751] Therefore, the notion of 'election' has not been applied rigorously by the courts and a replacement of it by 'estoppel' would probably not cause much upheaval of existing case law. Thirdly, Lord Denning, in the context of actual fundamental breach, several times openly advocated the estoppel view.[752] Turning to academic commentary, the scene is even more encouraging. Professor Treitel was a major proponent of the estoppel view of affirmation.[753] Professor Reynolds also questioned the wisdom of recognising an irrevocable election in the context of the law of agency.[754] Some of his criticism was clearly directed at 'election' in general and indicated that a mere representation, without being relied upon, should not generally be held to be binding.[755] Bower's seminal work on estoppel by representation, under its previous editorships, treated 'election' as a type of reliance-based 'semi-estoppel'.[756] There were similar suggestions in other parts of the common law world.[757] These works lend significant support to the estoppel view.

Interestingly, the courts have more readily endorsed the use of estoppel in a slightly different context. As shown previously in Chapter 5, a party in anticipatory breach may be estopped from insisting upon its contractual rights where the victim acts upon, but does not accept, the anticipatory breach and as a result is itself in breach of the contract.[758] An anticipatory breach does not of itself discharge a contract and therefore does not 'waive' the victim's subsequent breach; the contract-breaker is estopped from insisting upon a right or benefit under it. This was explicitly recognised in a dictum of Lord Ackner in *The Simona*,[759] where his Lordship stated that the victim, while not accepting the anticipatory breach, might nonetheless escape from such obligations by establishing an estoppel.[760] The High Court of Australia's decision in *Peter*

749 *Bentsen v Taylor, Sons & Co (No 2)* [1893] 2 QB 274 (CA).

750 n 614.

751 Treitel (n 693) 25.

752 *Charles Rickards v Oppenhaim* (n 676) 623, 626; *Panchaud v Etablissements* (n 444) 57, cited with approval *The Lorico* (n 442) 397–8 (Evans LJ).

753 Treitel (n 693). Also, *Treitel's Law of Contract* (n 276) [17–090].

754 FMB Reynolds, 'Election Distributed' [1970] 86 *LQR* 318. Also, FMB Reynolds, *Bowstead and Reynolds on Agency*, 18th edn (London, Sweet & Maxwell, 2006) [407–408], [415–416].

755 'Election Distributed' *ibid* 324, fn 31.

756 Bower and Turner (n 489). *cf* Feltham et al (n 488) 359 fn 1, 417.

757 Rossiter (n 733) 565, 566; Waddams (n 380) [610], cited with approval *Saskatchewan River Bungalows Ltd v Maritime Life Assurance Co* (1994) 115 DLR (4th) 478 (SCC) 486.

758 Ch 5, text to and after n 506 above.

759 n 386.

760 *Ibid* 805.

Turnbull v Mundus[761] is also best explained on the ground that the seller was estopped from requiring a ship at the port of Sydney.[762] Thus the anticipatory breach might raise an estoppel and therefore relieve the victim from a certain obligation if that breach contains an unequivocal representation that it is pointless for the victim to perform the obligation and the representation is then relied upon by the victim and thereby 'induces' its failure to perform the obligation.[763] Since the representation in these cases also involves a disposition of a contractual right and is thus not distinguishable in nature from the representation required for an affirmation, it can be argued that the notion of estoppel should equally be applied in adjudicating an affirmation case.

Generally speaking, an application of the doctrine of promissory estoppel to an affirmation following an anticipatory breach does not give rise to many special issues. There is a pre-existing contractual relationship and estoppel is used only as a shield, not a sword. Therefore debates on these two points can be put aside.[764] Two issues, however, require some further explanation. First, the presence of reliance is now central to the constitution of an affirmation. It must be established by the party alleging the existence of an affirmation. Reliance does not have to be detrimental; alteration of position is sufficient.[765] In an anticipatory breach case, it is possible to hypothesize acts of reliance by the contract-breaker that may well be beneficial, not detrimental, to it, such as resuming manufacturing, acquiring properties, or obtaining funds. Of course, if 'detriment' is used in a broader sense to mean the prejudice that the contract-breaker may suffer as a result of allowing the victim to resile from its representation, then reliance must be detrimental.[766] It is not superfluous to stress that the ultimate test is whether it is inequitable for the victim to resile from the representation. Reliance is a key factor but the courts have some latitude in both disallowing estoppel even though reliance is present[767] and, presumably, upholding estoppel where reliance is not shown. An act in reliance on a representation not to accept the anticipatory breach must be distinguished from a retraction of that breach. A retraction occurs when the victim is notified of the contract-breaker's change of attitude or position and is thus incapable of drawing a reasonable inference of a prospective fundamental breach. It quenches the anticipatory breach and disables the victim from accepting it. By contrast, reliance is not required to be communicated and does not affect the

[761] n 5.

[762] *Ibid* 245–6, 248 (Dixon CJ); 249 (Webb J). Also, *Austral Standard Cables Pty Ltd v Walker Nominees Pty Ltd* (1922) 26 NSWLR 524 (NSWCA).

[763] *Peter Turnbull* (n 5) 245 (Dixon CJ). Also, *The Simona* (n 386) 805 (Lord Ackner); *Foran v Wight* (n 155) 410 (Mason CJ).

[764] *High Trees* (n 735); *Combe v Combe* [1951] 2 KB 215 (CA). *cf Waltons Stores (Interstate) Ltd v Maher* (1988) 164 CLR 387 (HCA) 404 (Mason CJ and Wilson J); 425–6 (Brennan J).

[765] *WJ Alan & Co Ltd v El Nasr Export and Import Co* [1972] 2 QB 189 (CA) 213–14; *Société Italo-Belge pour le Commerce et l'Industrie v Palm and Vegetable Oils (Malaysia) Sdn Bhd (The 'Post Chaser')* [1982] 1 All ER 19 (Com Ct) 26–7 (Robert Goff J).

[766] *Verwayen* (n 489) 415 (Mason CJ). Also, Feltham et al (n 488) 481–2.

[767] Eg *D & C Builders v Rees* [1966] 2 QB 617 (CA).

existence of the breach. Secondly, a promissory estoppel is not irrevocable unless and until the promisee permanently alters its position.[768] Accordingly, the victim of an anticipatory breach may resile from its unequivocal representation not to accept that breach on giving reasonable notice before the contract-breaker permanently alters its position. The effect of estoppel may thus be temporary. The right to accept is only extinguished if the contract-breaker cannot resume its previous position. This enables the victim to regain that right if the contract-breaker's alteration of position is reversible. Where the victim, in an attempt to persuade the contract-breaker to retract the anticipatory breach, goes to the length of assuring the latter that the right of termination will not be exercised, it would be harsh to hold the victim to that assurance if the contract-breaker acts in reliance on it but fails to make real progress towards retracting the breach. Conversely, if the contract-breaker takes significant steps to perform the contract, it should be rewarded with an opportunity to correct its wrong. Whether the contract-breaker has done enough to make the victim's representation irrevocable must be determined under the general question whether it is inequitable to allow the victim to resile from that representation. Compared to the old rule that holds an affirmation as invariably irrevocable, this seems to be a more refined, flexible and balanced approach.

In conclusion, our survey in both the previous and this Chapter has cast serious doubt on the propriety of the use of 'election' in the context of the victim's choice between accepting the anticipatory breach and affirming the contract.[769] 'Election' is a fiction. The principle of 'election' disguises the fact that there are actually two distinct issues. The first issue is whether the victim effectively terminates the contract, which termination is justified by the anticipatory breach. This cannot be characterised as an act of election, as the victim's lack of knowledge of either the breach or its right of termination is wholly immaterial. The second issue is whether the victim is precluded, either temporarily or permanently, from relying upon the anticipatory breach as a ground for terminating the contract. An affirmative answer requires an unequivocal representation on the victim's part to abandon its right to accept the breach and reliance by the contract-breaker on that representation in such a way as to make it inequitable for the victim to resile from the representation. These two distinct issues cannot be accommodated into a single principle of 'election'. The use of 'election' in this context is thus an example of the form subduing the substance and the terminology eclipsing the principle. It is inappropriate, misleading and should consequently be discarded.

768 *Birmingham & District Land Co v London & North Western Rly Co* (1888) 40 Ch D 268 (CA) 286 (Bowen LJ); *Tool Metal Manufacturing Co Ltd v Tungsten Electric Co Ltd (No 3)* [1955] 1 WLR 761 (HL) 785 (Lord Tucker); *Ajayi v RT Briscoe (Nigeria) Ltd* [1964] 1 WLR 1326 (PC Nigeria) 1330 (Lord Hodson).

769 Indeed, much of what have been said applies equally to a party's decision whether or not to rescind the contract for a vitiating factor such as misrepresentation: *The Kanchenjunga* (n 614) 398 (Lord Goff).

Part IV

Remedying Anticipatory Breach

This Part explores the principal legal remedies available to the victim of an anticipatory breach. Its primary concern is with special issues brought about by the anticipatory nature of the breach. Chapter 7 deals with the remedy of damages. It examines when a right of action for damages accrues and how the damages are assessed. Chapter 8 turns to remedies available to a victim who does not accept the anticipatory breach. In particular, it considers a claim brought in debt to recover the contract price.

8

Claiming Damages

The primary remedy for an anticipatory breach is to claim damages at common law. The victim may, of course, seek liquidated damages in accordance with relevant contract provisions.[770] But the mere presence of such consensual remedies does not oust a common law claim.[771] Of course, where seeking both consensual and common law remedies leads to double recovery, the victim must make an election between them. In respect of an action for damages at common law, two distinct issues arise for consideration. The first issue concerns the victim's right to bring the action. The second issue concerns the assessment of damages. They are dealt with in separate sections.

A. The Right to Claim Damages

There are three interconnected points to be discussed in respect of the victim's right of action for damages. First, an appraisal is made of the peculiar relationship between that right of action and the victim's acceptance of the anticipatory breach. Secondly, the reason why the right of action must arise immediately after the acceptance, rather than being deferred until the time for performance, will be investigated. Lastly, both these points are influential in determining whether unilateral or one-sidedly executed contracts should be recognised as an exception to the doctrine of anticipatory breach.

1. The Conditional Damages Rule

It is trite law that following an anticipatory breach, the victim must accept the breach, thereby terminating the contract, in order to acquire a right of action for damages. We henceforth call this the 'conditional damages rule'. In Chapter 1, section C, we saw that a series of mistakes contributed to its inception. The seeds of the rule were perhaps sown in Lord Campbell's misreading of

770 *Robophone Facilities v Blank* [1966] 1 WLR 1428 (CA); *United Dominions v Ennis* (n 715).

771 *Gilbert Ash (Northern) Ltd v Modern Engineering (Bristol) Ltd* [1974] AC 689 (HL); *Stocznia v Latvian Shipping* [1998] 1 WLR 574; *Stocznia Gdynia SA v Gearbulk* (n 569) [20], [23] (Moore-Bick LJ).

Planché v Colburn[772] *in Hochster v De la Tour*.[773] The catalyst for its articulation was a substitution by the reporter of his Lordship's dictum for the ratio in the twin cases of *Avery v Bowden*[774] and *Reid v Hoskins*.[775] Since then the rule has been reasserted on numerous occasions. It must now be considered a well-established, distinctive part of the doctrine of anticipatory breach. The rule has long been confused with, but is in fact conceptually distinguishable from, the breach-conversion rule. It also has little to do with the victim's ability to continue with the contract and then to claim the contract price in debt[776] and must also be contrasted with the requirement that, for the victim to bring a restitutionary claim, the contract must be at an end.[777] The practical implications of the conditional damages rule are mainly two-fold. First, the chance of obtaining a right to claim damages for anticipatory breach may forever be lost where, before the breach could be accepted, the contract comes to an end. Secondly, under the rule the period of limitation starts to run[778] or a 'duty' to mitigate arises[779] not at the time of breach, but at the later time of acceptance. This may affect the viability of a claim for damages and the amount of damages recoverable.

The conditional damages rule has long been a subject of controversy. There has been a divergence of view as to whether it should be abandoned in favour of an automatic right of action for damages following an anticipatory breach. On the one hand, the rule has been criticised as historically ill-founded, contrary to common sense and unduly prejudicial to the victim.[780] On the other hand, defenders of the rule have endeavoured to argue that it works well in practice and that its abolition would serve no useful purpose but would send current law into turmoil. The true basis of the rule continues to be obscured and the mystery surrounding it remains to be dispelled. This has constantly bewildered contract lawyers and impeded a rational understanding of the doctrine of anticipatory breach.

[772] n 12.

[773] n 1.

[774] n 73.

[775] n 76.

[776] *Cf* Seddon & Ellinghaus (n 189) [23.21]. The authors relied upon the latter ground to explain a refusal by the Federal Court of Australia in *Hecec v Hydro-Electric* (n 92) [65] to strike out a claim for damages based on unaccepted anticipatory breaches.

[777] *Fibrosa v Fairbairn* (n 16). Restitution by subtraction for unjust enrichment is not available where an anticipatory breach is not accepted, for there is no total failure of consideration: *Morrison-Knudsen Co Inc v British Columbia Hydro & Power Authority* (1978) 85 DLR (3d) 186 (BCCA); *ERDC Construction Ltd v HM Love & Co* 1994 SC 620 (SD).

[778] *Wilkinson v Verity* (n 85); *Proctor & Gamble (Health and Beauty Care) Ltd v Carrier Holdings Ltd* [2003] EWHC 83 (TCC), [2003] BLR 255.

[779] *Kaines (UK) Ltd v Osterreichische Warrenhandelsgesellschaft Austrowaren Gesellschaft GmbH* [1993] 2 Lloyd's Rep 1 (CA).

[780] RA Lord (ed), *Williston on Contracts*, 4th edn (West, 2002) vol 23 § 63:51; Nienaber (n 37) 221; Vold (n 79) 508 *et seq*; Limburg (n 111) 140, 148 *et seq*.

a. Major Objections

Illogicality

We deal first with major attacks launched on the rule. The first line of attack is mounted in the name of logic. It is customarily assumed that a breach of contract always immediately gives rise to a right of action for damages. The conditional damages rule hence sounds like a heresy. This criticism, however, entails a blatant failure to recognise the fact that an anticipatory breach is distinct from an actual breach. It must also be noted that the conditional damages rule and the breach-conversion rule, although historically interwoven, are conceptually separable. The latter claims that an anticipatory breach is not a fully fledged breach unless and until accepted by the victim. This, as seen previously in Chapter 2, is demonstrably inappropriate as a party's wrongdoing cannot be said to be made up of some act of the other party. By contrast, it is no offence to logic to say that the victim must do something to earn a right to pursue the remedy of damages. An anticipatory breach is clearly in itself a wrong. Yet it does not follow that the law must respond to that wrong by immediately conferring upon the victim a right to claim damages. The question of wrong must thus be distinguished from the question of legal response. The conditional damages rule does not deny that an anticipatory breach constitutes a breach; it merely asserts that the breach is not by itself 'actionable'.[781] There is nothing illogical in this assertion.

Undue Prejudice

The second major objection to the conditional damages rule is that, by refusing to grant a right to claim damages before an anticipatory breach is accepted, the rule may unduly prejudice the victim. This argument sounds plausible but, upon closer analysis, is difficult to sustain. Let us examine some circumstances where the opportunity of accepting an anticipatory breach may be said to be unfairly removed from the victim before it is utilised. First, where, before the anticipatory breach can be accepted, the contract is frustrated or otherwise terminated without either party incurring a liability, the effect of the conditional damages rule is merely to deprive the victim of an empty claim for nominal damages. An automatic right of action does not give rise to substantial damages as the victim would have still lost the bargain but for the anticipatory breach. Secondly, where the contract-breaker terminates the contract for a breach by the victim before the anticipatory breach is accepted, even though no right of action accrues to the victim, the victim may still set off the loss caused by the anticipatory breach against damages recoverable by the contract-breaker. This usually means that the contract-breaker is entitled to nominal damages only. Thirdly, where the anticipatory breach evolves into an actual breach at the time for performance, the victim is

[781] *Manx Electricity v Morgan* (n 113) [38] (Rix LJ).

not put at a disadvantage by virtue of the fact that the only ground for it to claim damages is the actual breach as opposed to the antecedent anticipatory breach. The same can be said of a victim who terminates the contract by the time for performance for an actual breach of the contract-breaker. Lastly, where the contract-breaker retracts the anticipatory breach before it can be accepted, the wrong is put right and there is of course no basis for the victim to acquire a right of action against the contract-breaker. In none of these circumstances, therefore, can it be said that the victim is unduly prejudiced by the conditional damages rule.

Immediate Injury

A third objection to the conditional damages rule can be extracted from a dominant school of thought in the USA, which asserts that an anticipatory breach inflicts a present, immediate injury upon its victim by undermining its confidence in the security of contract performance and thus ruining its ability to rely on performance and plan accordingly.[782] It is thus said that a right of action for damages arises automatically from the breach and does not depend on a termination of the contract. This school of thought is based on a perception of an anticipatory breach as either an infringement of a property right or a tort. This 'contractual property' theory was criticised in Chapter 2 as an unwarranted departure from both legal principle and commercial reality. In a nutshell, the notion that an anticipatory breach constitutes a present wrong does not mean that it must also occasion a present loss. It is a fiction to regard every contract as having an intrinsic monetary value, the loss of which is recoverable in damages. People contract for performance,[783] not for the mere subsistence of a relationship. Although, according to socio-legal scholars, businessmen in reality value their mutual contractual relationship highly, these studies are a far cry from entertaining the proposition that the disruption of such a relationship should give rise to a claim in damages.[784] The value of a loss of performance must be measured by reference to the time when performance falls due. Further, a bargain is not entirely or irreversibly lost when an anticipatory breach is committed. The main injury inflicted by an anticipatory breach upon its victim is not some immediate injury, but a total loss of bargain that does not materialise until the time for performance. The third objection must therefore be dismissed.

b. *Justification*

As noted earlier, historically, the conditional damages rule had a precarious foundation. That the rule is of defective origin does not, of course, necessitate its

782 *Corbin on Contracts* (n 5) § 961, § 962, supp [(A)][(2)].

783 D Friedmann, 'The Performance Interest in Contract Damages' [1995] 111 *LQR* 628.

784 Eg S Macaulay, 'Non-Contractual Relations in Business: A Preliminary Study' (1963) 28 *American Sociological Review* 55; H Beale and T Dugdale, 'Contracts between Businessmen: Planning and the Use of Contractual Remedies' (1975) 2 *British Journal of Law and Society* 45.

abolition. Yet the origin of the rule is a good place from which to start to look for its underlying rationale. If we examine Lord Campbell's dicta in both *Avery v Bowden* and *Reid v Hoskins*,[785] they clearly postulated a situation where a frustrating event occurred before an anticipatory breach was accepted.[786] By disallowing the victim to sue for damages, the conditional damages rule could be said to protect the contract-breaker from an opportunistic claim. In truth, however, such a claim would have little chance of success in any event, even if the victim should be allowed to bring an action. No substantial damages would be available as the victim would still have sustained a total loss of bargain even if the anticipatory breach had not been committed.[787] It is thus unnecessary, for the purpose of avoiding a possible opportunistic claim, to adopt the conditional damages rule. It might further be argued that the rule has the benefit of restricting the number of claims brought for nominal damages. It is obvious, however, that this benefit cannot alone sufficiently justify the rule.

Where, then, does the true basis of the conditional damages rule lie? The answer must be found in an important proposition put forward earlier: the entire doctrine of anticipatory breach is founded upon the necessity of providing an exit route, in the victim's favour, from a bargain apparently doomed to fail. If such necessity does not arise or the right to terminate the contract is not exercised, there is no good reason to confer upon the victim a right of action in damages. This assertion entails two slightly different points. First, to claim damages for a prospective loss of performance is inconsistent with the subsistence of the underlying contract.[788] The victim cannot 'blow both hot and cold', recovering for its loss while maintaining that the contract-breaker is still bound by the contract.[789] The reason is that an anticipatory breach, as distinguished from an actual breach,[790] is invariably a fundamental breach and causes a total loss of bargain. For example, an anticipatory breach embodied in one specific instalment, once accepted, is regarded as a total breach that entitles the victim to damages measured not by the loss in relation to that specific instalment, but by the whole loss of profits under the entire contract.[791] Evidently such a loss cannot be recovered while the contract is still subsisting. The conditional damages rule thus reasserts the proposition that an 'anticipatory secondary obligation' to pay damages accrues to the contract-breaker only when the victim terminates the contract.[792] An anticipatory breach

[785] Ch 1, text to n 78 above.

[786] This also appears to be the 'supervening circumstance' adverted to by Cockburn CJ in *Frost v Knight* (n 87) 112–13.

[787] *Barley v Robertson* (n 5) 209 (McArthur J). Also, Lloyd (n 485) 130.

[788] *Reid v Hoskins* (n 76) 659 (Lord Campbell); *Johnstone v Milling* (n 88) 467 (Lord Esher MR), 473 (Bowen LJ); *Photo Production* (n 109) 844–5, 849 (Lord Diplock); *Ogle v Comboyuro* (n 696) 458 (Gibbs, Mason and Jacobs JJ); *Progressive Mailing House Pty Ltd v Tabali Pty Ltd* (1985) 157 CLR 17 (HCA) 31 (Mason J); *Sunbird v Maloney* (n 149) 260–1 (Mason CJ), 273 (Gaudron J).

[789] *Sudan v Société Générale* (n 709) 315 (Lord Evershed MR).

[790] *The Kanchenjunga* (n 614) 400 (Lord Goff); *Ogle v Comboyuro* (n 696) 450 (Barwick CJ).

[791] *Urquhart v Eastern Bank* (n 227) 324–5 (Rowlatt J).

[792] *Photo Production* (n 109) 848 (Lord Diplock).

might immediately cause a loss to its victim. For example, the victim might incur expenses to repair a defect in the contract-breaker's past performance. A ship owner might suffer a loss of extra profits when an imminent sale of its ship along with its right to future hire under a time charter is wrecked by a repudiation by the charterer.[793] A wrongfully dismissed employee might suffer financially from a loss of reputation, creditability or publicity.[794] None of these losses constitutes a total loss of bargain. The subsistence of the contract is no bar to recovery for them. However, this type of 'present loss' occurs mostly in the case of an actual breach[795] and is atypical in anticipatory breach cases. Where it is caused by an anticipatory breach, it can be recovered without the breach being accepted. This is, however, an exception to, rather than a refutation of, the conditional damages rule.

The second point is that an anticipatory breach, as long as it remains unaccepted, inherently carries a degree of uncertainty. An unaccepted anticipatory breach is a retractable wrong. This character is attributable to nothing but the fundamental nature of an anticipatory breach as an inferential breach of a future obligation.[796] As a result of its futurity, the loss of performance that the victim might sustain is in a state of flux. Accepting an anticipatory breach thus becomes a necessary step for the contract-breaker's liability to take root[797] and for the victim's loss to be fixed. In *Frost v Knight*, Cockburn CJ said that upon acceptance of an anticipatory breach the 'eventual non-performance' might, 'by anticipation, be treated as a cause of action' for damages.[798] This statement, endorsed in numerous later cases,[799] recognised that, in order for an anticipatory breach to constitute a valid cause of action, it should be accepted so as to render the anticipated breach in effect 'inevitable'. This reasoning might cause some difficulties where an anticipatory breach by itself renders future performance of the contract 'impossible', such as in the cases of a unique antique being destroyed by the seller before the date for delivery or an employee being wrongfully dismissed and excluded from

[793] *Golden Strait Corp v Nippon Yusen Kubishka Kaisha (The 'Golden Victory')* [2007] UKHL 12, [2007] 2 AC 353[37] (Lord Scott); [82] (Lord Brown); *cf* [7], [22] (Lord Bingham); [45] (Lord Walker). On the facts of the case, however, no evidence was adduced to show that such a sale was imminent.

[794] *Marbé v George Edwardes* [1928] 1 KB 269 (CA); *Clayton v Oliver* [1930] AC 209 (HL).

[795] Eg *Suisse Atlantique v NV Rotterdamsche* (n 393) 422 (Lord Upjohn); *Ets Soules & Cie v International Trade Development Co Ltd* [1980] 1 Lloyd's Rep 129 (CA) 137–8 (Megaw LJ); *CIC Insurance Ltd v Bankstown Football Club Ltd* (1994–1995) 8 ANZ Ins Cas 61–232 (NSWCA) 75 [571] (Priestley JA), rev'd on other grounds [1997] HCA 2, (1997) 187 CLR 384.

[796] *cf* G Lubbe, 'Retraction of Repudiation: A Doctrine Writ in Water?' (1996) 7 *Stellenbosch Law Review* 147, 158, 160–1. Lubbe argued that an anticipatory breach should not be regarded as retractable, because retractability was based on either the 'offer to rescind' theory or the breach-conversion rule and the contract-breaker should not be permitted unilaterally to deprive the victim of a right of termination which arose from a 'present breach of an existing duty'. This argument is clearly ill-founded.

[797] D Tiplady, 'A Comparative Analysis of the Discharge of Contracts by Anticipatory Breach and Actual Breach with Particular Reference to the Terminology of Frustration' (M Litt thesis, Oxford University, 1973) 40.

[798] *Frost v Knight* (n 87) 114.

[799] Eg *Citati* (n 2) 438 (Devlin J); *Manx Electricity v Morgan* (n 113) [38] (Rix LJ).

employment. Since future performance is made impossible, no uncertainty arises in such circumstances. It thus appears that a right of action for damages would accrue at the time when contract performance becomes impossible, rather than when the victim makes an attempt to accept the anticipatory breach. It does not, however, follow that the anticipatory breach should be immediately actionable and '[t]he subsequent acceptance ... would not create a new cause of action'.[800] The better explanation is that an acceptance should be 'easily infer[red]' where any other interpretation would be 'meaningless'.[801] The victim's inaction in such cases should generally be held to constitute an implied acceptance. The issue is thus not whether the conditional damages rule should be deserted or modified, but whether an acceptance could be identified. For these reasons the conditional damages rule must be upheld.

2. The Immediacy Rule

The necessity of accepting an anticipatory breach for the purpose of claiming damages must be distinguished from the issue whether the victim, having accepted the breach, needs to wait till the time for performance to bring such a claim. The immediacy of a right of termination following an anticipatory breach is firmly supported by the need to release the victim's resources from an apparently failed enterprise. Yet this does not by itself justify the immediacy of a right of action for damages once the anticipatory breach is accepted. The issue is, therefore, whether an immediate action or an action at the time for performance is more appropriate. Since the *Hochster* case English law has committed itself to the idea that a claim for damages may be brought immediately after an anticipatory breach is accepted. We call this the 'immediacy rule'. Yet little has been said in the English context why this should be so.

a. Criticisms

An immediate damages claim may at first sight appear to be unwarranted for a number of reasons.[802] First and foremost, historically speaking, such immediacy has a fallible foundation. The English doctrine of anticipatory breach was from the date of its birth impressed with a confusion between a right to terminate the contract and a right of action for damages.[803] So much can be gleaned from the court's reasoning in the *Hochster* case, where it was held that, since the victim had a right to terminate the contract, it necessarily obtained a right of action

800 *Gunton v Richmond* (n 218) 470 (Buckley LJ).

801 *Gunton ibid* 469 (Buckley LJ); *London Transport Executive v Clarke* [1981] ICR 355 (CA) 367 (Templeman LJ). *cf Boyo v Lambeth* (n 560) 743 (Ralph Gibson LJ).

802 *Corbin on Contracts* (n 5) § 961; *Farnsworth on Contracts* (n 137) 551–2.

803 Mustill (n 4) 45.

for damages immediately after the contract was terminated.[804] Yet there is no necessary link between the two. It was thus once suggested that counsel for the defendant in the *Hochster* case should have argued that although an anticipatory breach entitled the victim immediately to terminate the contract, a right of action for damages did not arise until the time for performance.[805] Yet if the contract was terminated, the defendant would be discharged from his obligation to employ the claimant—what, then, would be the cause of action for a claim in damages that does not arise until the time for performance? It is suggested that had counsel made the above argument in the *Hochster* case, it is unlikely that the court would have reached a different decision. It would be absurd to reject the claim simply because the action was commenced on 22 May 1852, rather than on or after the date for performance (1 July 1852).

Secondly, the principal objection to the immediacy rule, of which the main advocate is Williston,[806] is that it seems to do injustice to the contract-breaker by accelerating its contractual obligations without its consent. In a theoretical sense, the point is well made. Assuming that the monetary value of contract performance is readily realisable, if before the time for performance arrives the victim is put into a position it would be in should the performance be duly rendered, this does seem to cause an unjustified additional cost to the contract-breaker. The additional cost is derived from the fact that damages may be paid prior to the time for performance. It must, however, be noted that, given the reality of legal proceedings, this is by no means a common phenomenon. Besides, it is not true that such an additional cost is always incurred wherever damages are paid prior to the time for performance. Where the performance involves non-monetary obligations, it might not be easy to show that an early damages award results in any additional cost. At any rate, even if such additional cost is established, it is easily reversible by way of a judgment that the victim must pay interest for the use of money before the time for performance. In other words, a discount must be given for the immediate receipt of a lump sum as damages.[807]

Finally, the immediacy rule can be said to put both the courts and the victim (claimant) into a difficult position as a judgment on a loss is required prior to the time when the loss materialises. Although the courts are empowered to defer the assessment of damages until a further trial,[808] such a power is exercisable only

[804] *Hochster* (n 1) 693–4, 927–8 (Lord Campbell).

[805] Mustill (n 4) 41; *Corbin on Contracts* (n 5) § 960.

[806] S Williston, 'Repudiation of Contracts' (1900–1901) 14 *Harvard Law Review* 317, 432; *Williston on Contracts* (n 780) § 63:34, § 63:35. He seems to have changed his stance later when drafting the *Restatement (First) of Contracts* § 318.

[807] *Interoffice Telephones Ltd v Robert Freeman Co Ltd* [1958] 1 QB 190 (CA) 196 (Jenkins LJ), approved per curiam in *Robophone v Blank* (n 770).

[808] CPR 3.1(2): '… the court may … (e) direct that part of any proceedings (such as a counterclaim) be dealt with as separate proceedings; (f) stay the whole or part of any proceedings or judgment either generally or until a specified date or event; …'.

in exceptional cases.[809] The difficulty is, however, more perceived than real. Even if the assessment of a future loss is necessary, as is often the case with long-term contracts such as employment or insurance contracts, the victim is required only to prove that the loss is substantial, without the need to show its exact amount.[810] The courts have displayed a general propensity to come to the victim's aid 'in guessing as best it could a future loss'.[811] In many actual breach cases the courts are similarly called upon to assess a loss lying in the future, yet it cannot be said that the victim should be denied a legal action until the loss it claims has actually materialised. At any rate, the mere fact that it is difficult to quantify a future loss is no ground for rejecting an action in damages.

b. *Justification*

Having dismissed the above criticisms, we are now in search of a justification for the immediacy rule. Clearly, the rule cannot be justified either on the ground that an anticipatory breach inflicts an immediate injury upon the victim or that a 'duty' to mitigate arises as soon as the breach is accepted.[812] The loss caused by an anticipatory breach is, as a norm, a total loss of bargain that materialises in the future at the time for performance. Meanwhile, there is no compelling reason why the time when a 'duty' to mitigate arises should dictate the accrual of a right of action for damages. The true justification lies in the facilitation of 'an early settlement of the dispute and a timely payment of damages'.[813] The doctrine of anticipatory breach receives widespread recognition largely because of its practical convenience. It would be unfair to anyone who lawfully terminates a contract (especially a long-term one) at an early stage that an action should be suspended and evidence be allowed to dissipate until the time for performance arrives. This is particularly so when the victim is entitled under the contract to instalment performances at different future times. Without the immediacy rule the victim would be required to initiate multiple actions of a similar description. No court should sensibly tolerate such wasteful proceedings. This conversely illuminates the importance of granting an immediate action for damages and of enabling the parties to resolve their disputes expeditiously. An immediate action would ensure a timely intervention by the judicial system. Indeed, without it, the doctrine of anticipatory breach would lose much of its attraction. The option of extricating oneself from the contract would be less frequently used and hence become less

[809] *A v National Blood Authority (No 2)* [2002] Lloyd's Rep Med 487 (QB) 492 (Burton J). Also, *Trans Trust SPRL v Danubian Trading Co LD* [1952] 2 QB 297 (CA) 307 (Denning LJ), 303 (Somervell LJ); *Deeny v Gooda Walker (No 3)* [1995] 1 WLR 1206 (Com Ct).

[810] H McGregor, *McGregor on Damages*, 17th edn (London, Sweet & Maxwell, 2003) [8–002].

[811] *Melachrino v Nickoll & Knight* [1920] 1 KB 693, 699 (Bailhache J); *Shindler v Northern Raincoat Co Ltd* [1960] 1 WLR 1038 (Manchester Assizes) 1050 (Diplock J); *Tai Hing v Kamsing* (n 145) 106. Also, *Applied Computer v Parallellweb* (n 372).

[812] *Cf Smith's Leading Cases* (n 14) 36, 149.

[813] *Corbin on Contracts* (n 5) § 961, especially fn 4. Further, Franklin (n 5) suggests that an immediate action for damages has the effect of encouraging actual performance of the contract.

effective in achieving its intended goal of conserving resources and preventing waste.[814] Even if that option is exercised, the fact that the dispute is yet to be settled may prevent the victim from committing its resources elsewhere. It is thus imperative that an anticipatory breach must confer upon its victim, along with a right immediately to terminate the contract, an immediate right of action for damages.

3. Unilateral or One-sidedly Executed Contracts

It is clear from the preceding discussion that the immediacy rule is premised on the conditional damages rule. Generally, an anticipatory breach triggers no right of action to damages at all, let alone prior to the time for performance, unless it is accepted. This fact has been relied upon to support a supposed exception to the doctrine of anticipatory breach. It is thus appropriate to take a closer look at the exception before we conclude this section. The exception, hardly visible in English law but widely recognised in the USA,[815] holds that where the contract is unilateral or executed on one party's side when the other party commits an anticipatory breach, namely, where the victim of an anticipatory breach is under no outstanding obligation at the time of the breach, no action in damages lies before the contract-breaker's performance falls due. To illustrate, on 1 January A and B execute a deed[816] under which A promises to pay B £100 on the first day of each of the remaining 11 months of the year if B swims across the River Thames on 10 January. The contract is unilateral. B is not obliged to swim. A is the only party bound under the contract. When B is just about to jump into the water, A renounces the contract. According to the exception, the earliest date on which B is allowed to file an action in damages is 1 February. Since the courts are generally not empowered to award damages by way of periodic payments,[817] if B does not want to bring separate actions on the first day of each of the remaining months, he has to wait until 1 December to claim his total loss. B's cause of action is not A's renunciation, but A's actual failure to make payment when due. The renunciation is transformed into an actual breach on each of the due days. The exception is said to be at its strongest where the future obligation anticipatorily breached is to pay money and there is formal

[814] L Vold, 'Repudiation of Contracts' (1927) 5 *Nebraska Law Bulletin* 269, 279–85.

[815] *General American Tank Car Corp v Goree (No 2114)* 296 F 32 (4th Cir 1924) 36. Also, *Farnsworth on Contracts* (n 137) 554 *et seq*. The exception has also been adopted by courts in some other common law jurisdictions, such as Australia and Canada: *Mackenzie v Rees* (1941) 65 CLR 1 (HCA) 15–16 (Dixon J); *Long Island Rail Road Co v Northville Industries Corp* 362 NE (2d) 558, 563 (1977) (Cooke J). Also, Dawson (n 61) 101.

[816] The primary reason for having a deed executed between the parties in the illustration is to eliminate any dispute over the existence of a binding and enforceable contract. It also ensures that the illustration represents the strongest scenario to which the exception is said to apply.

[817] *McGregor on Damages* (n 810) [1–013]. Periodic payments are awarded by the American courts in cases where, say, a disability insurer anticipatorily breaches its obligation to pay upon the insured's incurring a disability: *Corbin on Contracts* (n 5) § 969.

evidence of a debt.[818] Yet even in such circumstances it is by no means immune from controversy.[819] Courts and academics alike struggle to come up with a convincing explanation. As a result exceptions to the exception are created. The doctrine of anticipatory breach is said to apply where the contract in question is an option contract, a life insurance contract or a unilateral contract under which the contract-breaker's future obligation is due to be performed once the victim fulfils a non-promissory condition precedent.[820] The last type of contract can be illustrated by supposing that A's promise is to pay B the entire sum of money once he swims across the River Thames and there is no time fixed for A's payment. In such a case B would be entitled to sue A immediately following the renunciation, without the need either to complete the act of swimming or to wait for a certain period of time.

The possible justification for the exception can be examined in three steps. First, it is obvious that the exception does not claim that no anticipatory breach can be constituted under a unilateral or one-sidedly executed contract. It would be ludicrous to suggest that the contract-breaker's conduct should be treated differently according simply to whether the victim has any outstanding obligations under the contract. If the conduct constitutes an anticipatory breach under a bilateral executory contract, it must equally constitute an anticipatory breach under a contract which is unilateral or executed on the victim's side. Secondly, the exception can be said to rest upon the fact that under a unilateral or one-sidedly executed contract, it is not open for the victim of an anticipatory breach to terminate the contract and thus, according to the conditional damages rule, the breach gives rise to no right of action in damages. This is perhaps the principal justification thus far advanced for the exception. Nevertheless, it is distinctly dubious that the argument can be sustained. If the reasoning is that it is not open for the victim to terminate the contract as there is no outstanding obligation from which it may extricate itself, the argument is clearly misconceived. The termination of a contract does not depend upon the existence of some future obligations on the terminating party. It can be invoked solely for the purpose of putting an end to the other party's future primary obligations and substituting them with a secondary obligation to pay damages for the total loss of bargain. The victim may, therefore, terminate the contract even though it has no future obligations to perform. It might be further argued that the doctrine of anticipatory breach should have no application and an immediate right of termination (and hence an immediate right of action in damages) should not be granted where the main policy factor underlying that doctrine, namely, the need to

[818] Eg a formal bond, a promissory note, a bill of exchange, or other formal commercial paper: *Roehm v Horst* (n 5) 17–18; *Thomas J Daniels v Samuel F J Newton* 114 Mass 530 (1874) 532; *John A Nichols v The Scranton Steel Co* 137 NY 471 (1893) 487. Also, *Corbin on Contracts* (n 5) § 963.

[819] *Corbin on Contracts ibid* § 962; *Farnsworth on Contracts* (n 137) 555; DA Wiesner and J Klotchman, 'Anticipatory Breach and the Unilateral Contract: A Decade of the Status Quo?' (1982–1983) 8 *University of Dayton Law Review* 61.

[820] *Corbin on Contracts ibid* § 967; *Farnsworth on Contracts ibid* 556.

prevent future wasteful performance, is not present in a case involving a unilateral or one-sidedly executed contract. Yet the fact that the victim is under no future obligation does not mean that it is not susceptible to future wasteful performance. Under a unilateral contract, for example, the victim's future performance of a non-promissory condition may equally be wasteful in view of the anticipatory breach. Thus, in our illustration, there is a need to save B's time and energy in completing the swim. More importantly, the argument assumes that the doctrine of anticipatory breach is concerned only with future waste, not with past waste. There is no foundation for such an assumption. The need to alleviate or eliminate past waste, just as the need to avoid future waste, equally justifies immediate remedies. Besides, is it not true that where the victim has already executed its part of the contract, it is in greater need for swift protection than where it has yet to perform some or all of its obligations? The victim would be put 'at the mercy of the reneging party who may toy with [it] as he will'[821] if its only option is to wait for the contract to run its course and then claim damages when an actual breach arises. Further, the exception 'almost always operates in favour of the rich and powerful, and tramples on the poor and helpless',[822] for those who are due to perform at a later time than the counter parties are likely to have stronger bargaining power. For these reasons the conditional damages rule ought not to be considered to warrant the exception. Indeed, the fact that the operation of the doctrine of anticipatory breach requires 'some dependence of performances'[823] must not be taken to require the contract to be wholly or partially executory on the victim's side. Thirdly, it might be said that unless the victim has immediate remedies incorporated into the contract, such as in the form of an acceleration clause in loan contracts,[824] the contract-breaker would be unduly penalised by an immediate action by the victim.[825] This 'acceleration of obligation' argument has previously been dismissed as an objection to the immediacy rule in the context of a bilateral executory contract. It fares no better in the context of a unilateral or one-sidedly executed contract. As noted by Corbin, an immediate action in damages does not involve bringing forward the 'date of maturity' for the contract-breaker's performance; a judgment for damages must be distinguished from an order of specific performance, even where the performance specifically enforced is the payment of money.[826] When assessing damages the courts normally deduct interest that reflects the victim's earlier use of money. In this way an acceleration of the contract-breaker's obligations is

[821] *Corbin on Contracts ibid* § 962, supp [(A)][(2)].

[822] *Ibid.*

[823] *Restatement (Second) of Contracts* § 318. The doctrine has no application where the parties' performances are independent of each other: *Williston on Contracts* (n 780) § 63:60.

[824] *Farnsworth on Contracts* (n 137) 555.

[825] *Williston on Contracts* (n 780) 686: 'allowing the promisee immediate recovery is truly nothing but a direct bonus to the promisee beyond what was promised and a direct penalty to the promisor.'

[826] *Corbin on Contracts* (n 5) § 965.

avoided. To summarise this critique of the exception, it is fitting to quote in full the following remarks of Brennan J in the High Court of Australia:

> The principles relating to anticipatory breach put both a shield and a sword in the hands of an innocent party who accepts the other party's repudiation. His shield is the ending of his executory obligations; his sword is an immediate right to damages. … [A victim whose side of the contract is executed] has no need of a shield. But he may wish to brandish a sword. Although the paradigm case in which the principles are applied involves interdependent executor obligations, anomalies would occur if there were an unqualified rule that damages for repudiation by anticipatory breach should be refused where the innocent party has fully performed his obligations, but granted where he has not. Whether the contract be executed or executory, it can be said that repudiation causes the innocent party loss of the benefit of the contract. Indeed, where the innocent party has fully performed his obligations, a repudiation by the other party deprives him not only of the profit to which his bargain entitled him but also of compensation for the cost incurred in performing his obligations.[827]

In our illustration, although B is not bound to swim, he is allowed to brandish the sword and bring an action to recover for his total loss of bargain immediately after he accepts A's anticipatory breach.

To conclude this section, in order to claim damages for a total loss of bargain, the victim of an anticipatory breach must first have terminated the contract. Once the contract is terminated, the victim may immediately make the claim without having to wait for the time for the contract-breaker's performance to arrive. The conditional damages rule and the immediacy rule are both amply justified. They do not support the view that a unilateral or one-sidedly executed contract constitutes an exception to the doctrine of anticipatory breach.

B. Assessing Damages

The assessment of contractual damages is an enormous subject. Fortunately, the majority of the rules governing that subject apply irrespective of whether the breach in question is anticipatory or actual. Thus, we need only dwell on those rules that bring out the distinctiveness of an anticipatory breach. This section concentrates on three such rules. First, we consider the time by reference to which damages are assessed in anticipatory breach cases. Secondly, we explore whether an event which would or might have occurred had the anticipatory breach not been accepted should be taken into account in assessing damages. Lastly, the issue how the loss of a chance should be evaluated in the context of anticipatory breach is pursued.

[827] *Progressive Mailing v Tabali* (n 788) 44–5 (Brennan J).

1. The Time for Assessment

The time by reference to which damages are assessed in anticipatory breach cases is normally the time when the loss is sustained (hereinafter 'the time of loss'). This may, however, be altered should a 'duty' to mitigate arise before the time of loss.

a. The Time of Loss

Commensurate with the two limbs of the rule in *Hadley v Baxendale*,[828] the loss caused by an anticipatory breach can be divided into 'normal loss' and 'consequential loss'. Normal loss befalls 'every claimant in a like situation'; in contrast, consequential loss is 'special to the circumstances of the particular claimant'.[829] Accordingly, the time of loss can be ascertained by two different sets of rules.

First, since the normal loss caused by an anticipatory breach is a prospective loss of performance, the default rule is that the time of loss is the time fixed for the contract-breaker's performance. This must be contrasted to the case of actual breach, where the time of breach dictates the assessment of damages.[830] In *Michael v Hart*,[831] for example, where the claimant pledged with the defendant brokers certain stocks by way of security and the defendant before the date for settlement wrongly sold the stocks, it was held that the claimant, who duly accepted the anticipatory breach, was entitled to have the market value of the stocks fixed by reference to the date for settlement, rather than the date when they were wrongly sold. Since the market value was higher at the former date, the claimant was granted a larger sum of damages. Where the case involves an instalment contract, the market value must be calculated by reference to each of the dates on which performance falls due.[832] It has been held that the default rule still applies even though a substitute contract entered into at the time of performance is not to be performed until a later time.[833] It is also clear that the time of loss is generally the same whether an anticipatory breach is accepted or allowed to mature into an actual breach.[834] In a case with similar facts to *Michael v Hart*, *Ellis & Co's Trustee v Dixon-Johnson*,[835] where the anticipatory breach in question remained unaccepted, damages were also assessed by reference to the date when the pledged shares should have been returned—although on appeal there was some

[828] *Hadley v Baxendale* (1854) 9 Exch 341, 156 ER 145.

[829] *McGregor on Damages* (n 810) [1–036].

[830] *The Golden Victory* (n 793) [11] (Lord Bingham); [57] (Lord Carswell); [79]–[81] (Lord Brown); *cf* [34]–[36] (Lord Scott).

[831] n 145.

[832] *Roper v Johnson* (n 145); *Brown v Muller* (1871–72) LR 7 Ex 319.

[833] *Glencore Energy UK Ltd v Transworld Oil Ltd* [2010] EWHC 141 (Comm) [73] (Blair J).

[834] *Garnac Grain v Faure* (n 246) 1140 (Lord Pearson). Also, *Roper v Johnson* (n 145) 175–6 (Keating J)); 180 (Brett J). The action in *Roper* was brought before the final date of delivery, but the court in assessing damages applied 'cy près' *Brown v Muller* (n 832), where the action was brought after the final date of delivery.

[835] (n 328) 356 (Lawrence J).

disagreement as to when that date would be—rather than the date when they were wrongly disposed of.

Where the time for performance is not fixed by the contract, the identification of the reference time can cause difficulties. The issue has been raised in the context of a contract for the sale of goods, in relation to the applicability of the second limb of section 51(3) of the Sale of Goods Act 1893[836] to an anticipatory breach case. The first limb of that section, which generally designates the time for delivery as the time by reference to which damages are assessed, is clearly in conformity with the default rule discussed in the previous paragraph. It applies equally to both actual and anticipatory breach cases where the time for delivery is fixed. Where, however, no time is fixed for delivery,[837] according to the second limb, damages are to be assessed by reference to 'the time of the refusal to deliver'. This obviously clashes with the default rule. Yet it has long been settled that the second limb should have no application to an anticipatory breach. The leading case is *Tai Hing v Kamsing*.[838] On 23 March 1971, the parties entered into a contract for the sale of 1,500 bales of cotton yarn at HK$1,335 per bale, under which delivery was to be made upon one month's notice by the buyers. On 31 July 1973, the sellers wrongfully terminated the contract. The buyers accepted the anticipatory breach on 28 November 1973 and claimed damages. The market price for cotton yarn had fallen significantly. The buyers argued that the market price on the date of the anticipatory breach (31 July 1973), namely, HK$3,325 per bale, should be adopted for the purpose of assessing the damages, whilst the sellers contended that the time for assessment should be 28 December 1973, one month after the date when the breach was accepted, as the date of acceptance was the last day on which the buyers could have given one month's notice requiring delivery of the yarn. Lord Keith, in giving the advice of the Judicial Committee of the Privy Council and allowing the sellers' appeal, held that the second limb of the Hong Kong equivalent of section 51(3)[839] did not apply in an anticipatory breach case like the present and that damages should be assessed by reference to the date for delivery rather than the date of breach. The main reason given was that, since the market continued to fall following the acceptance up to the date for delivery, an application of the second limb would place the buyers 'in a better position than if there had been due performance' and would therefore 'represent an important inroad on' the compensatory nature of damages.[840] The sellers' submission that 28

[836] Now SGA 1979 s 51(3): 'Where there is an available market for the goods in question the measure of damages is prima facie to be ascertained by the difference between the contract price and the market or current price of the goods at the time or times when they ought to have been delivered or (if no time was fixed) at the time of the refusal to deliver'. There is a compatible provision in s 50(3) for non-acceptance of goods. Therefore, what is to be said of s 51(3) below applies equally to s 50(3).

[837] It might not always be easy to tell whether the time for delivery is fixed. eg *Melachrino v Nickoll* (n 811), where the first limb was held to apply where the contract stipulated that delivery was due when a nominated ship arrived in London. Compare this to cases discussed below.

[838] n 145.

[839] The Hong Kong Sale of Goods Ordinance s 53(3).

[840] *Tai Hing v Kamsing* (n 145) 104. Also, *Melachrino v Nickoll* (n 811) 698 (Bailhache J).

December 1973 should be the time for assessment was thus accepted.[841] The fact that no evidence was adduced as to the market price on that date did not worry their Lordships. They fixed the market price as HK$2,900 according to evidence as to the market price both prior to and subsequent to that date.[842] This case thus illustrates the principle that the time for performance does not have to be fixed by the contract, but must be capable of being ascertained by the court. In *Synge v Synge*,[843] for example, where a husband promised to make in his will a disposition of his house in favour of his wife for her life but conveyed the house to a third party during his lifetime, the wife was allowed to sue at once for damages based on 'the value of the possible life estate which she would be entitled to if she survived her husband'.[844] In coming to that value, the court would anticipate the time when the promised conveyance became due, taking into account the parties' comparative ages. Similarly, the fact that delivery is to be made within a reasonable time following an uncertain event, such as the lifting of a governmental export ban,[845] is no ground for setting a time other than the time for delivery as the time for assessing damages.

Secondly, where the victim of an anticipatory breach seeks to recover for a consequential loss, the time of loss is the time when that loss is actually sustained and may differ from the time for performance. A consequential loss may be recoverable either in addition to or as an alternative to the normal loss. An example of the latter is where a consequential loss is recovered as a head of reliance damages. The victim of an anticipatory breach may thus recover expenses incurred up to the time of acceptance,[846] which expenses are rendered futile by its acceptance of the breach, unless the contract-breaker proves that such expenses would not have been recouped had the contract been duly performed.[847] In this respect an anticipatory breach does not differ from an actual breach. However, an anticipatory breach must be distinguished from the future actual breach it foreshadows in that a consequential loss caused by the former may occur even prior to the time for performance. For example, as a result of accepting an anticipatory breach, the victim may incur additional expenses in reasonable attempts to mitigate loss. In *Gebruder Metelmann GmbH & Co v NBR (London) Ltd*,[848] the seller accepted an anticipatory breach by the buyer and immediately resold the goods. The resale price was lower than the market price at the date fixed for delivery. So the resale actually aggravated the seller's loss. It was nevertheless held that the resale was

[841] *Tai Hing v Kamsing* (n 145) 105.

[842] *Ibid* 106.

[843] *Synge v Synge* [1894] 1 QB 466 (CA).

[844] *Ibid* 472.

[845] *Millett v Van Heek* (n 145).

[846] *Anglia Television v Reed* [1972] 1 QB 60 (CA).

[847] *C & P Haulage v Middleton* [1983] 1 WLR 1461 (CA); *CCC Films (London) v Impact Quadrant Films* [1985] QB 16; *The Commonwealth of Australia v Amann Aviation Pty Ltd* [1991] 174 CLR 64 (HCA).

[848] *Gebruder Metelmann GmbH & Co v NBR (London) Ltd* [1984] 1 Lloyd's Rep 614 (CA). Also, *Banco de Portugal v Waterlow* [1932] AC 452 (HL); *Kaines v Osterreichische* (n 779) 12 (Bingham LJ).

a reasonable step taken by the seller to mitigate loss and therefore entitled it to recover the additional loss as a consequential loss.[849] For another example, in the rare circumstances where an anticipatory breach inflicts an immediate injury on the victim, the time of loss is the time of breach and invariably precedes the time for performance. In these cases, damages must be assessed by reference to the time when the consequential loss is actually sustained.

b. 'Duty' to Mitigate

That damages must be assessed by reference to the time of loss is qualified by the fact that a 'duty' to mitigate loss emerges. In such a case the time when that duty arises, rather than the time of loss, may sometimes be adopted as the time for assessment. The word 'duty' is, of course, a misnomer. The victim does not commit a wrong by failing to mitigate.[850] Instead, the victim is precluded from recovering for losses that it could reasonably have avoided. In the case of anticipatory breach, this has given rise to the issue whether the time of breach or the time of acceptance should be taken as the time from which mitigatory measures are required. Prior to the *Hochster* case it had already been settled that mitigatory measures, if they ought to be taken at all, should be taken at or shortly after the time of breach, which was the same as the time for performance.[851] The inception of the doctrine of anticipatory breach, however, posed a major challenge to this rule of law. Without doubt, in anticipatory breach cases a duty to mitigate should arise prior to the time for performance. But the real issue was whether a duty to mitigate arose at the time of breach or the time of acceptance. As early as *Frost v Knight*, Cockburn CJ in his famous dictum recognised that, as a matter of general principle, mitigatory measures might be required when, and only when, an anticipatory breach was accepted.[852] This was confirmed in a series of subsequent cases, mostly sale of goods cases, at the turn of the 20th century and the time of acceptance became firmly established as the time when a duty to mitigate arose.[853] It has been argued that it was unfair to impose on the victim a duty to mitigate at the time of acceptance as this duty would require the victim to forecast the unknown future for the benefit of the contract-breaker and to take the risk

[849] *Cf* the situation where the victim acts unreasonably, say, by contracting with 'a person who proved insolvent', *Brown v Muller* (n 832) 322–3 (Kelly CB).

[850] *Sotiros Shipping Inc v Sameiet Solholt (The 'Solholt')* [1983] 1 Lloyd's Rep 605 (CA) 608 (Sir John Donaldson MR).

[851] *Leigh v Paterson* (n 609); *Startup v Cortazzi* (1835) 2 Cr, M & R 165, 150 ER 71; *Phillpotts v Evans* (n 11) 476–7, 201 (Lord Abinger CB).

[852] *Frost v Knight* (n 87) 114.

[853] *Brown v Muller* (n 832) 322–3 (Kelly CB); *Roth & Co v Taysen Townsend & Co* (1895) 1 Com Cas 240 (QB) 242–3 (Mathew J), aff'd (1896) 12 TLR 211 (CA) 212 (Lord Esher MR); *Tredegar Iron and Coal Co Ltd v Hawthorne* (1902) 18 TLR 716 (CA) 716 (Collins MR); *Melachrino v Nickoll* (n 811) 697 (Bailhache J). Also, in Scotland, *Howie v Anderson* (1848) 10 D 355, 357–8 (Hope LJC), 359 (Lord Medwyn). *cf Nickoll & Knight v Ashton Edridge & Co* (1900) 2 QB 298, 305 (Mathew J), aff'd on other grounds [1901] 2 KB 126 (CA).

that the forecast might turn out to be wrong.[854] According to this view, a duty to mitigate should not arise until the time for performance. Clearly, this would defeat much of the purpose of the doctrine of anticipatory breach. The better view is that the difficulty in forecasting a future loss is a relevant factor to be taken into account when the courts consider whether the victim acts reasonably in seeking to mitigate that loss. It can be trumped by factors pointing in the opposite direction.[855] This means that the difficulty goes to the issue whether a duty to mitigate is complied with, rather than the issue whether that duty accrues to the victim. It does not by itself prevent a duty to mitigate from arising at (or shortly after) the time of acceptance.

Thus, where a duty to mitigate arises at all, as is normally the case where there is a readily accessible market, it arises when an anticipatory breach is accepted. An important, although not inevitable, consequence arising from the emergence of a duty to mitigate is that the courts would often replace the time for performance with the time of acceptance as the time for assessing damages. This consequence is illustrated by two modern cases. In *Koch Marine Inc v D'Amica Societa di Navigazione ARL (The 'Elena d'Amico')*,[856] the owners in March 1973 repudiated a three-year time charter that started to run from 10 January 1972. The charterers accepted the anticipatory breach but did not charter another vessel. In an action by the charterers for damages, Robert Goff J faced a choice between two methods of assessing the damages: (1) the difference between the market rate at the time of the acceptance and the contract rate for the balance of the charter period; or, (2) the profits which the charterers would have earned but for the anticipatory breach.[857] His Lordship adopted (1), rather than (2), as the 'normal measure of recovery' for the owners' anticipatory breach on the ground that, since an available market existed at the time of the acceptance, the charterers were under a duty to mitigate by chartering a substitute vessel.[858] The other case is *Kaines v Osterreichische*.[859] On 17 June 1987 the sellers repudiated a contract for the sale of 600,000 barrels of Brent crude oil for September lifting at \$18.48 per barrel, which repudiation the buyers promptly accepted on 18 June. The buyers bought in at the price of \$19.30 per barrel on 29 June. The buyers submitted that the relevant market price to be adopted for the purpose of assessing damages should be that at the date of the acceptance or shortly thereafter, namely, \$18.72 per barrel on 18 June or \$18.74 per barrel on 19 June. The sellers contended that the buyers were entitled to nominal damages only since no evidence was adduced as to the market

[854] *Brown v Muller* (n 832) 322–3 (Kelly CB); *Roper v Johnson* (n 145) 182 (Brett J); *Jewelowski v Propp* [1944] KB 510. Also, *Corbin on Contracts* (n 5) § 1053.

[855] *Corbin on Contracts ibid* § 1043–4; AL Goodhart, 'Measure of Damages When a Contract is Repudiated' (1962) 78 *LQR* 263, 270.

[856] *Koch Marine Inc v D'Amica Societa di Navigazione ARL (The 'Elena d'Amico')* [1980] 1 Lloyd's Rep 75 (Com Ct).

[857] According to the arbitrator, method (1) yielded £167,786 as damages whilst method (2) came up to a figure of £348,621.

[858] *The Elena d'Amico* (n 856) 81, 87, 90.

[859] n 779.

price at the date for performance and, alternatively, the reference date should be 25 June, the date when the market price fell to the lowest point between the date of acceptance and the date for performance, namely, $18.38 per barrel. The Court of Appeal affirmed Steyn J's decision that a duty to mitigate accrued to the buyers on 19 June, which followed immediately—allowing for some time for deliberation—the date of the acceptance.[860] Since the date of mitigation ought not to be fixed with the benefit of hindsight, 25 June was held to be irrelevant.[861] The court thus concluded that the damages should be assessed by reference to the date of mitigation, namely, 19 June, rather than the date for delivery in September. A mitigatory measure is, of course, not confined to a substitute transaction in the physical market. Where after making the contract a party seeks to hedge its market exposure by entering into a reverse transaction in the futures market, it may be required upon acceptance of the other party's anticipatory breach to close out the hedge if to do so is likely to reduce its losses.[862] In such a case the time of acceptance will again supersede the time for performance as the time for assessment.

To sum up, a distinctive feature of the doctrine of anticipatory breach is that damages are generally assessed by reference not to the time of breach, but to the time for performance. Sometimes when a consequential loss is claimed, the time for assessment may be brought forward to the time when that loss is actually sustained. Where a duty to mitigate arises the courts may assess the damages by reference to the time when that duty arises. In contrast to actual breach cases, a duty to mitigate arises not at the time of breach, but at the time of acceptance. These principles are critical to a proper understanding of the relevance of supervening events to the assessment of damages, to which we must now turn.

2. Supervening Events

By 'supervening event', we refer to an event unprovided for under the contract and not causally linked to the anticipatory breach in question. It is an event that would or might have caused the victim's loss to waver had the anticipatory breach not been accepted.[863] As aptly stated by Diplock LJ, '[w]here there is an anticipatory breach by wrongful repudiation, [assessment of damages] can at best be an estimate, whatever the date of the hearing. It involves assuming that what has not occurred and never will occur has occurred or will occur'.[864] Therefore, the courts are asked to look not only into the future, but also at the hypothetical. This

860 *Ibid* 8 (Steyn J).
861 *Ibid*; 11 (Bingham LJ); 12 (Dillon LJ).
862 *Glencore v Transworld* (n 833) [78].
863 We are thus not concerned with an event like the embargo of the Turkish Government in Watts, *Watts Ltd v Mitsui Ltd* [1917] AC 227 (HL), which, albeit it prevented the contracted journey of carriage of goods, could not be relied upon in reduction of the cargo owners' damages, because the carriers' prior repudiation had robbed them of an opportunity to insure against such an event. Further, Lloyd (n 485).
864 *Lavarack v Woods of Colchester Ltd* [1967] 1 QB 278 (CA) 294.

may give rise to uncertainty in assessing damages. Ingenious efforts apparently motivated by a desire for certainty have been made to deny any relevance of a supervening event to the assessment of damages by way of, say, locating either the time of loss or the time of assessment (namely, the time when the loss is assessed) at the time of acceptance. Nevertheless, it is submitted that the problem of uncertainty in this context is largely an invented one. As far as the assessment of damages is concerned, priority must be given to fair and just compensation. The central issue is: ought a supervening event to be taken into account at all in assessing damages? This subsection examines four theories that favour a negative answer. It will be shown that they actually mystify rather than clarify the doctrine of anticipatory breach. The first two theories concern supervening events in general. The last two are confined to two specific supervening events.

a. The 'Fictitious Breach' Theory

This theory claims that damages sought on the basis of an accepted anticipatory breach must be assessed as if the anticipatory breach had not been accepted and had matured into the anticipated actual breach and any supervening event inconsistent with this assumption must be disregarded. The most salient enunciation of this theory can be found in *The Mihalis Angelos.*[865] Clause 11 of a charterparty entitled the charterers to 'cancel' the contract 'should the vessel not be ready to load … on or before 20 July 1965'. On 17 July 1965, when the vessel was at such a distance away from the loading port that its timely arrival became virtually an impossibility, the charterers purported to terminate the contract on an invalid ground (force majeure). The owners immediately accepted this conduct as an anticipatory breach and lodged a claim for damages. The dispute centred on whether, the charterers' termination having been adjudicated as wrongful, the owners were nevertheless entitled to nominal damages only given the arbitrator's finding that the charterers would have exercised their right of termination under Clause 11 had the vessel proceeded to the loading port. In the Queen's Bench Division, Mocatta J held that since the charterers' wrongful termination constituted an anticipatory breach, their future exercise of the right under Clause 11 was irrelevant to the assessment of damages. Accordingly, the owners were awarded substantial damages.

In so holding the learned judge was persuaded by Robert Goff QC, who advocated the 'fictitious breach' theory. It was thus reasoned that since the charterers' 'assumed future breach', namely, a total failure to perform any of their contractual obligations when due, should be regarded in law as 'inevitable', the owners' damages were to be assessed as if they had duly tendered a ship ready to load on or before 20 July and had consequently suffered a total loss of bargain as a result of that breach.[866] This 'fictitious breach' theory was said to be 'compelled' by the

[865] n 136.
[866] *Ibid* 179, 182 (Mocatta J).

'artificial' doctrine of anticipatory breach.[867] Mocatta J placed primary reliance on Cockburn CJ's following words in *Frost v Knight*:

> The contract having been thus broken by the promisor, and treated as broken by the promisee, performance at the appointed time becomes excluded, and the breach by reason of the future non-performance becomes virtually involved in the action as one of the consequences of the repudiation of the contract; and *the eventual non-performance may therefore, by anticipation, be treated as a cause of action, and damages be assessed and recovered in respect of it, though the time for performance may yet be remote.*[868] (Emphasis added.)

Resort was also had to Devlin J's observation in the *Citati* case that the victim was allowed to 'anticipate an inevitable breach'.[869] Mocatta J believed that both statements supported his decision that the charterers' almost certain termination on 20 July was wholly irrelevant to the assessment of damages and the owners should be put into the position they would have been in had a cargo been loaded.[870]

In view of the fact that a previous, less sophisticated, dictum to similar effect by Collins MR in *Braithwaite's* case had been roundly rejected by the House of Lords,[871] it is not at all surprising that Mocatta J's decision was unanimously reversed by the Court of Appeal.[872] The appellate judges adopted three separate lines of reasoning. First, perhaps most significantly, the dominant role of the compensatory principle in assessing damages was asserted. Damages for breach of contract should accordingly be measured by 'the true value of the contractual rights which [the victim] has thereby lost'.[873] To that end the court 'must take into account all contingencies which might have reduced or extinguished the loss'.[874] Secondly, to require one to 'always anticipate not only a breach, but the worst breach' would lead to a 'manifestly unrealistic' result.[875] It was indeed a novel idea to use the charterers' anticipatory breach to support an assumption that the owners would have tendered a ship timeously. The charterers were entitled to have damages assessed in accordance with the least burdensome mode of performance for them, namely, terminating the contract when the ship was not ready to load on 20 July.[876] Thirdly, Lord Denning criticised the 'fictitious breach' theory as 'rooted in fallacy'.[877] The term 'anticipatory breach' was said to be 'misleading' because the 'cause of action' consisted in 'not the

[867] *Ibid* 177, 182: 'the doctrine of anticipatory breach is an artificial one. It may be said to be one of the legal fictions which remains very much alive'.

[868] *Frost v Knight* (n 87) 114.

[869] *Citati* (n 2) 437.

[870] *The Mihalis Angelos* (n 136) 182–3.

[871] Ch 5, text to n 479 above.

[872] This was by way of dicta. The appeal was allowed on the ground that the charterers were justified in terminating the contract for the owners' actual breach of a condition (in its strict, technical sense) by making a misdescription of the vessel on 17 July.

[873] *The Mihalis Angelos* (n 136) 210 (Megaw LJ).

[874] *Ibid* 196–7, 196 (Lord Denning MR).

[875] *Ibid* 202 (Edmund Davies LJ).

[876] *Ibid* 209 (Megaw LJ).

[877] *Ibid* 196.

future breach', but 'the renunciation itself'.[878] This attack on 'anticipatory breach' was shown in Chapter 2 to be too harsh. The word 'anticipatory' should not read as 'anticipated'. However, his Lordship's criticism over the 'fictitious breach' theory in the context of damages assessment is plainly correct. The Court of Appeal's decision in *The Mihalis Angelos* was followed two years later by Kerr J, who put another nail in the coffin of 'fictitious breach' by ruling that, where the owners under a charterparty withdrew their ship in anticipation of a prospective frustrating delay in the charterers' performance of their obligation to provide and load a cargo, the damages should not put the owners 'in a better position than if the ship had gone to [the port of loading] and waited', nor should the charterers be deprived of 'defences which would in that event have been available to' them.[879]

The main fallacy of the 'fictitious breach' theory lies in the fact that in effect it brings forth an acceleration of the anticipated breach rather than the remedies for it and thus treats an anticipatory breach as of 'the same character' as the anticipated breach.[880] This involves two types of confusion. First, the assessment of damages is a distinct issue from the constitution of a breach. In respect of the latter, an anticipatory breach is constituted by a reasonable inference of the anticipated breach. This inference, as shown previously, has a conclusive force. Its correctness is not susceptible to attack. A right of termination arising from the inference cannot be controverted by a supervening event. In this sense the anticipatory breach can be said to be 'fictitious', 'notional'[881] or 'assumed'. The reason underpinning the conclusiveness of the inference is that the putative victim needs to know with certainty whether or not it is bound by the contract. The same, however, cannot be said of the assessment of damages. With respect to the latter, certainty must give way to fair and just compensation. In assessing damages the central task of the court is to arrive at a figure that reflects as accurately as possible the loss sustained by the victim. It is not concerned with providing the victim with the certainty of knowing whether or not it is bound by the contract. Mocatta J's reliance on Devlin J's statement in the *Citati* case was thus clearly misplaced. Devlin J's statement was concerned with the constitution of an anticipatory breach only. It had no relevance to the assessment of damages.[882] Secondly, the general rule that in an anticipatory breach case damages are assessed by reference to the time for performance does not support the assumption that the anticipatory breach would have matured into the anticipated actual breach at that time had it not been accepted earlier. On the contrary, it dictates that all supervening events that may affect the value of the lost prospective performance must be taken into account.[883] In this respect, Mocatta J seemed to have misread Cockburn CJ's statement in *Frost v Knight* that damages

[878] *Ibid.*

[879] *The Angelia* (n 299) 229.

[880] *Citati* (n 2) 438 (Devlin J).

[881] D Tiplady, '*The Angelia*' (case note) [1973] 89 *LQR* 465, 466.

[882] Also, Carter (n 166) 426–7.

[883] Also, R Stevens, 'Damages and the Right to Performance: A Golden Victory or Not?' in JW Neyers, R Bronaugh and SGA Pitel (eds), *Exploring Contract Law* (Oxford, Hart Publishing, 2009) 196–7.

should be assessed 'in respect of ... the eventual non-performance'. Cockburn CJ apparently referred only to the default rule as to the time by reference to which damages are assessed. He said later in his judgment that the victim fiancée was entitled to damages 'in respect of the non-performance of the promise as though the death of the defendant's father—the event on which the fulfilment was to depend—had actually occurred'.[884] This is better to be interpreted as saying that the fact that the defendant's father was still alive should not preclude the court from assessing damages by reference to the end of his expected lifespan. The Chief Justice did not seem to be intending to say that the defendant's prospective breach should be accelerated to the present time and any supervening event that might have altered the value of his promise, such as the fact that he might be outlived by his father, should be disregarded for the purpose of assessing damages. It follows that, although by accepting the anticipatory breach the victim is absolved from further performance, it should not thus be treated as if it would have duly performed its part of the contract had the anticipatory breach not been accepted.[885] For these reasons, the 'fictitious breach' theory was rightfully dismissed in *The Mihalis Angelos*.

b. The 'Crystallisation' Theory

The 'fictitious breach' theory must be considered dead and buried since *The Mihalis Angelos*. Yet its phantom still managed to find a way into later cases. This time it was dressed up as a theory in relation to the 'crystallising' effect of a duty to mitigate upon the quantum of damages. The leading statement was made by Dillon LJ in *Kaines v Osterreichische*:

> [The date of mitigation] crystallises the position so far as the basis of a capital award of damages is concerned. The date so fixed by the Judge takes the place of the contractual delivery date as the date at which the damages are to be assessed. *Any further fluctuations of the market after the date so fixed are irrelevant*.[886] (Emphasis added.)

Notwithstanding the fact that Dillon LJ confined his observation unequivocally to market fluctuations only, the word 'crystallise' was later picked up and developed into a theory which drove any supervening event, market related or not, completely out of the damages assessment. Most strikingly, in *The Golden Victory*,[887] the theory was even relied upon to support a claim for damages greatly in excess of the victim's actual loss.

In *The Golden Victory*, the charterers under a time charter committed an anticipatory breach by prematurely redelivering the vessel, a breach promptly accepted by the owners at a time when the charter had still approximately four

[884] *Frost v Knight* (n 87) 117.

[885] *Cf* B Coote, 'Breach, Anticipatory Breach, or the Breach Anticipated?' (2007) 123 *LQR* 503, 509.

[886] *Kaines v Osterreichische* (n 779) 13. Also, SM Waddams, 'The Date for the Assessment of Damages' [1981] 97 *LQR* 445, 446–50.

[887] n 793.

years to run.[888] Thereafter the owners did not re-charter the vessel. Some 14 months after the acceptance took place, a second Gulf War, as described under Clause 33 of the charter, broke out. According to that clause, the War would have entitled either party to terminate the charter had it not been brought to an end earlier. The only dispute between the parties was whether damages should cover the owners' loss of future hire during the whole remaining four years or during the 14-month period up to the outbreak of the war. The House of Lords, by a bare majority (Lord Bingham and Lord Walker dissenting), held that a lesser award by reference to the 14-month period should be given.

The minority, however, took the view that the owners were entitled to have their damages assessed by reference to the date of the acceptance and thus to recover for their full loss during the rest of the contract. The dissenting judges' view rested on two different lines of reasoning. The first line of reasoning was that a duty to mitigate accrued to the owners on the date of the acceptance and crystallised their losses, thereby rendering the war completely irrelevant to the assessment of the damages. It is submitted that this line of reasoning was based on a misunderstanding of Dillon LJ's statement cited above and must be firmly rejected as it has fundamentally deviated from the mitigation principle in two important respects. First, any suggestion of 'crystallisation' in the sense of allowing recovery in excess of the actual loss inevitably runs straight into the compensatory principle, namely, that damages aim to compensate loss, not to enrich the victim.[889] A duty to mitigate merely places a ceiling on the recovery of actual loss.[890] It has been argued, however, that where the ambit of the 'crystallisation' theory is restricted to future market fluctuations, there is good reason for allowing recovery in excess of actual loss. It is thus said that the victim of an anticipatory breach is prima facie entitled to have damages assessed by reference to the time of acceptance, even though it later enters into an equivalent contract with a third party in a more favourable market.[891] This is mainly explained on the grounds that the victim speculates on its own account and should not be allowed to do so at the contract-breaker's expense,[892] and, under what is dubbed 'the reciprocity principle', the victim must

[888] Prior decision by Morison J in *Nippon Yusen Kaisha v Golden Strait Corp (The 'Golden Victory')* [2003] EWHC 16, [2003] 2 Lloyd's Rep 592 (QB). The charterers' breach is best seen as an anticipatory breach, as it is artificial to conjure up a present (most likely implied) obligation that would form the object of the breach. *cf* GH Treitel, 'Assessment of Damages for Wrongful Repudiation' (2007) 123 *LQR* 9, 10.

[889] *Longden v British Coal Corp* [1998] AC 653 (HL) 662 (Lord Hope).

[890] *Compania Financiera Soleada SA v Hamoor Tanker Corp Inc (The 'Borag')* [1981] 1 WLR 274, [1981] 1 Lloyd's Rep 483 (CA).

[891] The proposition originated in actual breach cases: *AKAS Jamal v Moolla Dawood, Sons & Co* [1916] 1 AC 175 (PC Burma), applied *Campbell Mostyn (Provisions) Ltd v Barnett Trading Co* [1954] 1 Lloyd's Rep 65 (CA); then extended to the context of anticipatory breach: *Melachrino v Nickoll* (n 811) 698–9 (Bailhache J); *The Elena d'Amico* (n 856) 89–90 (Goff J); *Johnson v Agnew* (n 180) 400–1 (Lord Wilberforce); *Kaines v Osterreichische* (n 779) 11 (Bingham LJ); *Dampskibsselskabet 'Norden' A/S v Andres & Cie SA* [2003] EWHC 84 (Comm), [2003] 1 Lloyd's Rep 287 [41] (Toulson J).

[892] *Jamal v Moolla ibid* 179 (Lord Wrenbury); *The Elena d'Amico ibid*. Also, MG Bridge, 'Mitigation of Damages in Contract and the Meaning of Avoidable Loss' (1989) 105 *LQR* 398, 408.

bear 'the risk of an adverse turn in the market' while it is in a position of taking 'advantage of a favourable turn'.[893] This proposition is, however, better viewed as being based on the fact that the equivalent contract entered into by the victim does not reduce its loss because it is *res inter alios acta* (a thing done between others),[894] or, in other words, 'an independent or disconnected transaction'[895] that generates 'an entirely collateral benefit',[896] rather than a 'substitute transaction'.[897] If the equivalent contract is shown to constitute a 'substitute transaction', clearly it must be taken into account when assessing the damages. Therefore, in so far as it is argued that a duty to mitigate 'crystallises' the victim's loss despite the fact that, by failing to comply with that duty, the victim has reduced the loss that it suffers,[898] the argument must fail. In effect, the argument allows the victim, precisely by admitting its own unreasonable conduct, to be put into a better position than if the contract had been duly performed. This is a draconian result. A duty to mitigate prevents the victim from profiting from its own unreasonable conduct. The 'crystallisation' theory does the converse, namely, to give the victim a windfall for failing to act reasonably. Therefore, 'crystallisation', if that word should be used at all, must be confined to the situation where, due to an unfavourable market movement, the victim's failure to mitigate increases its loss. The mitigation principle, by its nature, cannot be a justifiable ground for the victim to recover in excess of its actual loss.

Secondly, it is utterly unwarranted to extend the 'crystallisation' theory beyond Dillon LJ's clearly-worded ambit of 'market fluctuations' in the way the minority in *The Golden Victory* did. The mitigation principle prevents recovery of an aggravated but avoidable loss. However, not every aggravated loss is avoidable. In anticipatory breach cases, the most common scenario of an avoidable loss is where there is an available market at the time of acceptance. If the loss is a loss of an unmarketable contract performance, it may not be an avoidable loss and may not, therefore, be subject to the mitigation principle. In *The Golden Victory*, the majority recognised that, while a loss associated with the 'rate' of the hire was avoidable, a loss associated with the 'duration' of the charter was not.[899] Plainly, there was no loss to mitigate in that case, as it was not only impractical, but also unreasonable, to require the owners to find a substitute charter with a four years'

893 EA Farnsworth, 'Your Loss or My Gain? The Dilemma of the Disgorgement Principle in Breach of Contract' (1985) 94 *Yale Law Journal* 1339, 1374.

894 *British Westinghouse Electric & Manufacturing Co Ltd v Underground Electric Railways Co of London Ltd* [1912] AC 673 (HL) 691(Viscount Haldane LC).

895 *R Pagnan & Fratelli v Corbisa Industrial Agropacuaria Limitada* [1970] 1 WLR 1306 (CA) 1315 (Salmon LJ).

896 *Lavarack v Colchester* (n 864) 290 (Lord Denning MR); 301 (Russell LJ).

897 *Restatement (Second) of Contracts* § 347. Also, *Hussey v Eels* [1990] 2 QB 227 (CA) 239–40 (Mustill LJ); *Earls Terrace Properties Ltd v Nilsson Design Ltd* [2004] EWHC 136 (TCC), [2004] BLR 273; *McGregor on Damages* (n 810) [7–113]. *cf* D Simon, 'A Critique of the Treatment of Market Damages in the *Restatement (Second) of Contracts*' (1981) 81 *Columbia Law Review* 80, 88 fn 47.

898 Eg *Melachrino v Nickoll* (n 811) 699 (Bailhache J). Also, Farnsworth (n 893) 1374 fn 136.

899 *The Golden Victory* (n 793) [35]–[36] (Lord Scott); [64] (Lord Carswell); [83] (Lord Brown).

duration without an equivalent war clause.[900] In short, in a case like *The Golden Victory*, even if the victim's loss is aggravated by a supervening event, the victim is not ex post to be put under a duty to mitigate the loss. It is, therefore, sensible to confine the 'crystallisation' theory strictly to anticipatory breach cases where the loss to be sustained by the victim is avoidable. Dillon LJ's reference to 'market fluctuations' is a rough but convenient way of articulating this restraint.

The second line of reasoning adopted by the minority in *The Golden Victory* was a qualification to the 'crystallisation' theory and was employed to temper its vigour. It was suggested that, even though the owners' loss was 'crystallised' at the date of the acceptance, this did not exclude all supervening events from the assessment of the damages; the war should be excluded only because it was not 'predestined' at that date to happen.[901] In this way the Court of Appeal's decision in *The Mihalis Angelos* appeared to be distinguished. Whilst the charterers' cancellation of the charter in *The Mihalis Angelos* was at the date of the acceptance 'predestined' or 'inevitably bound' to happen, in *The Golden Victory* a reasonably well-informed person, viewing from the date of the acceptance, would have considered the war, far from being 'certain'[902] or 'completely certain',[903] to be 'merely a possibility'.[904] This test of 'predestination', when first presented to the arbitrator in *The Golden Victory*, was 'preferred', failing solely because he felt that he was constrained by prior authority to decide otherwise.[905] In *The Mihalis Angelos*, however, only Megaw LJ seemed to suggest that later events should be excluded from consideration if they were at the date of acceptance 'predestined to happen'.[906] By contrast, Lord Denning MR and Edmund Davies LJ merely said respectively that it was 'beyond doubt' or 'clear' that the charterers would have cancelled the charter at the end of 20 July, without indicating whether or not this was judged from 17 July, the date when the acceptance took place.[907] In *The Golden Victory*, Lord Bingham regarded all three judges as 'viewing the case as from the date of acceptance of the repudiation' and 'not taking account of later events'.[908] Yet in *The Seaflower*, Timothy Walker J explicitly distinguished Lord Denning's and Edmund Davies LJ's statements from, and followed them in preference to, that of Megaw LJ and clearly judged the 'inevitability' of the charterers' cancellation of the charter

[900] *Cf* D McLauchlan and N Hegan, 'Contract Damages: Fundamental Principle, Fundamental Disagreement' (2008) 46 *Canadian Business Law Journal* 89, 91.

[901] *The Golden Victory* (n 793) [14], [19] (Lord Bingham); [39]–[40] (Lord Walker).

[902] *Ibid* [30] (Lord Scott).

[903] *Ibid* [61] (Lord Carswell).

[904] *The Golden Victory* [2005] EWCA Civ 1190, [2005] 1 Lloyd's Rep 443, [9] (Lord Mance). Also, *ibid* [7], [22] (Lord Bingham); [45] (Lord Walker).

[905] *The Golden Victory* [2005] EWCA Civ 1190 [10] (Lord Mance). The prior authority was *BS & N Ltd (BVI) v Micado Shipping Ltd (Malta) (The 'Seaflower') (No 2)* [2000] 2 All ER (Comm) 169, [2000] 2 Lloyd's Rep 37 (QB).

[906] *The Mihalis Angelos* (n 136) 209–10, applied *North Sea Energy* (n 484) 496 (Waller LJ). Also, *Amann* (n 847) 114 (Brennan J).

[907] *The Mihalis Angelos ibid* 197 (Lord Denning MR); 202 (Edmund Davies LJ).

[908] *The Golden Victory* (n 793) [14] (Lord Bingham).

not from the date of breach or acceptance, but from some later date.[909] In fact, the test of 'predestination' does not seem to find favour with either conventional wisdom or established legal authorities. It was argued that defences that accrued before the acceptance should be made available to the contract-breaker.[910] Yet this fails to explain why only 'predestined' events may provide the contract-breaker with a defence. The test creates unnecessary complexities and is liable to give rise to the absurdity that, where an event 'predestined to happen' at the time of acceptance does not eventuate, damages must none the less be calculated as if it had occurred.[911] With respect to legal authorities, we need not look further than the *Hochster* case itself where it was proclaimed that the court 'would be justified in looking to all that had happened, or was likely to happen, to increase or mitigate the loss of the plaintiff down to the day of trial'.[912] In *The Golden Victory*, the majority readily accepted the long-standing 'Bwllfa principle', namely, that known facts should supersede any previous estimate and conjecture,[913] and confirmed that damages should be assessed with the benefit of hindsight. The test in that case was not whether the war should be regarded as 'inevitable' or 'probable' at the date of the acceptance,[914] but how it has turned out at the date of the trial.[915]

A principal consideration underpinning the 'crystallisation' theory and the minority's reasoning in *The Golden Victory* is that certainty and finality is too vital in commercial cases to be subdued by the compensatory principle and thus dictates that damages must be assessed conclusively by reference to the time of acceptance.[916] Similarly, Treitel also doubted why certainty and finality had, as suggested by Lord Mance in the Court of Appeal in *The Golden Victory*, to 'yield to the greater importance of' the compensatory principle.[917] The 'desideratum' of certainty and finality,[918] in fact, has a beguiling, yet deceptive, force. Its role in assessing damages is often overstated. *The Golden Victory* is not a case where the owners had to rely on a projection of future events in order to decide how to act. It does not concern, for example, whether, in the absence of the charterers' breach, the owners might, in anticipation of the war, extricate themselves from the contract.[919] The vitality of certainty and finality in that hypothetical situation could be justified by the practical imperative that compels the owners to lose

909 *The Seaflower* (n 905) 44. Also, *ibid* [62] (Lord Carswell).

910 Coote (n 885) 510.

911 *The Golden Victory* (n 793) [84] (Lord Brown).

912 *Hochster* (n 1) 691, 927 (Lord Campbell).

913 *The Golden Victory* (n 793) [30] (Lord Scott); [61]–[62] (Lord Carswell), approving *Bwllfa and Merthyr Dare Steam Collieries (1891) Ltd v Pontypridd Waterworks Co* [1903] AC 426 (HL), 432 (Lord Robertson); 431 (Lord Macnaghten).

914 *The Golden Victory* (n 793) [73] (Lord Brown).

915 *Ibid* [76], [78] (Lord Brown).

916 *Ibid* [1], [11]–[13], [17], [23] (Lord Bingham); [39] (Lord Walker). Also, Bridge (n 892) 409.

917 *The Golden Victory* [2005] EWCA Civ 1190 [24] (Lord Mance). Treitel (n 888) 10.

918 *The Golden Victory* (n 793) [38] (Lord Scott).

919 A shipowner might sail away on the ground of a reasonable inference that an event would frustrate the contract: *Geipel v Smith* (1872) LR 7 QB 404, 412, 414 (Blackburn J); *Hirji Mulji v Cheong Yue* (n 410) 508 (Lord Sumner); *Bank Line v Arthur Capel* (n 410) 454–5 (Lord Sumner).

no time in deciding whether or not to withdraw from the charter. The same consideration does not require damages to be 'crystallised' at the time of acceptance.[920] By contrast, in respect of the assessment of damages, the more fundamental consideration seems to be to avoid unfair overcompensation.[921] Consequently, *The Golden Victory* should be regarded as authority for a broad principle that a court in assessing damages ought to take account of all relevant supervening events. The time of assessment is the time of trial, not any earlier time. Although *The Golden Victory* itself involved an extraneous event, this broad principle is equally applicable to a supervening event that would have been brought about by either party had the contract continued. The next two theories relate to the latter type of event.

c. The 'Obligation Only' Theory

This theory concerns a supervening event that would have been brought about by the contract-breaker had the contract continued. It has long been settled that the contract-breaker is entitled to have damages assessed on the assumption that it will perform the contract in a way most beneficial to itself and not a way that is most beneficial to the victim.[922] The application of this seemingly entrenched principle to two differing situations has, however, caused some disparity of reasoning. On the one hand, where it is raised as a complete or partial defence against the victim's claim for damages, the supervening event is normally taken into account. In *The Mihalis Angelos* the Court of Appeal employed this principle to reject the owners' claim for substantial damages on the ground that the charterers would have exercised their contractual right to cancel the charter.[923] In this respect, it does not seem to matter whether the contract-breaker has a legal right or a mere freedom to bring about the event that diminishes or eliminates the victim's loss. On the other hand, if a supervening event is relied upon to prove an enlarged loss, then entitlement or freedom and propensity on the contract breaker's part to bring it about seems to be insufficient. The currently prevailing view is that in order for the event to be factored into the damages assessment, the contract-breaker must be contractually or otherwise legally bound to bring it about. We call this the 'obligation only' theory.

[920] *Cf* Mustill (n 95) 585. For a defence of the majority's decision from the perspective of economic analysis, Q Zhou, 'Damages for Wrongful Repudiation of Contract: An Ex Ante Perspective on Golden Victory' www.ssrn.com/abstract=1525469 (unpublished, forthcoming).

[921] *Tai Hing v Kamsing* (n 145) 104; *The Golden Victory* (n 793) [38] (Lord Scott), [63] (Lord Carswell). Also, JW Carter and E Peden, 'Damages Following Termination for Repudiation: Taking Account of Later Events' (2008) 24 *Journal of Contract Law* 145; D Capper, 'A "Golden Victory" for Freedom of Contract' (2008) 24 *Journal of Contract Law* 176.

[922] *Cockburn v Alexander* (1848) 6 CB 791, 814, 136 ER 1459, 1468–9 (Maule J). Also, *McGregor on Damages* (n 810) [8–060].

[923] *The Mihalis Angelos* (n 136) 202 (Edmund Davies LJ); 209 (Megaw LJ). Also, *Gunton v Richmond* (n 218) 469 (Buckley LJ); *The Seaflower* (n 905); *Littlehampton v Dorling* (n 351).

The principal authority is *Lavarack v Woods of Colchester Ltd*,[924] in which the claimant employee was wrongfully dismissed by the defendant employer when his contract had still two years and eight months to run. At the date of the dismissal the claimant earned an annual salary of £4,000 and a bonus. One year after the dismissal, the defendant increased the annual salary of all employees of the claimant's grade by £1,000 and cancelled the bonus. The key issue was whether the court in assessing the claimant's damages should take account of the salary increase of £1,000 per annum[925] in respect of the one-year-and-eight-month period of his contract during which the increase would have applied had the contract continued. The three appellate judges differed on this issue. The majority (Diplock and Russell LJJ) held that the increase should not be taken into account because the defendant was not bound under the contract to increase the salaries.[926] By contrast, Lord Denning MR adopted a test of 'probabilities and reasonable expectation'—a test based on 'the probabilities of the case' and 'the remuneration which the claimant might reasonably be expected to receive'[927]—in preference to the 'obligation only' theory, and concluded that the claimant was entitled to the salary increase.

According to the majority, the decisive factor was not the claimant's reasonable expectation but the defendant's legal obligation.[928] Consequently, a possible voluntary renewal by the defendant of the contract upon its expiry,[929] for example, should not be allowed to work in the claimant's favour. Diplock LJ contrasted the increase in salaries in the present case with the discontinuance of a pension scheme in a previous wrongful dismissal case.[930] Only the latter was said to affect damages as it was 'not a discretion as to the manner of performing' the particular contract between the parties 'but a discretion as to the way in which [the employers] would conduct their business as a whole'.[931] So the distinction was one between voluntary acts of the contract-breaker in performing the particular contract and those considered to be an 'extraneous event' to that contract.[932] In respect of an 'extraneous event', the test was evidently one of 'reasonable expectation'. It was thus said that 'one must not assume that [the contract-breaker] will cut off his nose to spite his face and so control these events as to reduce his legal obligations to the claimant by incurring greater loss in other aspects'.[933] On the

924 n 864.

925 The bonus was considered as too speculative to be included into the assessment.

926 Similarly, *Beach v Reed Corrugated Cases Ltd* [1956] 1 WLR 807 (QB).

927 *Lavarack* (n 864) 288.

928 *Ibid* 294 (Diplock LJ), citing with approval *Abrahams v Reiach (Herbert) Ltd* [1922] 1 KB 477 (CA) 482 (Scrutton LJ); *Withers v General Theatre Corp Ltd* [1933] 2 KB 536 (CA) 551 (Scrutton LJ), 298 (Russell LJ).

929 *Lavarack* (n 864) 297 (Diplock LJ).

930 *Bold v Brough, Nicholson & Hall Ltd* [1964] 1 WLR 201 (QB).

931 *Lavarack* (n 864) 296 (Diplock LJ). Also, *Mulvenna v Royal Bank of Scotland plc* [2003] EWCA Civ 1112 [34] (Sir Anthony Evans), [2003] All ER (D) 439 (Jul).

932 *Lavarack ibid* 294 (Diplock LJ), cited with approval *HSS v BMB* (n 173) [2006] EWHC 3677 [10], [11].

933 *Lavarack ibid* 295.

other hand, the 'obligation only' test would apply where the contract breaker's acts related only to the particular contract. On the facts of *Lavarack*, however, it is difficult to see why the increase in salaries should be regarded as something connected only with the particular contract between the parties rather than a general business decision, as it was applied to all employees of the same grade. At any rate, it will be shown that such a delicate distinction should not be retained and voluntary acts reasonably expected from the contract-breaker in performing the particular contract should be taken into account in assessing damages.

The 'obligation only' theory embraced by the majority in *Lavarack* has not been received warmly in later cases. In *Paula Lee Ltd v Robert Zehil Ltd*, for example, Mustill J opined that the critical distinction should be that, in valuing a promise, the court might take account not only of what the promisor could have done, but also of what it would have done, had the contract been carried out, whereas in fixing the content of a promise it was legitimate to look only at what the promisor could have done.[934] Even in the latter case, it was suggested, the 'obligation only' theory did not apply where the point in issue was not a choice between alternative modes of performance, but a determination of 'a single obligation expressed in an indefinite way'.[935] In respect of the assessment of damages, the correct test should be one of reasonable expectation and no role should be given to the 'obligation only' theory.[936] In *North Sea Energy v Petroleum Authority of Thailand*,[937] the claimant contracted to sell to the defendant a large quantity of Saudi Arabian oil throughout a five-year period. The delivery of the oil was conditional on the provision by the claimant of an official confirmation from Saudi Arabian suppliers that the oil might be used without destination restrictions. On 17 August 1994, the defendant repudiated the contract by prematurely insisting upon the immediate provision of the confirmation. The claimant maintained that it should be compensated for the value of a chance that the confirmation would have been given and it would have earned the profits under the contract. One major difficulty with this claim was that the defendant was under no duty to specify all the destinations where its end users had processing facilities and, if it did not specify the destinations, the Saudi Arabian suppliers would not provide the confirmation and the sales contract would not go ahead. Waller LJ, with whom Ward and Roch LJJ concurred, held that the claim should be rejected on the ground that the defendant could not have specified the destinations had there been no repudiation. In arriving at that decision his Lordship dismissed in principle the notion that the absence of obligation on the defendant's part in that respect should be an obstacle to the claim[938] and applied Lord Denning's 'reasonable expectation' test in *Lavarack* in preference to the 'obligation only' theory.[939]

[934] *Paula Lee Ltd v Robert Zehil Ltd* [1983] 2 All ER 390 (QB) 393.
[935] *Ibid* 394.
[936] *Mulvenna v Royal Bank of Scotland* (n 931) [35] (Sir Anthony Evans); *cf* [19] (Waller LJ).
[937] n 601.
[938] *Ibid* 483, 495.
[939] *Ibid* 494–5. The theory was also discredited in Australia: *Amann* (n 847).

It is submitted that the 'obligation only' theory should not be supported. There are three main reasons. First, the theory causes inconsistency in law and impedes even-handed justice. The contract-breaker should not be permitted to take advantage of a voluntary act of its own in reduction of damages and in the same breath distance itself from the act if it increases damages. The relevance of a supervening event to the assessment of damages must not be made dependent on the matter of in which party's favour it turns out to be. Secondly, as exposed by Mustill J's distinction in *Paula Lee*, the 'obligation only' theory may be considered as valid only where the issue is to define the content of a promise, rather than ascertaining its value. Whether the contract-breaker is obliged to bring about an event seems to have little bearing on whether the victim receives just and fair compensation for the loss sustained by it. Thirdly, the 'obligation only' theory overly favours the contract-breaker and unjustifiably prevents the victim from fully recovering for its actual loss.[940] Given that the victim establishes the course of action that the contract-breaker is reasonably expected to have followed had the contract continued, there is no need to create a fiction that the contract-breaker would perform the contract only in a way most beneficial to itself. Besides, the most beneficial way of performing the contract is not necessarily doing merely what one is contractually bound to do. Instead, the principle in *The Golden Victory* ought to be applied to ensure that the victim is fully compensated for its actual loss. The test of 'reasonable expectation' advocated by Lord Denning in *Lavarack* is generally consistent with that principle and should be preferred.

d. The 'Innocence–Guilt' Dichotomy

Where the victim of an anticipatory breach satisfies the court that it would have brought about a supervening event had the contract continued, which event augments its damages, there seems to be nothing precluding the principle in *The Golden Victory* from applying to this situation or preventing the victim from recovering the augmented damages, provided that its act of bringing about the event is not unlawful. In *Michael v Hart*, for example, one issue, which was left undecided because the parties came to a compromise, was whether the claimant client was entitled to have the damages assessed by reference to the highest market price between the time of the wrongful disposition and the time for settlement.[941] It seems that, if the claimant shows that he would have given the defendant broker an instruction to sell the stocks at the time when the market reached its peak but for the wrongful disposition, there would be no good reason why the damages could not be assessed by reference to that highest market price. Difficulties arise, however, where the event tends to decrease the amount of losses the victim sustains. A typical scenario

940 *Amann* (n 847) 136, 145 (Toohey J); *cf* 91 (Mason CJ and Dawson J).
941 *Michael v Hart* (n 145) 493 (Collins MR).

is where the victim would have committed a breach itself had the contract continued. In answering the question whether the victim's breach should be taken into account in assessing damages, the common law traditionally adopts an all-or-nothing approach.[942] Under this approach, the court's only task is to identify an innocent party and a guilty party. The guilty party is made solely responsible for the failure of the entire venture. The innocent party cannot be sued for damages even if it would have been in breach had the contract continued. Accordingly, if the victim is characterised as the innocent party, its future breach would be excluded from the assessment of damages. We call this the 'innocence—guilt' dichotomy.

The principal grounds for the 'innocence—guilt' dichotomy are said to be certainty and the reduction of litigation. To some extent this argument is identical to that underlying the debate on the suitability of contributory negligence as a defence to breach of contract claims. Of course we are concerned not with 'negligence',[943] but with a future breach, on the victim's part. Under the rules of contributory negligence, apportionment is permitted only where the defendant is concurrently in breach of a contractual and a tortious duty of care.[944] This instantly rules out the vast majority of anticipatory breach cases. The current law of contributory negligence has been criticised for its conservativeness and insensitivity to justice.[945] Although apportionment means that the court may have an increased workload and may be required to make difficult decisions as to how to divide the total loss between the parties, this does not by itself justify a bar against apportionment. In fact, apportionment does not seem to be liable to encourage litigation, because the parties' responsibilities under the contract should be, and normally are, dealt with in the same litigation. As for uncertainty resulting from an apportionment of damages, this seems to be more assumed than demonstrated. As noted earlier while discussing *The Golden Victory*, just and fair compensation should be recognised as the first principle in the assessment of damages and should trump any concern over uncertainty. The 'innocence—guilt' dichotomy is based on a false assumption that one of the parties must be innocent and the other must be guilty. Whether a party is innocent or guilty is often decided fortuitously

[942] Eg *DTR Nominees v Mona* (n 194) 433 (Stephen, Mason and Jacobs JJ).

[943] For a discussion of eight different types of 'negligence' on the claimant/plaintiff's part, A Porat, 'Contributory Negligence in Contract Law: Toward A Principled Approach' (1994) 28 *University of British Columbia Law Review* 141.

[944] The Law Reform (Contributory Negligence) Act 1945 s 1(1); *Forsikringsaktieselskapet Vesta v Butcher* [1989] AC 852 (CA), aff'd on other grounds [1989] AC 880 (HL); *UCB Bank plc v Hepherd Winstanley and Pugh*, The Times, 25 August 1999 (CA). *cf* statutes in Australian states and territories, especially Law Reform (Contributory Negligence and Apportionment of Liability) Act 2001 (SA) ss 3 and 7(2).

[945] A Burrows, 'Limitations on Compensation' in A Burrows and E Peel (eds), *Commercial Remedies Current Issues and Problems* (Oxford, OUP, 2003) 27, 37–43; TM FitzPatrick, 'Contributory Negligence and Contract—A Critical Reassessment Part II: At Common Law' (2001) 30 *Common Law World Review* 412.

on which party breaches, terminates or sues first in time. Evidently, a disregard for the 'innocent' party's future breach would lead to that party being overcompensated. This is so especially in view of the fact that the other party would not be able to bring a counterclaim for that breach unless it establishes an anticipatory breach on the part of the 'innocent' party. Furthermore, this also causes an inequality between the two parties. It cannot be said that, whilst the victim may rely upon a self-induced supervening event in augmentation of its damages, the contract-breaker may not raise the victim's future breach as a defence. For these reasons, the 'innocence—guilt' dichotomy must be rejected in the context of assessing damages.

The more rational approach, it is submitted, is to recognise that a party is liable to pay damages only to the extent of its share in the responsibility for the other party's loss. To prove that a party has committed a wrong does not automatically transfer all the blameworthiness to it. The establishment of liability must be severed from the assessment of damages. In other words, the courts should apportion damages between the parties, provided that it does not undermine the contractual allocation of risk. This is in fact not something entirely new to English law. In *Braithwaite's* case, for example, it was held that a deduction should be made to the seller's damages for the buyers' wrongful termination on the ground that some goods were inferior.[946] Collins MR, although he eventually came to the same decision, said that as a matter of 'strict law' no deduction should be allowed.[947] This view has been decisively rejected in a series of subsequent cases,[948] which in turn seemed to suggest the viability of apportioning damages. Lord Sumner, in particular, acknowledged that the victim's prospective inability might serve as a 'defence either as to the whole or as to part' of the contract-breaker's liability.[949] This seems to indicate that the contract-breaker might rely upon the victim's future breach in reduction of the damages payable. Furthermore, the principle in *The Golden Victory*, namely, that it is legitimate for a court to take into account all relevant supervening events in assessing damages, treats likewise the victim's future breach as a supervening event and is thus strongly in favour of limiting damages payable by the contract-breaker to the extent of its share of liability.

A rejection of each of the above four theories means that in anticipatory breach cases, all supervening events, except a failure by the victim to comply with a duty to mitigate resulting in an aggravated loss, should in principle be taken into account in assessing the damages. The issue how such events are to be factored into damages where they are not certain to occur is considered in the next subsection.

[946] *Braithwaite* (n 436).

[947] *Ibid* 552.

[948] *British & Beningtons* (n 207) 71 (Lord Sumner); *Esmail v Rosenthal* (n 457) 466 (Salmon LJ); *The Simona* (n 386) 803–5 (Lord Ackner).

[949] *British & Beningtons ibid.*

3. The Valuation of a Chance

Since in anticipatory breach cases the victim's normal loss is a prospective loss of performance and the courts are routinely called upon to look at the hypothetical, it is natural that the assessment of damages in such cases often involves putting a monetary value to a lost chance. It is, for example, usual that a supervening event is not certain, but merely has a chance, to occur. If such an event ought to, as argued earlier, be taken into account in assessing the damages, how should the chance of it occurring be evaluated? In response to this question, two possible answers may be given. The supervening event may be factored into damages according to either the normal test in civil actions, the 'balance of probabilities test',[950] or on the basis of the actual probability of its occurrence (the probabilistic test). The currently prevailing view is to apply the 'balance of probabilities test', which allows account to be taken only of an event that has a 51 per cent or more chance to occur and, in that case, treats the event as a certainty.[951] Lord Denning's test of 'reasonable expectation' in *Lavarack*, for example, seems to accord with this approach. By contrast, the probabilistic test insists that, whether a supervening event has a more or less than 50 per cent chance to occur, damages must be assessed commensurate with the actual degree of that chance. Where it is shown that there is a 51 per cent or more chance, this test may cause unnecessary complexities. In such a case the balance of probabilities test is more appropriate. When it comes to a 50 per cent or less chance, however, the probabilistic test should be favoured. The better view seems to be that the event, even if it has a 50 per cent or less chance of occurring, should be factored into damages on the basis of the actual probability of its occurrence. In the following paragraphs, we look briefly at some anticipatory breach cases which lend support to the application of the probabilistic test to a 50 per cent or less chance.

The question whether a loss of a 50 per cent or less chance might be compensated for was answered in the affirmative in the well-known case of *Chaplin v Hicks*.[952] That case involved an actual rather than anticipatory breach. It was held that the defendant, a theatre seeking actresses, failed unreasonably to give the claimant, one of the 50 shortlisted candidates, an opportunity to attend an interview and to compete with the others for one of the 12 posts advertised and was thus liable in damages. The same principle should apply to an anticipatory breach case. Thus, in an illustrative case given by one of the judges in the case, a wrongfully dismissed clerk, who was among five clerks out of whom two would be promoted at the end of the contract period, was said to be entitled to recover for the value of his contractual 'right to belong to a limited class

[950] *Miller v Minister of Pensions* (n 366) 374 (Denning J).

[951] *Amann* (n 847) 94 (Mason CJ and Dawson J); 111–13 (Brennan J); 130–1 (Deane J); 158 (Gaudron J).

[952] *Chaplin v Hicks* [1911] 2 KB 786 (CA).

of competitors'.[953] The unsolved problem is how far this principle should be pressed. It has been suggested that in pleading for a loss of a 50 per cent or less chance, the claimant must prove on the balance of probabilities the existence of the chance.[954] Another way of saying the same thing is that although the lost chance needs not to be more than 50 per cent, it must be 'real', 'substantial' or 'significant', not 'speculative',[955] and must have some assessable economic value.[956] It has also been said that a loss of a 50 per cent or less chance may be recoverable only where it does not flow from an event that may be brought about by the victim.[957] Yet, with respect to the applicability of the probabilistic test, there does not seem to be any difference in principle between such an event and an extraneous event like the war in *The Golden Victory*. Given that the occurrence of the event is based on the hypothesis that the contract had continued, it is immaterial whether it is the victim's making.[958] Therefore, in *The Seaflower*,[959] a case involving the victim's prospective failure to fulfil a condition precedent, Timothy Walker J applied the probabilistic test to determine the chance of that event occurring. Similarly, in *Applied Computer Expertise v Parallellweb Ltd*, where the claimant contracted to promote the defendant's internet connectivity service to the barrister market and that contract was prematurely terminated by the defendant, the claimant was held to be entitled to claim the value of its chance of earning the commissions.[960] The above anticipatory breach cases thus demonstrated the court's growing preparedness to depart from the balance of probabilities test and to give more scope to the probabilistic test.[961] A strong case in favour of the latter test was made by some members of the High Court of Australia in *The Commonwealth of Australia v Amann Aviation Pty Ltd*.[962] It is necessary to take a closer look at this leading Australian authority.

The Commonwealth government engaged Amann to conduct aerial coastal surveillance under a three-year contract. On the day when Amann commenced performance the Commonwealth, in breach of a contract provision which required it to follow a 'show case' procedure to explain its reasons before making any attempt to terminate the contract, purported to terminate the contract

[953] *Ibid* 795–6 (Moulton LJ).

[954] Coote (n 154) 768.

[955] *Chaplin v Hicks* (n 952) 792 (Vaughan Williams LJ); *North Sea Energy* (n 484) 495 (Waller LJ).

[956] *McRae v Commonwealth Disposals Commission* (1951) 84 CLR 377 (HCA). Also, Coote (n 154) 768.

[957] *North Sea Energy* (n 484) 495 (Waller LJ). Also, Coote (n 154) 768; *McGregor on Damages* (n 810) [8–035].

[958] *Cf* in respect of an extraneous event, *The Golden Victory* [2005] 1 Lloyd's Rep 443, [34] (Langley J); J Cooke et al *Voyage Charters*, 2nd edn (London, LLP, 2001), paras 21.14–15.

[959] (n 905) 44.

[960] *Applied Computer Expertise v Parallellweb* (n 372), citing *Trollope v Caplan* [1936] 2 KB 382, 401 (Lord Green), [1936] 2 All ER 842.

[961] Also, *McGregor on Damages* (n 810) [8–037]: 'a widening of the loss of a chance doctrine may be in the air'.

[962] n 847.

with immediate effect. Amann accepted this anticipatory breach and claimed damages for the difference between its wasted expenditure in acquiring and fitting specially designed aeroplanes, which expenditure clearly could not be recouped during the contract period, and a substantially lower price at which it disposed of the aeroplanes. When the case went up to the High Court of Australia, the only issue was about the quantum of Amann's damages. A majority of the High Court (McHugh J dissenting) affirmed the decision of the lower court[963] and awarded the substantial damages claimed by Amann. The matter that interests us most was the court's treatment of two supervening events. The first event was a possible renewal of the contract at its expiry. Amann alleged that, had the contract gone ahead, Amann would have been in a strong position, as compared to any new tenderers, to obtain a renewal and would have been able to recoup its expenditure and make a profit during the course of the second contract. The second event was a possible termination by the Commonwealth of the contract before it expired. The Commonwealth contended that it would have lawfully terminated the contract in conformity to the 'show case' procedure but for the wrongful termination.

As regards the renewal of the contract, all the majority judges were of the view that the 'obligation only' theory should not be an obstacle and it was immaterial that Amann had no right to renew. With the exception of Toohey J, all of them opined that the Commonwealth was bound, and failed, to prove on the balance of probabilities that Amann would not have been able to obtain a renewal and thus recoup its expenditure.[964] Toohey J, by contrast, believed that imposing on the Commonwealth such a 'strict onus of proof' would not necessarily lead to fair and just compensation.[965] He advocated an approach under which all 'significant contingencies' were 'balanced'.[966] A non-renewal, it was held, although it 'may have been unlikely' to eventuate, remained 'a distinct possibility' and should correspondingly be factored into the damages.[967] Toohey J applied the same approach to the second event, namely, the possible termination by the Commonwealth, and concluded that on the whole only half of Amann's wasted expenditure could be claimed.

In respect of that second event Toohey J had the support of Deane J, both of whom relied upon a distinction between past and future or hypothetical events.[968] Deane J was of the view that the balance of probabilities test, under which 'a 50 per cent probability represents a dividing line between certainty

[963] *Amann Aviation Pty Ltd v The Commonwealth of Australia* (1990) 22 FCR 527 (FCA, Full Court).

[964] *Amann* (n 847) 94 (Mason CJ and Dawson J); 111–13 (Brennan J); 130–1 (Deane J); 158 (Gaudron J).

[965] *Ibid* 142, 143.

[966] *Ibid* 143.

[967] *Ibid* 146.

[968] *Ibid* 122–4 (Deane J); 143–4 (Toohey J). Also, Coote (n 154) 766–7; *McGregor on Damages* (n 810) [8–028].

and non-existence or irrelevance', while it, if properly qualified, was generally applicable in the case of past events, 'would inevitably lead to injustice and a degree of absurdity' in the case of future or hypothetical events.[969] The probabilistic test should therefore be applied to the Commonwealth's possible termination of the contract. In order for a 50 per cent or less chance to be taken into account, its 'precise or approximate' proportion should be capable of being identified or estimated.[970] In the case the chance of the second event was fixed by the lower court at 20 per cent, which was unanimously endorsed by the High Court. Nevertheless, given that the renewal of the contract was as a future or hypothetical event as the Commonwealth's termination of the contract, Deane J's decision not to apply the probabilistic test to the former was difficult to justify. The reason could perhaps be found in the judgments of Brennan and Gaudron JJ, where it was said that, since Amann's claim was a claim for reliance damages, the Commonwealth had the onus to prove on the balance of probabilities Amann's inability to recoup its expenditure.[971] Had Amann claimed for expectation damages,[972] their opinions might have been different. The distinction between expectation and reliance damages in this regard was, however, unsatisfactory. It did not seem that the location of the onus of proof should determine on which of the two tests that proof should be made. At any rate the distinction did not sit easily with a proclamation by all the judges that both heads of damages were merely 'manifestations' of the compensatory principle.[973]

Notwithstanding the general adhesion by a majority of the court to the balance of probabilities test in the case, the approach adopted by Toohey J, and by Deane J in respect of the second event, is preferable. There is much to be said for the suggestion that in assessing damages the courts must refrain from being preoccupied by the balance of probabilities test and be more open-minded towards a real, non-speculative loss of chance established by the victim.[974] Since certainty is not a commanding consideration in damages assessment, to attain fair and just compensation, the probabilistic test ought to be applied where a supervening event has a 50 per cent or less chance to occur.[975]

To sum up this Chapter, a number of special rules apply when the victim of an anticipatory breach pursues the remedy of common law damages. We argued that both the conditional damages rule and the immediacy rule should be supported. Damages may be claimed immediately after the breach is accepted to recover for

969 *Ibid* 123, 124 (Deane J).

970 *Ibid* 120.

971 *Ibid* 114 (Brennan J); 151 (Gaudron J).

972 This was actually the decision of the dissenting judge, McHugh J, who hence applied the probabilistic test, *ibid* 176–7.

973 *Amann* (n 847) 82 (Mason CJ and Dawson J); 107 (Brennan J); 126–7 (Deane J); 134–5 (Toohey J); 154–5 (Gaudron J); 162–3 (McHugh J).

974 MA Eisenberg, 'Probability and Chance in Contract Law' (1997–1998) 45 *UCLA Law Review* 1005, 1052 *et seq*. Also, SM Waddams, 'The Valuation of Chances' (1998) 30 *Canadian Business Law Journal* 86.

975 Coote (n 154) 771, 773.

the loss of bargain even in the case where the victim has no future obligation to perform under the contract. Subject to a different measurement necessitated by a duty to mitigate, damages are generally assessed by reference to the time for performance. The natural gap between the time of acceptance and the time for performance sparks off a debate over whether a supervening event during that gap ought to be taken into account in assessing damages. Four theories have been advanced to support a negative answer. None of them should be allowed to stand. Indeed, the general rule that the time for performance is the time for assessment strongly suggests that an affirmative answer should be adopted. Where a supervening event has a less than 50 per cent chance to occur, it should still be factored into damages in proportion to the actual probability of that chance.

9

Specific Relief

In this Chapter, we look at the principal remedies available to a victim who does not accept the anticipatory breach. We call these remedies 'specific relief', as they all involve some form of actual enforcement of the contract. Our attention is primarily focused on a claim in debt for the contract price. It is in respect of this type of claim that the anticipatory nature of a breach is brought into the spotlight. It gives rise to the issue whether, and when, the victim may continue to perform the contract following an anticipatory breach and thereby earn the contract price. It is the task of section A to resolve this debate. Section B then briefly discusses the availability of a claim for specific performance or an injunction before the time for performance.

A. A Claim for the Contract Price

1. The *White & Carter* Principle

Where a party commits an anticipatory breach of its obligation to pay a fixed sum at a future time, is the other party entitled to continue to perform the contract and then claim that sum when it falls due? This question has received intense attention since the House of Lords' controversial decision in *White & Carter (Councils) Ltd v McGregor*.[976] Although the case is strictly a Scottish one, the subsequent development by English courts of the principle originating therein means that that principle (the *White & Carter* principle) can be properly regarded as part of English law. It is necessary first to look more closely at the case itself.

The pursuers were a company supplying litter bins to local councils and were paid by businesses like the defender in return for displaying the latter's advertisements on the bins. On 26 June 1957, when a three-year contract for displaying advertisements between the two parties was about to expire, the sales manager of the defender renewed it with the pursuers for a further term. On the same day the defender purported to cancel the deal, stating that the manager acted

[976] *White & Carter (Councils) Ltd v McGregor* [1962] AC 413 (HL Sc), 1962 SC (HL) 1. The Appeal Cases report will be cited thereafter.

without valid authority. The pursuers nonetheless proceeded with the contract and had the defender's advertisements displayed as contracted for. When the first few payments under the contract were not paid within the specified times, the pursuers brought a claim for the whole contract price pursuant to condition 8 of the contract, which provided that all of the defender's future payments would accrue immediately upon a failure to make any payment timeously. The claim was refused on two occasions in Scotland,[977] only to be allowed on appeal to the House of Lords by a narrow 3:2 margin. Both parties had prior authority on which they could rely. The pursuers relied upon *White & Carter (Councils) Ltd v Harding*,[978] a case where they had successfully enforced an identical clause against a different client. The defender looked instead to a then leading Scottish authority, *Langford & Co Ltd v Dutch*, where Lord President Cooper said that the victim of a repudiation could not force its performance upon the repudiator and 'the only reasonable and proper course' for it to take was to accept the repudiation and be content with a claim for damages.[979]

In upholding the pursuers' claim, their Lordships in the majority adopted two distinct approaches. They all started from the general principle that the victim of an anticipatory breach had an unfettered option whether to accept it or not and that it was under no duty to enforce its contractual rights in a reasonable way.[980] However, while Lord Hodson denied any room for an exception to the general principle and rejected any role for equity in this regard,[981] Lord Reid admitted two grounds on which the general principle could be departed from. First, the present case belonged to a small number of cases where the victim could perform its side of the contract without any co-operation from the contract-breaker; otherwise the claim would fail right away as the defender could not be compelled to co-operate.[982] We henceforth call this the 'co-operation qualification'. Secondly, the victim's contractual rights might be restrained on the ground of 'some general equitable principle or element of public policy', where the contract-breaker should be able to show that the victim 'has no legitimate interest, financial or otherwise, in performing the contract rather than claiming damages'.[983] We henceforth call this the 'legitimate interest qualification'. The defender's ignorance of the need, and hence its failure, to show a lack of 'legitimate interest' on the victim's part eventually cost it the case.

977 First by the Sheriff Court and then: *White & Carter (Councils) Ltd v McGregor* 1960 SC 276 (CSIH).

978 (unreported, CA, 21 May 1958). The only factual difference with *McGregor* was that in *Harding* repudiation occurred some two months after the pursuers had started to display advertisements. But this hardly matters as in both cases the victim continued to perform the contract after the repudiation.

979 1952 SC 15 (CSIH) 18.

980 *White & Carter* (n 976) 427, 430 (Lord Reid); 445 (Lord Hodson). Lord Tucker concurred with Lord Hodson.

981 *Ibid* 445.

982 *Ibid* 429.

983 *Ibid* 430–31.

The two judges in the minority, in contrast, relying as they did upon a range of different legal grounds, expressed a concern that the pursuers had engaged in an 'unreasonable and oppressive' course of action.[984] There appeared to be two distinct lines of reasoning. First, the pursuers were in effect 'claiming a kind of inverted specific performance',[985] whilst specific performance could not be decreed in the present case. When making this observation their Lordships referred to the Scottish law of specific implement, which is very different from, and probably more generous to the claimant/pursuer than, the English law of specific performance. Nevertheless, the argument can be equally raised in the English context. According to English law, the contract in *White & Carter* was clearly not one in respect of which specific performance was available. It can thus be said that the pursuers' claim for the contract price, if permitted, would achieve what a claim for specific performance would not achieve and would therefore defeat the policing reasons that necessitated the rejection of the latter claim. Secondly, the minority also argued that the pursuers in carrying on performance contravened a duty to mitigate their losses.[986] Lord Keith, in addition, raised three points in support of his decision, namely, automatic termination,[987] the mutuality of contract[988] and an analogy with a contract of personal service.[989] All three points were, in fact, as shall be shown in due course, of very limited assistance to his Lordship's cause.

A hypothetical example relied upon by counsel for the defender, adverted to by their Lordships,[990] well illustrated their differences in opinion. A company commissioned an expert to write a report and, before he could incur any expenses, repudiated the contract. Was the expert entitled to proceed to finish the report and claim the agreed remuneration? Whilst Lord Reid left the matter open by saying that it 'might be' that the company could show a lack of 'legitimate interest' on the expert's part,[991] it was said to be 'strange'[992] or 'startling',[993] by Lord Morton and Lord Keith respectively, that an affirmative answer would be given.

The decision in *White & Carter* has not been warmly received by lower courts and has stirred up a great deal of controversy among commentators. There has been, for example, some uncertainty as to whether Lord Reid's two qualifications formed part of the ratio of the case. The other two majority judges did not endorse the qualifications. In this respect, they should therefore be regarded as dicta only.[994] Yet it can of course be said that without Lord Reid there would be

984 *Ibid* 434 (Lord Morton).
985 *Ibid* 433. Also, 438 (Lord Keith).
986 *Ibid* 433 (Lord Morton); 439 (Lord Keith).
987 *Ibid* 436.
988 *Ibid* 439.
989 *Ibid*.
990 *Ibid* 428–9 (Lord Reid); 432 (Lord Morton); 442 (Lord Keith).
991 *Ibid* 431.
992 *Ibid* 432 (Lord Morton).
993 *Ibid* 442 (Lord Keith).
994 *Clea Shipping Corp v Bulk Oil International Ltd (The 'Alaskan Trader') (No 2)* [1984] 1 All ER 129 (QB) 133 (Lloyd J).

no majority.[995] Therefore the qualifications are better seen as part of the ratio. In any event, having been repeatedly adopted or applied by lower courts including the Court of Appeal, they are now incontrovertibly seen as an integral component of the *White & Carter* principle. Nevertheless, the decision in *White & Carter*, albeit constantly followed, has been described as 'a striking decision'[996] and one which should be kept to a case that is 'precisely on all fours with' its facts.[997] It was also both criticised as 'grotesque'[998] and defended as 'both legally and logically inevitable'.[999] Was *White & Carter* correctly decided, in terms of both legal principle and its application to the facts? Should any of their Lordships' speeches, especially that of Lord Reid, be regarded as embodying the most appropriate approach to future like cases? In order to attain a balanced view, we must start with a broad exploration of the critical issue raised by the case and the competing values and policies underpinning it.

2. Identifying the Issue

The legal issue posed in a factual situation akin to *White & Carter* has been variously stated. In general, it can be put in three different ways. First, the issue has been seen as one relating to the availability of an option to keep the contract alive.[1000] There is a theory that, where a contract is or is analogous to a contract of personal service, it should automatically come to an end once an anticipatory breach is communicated. Secondly, there have been suggestions that *White & Carter* was concerned not with the victim's option, but with its ability to resort to a claim for the contract price.[1001] As Sachs LJ succinctly put it, 'it is the range of remedies that is limited, not the right to elect'.[1002] Thus, '[t]he court is not exercising a dispensing power; nor is it rewriting an improvident contract. It is simply refusing a certain kind of relief'.[1003] Thirdly, it can be argued that the real issue concerns whether, and to what extent, a party is allowed, in the face of an anticipatory breach by the other party, to persist in a wasteful performance.[1004] In other words, it is on this third view the appropriateness of the continuance

[995] *Hounslow LBC v Twickenham Garden Developments Ltd* [1971] Ch 233, 254 (Megarry J).

[996] *Ibid* 251.

[997] *Attica Sea Carriers Corp v Ferrostaal Poseidon Bulk Reederei GMBH (The 'Puerto Buitrago')* [1976] 1 Lloyd's Rep 250 (CA) 255 (Lord Denning MR). Also, *ibid* 253: the decision should be confined to a case 'fairly within the contemplation of their Lordships'; *Ministry of Sound (Ireland) Ltd v World Online Ltd* [2003] EWHC 2178 (Ch), [2003] 2 All ER (Comm) 823 [71] (Mr Nicholas Strauss QC): 'a degree of judicial reluctance over the last 40 years to apply White and Carter outside the strict limits of its ratio'.

[998] Furmston (n 151) 782.

[999] E Tabachnik, 'Anticipatory Breach of Contract' (1972) 25 *Current Legal Problems* 149, 166.

[1000] *White & Carter* (n 976) 439 (Lord Keith); 444–5 (Lord Hodson).

[1001] *Decro-Wall* (n 201) 370 (Salmon LJ); 375–6 (Sachs LJ); 381 (Buckley LJ).

[1002] *Ibid* 375.

[1003] *The Alaskan Trader* (n 994) 137 (Lloyd J). Also, *The Odenfeld* (n 588) 373 (Kerr J).

[1004] Eg JW Carter, A Phang and SY Phang, 'Performance Following Repudiation: Legal and Economic Interests' (1999) 15 *Journal of Contract Law* 1, 98–9.

of performance, rather than the freedom to continue with the contract or the availability of a claim for the contract price, that sits at the distinctive core of the *White & Carter* principle. The above three formulations of the issue in *White & Carter* have obvious connections. If an anticipatory breach automatically terminates the contract, thereby giving rise to a right to claim damages only, the other two formulations would be irrelevant. The ability to claim the contract price, albeit distinct from the appropriateness of continuing performance, depends in large part on the latter. It will be shown below that these three formulations must be either rejected or substantially improved.

a. Automatic Termination

The first formulation stems from a debate as to whether a contract of personal service forms an exception to the general rule that an anticipatory breach does not automatically terminate the contract but merely vests in the victim a power to terminate. Two opposing views present themselves.[1005] One, usually dubbed the 'elective (or acceptance) view', treats a contract of personal service as no different from other types of contracts. The other, usually dubbed the 'unilateral (or automatic termination) view', excludes such a contract from the general rule. The legal authorities are divided, but as a matter of precedent it seems to be the 'elective view' that has thus far gained the upper hand.[1006] In view of this conflicting line of authority, it has been thus admitted that this area of law was 'distinctly lacking in rhyme and reason'.[1007] The first formulation assumes that the unilateral view is tenable at least in some cases. If that view is based on the fact that a wrongful dismissal destroys the victim's status as an employee and thus disentitles him to claim wages,[1008] then a contract of personal service should be regarded as sui generis in this respect. However, if the unilateral view is founded on a more general basis, this would open the door to an enquiry into whether an anticipatory breach in a given case is such that it would automatically terminate the contract and thus vaporise any hope of the victim claiming the contract price. Two such general arguments emerge.

The first argument is that, where an employee is wrongfully dismissed, since s/he is generally not entitled to specific relief,[1009] including a claim for unearned

1005 These two views were helpfully summarised in *Robert Cort & Son Ltd v Charman* [1981] ICR 816 (EAT) 819 (Browne-Wilkinson J). Also, *Dietman v Brent* (n 561) 753 (Hodgson J).

1006 This view was adopted and applied by a majority of the Court of Appeal as *ratio* in *Gunton v Richmond* (n 218) and by the High Court in two later cases: *Thomas Marshall v Guinle* (n 314); *Dietman v Brent* (n 561). By contrast, the most significant recognition of the 'unilateral view' has been Viscount Kilmuir LC's dictum in *Vine v National Dock Labour Board* [1957] AC 488 (HL) 500, endorsing Jenkins LJ's statement in the first appeal: [1956] 1 QB 658 (CA) 674, and the ratio of the decision of the National Industrial Relations Court (since abolished by the Trade Union and Labour Relations Act 1974) in *Sanders v Ernest A Neale Ltd* [1974] ICR 565.

1007 *Boyo v Lambeth* (n 560) 748 (Staughton J).

1008 *Ministry of Sound v World Online* (n 997) [58] (Strauss QC), citing with approval *Gunton v Richmond* (n 218) 778 (Brightman LJ).

1009 *Jerome Francis v The Municipal Councillors of Kuala Lumpur* [1962] 1 WLR 1411 (PC Federated Malay States) 1417–18; *Boyo v Lambeth* (n 560) 743 (Ralph Gibson LJ), 747 (Staughton J), 749–50 (Sir

wages,[1010] the wrongful dismissal must have automatically terminated the contract, leaving the employee with a claim for damages only. This argument can be extended to other types of contracts. Accordingly, whether an anticipatory breach automatically terminates the contract would depend on the availability of specific relief. Where specific relief is not available to the victim, the contract is automatically terminated and the victim has no option to keep it alive. This argument, however, seems to put the cart before the horse. Furthermore, its logic is evidently flawed. The subsistence of a contract is a necessary, but not sufficient, reason for seeking specific relief. Conversely, even where specific relief is unavailable, the victim may still have 'good reasons' to keep the contract alive.[1011] An option to preserve the contract following an anticipatory breach is thus not, as Shaw LJ once suggested, 'an empty formality'.[1012]

The second argument in support of the unilateral view is that automatic termination hinges on the seriousness of an anticipatory breach. This is one possible interpretation of the assertion that a wrongful dismissal, if it destroys the relationship of trust and confidence between the parties, would automatically terminate the contract.[1013] More generally, Lord Denning once observed that, whilst certain actual breaches might automatically terminate the contract, no anticipatory breach could have such an effect.[1014] Presumably, the second part of this observation is attributable to the fact that an anticipatory breach is a retractable wrong. However, if the first part of his Lordship's observation is explicable on the ground that an actual breach might be so serious that it should be treated in the same way as a frustrating event,[1015] it is arguable that the same could be said of an anticipatory breach, such as where it renders further performance of the contract impossible. If the seller under a contract for the sale of a unique painting burns it to ashes, it does not seem to matter whether the incident happens before or after the

Francis Purchas). For specific performance or injunctions, *Chappell v Times Newspapers Ltd* [1975] ICR 145 (CA); *Marsh v National Autistic Society* [1993] ICR 453 (EAT). For declaratory judgment, RSC Ord 25 r5; *R v East Berkshire Health Authority, ex parte Walsh* [1984] ICR 743 (CA) 757 (May LJ); *cf Howard v Pickford* (n 94).

1010 *Mackay v Dick* (1881) 6 App Cas 251 (HL); *Vine v National Dock* (n 1006) 674 (Jenkins LJ); *Denmark Productions v Boscobel* (n 435) 732 (Winn LJ); *Gunton v Richmond* (n 218) 468 (Buckley LJ).

1011 *Hill v Parsons* [1972] Ch 305 (CA) 319–20 (Sachs LJ), *cf* 314 (Lord Denning MR); *Gunton v Richmond* (n 218) 469 (Buckley LJ), 475 (Brightman LJ); *London Transport v Clarke* (n 801) 366 (Templeman LJ); *Rigby v Ferodo Ltd* [1988] ICR 29 (HL) 34 (Lord Oliver).

1012 *Gunton ibid*, 459.

1013 *Ibid*; *Hill v Parsons* (n 1011) 314 (Lord Denning MR), 474 (Brightman LJ); *Chappell v Times Newspapers* (n 1009) 178 (Geoffrey Lane LJ). Also, Perrins (n 259) [2229], [2261]–[2262].

1014 *London Transport v Clarke* (n 801) 362. His Lordship used two examples to illustrate the point: while an employee might retract a previous refusal to work, the contract of employment was automatically terminated when he walked off and worked for another employer (362–3).

1015 *Ibid*. His Lordship cited Blackburn J's statement in *Poussard v Spiers & Pond* (1876) 1 QBD 410, 414–15. But Blackburn J spoke loosely of a breach 'discharging' the parties and did not seem to turn his mind to whether the 'discharge' was effected automatically or as a result of the victim's exercise of its right of termination. Also, *Jackson v Union Marine Insurance Co Ltd* (1874) LR 10 CP 125 (EC) 145 (Bramwell B); Carter (n 166) 432.

time for delivery. There are several responses to this argument.[1016] First, not only is it hard to discern any rational basis for linking the seriousness of a breach with the legal effect of automatic termination, but it also seems to contradict established authority to regard frustration cases as resting upon a more stringent test of seriousness than that applied in termination for breach cases.[1017] As noted earlier, the reason why the victim of an anticipatory breach should be given a choice whether or not to terminate the contract is to prevent the contract-breaker from taking advantage of its own wrong and to protect the victim. Secondly, a realistic propensity to terminate must not be confused with a legal right to terminate. In particular, an anticipatory breach that destroys a relationship of trust and confidence between the parties and thus extinguishes the 'de facto' employment does not necessarily also terminate the 'de jure' employment, namely, the contract.[1018] It does not reduce the number of options open to the victim; it merely makes the option of termination practically more plausible for it.[1019] The fact that a degree of co-operation is required for most contracts to be performed does not derogate from the root principle that the victim has an option whether or not to accept a repudiation.[1020] Thirdly, the 'impossibility' cases are commonly solved, as said earlier, by holding the victim to have impliedly accepted the anticipatory breach. This is so especially if the courts take the view that the time has arrived for 'deadlocked situations' created by two uncompromising parties to come to an end.[1021]

All in all, the 'unilateral view' was rightly condemned by Templeman LJ as 'contrary to principle, unsupported by authority … and undesirable in practice'.[1022] What lies between a contract of personal service and other types of contract is 'a difference in procedure, not in principle'.[1023] The first formulation of the issue in *White & Carter* is both illusory and futile and must thus be rejected. It is illusory because it should be accepted that the victim of an anticipatory breach has an option whether or not to terminate the contract. It is futile because if the victim decides not to terminate the contract, it does not necessarily follow that it is entitled to the contract price.

b. Availability of Specific Relief

The second formulation of the issue in *White & Carter* postulates that an enquiry should be had into whether a claim for the contract price is available to the victim of an anticipatory breach. This formulation has two dimensions. First, the

1016 The argument was rejected, for instance, by Moore-Bick J in *Portaga v Brazil* (n 374).

1017 *Poussard* (n 1015); *Hongkong Fir* (n 203) 66 (Diplock LJ).

1018 *Dellys v Elderslie Finance Corp Ltd* [2002] WASCA 161 [38] (Anderson J).

1019 *Decro-Wall* (n 201) 369–70 (Salmon LJ), 376 (Sachs LJ); *Gunton v Richmond* (n 218) 468 (Buckley LJ).

1020 *Regent International Hotels (UK) Ltd v Pageguide Ltd* (unreported, QB, 6 March 1985).

1021 *The Odenfeld* (n 588) 375, 379 (Kerr J).

1022 *London Transport v Clarke* (n 801) 368. Also, FD Rose, 'The Effects of Repudiatory Breaches of Contract' (1981) 34 *Current Legal Problems* 235.

1023 Perrins (n 259) [2264].

contract price, as a debt, is payable only if all conditions precedent are fulfilled. The co-operation qualification is testimony to this point. In most cases, the victim's performance is necessary for the contractual debt to accrue and without the contract-breaker's co-operation no such performance is possible. A typical example is that of a wrongfully dismissed employee who cannot claim future wages because he needs the employer's co-operation to earn the wages and is incapable of doing so by simply presenting his services to the employer.[1024] The issue is thus sometimes transformed into whether the contract in question, such as a charterparty, should be treated as analogous to a contract of personal service in this respect.[1025] However, the clearance of the co-operation hurdle is not sufficient for the claim to be allowed. The legitimate interest qualification, which does not concern the fulfilment of a condition precedent to the payment of the contract price, must also be satisfied. Indeed, the *White & Carter* principle is not concerned with the accrual of a contractual debt as such. Its distinctiveness lies in a different question: is it appropriate to allow the victim to go on and fulfil all the conditions precedent to the payment of the contract price, thereby putting itself in a position to claim an accrued debt?

Secondly, there were suggestions that a claim for the contract price was not only a claim in debt, but should also be treated as a form of specific performance.[1026] As noted earlier, one of the grounds on which the minority rejected the claim in *White & Carter* was that it might outflank and undermine the court's jurisdiction over the sanctioning of specific implement/performance.[1027] None of the judges in that case, however, treated the claim as analogous to a claim for specific implement/performance.[1028] Nevertheless, the minority's argument was later relied upon by some English courts to draw the analogy and consequently the adequacy of damages was accepted as a principal test for 'legitimate interest'. This analogy, drawn in the English context, is, however, both a lax and a dangerous analogy. Once the victim fulfils all conditions precedent to the payment of the contract price, it is entitled to that price. It is thus well established that where a payment falls due before an anticipatory breach is committed it is recoverable irrespective of whether or not the breach is accepted.[1029] The courts have no discretion to encumber the victim's entitlement to the contract price. Admittedly, Lord Reid's legitimate interest qualification confers on the courts an equitable jurisdiction to constrain the accrual of that entitlement.[1030] Yet this is demonstrably distinct from the courts' more general jurisdiction to grant an order of specific performance.[1031]

[1024] Eg *Henderson-Williams (t/a F Henderson-Williams & Co) v Davis* (unreported, CA, 17 June 1999); *Masood v Zahoor* [2008] EWHC 1034 (Ch) at [279] (Peter Smith J).

[1025] *The Alaskan Trader* (n 994) 139 (Lloyd J): yes; *The Odenfeld* (n 588) 374 (Kerr J): no.

[1026] *Ministry of Sound v World Online* (n 997) [67] *et seq* (Strauss QC).

[1027] *White & Carter* (n 976) 433 (Lord Morton); 438 (Lord Keith).

[1028] *Ibid* 427, 430 (Lord Reid); 433 (Lord Morton); 438 (Lord Keith); 445 (Lord Hodson).

[1029] *Ministry of Sound v World Online* (n 997) [32]. Also, *Corbin on Contracts* (n 5) § 983.

[1030] *White & Carter* (n 976) 431 (Lord Reid); *The Alaskan Trader* (n 994) 137 (Lloyd J).

[1031] *Cf Ministry of Sound v World Online* (n 997) [67] *et seq* (Strauss QC).

The factors that mould the equitable jurisdiction to decree specific performance, such as the preservation of personal liberty and the impracticability of supervision, have no role in the *White & Carter* principle. It was once held that the lack of mutuality, a factor militating against specific performance, would equally defeat a claim for the contract price.[1032] It was said that the victim, if its outstanding performance was not specifically enforceable, might not force the contract-breaker to pay the contract price. Yet clearly a simple explanation for this is that unless the victim fulfils all the conditions precedent, including some or all of its outstanding performance, the contract price is not payable. The issue in *White & Carter* is not whether the victim, having fulfilled all the conditions precedent, should be awarded the contract price, but whether it should be allowed to fulfil those conditions in the first place, or, whether its conduct in fulfilment of those conditions should be regarded as inappropriate and thus incapable of giving rise to an entitlement to the contract price. In short, the *White & Carter* principle is not concerned with the appropriateness of a claim for the contract price, whether it is seen as a claim in debt or a claim for specific performance, but with the appropriateness of the victim's continuing performance. It is for this reason that the second formulation must be rejected.

c. *Wasteful Performance*

The issue in *White & Carter* does not lie in whether the victim of an anticipatory breach may keep the contract alive or, if it continues and completes its performance, it is entitled to the contract price. Instead, the third formulation asserts that it is the wastefulness of the victim's continuing performance that constitutes the heart and soul of the *White & Carter* principle. A wrongfully dismissed employee's inability to claim unearned wages, for example, has been explained on the ground of the wastefulness of his continuance with the contract.[1033] Two comments to different effects can be made. The first comment is that the third formulation correctly pinpoints the wastefulness of the victim's continuing performance as a key factor in the application of the *White & Carter* principle. In *White & Carter*, the judges who took that view actually formed a majority. Lord Morton and Lord Keith rested their dissenting decisions principally upon the wastefulness of the pursuers' conduct.[1034] Lord Reid's legitimate interest qualification also centred effectively on it. It was once argued that *White & Carter* involved unwanted but not necessarily wasteful performance.[1035] The reason seems to be that the defender would reap benefits, such as good publicity, from the unwanted advertisements. This argument is, however, based on too restrictive a view of 'waste'. A performance is wasteful when its costs exceed the benefits.

[1032] *Ibid* [73].
[1033] *The Puerto Buitrago* (n 997) 255 (Lord Denning MR). Also, Nienaber (n 37) 232.
[1034] *White & Carter* (n 976) 433 (Lord Morton); 439 (Lord Keith).
[1035] Bridge (n 892) 405; Nienaber (n 37) 232–3.

Yet the wastefulness must not be assessed solely from the perspective of one of the parties. Rather, full regard must be had to the interests of both parties and even to the interests of the wider community. Thus, an unwanted performance will not generally lead to an effective allocation of resources, namely, resources being moved to the person in most need of them.[1036] In this sense, it is economically inefficient and is thus wasteful. On the facts of *White & Carter*, the pursuers ought, on learning of the repudiation, to have realised that their advertising services would find better use in a desirous party and would thus be wasteful if imposed upon the defender. Conversely, suppose the defender wanted the advertisements but showed a marked inability to pay, the pursuers' continuance with the contract would be less likely to be wasteful. The wastefulness of the victim's continuing performance is in fact essential to the *White & Carter* principle. There is no need to encumber the victim's right to earn the contract price by continuing performance if the performance is not wasteful.[1037] For example, a tenant cannot rely upon the *White & Carter* principle to facilitate an argument that the landlord has no legitimate interest to sue it rather than the under-tenant to whom the tenancy has been assigned.[1038] No wasteful performance is involved and there is thus no question of legitimate interest.

The second comment is that if the third formulation is concerned only with the wastefulness of the victim's continuing performance, then it misses the full picture. Wastefulness alone does not necessarily mean that the victim is not entitled to earn the contract price by continuing performance. That entitlement hinges on the weighing of two competing values, namely, the certainty or sanctity of a contractual right and economic efficiency in the form of waste avoidance. English contract law has traditionally prioritised certainty ahead of efficiency. In order to achieve certainty, it was even said to be 'hardly uncommon' for a court to deviate from a 'commercially just result',[1039] which can often be equated with an efficient result. Thus, a lessee of equipment who has no further use for it remains liable for the rent for the rest of the contract period, even though the lessor is thus saved from maintaining the equipment.[1040] This prioritisation tends to lead to the extreme view that efficiency should be entirely left out of consideration. In *White & Carter*, Lord Hodson thus held that the pursuers were entitled to the contract price simply because they had given what the defender contracted for, namely, the advertising service, and it was irrelevant that their continuing performance was unreasonable or wasteful.[1041] However, as Lloyd J observed, 'absolute certainty

1036 Carter, Phang and Phang (n 1004) 80, 98–9.

1037 *Ministry of Sound v World Online* (n 997) [66] (Strauss QC). *cf Asamera Oil Corp v Sea Oil & General Corp* [1979] 1 SCR 633, 668, (1978) 89 DLR (3d) 1 (SCC) 68 (Estey J); SM Waddams, 'Damages for Failure to Return Shares' (1978–1979) 3 *Canadian Business Law Journal* 398, 405–6.

1038 *Norwich Union Life Insurance Society v Low Profile Fashions Ltd* [1992] 1 EGLR 86 (CA).

1039 *Ministry of Sound v World Online* (n 997) [26], [61] (Strauss QC).

1040 *Ibid* [26].

1041 *White & Carter* (n 976) 445.

can never be attained'.[1042] The better view seems not to dismiss efficiency entirely but to accept that it may, in certain circumstances, triumph over certainty. To identify such circumstances, the enquiry must not stop at the discovery of a wasteful performance. The existence of waste is a necessary, but not sufficient, reason for the victim to be precluded from earning the contract price by continuing performance. Indeed, it is clear from Lord Reid's decision in *White & Carter* that only in exceptional cases is the victim regarded as having no legitimate interest in continuing to perform the contract. The appropriate legal test is whether the wastefulness of the victim's continuing performance is so serious as to outweigh the certainty of preserving its right to earn the contract price by continuing performance. As will be seen, Lord Reid's legitimate interest qualification ought to be recast on the basis of this legal test. In applying the *White & Carter* principle, the courts will take account of a wide range of factors in weighing wastefulness against certainty. Consequently, this is an equitable principle that comes to the contract-breaker's aid only where wastefulness outweighs certainty.[1043]

3. Building the Solution

a. The Onus of Proof

We first look at the onus of proof under the *White & Carter* principle. It is clear from the foregoing discussion that the issue in *White & Carter* concerns the circumstances in which the victim is not entitled to earn the contract price by continuing performance, rather than the circumstances in which it is. The victim's entitlement is the general rule and only exceptionally is that entitlement taken away from it. This is not only a reflection of the traditional prioritisation of certainty ahead of efficiency, but is also necessitated by the placement of the onus of proof on the contract-breaker. The victim, who simply follows the terms of the contract, should not be required to justify its conduct. It is for the contract-breaker to establish that the victim's continuing performance is so wasteful as to outweigh the certainty of its right to earn the contract price. Lord Reid, when formulating the legitimate interest qualification in *White & Carter*, explicitly adopted this placement.[1044] Later cases followed suit.[1045] As will be seen, the onus in respect of this qualification is an extremely heavy one. As regards the co-operation qualification, once the victim makes out a prima facie case that the contract price is

1042 *The Alaskan Trader* (n 994) 137 (Lloyd J).

1043 *Cf Scandinavian Trading Tanker Co AB v Flota Petrolera Ecuatoriana (The 'Scaptrade')* [1983] QB 529 (CA), [1983] 1 Lloyd's Rep 146, where the existence of an equity was rejected as there was no countervailing value such as efficiency that competed with certainty in that case.

1044 *White & Carter* (n 976) 430–1.

1045 *The Puerto Buitrago* (n 997) 256 (Orr LJ); *Stocznia v Latvian Shipping* [1995] 2 Lloyd's Rep 592, 602 (Clarke J); *Ocean Marine Navigation Ltd v Koch Carbon Inc (The 'Dynamic')* [2003] EWHC 1936 (Comm), [2003] 2 Lloyd's Rep 693 [23] (Simon J). Also, *Salaried Staff London Loan Co Ltd v Swears & Wells Ltd* 1985 SC 189, 1985 SLT 326 (CSIH).

payable, it is also for the contract-breaker to show that the victim's performance requires its co-operation and has been rendered without it. The onus on this matter is generally not a heavy one.

b. Co-operation

The victim must be able to continue to perform the contract without co-operation from the contract-breaker. Only when this co-operation hurdle is overcome does the issue of wastefulness arise. The practical significance of the co-operation qualification is plain to see. In most cases the contract-breaker can prevent a claim for the contract price by simply withholding its co-operation. The absence of co-operation does not have to render the victim's performance physically impossible. All that matters is that the contract-breaker's co-operation is necessary for the victim to perform in conformity with the terms of the contract. Thus, if a contract for building a machine stipulates that the machine must be built in accordance with special specifications given by the owner, to build the machine single-handedly without the specifications is not a conforming performance and therefore does not trigger the owner's obligation to pay. Below we look at two concepts affecting the scope of application of this qualification.

Dependency of Performance

The co-operation qualification has no application where the victim's continuing performance is not a condition precedent to the payment of the contract price. In other words, if the contract is independent, or, more accurately, if the parties' performances are independent of each other,[1046] neither the victim's performance nor the contract-breaker's co-operation is necessary for the accrual of the obligation to pay the contract price.

This is made clear in *Ministry of Sound v World Online*.[1047] Under a contract that was set to expire in February 2002, the claimant undertook to promote the defendant's internet service by associating it to the brand of 'Ministry of Sound'. This undertaking included packaging and distributing Access CDs to be supplied by the defendant and maintaining and publicising the defendant's service on the claimant's website. In return the defendant promised to pay the claimant in instalments. A substantial final instalment was due on 3 October 2001. Since August 2000 the defendant had ceased to supply any Access CDs. As a result, the claimant did not package or distribute any such CDs after August 2000. On 20 September 2001, the defendant without lawful excuse refused to pay the final instalment. Nevertheless, the claimant continued to maintain and publicise the defendant's

[1046] For earlier independent contract cases, (1500) *Anon* YB 15 Hen VII fo 10b pl 17 (Fineux CJ); *West v Stowel* (1577) 2 Leo 154, 74 ER 437; *Nichols v Raynbred* (1615) Hob 89, 80 ER 238. Also, Simpson (n 29) 576; Stoljar (n 129) 150; Dawson (n 61) 87 fn 16.

[1047] n 997.

service on its website and brought an action for that instalment when it was not paid on 3 October. The defendant contended that the claimant was not entitled to the final instalment as it had not packaged or distributed any Access CDs since August 2000. Mr Nicholas Strauss QC, sitting as a Deputy Judge in the Chancery Division, held that the defendant was liable to pay the final instalment.

The major ground on which the learned judge arrived at this decision was that under the contract payments 'are due on specified calendar dates and not (as in both *Langford* and *White & Carter*) dependent on the prior performance of specific contractual obligations'.[1048] His Lordship distinguished the reciprocity of consideration from the dependency of performance in that the latter 'denotes a pre-condition to the right of payment'.[1049] The packaging and distribution of Access CDs was apparently part of the consideration given in exchange for the final instalment. It was, however, not a condition precedent to the payment of that instalment. For this reason, it was immaterial that the claimant's inability to package or distribute any CDs amounted to a substantial failure to perform the contract.[1050] The defendant was bound to pay the final instalment on 3 October and was left to a counterclaim based on a total or a partial failure of consideration.[1051] As the learned judge pointed out, dependent performances were the norm in modern contracts. In a contract for the sale of goods, for instance, until goods were accepted 'there is no indebtedness'.[1052] But at the same time exceptions existed: an example was the SGA 1979 section 49(1), under which the price for goods was payable on a certain day irrespective of delivery.[1053] In such cases the co-operation qualification would be irrelevant.

The facts of *Ministry of Sound* also gave rise to another issue: if the parties' performances under the contract were dependent, should it matter which party's performance fell due first in time? In *White & Carter*, Lord Keith stated that it was 'an arbitrary distinction' and contrary to the 'mutuality of contracts' that a claim for the contract price should be allowed where the victim's performance became due first in time but not where the contract-breaker was first called for to pay under the contract.[1054] There is, however, no reason why this should necessarily be so. It has been settled since the late 18th century that the victim must aver its willingness and readiness to perform when the contract-breaker puts it in issue.[1055] Where the contract-breaker's obligation to pay falls due first,

1048 *Ibid* [45]. Also [33].
1049 *Ibid* [50].
1050 *Ibid* [34], [53].
1051 *Ibid* [42], [63].
1052 *Ibid* [51], citing *Automatic Fire Sprinklers Proprietary Ltd v Watson* (1946) 72 CLR 435 (HCA) 464 (Dixon J).
1053 *Ibid* [52]. The section was held to be inapplicable in *Otis Vehicle Rentals Ltd (formerly Brandrick Hire (Birmingham) Ltd) v Ciceley Commercials Ltd* [2002] All ER (D) 203 (July) (CA Civ). For a similar decision featuring the Australian equivalent of the section, *Kim Francis Ledger v Cleveland Nominees Pty Ltd* [2001] WASCA 269.
1054 *White & Carter* (n 976) 436.
1055 Ch 5, text before n 524 above.

the victim is, subject to Lord Reid's two qualifications, entitled to the payment if, and only if, it is willing and ready to continue to perform the contract. It is open for the contract-breaker to argue that the victim will not be ready to perform later as the contract-breaker will withhold its co-operation which is essential to the victim's performance. Thus, a seller cannot sue the repudiating buyer who is first obliged to pay for the price, or a school cannot sue the repudiating parents who are first obliged to pay for the tuition—not because the payment precedes the performance, but because in both cases the victim's readiness cannot be averred in the absence of the repudiating party's co-operation.[1056] Consequently, the 'arbitrary distinction' alleged by Lord Keith is in fact illusory. The same legal rules apply whether it is the contract-breaker or the victim who is bound to perform first.

Passive Co-operation

Co-operation does not necessarily require active steps to be taken. A buyer, by refusing to take delivery, thus withholds its co-operation necessary for the delivery to take place.[1057] In *Hounslow LBC v Twickenham*,[1058] Megarry J went further and held that mere legal ownership, irrespective of physical control, of property would inevitably make the owner's co-operation a prerequisite for any performance involving that property. In this case the council, the employer in a building contract, purported to terminate the contract before the construction work was due to be completed. The contractor refused to vacate the site and proceeded with the work. The council sought an injunction to restrain a trespass. Assuming the termination was wrongful, the legal issue was whether the *White & Carter* principle was applicable so as to confer on the contractor a right to insist upon continuing its performance. Megarry J declined to apply that principle on the ground that the contractor could not perform the contract without the council's co-operation. His Lordship distinguished two types of co-operation. First, the contractor's performance of its contractual obligations required 'active co-operation' by the council as '[t]he whole machinery of the contract is geared to acts by the architect and quantity surveyor'[1059] and the council was involved in this process. Secondly, even without such active co-operation, the need for the council's 'passive co-operation' alone would suffice to deny the contractor a right to earn the contract price. Passive co-operation was required simply because the council owned the property. It was immaterial whether the council was also in possession of it. To illustrate, where B contracted to restore A's picture and A repudiated the contract before the work started, B could not be heard to insist on performing the contract, even

[1056] *Corbin on Contracts* (n 5) § 983.

[1057] *The Alaskan Trader* (n 994) 133 (Lloyd J). The same can be said where a hirer rejects the hired equipment, *Telephone Rentals plc v Burges Salmon & Co* (unreported, CA, 9 April 1987), adopting *National Cash Register Co Ltd v Stanley* [1921] 3 KB 292 (CA).

[1058] n 995.

[1059] *Ibid* 253.

though B had full physical control of the picture.[1060] It would also seem that in *White & Carter* had the defender owned some of the sites on which the advertisements should be displayed, it would have been able to resist the pursuers' claim to the extent of the price payable for services rendered on those sites.[1061] It must be noted that passive co-operation is not required where it is the victim, not the contract-breaker, who has a superior proprietary right over the property in question. Therefore, it cannot be alleged against a ship-owner who sues a repudiating charterer[1062] or a landlord who sues a repudiating tenant.[1063] The endorsement of the notion of 'passive co-operation' testifies to the courts' rather liberal approach towards the co-operation qualification. It is, however, in respect of cases where the contract-breaker's co-operation is not required that the distinctive identity of the *White & Carter* principle comes to the force.

c. Legitimate Interest

The legitimate interest qualification brings out conspicuously the clash between certainty and efficiency. Although it remains somewhat underdeveloped, it certainly points in the right direction—the contract-breaker must show that the wastefulness of the victim's continuing performance outweighs the certainty of its right to earn the contract price. Three specific tests have been proposed, either individually or jointly, to determine the existence of a legitimate interest. They must first be examined separately.

Adequacy of Damages

The first test, alluded to by Lord Reid in *White & Carter* and adopted by English courts subsequently, states that in order to show the absence of a legitimate interest on the victim's part, the contract-breaker must satisfy the court that damages are an adequate remedy for the victim. This test was sometimes said to be the dominant test.[1064] More commonly, the test was seen as controlling one of the two essential elements to a successful defence against a claim for the contract price: the contract-breaker must show not only the adequacy of damages, but also that the victim's continuing performance would be 'wholly unreasonable'.[1065]

In either case, an analogy has been drawn by English courts between a claim for the contract price and a claim for specific performance. The adequacy of damages test, the principal test for the availability of specific performance in anticipatory

[1060] *Ibid.*

[1061] *Ministry of Sound v World Online* (n 997) [43] (Strauss QC).

[1062] *The Alaskan Trader* (n 994); *The Odenfeld* (n 588).

[1063] *Reichman v Beveridge* [2006] EWCA Civ 1659, [2006] All ER (D) 186 (Dec).

[1064] *The Puerto Buitrago* (n 997) 255 (Lord Denning MR); A Burrows, *Remedies for Torts and Breach of Contract*, 3rd edn (Oxford, OUP, 2004) 440.

[1065] *The Odenfeld* (n 588) 374 (Kerr J); *The Dynamic* (n 1045) [23] (Simon J); *Reichman v Beveridge* (n 1063) [17] (Lloyd LJ).

breach[1066] as well as actual breach cases, has consequently been adopted. However, the analogy, as shown previously, is a dangerous one. The claim in *White & Carter* is a claim in debt, rather than a claim for specific performance. The adequacy of damages test in specific performance cases must not be applied unbendingly to a case such as *White & Carter*. The adequacy of damages is distinguishable from the wastefulness of the victim's continuing performance in that it is not concerned with whether the costs of that performance exceed its benefits, but with whether the victim might be compensated for the difference between the contract price and those costs. This does not, however, mean that in the latter case it is wholly irrelevant whether damages are an adequate remedy. Coupled with the wastefulness of the victim's continuing performance, the adequacy of damages would militate strongly in favour of a finding of no legitimate interest. Nevertheless, it is neither necessary nor sufficient for the contract-breaker to show the adequacy of damages. It must show that the victim has a real alternative other than to continue to perform the contract. If no such alternative exists, the certainty of conserving the victim's contractual right must prevail over any wastefulness involved in its continuing performance. The adequacy of damages means that the principal alternative, namely, terminating the contract and claiming damages, is open to the victim. It does not, however, necessarily lead to the conclusion that the victim is disentitled from earning the contract price. Nor does it follow from the inadequacy of damages that the victim has no real alternative other than to continue to perform. The victim may terminate the contract and seek other remedies, such as restitution. The adequacy of damages test has been explicitly applied in two cases. In neither case was damages held to be an adequate remedy. In *The Odenfeld*, Kerr J rested his conclusion on the ground that the assessment of damages in the case, which involved ascertaining the owners' lost profits in the remaining six and a half years of a time charter, was 'an extremely difficult and lengthy process'.[1067] In *Reichman v Beveridge*, Lloyd LJ held that English law had not yet reached the stage where damages for the loss of future rents could be recovered in a case where the landlord re-entered for the tenant's repudiation and re-let at a lower market rent.[1068] In both cases the adequacy of damages test was applied in conjunction with the 'wholly unreasonable' test. The victim's continuing performance was held not even to be 'unreasonable'. It was thus entitled to the contract price.

[1066] *Lumley v Wagner* (1852) 1 De GM & G 604, 42 ER 687; *Warner Brothers Pictures v Nelson* [1937] 1 KB 209; *Taylor v National Union of Seaman* [1967] 1 WLR 532 (Ch); *Page One Records Ltd v Britton* [1968] 1 WLR 157 (Ch) 166 (Stamp J); *Hill v Parsons* (n 1011) 314 (Lord Denning MR); *Ivory v Palmer* (n 561); *Irani v Southampton and South West Hampshire Health Authority* [1985] ICR 590 (Ch); *Evening Standard Co Ltd v Henderson* [1987] ICR 588 (CA). Further, authorities cited *Dietman v Brent* (n 561) 754 (Hodgson J).

[1067] *The Odenfeld* (n 588) 374. The learned judge distinguished the case from *The Puerto Buitrago* (n 997), which he said involved no difficulty in assessing damages since there was probably no loss.

[1068] *Reichman v Beveridge* (n 1063) [27]. *cf* Australian law: *Progressive Mailing v Tabali* (n 788); *J & S Chan Pty Ltd v McKenzie* [1994] ANZ ConvR 610 (ACTSC). Canadian law: *Highway Properties Ltd v Kelly, Douglas & Co Ltd* (1971) 17 DLR (3d) 710 (SCC).

Duty to Mitigate

The second test, relied upon by the two dissenting judges in *White & Carter*,[1069] is to use the victim's duty to mitigate to scrutinise the victim's right to earn the contract price by continuing performance. A formidable obstacle for this test is a long-standing line of authorities that fix the time when a duty to mitigate arises in anticipatory breach cases at the time when the victim accepts the breach. It was suggested that this rule of law has caused a major anomaly in practice, as the victim might freely continue to perform the contract and thus shift the cost of wasted resources to the contract-breaker.[1070] Consequently, critics argued that American law should be preferred, under which a duty to mitigate arose in the victim as soon as the anticipatory breach was communicated and held the victim's continuing performance in check.[1071] Even some members of the English judiciary have been attracted to this 'uncomplicated view'.[1072] To be sure, the mitigation principle and the *White & Carter* principle do share in common a commendable desire to avoid waste. It is thus no great offence to refer to the latter as being analogous to the former.[1073] What is objectionable is the suggestion that the distinction between the two should be removed entirely and the mitigation principle should be applied to a victim who chooses to continue to perform to earn the contract price in the same way as it is applied in assessing damages.[1074] It is submitted that, for the following two reasons, the reliance on the mitigation principle is gravely misplaced.

First, the standard of unreasonableness applied in mitigation cases seems to be ill-suited as an appropriate yardstick for determining the victim's right to earn the contract price by continuing performance. Critically, the courts, while driven by the same desire to avoid waste, are looking at quite different things. In mitigation cases, the courts are looking at acts that fall outside of the contract, such as buying or selling against the contract in the market, which the victim is neither obliged nor entitled to do. By contrast, in a *White & Carter* scenario, the victim is not only entitled but also obliged to perform the contract.[1075] To apply the mitigation principle indiscriminately to the latter would in effect impose upon the victim a

1069 *White & Carter* (n 976) 433 (Lord Morton); 439 (Lord Keith).

1070 Goodhart (n 855) 267 *et seq*; S Stoljar, 'Some Problems of Anticipatory Breach' [1974] 9 *Melbourne University Law Review* 355; Carter, Phang and Phang (n 1004) 97; Burrows (n 1064) 440.

1071 *Clark v Marsiglia* 1 Denio 317 (NY 1845); *Rockingham County v Luten Bridge Co* 35 F 2d 301 (1929); *Restatement (Second) Contracts* § 257. Also, *Farnsworth on Contracts* (n 137) § 8.22.

1072 *The Alaskan Trader* (n 994) 137 (Lloyd J). To similar effect, *Stocznia v Latvian Shipping* [2001] 1 Lloyd's Rep 537 [175] (Thomas J). In Australia, Priestley JA has written extrajudicially in favour of the American position: LJ Priestley, 'Conduct after Breach: the Position of the Party not in Breach' (1991) 3 *Journal of Contract Law* 218, 230–1.

1073 *Reichman v Beveridge* (n 1063) [12]. Also, Furmston (n 151) 783.

1074 *Cf* Carter, Phang and Phang (n 1004) 80, 98–9, 103.

1075 *Cf* Goodhart (n 855) 264: 'by repudiating his own duty the repudiator must lose his right to enforce the other party's obligation'; Priestley (n 1072) 229: the victim impliedly promised not to continue if while the contract remains wholly executory the other party 'for good reason' notifies that its performance is no longer required, criticised in K Mason, 'Commentary on "Conduct after Breach: the Position of the Party not in Breach' (1991) 3 *Journal of Contract Law* 232, 236.

general obligation to perform its contract 'reasonably' and deny it a bargained-for right to earn the contract price, an approach clearly not favoured by common law tradition.[1076] Sir John Donaldson MR thus warned against a confusion of

> the proposition that in deciding whether to rescind or affirm a contract the innocent party need have no regard to considerations of mitigation of loss with the proposition that, having made such an election, he will be able to recover such loss as was unavoidable following that election.[1077]

Consequently, the yardstick for a legitimate interest under the *White & Carter* principle must be distinguished from that in mitigation cases. Although the onus on the contract-breaker to show that the victim acts 'unreasonably' in not mitigating is not a light one,[1078] the onus must be even heavier when the contract-breaker aims not to reduce the amount of damages payable, but to thwart in its entirety a claim for the contract price. In fact, the courts, as will be seen, have been alert to this distinction and have thus pitched the level of the contract-breaker's onus under the *White & Carter* principle at 'wholly unreasonable'.

Secondly, the position in American law seems to be based on a misunderstanding of the nature of anticipatory breach as a reversible wrong. The American jurisprudence correctly views an anticipatory breach as in itself a wrong. However, it does not follow from this that a duty to mitigate immediately follows an anticipatory breach. Mitigation presupposes a wrong[1079] but the committing of a wrong does not always necessitate mitigation. In *Shindler v Northern Raincoat Co Ltd*,[1080] for instance, a wrongfully dismissed employee was held not to be required in mitigation to accept alternative offers of employment, for the very reason that the employer had a locus poenitentiae to retract the unaccepted anticipatory breach. In other words, it is the fact that a party in anticipatory breach 'may reinstate himself' prior to acceptance that makes acceptance a prerequisite for both a right of action for damages and a duty to mitigate.[1081] It should be added that, although it seems that the mitigation principle can be applied retrospectively to the victim's conduct after the time of breach once an anticipatory breach is accepted, such conduct cannot, for the first reason stated above, encompass attempts to perform the contract.

In rejecting the mitigation principle as an appropriate test we have omitted the usual argument that that principle has application only in a claim for damages, not in a claim in debt.[1082] This argument has been criticised for putting form

[1076] *White & Carter* (n 976) 427, 431 (Lord Reid); 444–5 (Lord Hodson).
[1077] *The Solholt* (n 850) 609.
[1078] *McGregor on Damages* (n 810) [7–064].
[1079] Eg *Abrahams v Performing Right Society* [1995] ICR 1028 (CA).
[1080] (n 811) 1048 (Diplock J). Also, *Cerberus Software v Rowley* [2001] ICR 376 (CA).
[1081] Bridge (n 892) 402. *cf* Priestley (n 1072) 229.
[1082] Eg *Swallow Securities Ltd v Brand* (1981) 45 P & CR 328; *Sorgato v Khalili* (unreported, QB, 30 July 1992); *Royscot Commercial Leasing Ltd v Ismail* (unreported, CA, 29 April 1993) per Hirst LJ. Also, Nienaber (n 37) 227–8; E McKendrick, *Contract Law: Text, Cases, and Materials*, 2nd edn (Oxford, OUP, 2005) 1000.

above substance.[1083] As a point of substance, we have shown that the *White & Carter* principle, albeit broadly sharing the same goal of waste avoidance as the mitigation principle, addresses the victim's right to earn the contract price by continuing performance, rather than its right to recover for certain avoidable loss, and must thus embrace a different legal test, a test with a heavier onus on the contract-breaker of showing the absence of a legitimate interest.

'Wholly Unreasonable'

The third test, reasserted many times by English courts subsequent to *White & Carter*, asks whether the victim's continuing performance is 'wholly unreasonable'. Lord Reid's unhesitating rejection of Lord Cooper's prior observation that 'the only reasonable and proper course' for the victim to take was to accept the breach[1084] was a clear indication that a test of 'unreasonableness', inclusive of that applied under the mitigation principle, was too broad to strike a sensible balance between certainty and efficiency in a case like *White & Carter*. Taking up this strand of reasoning, the courts in later cases stressed that the equity to refuse a claim for the contract price should be administered in 'extreme cases' only.[1085] The contract-breaker must show that the victim acts 'wholly unreasonably' in continuing to perform the contract. The distinction between merely unreasonable and wholly unreasonable is nowhere more prominently depicted than in a judgment of Lloyd J in *The Alaskan Trader*.[1086] It is necessary to quote the learned judge's statement in full:

> [T]here comes a point at which the court will cease, on general equitable principles, to allow the innocent party to enforce his contract according to its strict legal terms. How one defines that point is obviously a matter of some difficulty, for it involves drawing a line between conduct which is merely unreasonable (see per Lord Reid in *White & Carter v McGregor* [1961] 3 All ER 1178 at 1182, [1962] AC 473 at 429–430, criticising the Lord President in *Langford & Co Ltd v Dutch* 1952 SC 15) and conduct which is wholly unreasonable (see per Kerr J in *The Odenfeld* [1978] 2 Lloyd's Rep 357 at 374). But however difficult it may be to define the point, that there is such a point seems to me to have been accepted both by the Court of Appeal in *The Puerto Buitrago* and by Kerr J in *The Odenfeld*.[1087]

The legal test expressed in this form was, however, said to be 'somewhat vague'.[1088] The word 'wholly' was dismissed as 'add[ing] nothing to the test'.[1089] These negative comments were apparently aimed at the difficulty in defining the meaning of

[1083] Carter, Phang and Phang (n 1004) 17, 69–70, 103; Priestley (n 1072) 229–30.

[1084] *White & Carter* (n 976) 429, 430.

[1085] *The Odenfeld* (n 588) 374 (Kerr J); *The Dynamic* (n 1045) [23] (Simon J); *Reichman v Beveridge* (n 1063) [16], [17], [40].

[1086] n 994.

[1087] *Ibid* 136–7.

[1088] Nienaber (n 37) 231.

[1089] *The Dynamic* (n 1045) [22] (Simon J). Also, Carter, Phang and Phang (n 1004) 80.

'wholly'. The problem is, however, not only with the word 'wholly', but also with the word 'unreasonable'. It is submitted that the apposite test under the *White & Carter* principle should not be broadly directed at the unreasonableness of the victim's continuing performance at all. A test of 'unreasonableness' fails to capture the critical issue in *White & Carter* and tends to cause obscurity and to expand unduly the range of factors to be taken into account. The better and more refined approach is to confine the courts' discretion to those factors that affect the weighing of wastefulness against certainty. Consequently, the legal test for 'legitimate interest' must be reformulated.

The New Test

The apposite test for 'legitimate interest' to be suggested here will not cause an upheaval to existing case law. Instead, it requires cases decided under the 'wholly unreasonable' test to be restated. Rather than probing the cases chronologically, we analyse them in different categories according to the dominant reasons leading to each decision.

The first category of cases addresses directly the issue of wastefulness and is characterised by manifest idleness. In *The Puerto Buitrago*,[1090] the charterers redelivered the vessel unrepaired when the time charter finished. It was held that this constituted a breach of their duty to keep the vessel in repair, a breach sounding in damages only. Assuming, however, that the redelivery was wrongful and ineffectual, the Court of Appeal firmly rejected an argument on behalf of the owners that they were entitled to reject the vessel and sue for the hire month by month until the charterers had it repaired.[1091] Lord Denning, in particular, pointed out that to decide otherwise would be to require the charterers either to pay the hire 'while the vessel lies idle and useless for want of repair' or to repair it at a cost twice as much as its value.[1092] In another case, *The Alaskan Trader*,[1093] the charterers wrongfully cancelled a time charter a few months before its expiry and refused to give the master any orders. The owners nevertheless kept the vessel with a full crew on board, ready to sail but idle. The charterers paid the remaining monthly hire and then brought a claim to recover it. Lloyd J held that the owners' conduct was 'wholly unreasonable' and the charterers were thus entitled to recover the hire subject to an offset by damages recoverable by the owners. This should be contrasted with the learned judge's decision that the owners were fully justified in continuing with the contract during a short period following the charterers' repudiation, when the vessel was off-hire for repair.[1094] The above two cases were analogous to the case of a wrongfully dismissed employee, who was not entitled to earn his wages simply by remaining idle and allowing the employer to '[have]

1090 n 997.
1091 *Ibid* 255 (Lord Denning); 256 (Orr LJ); 256 (Browne LJ).
1092 *Ibid* 255.
1093 n 994.
1094 *Ibid* 138.

a call on his services'.[1095] In both cases, therefore, the victim's continuing performance was extravagantly wasteful and, unlike in *White & Carter*, it was not even arguable that that performance could still confer, albeit forcibly, some benefits upon the contract-breaker.

The second category of cases asks the question whether the contract-breaker could have reduced or avoided the waste. In *Reichman v Beveridge*,[1096] the landlord, when the tenant unlawfully vacated the property and ceased to pay the rent some two years before the tenancy was set to expire, did not re-enter until about a year later, when it sued for the arrears due up until then. Lloyd LJ, delivering the judgment of the Court of Appeal, found that the landlord's conduct had not been shown to be 'unreasonable, still less wholly unreasonable'.[1097] This was because 'it is not only the landlord who can take steps to fill the space'.[1098] The tenant, a wrongdoer, 'should bear the burden' of assigning the tenancy or subletting the property, provided the landlord did not unreasonably withhold its consent.[1099] In view of this, it was virtually impossible to conclude that the landlord's continuance with the contract was wasteful.

The third category of cases concerns whether the victim has any real alternative other than to continue its performance. If there is no such alternative, the victim must be held to have a legitimate interest in continuing to perform. In *The Odenfeld*, Kerr J, in holding that the owners did not act wholly unreasonably in keeping a time charter alive, relied upon, inter alia, the impracticability of finding an alternative comparable employment of the vessel.[1100] In *The Dynamic*,[1101] the owners of the vessel alleged that they were entitled to hire during the period when the charterers wrongfully arrested her. While critical of the 'wholly unreasonable' test, Simon J remitted the case to the arbitrator on the ground that the latter had failed to deal adequately with the argument that the owners could not accept the anticipatory breach and re-charter the vessel for she was under arrest.[1102] As stated above, the cases that applied the adequacy of damages test also fall within this category.[1103]

The fourth category consists of cases where the victim, as Lord Reid recognised in *White & Carter*, has an other than 'immediate financial interest' in continuing its performance.[1104] There is only one decided case. In *Ministry of Sound v World Online*, where the claimant continued to maintain and publicise on its website the defendant's internet service as contracted despite the defendant's clear refusal to pay, it was opined that, had the claimant's continuing performance been

1095 Nienaber (n 37) 232.
1096 n 1063.
1097 *Ibid* [42].
1098 *Ibid* [39].
1099 *Ibid* [31].
1100 *The Odenfeld* (n 588) 374.
1101 n 1045.
1102 *Ibid* [25]–[26].
1103 Text before n 1067 above.
1104 *White & Carter* (n 976) 431 (Lord Reid).

adjudicated as wasteful and thus invoking the *White & Carter* principle, it would on the facts have had a legitimate 'non-financial interest' in proceeding with the contract 'since its name was associated with World Online's publicity' and a termination might therefore be detrimental to both parties.[1105] It is not difficult to envisage a similar situation where such a non-pecuniary interest might justify continuing performance. An animal rights activist contracts with an international agency to give a public lecture in Tokyo on whale conservation but, before he can even start preparing a draft of the speech, the agency states that they no longer want the lecture to take place. It seems that the activist's special interest in presenting his views and possibly influencing a Japanese audience militates strongly in favour of a holding that he ought to be allowed to go ahead with the contract, provided no co-operation from the agency is required. Likewise, to protect or enhance one's professional reputation may also constitute a good reason for the victim to disregard an anticipatory breach.[1106]

The fifth category of cases is marked by the involvement of an innocent third party. There are two cases. The first case, *Anglo-African Shipping Co of New York Inc v J Mortner Ltd*,[1107] was decided in the same year as *White & Carter*. The defendants, a London-based company, engaged the claimants as both a confirming house and a shipping agent for the purchase of some sheeting from a New York supplier. Before the contract period for delivery elapsed, the defendants wrongfully terminated the contract. The interesting issue, argued before Megaw J but dropped on appeal, was whether the claimants might proceed with the shipment and then claim the agreed remuneration from the defendants. Megaw J, discerning 'the practical justice' of the decision in *White & Carter* on the facts of the case,[1108] answered the question affirmatively. Although the defendants' case was framed on the basis of a duty to mitigate on the claimants' part, it is important to analyse the learned judge's reasoning leading to a finding that no such duty arose upon the claimants. Aside from the difficulty and controversy in determining the reasonableness of a possible resale by the claimants of the goods, he relied principally on the fact that the claimants had in reliance on the defendants' promise entered into 'various sub-contracts', such as with a cargo carrier, and it 'might be extremely damaging commercially' to the claimants if they were required to cancel all those sub-contracts.[1109] The second case is *The Odenfeld*.[1110] The defendants chartered the vessel for 10 years. The claimants agreed to provide the owners with a loan, which was secured by way of an assignment by the owners of their right to all future hire under the charter to the claimants. The loan contract bound the owners to 'take all necessary steps to procure due performance' by the defendants of the

[1105] *Ministry of Sound v World Online* (n 997) [47].

[1106] Nienaber (n 37) 231; Carter, Phang and Phang (n 1004) 39–40.

[1107] *Anglo-African Shipping Co of New York Inc v J Mortner Ltd* [1962] 1 Lloyd's Rep 81 (QB), aff'd on other grounds [1962] 1 Lloyd's Rep 610 (CA).

[1108] *Ibid* 94.

[1109] *Ibid.*

[1110] n 588.

charter. In January 1976, the defendants purported, wrongfully, to terminate the charter. The claimants required the owners to, and they did, hold the defendants to the charter. The charter was kept in force until September 1976, when an agreement was reached to transfer the title of the vessel to the claimants. The claimants sued to recover the hire due between January and September 1976. The defendants contended that the owners ought to have accepted the repudiation in January and their only liability was in damages. It was held by Kerr J that the owners were not shown to have acted 'wholly unreasonably' in continuing with the charter, for they were bound by the loan contract to do so and a termination of the charter would be unfairly prejudicial to the claimants, 'an entirely innocent party'.[1111]

The sixth, and final, category is occupied by one case only, *Stocznia v Latvian Shipping*, a case extensively explored in Chapter 7 above. In its complex legal proceedings, an argument was once afloat that, where the buyers under a shipbuilding contract repudiated it before the yard completed the keel-laying, the latter's continuance with the keel-laying following the repudiation contradicted a duty to mitigate and was thus incapable of triggering the buyers' contractual obligation to pay progressive instalments.[1112] Clarke J held that the correct test was one of 'wholly unreasonable' and the yard did not act unreasonably, let alone wholly unreasonably, in laying the keel, for the reason that the yard had insufficient evidence at that time to establish an anticipatory breach on the buyers' part.[1113] This decision was fully adopted by the Court of Appeal, where Staughton LJ explained that 'it was not at the time plain beyond all argument that the owners were repudiating the contracts, although … it was common ground later'.[1114] Accordingly, the fact that an anticipatory breach can be established only on post-acceptance evidence tends to show that the victim does not act wholly unreasonably in continuing to perform the contract.

On the basis of this restatement of existing case law, it is possible to reformulate the 'wholly unreasonable' test as follows. (1) The principal test for a legitimate interest is whether, in the particular circumstances of the case, the wastefulness of the victim's continuing performance outweighs the certainty of its right to earn the contract price by such performance. By its nature this test is equitable and confers on the court a discretionary power, which is exercised only in exceptional cases, to hold that the victim has no legitimate interest in continuing to perform and is thus not entitled to the contract price. There must be some 'very cogent reason' for doing so, as the victim would otherwise suffer 'inconvenience and injustice'.[1115] (2) In applying the 'wholly unreasonable' test, the courts seem to

[1111] *Ibid* 374.

[1112] The point was subsequently dropped on appeal to the House of Lords: *Stocznia v Latvian Shipping* [1998] 1 WLR 574, 581 (Lord Goff).

[1113] *Stocznia v Latvian Shipping* [1995] 2 Lloyd's Rep 592, 604.

[1114] *Stocznia v Latvian Shipping* [1996] 2 Lloyd's Rep 132, 139.

[1115] *Highland & Universal Properties Ltd v Safeway Properties Ltd* [2000] 3 EGLR 110 (CSIH) 111 (Lord President Rodger), adopting *Grahame v Magistrates of Kirkcaldy* (1882) 9 R (HL) 91, 91–2 (Lord Watson); *White & Carter*, above n 976, 430 (Lord Reid).

be looking for a further good reason, in addition to the fact that the victim has a bargained-for right to earn the contract price, for its continuing performance. The new test recognises more directly and clearly the significance of such a reason. This is not to say that a further good reason is required and without it the victim cannot have a legitimate interest in continuing to perform. Rather, the existence of such a reason may very easily tip the scale in favour of certainty. A further good reason can be a non-pecuniary interest in the performance of the contract (category four) or a legal liability to a third party consequent on non-performance (category five). It can also be the lack of a real alternative for the victim other than continuing to perform (category three). Another example may be that the victim's continuing performance is necessitated by trade practices or statutes or regulations.[1116] (3) Since the main countervailing factor for the victim's right to earn the contract price is the wastefulness of its continuing performance, regard must be had not only to the victim's interests, but also to the contract-breaker's interests.[1117] It is not sufficient for the contract-breaker to show the mere fact of wastefulness, namely, that the benefits of the victim's continuing performance are small in comparison with its costs.[1118] The benefit-cost gap must be 'completely out of proportion'.[1119] The excessiveness of the wastefulness is necessary for the victim's claim for the contract price to be resisted (category one). (4) The principal test is subject to a defence that the victim has no knowledge of the anticipatory breach at the time when it continues to perform the contract (category six). It is, however, debatable whether the victim's lack of knowledge of the wastefulness of its continuing performance also constitutes a good defence. There were suggestions that the 'wholly unreasonable' test should be applied from the victim's point of view and therefore the latter's knowledge should be taken into account.[1120] The decision in *White & Carter* was thus said to be justified by the pursuers' apparent ignorance of any waste.[1121] Accordingly, it was argued that in the expert report illustration, the expert might go on and make the report if the company wished to engage another expert but not if to his knowledge the report had become superfluous.[1122] It is submitted, however, that the victim's lack of knowledge of waste should not be recognised as a defence. If the contract-breaker shows that wastefulness outweighs certainty, it is difficult to see why the victim's continuing performance should be justifiable by reason of its ignorance of the waste. The *White & Carter* principle is not invoked to impose a legal liability upon an intentional wrongdoer. It discourages the victim from continuing to perform

[1116] Eg *MP-Bilt Pte Ltd v Oey Widarto* [1999] 3 SLR 592, [1999] SGHC 70, discussed in Carter, Phang and Phang (n 1004) 88 *et seq.*

[1117] *Stocznia v Latvian Shipping* [1996] 2 Lloyd's Rep 132, 139 (Staughton LJ). Also, Nienaber (n 37) 231; Carter, Phang and Phang (n 1004) 66, 100–1. *cf McGregor on Damages* (n 810) [7–030].

[1118] *White & Carter* (n 976) 431 (Lord Reid); *The Dynamic* (n 1045) [23] (Simon J).

[1119] Nienaber (n 37) 232.

[1120] *Ibid.*

[1121] *Ibid* 233.

[1122] *Ibid* 232–3.

the contract if to do so is adjudged to be overly wasteful and hence inappropriate. Thus, if the inappropriateness of the continuance with the contract is established, it is irrelevant that it is unknown to the victim. For similar reasons, whether the victim's intention is to embarrass the contract-breaker[1123] or to improve its bargaining position[1124] seems to be immaterial.

Needless to say, the list of six categories is a non-exhaustive one. Additional good reasons for a finding of no legitimate interest may be discovered and recognised in future cases. But hopefully the above analysis has demonstrated that the new test is not based on the general concept of equitability or reasonableness. The equity precluding continuous performance must be exercised in a controlled way. The central issue is whether the victim's continuance with its performance is so wasteful as to outweigh the certainty of its contractual right to earn the contract price. This formulation puts a limit on the range of facts that may be taken into account in determining the existence of a legitimate interest. Was *White & Carter* correctly decided in view of this newly articulated test? Since the pursuers' ignorance of the wastefulness of their continuing performance was irrelevant and there was apparently no further good reason for that performance, the answer should hinge on whether the wastefulness was excessive. However, given that counsel for the defender was not informed of the necessity of showing the extent of the wastefulness, it might not be possible now to say whether the decision should have gone one way or the other. Had the new test suggested in this article been accepted by then, the House of Lords' approach would have been more coordinated, more apprehensible and, above all, more rational.

B. Specific Performance and Injunctions

In comparison with a claim for the contract price, a claim for specific performance or injunction raises fewer special issues in the context of anticipatory breach. The primary issue is whether the victim must wait for the contract-breaker's performance to fall due before applying for an order of specific performance or an injunction. In the leading case of *Hasham v Zenab*,[1125] a question was asked whether, where the vendor tore up a contract for the sale of land immediately after signing it, it was premature for the purchaser, who did not accept the anticipatory breach, to lodge an application for specific performance prior to the date for completion. Lord Tucker, giving the advice of the Privy Council, answered the question in the negative. In reliance on a previous decision of Vaisey J[1126] and

[1123] *Ibid* 231.
[1124] MP Furmston, 'The Case of the Insistent Performer' (1962) 25 *MLR* 364, 367.
[1125] n 116.
[1126] *Marks v Lilley* [1959] 1 WLR 749 (Ch) 753.

Canadian and American jurisprudence,[1127] his Lordship held that specific performance, as an equitable remedy, did not necessarily depend on the accrual of a cause of action for damages at common law.[1128] An order of specific performance might thus be granted before the time for performance, in the absence of an acceptance of the anticipatory breach. The order so granted was of a declaratory nature only. Consequential directions for performance would not be implemented until the time for performance arrived, for which no fresh action would be necessary. In the event that the contract is frustrated by the time for performance, the court might grant relief from the order.[1129] These observations are plainly correct. While a deferral of the execution of the order to the time for performance ensures that no injustice is done to the contract-breaker, to make an early order available restores to the victim its bargained-for security under the contract to arrange its affairs in the light of a future conveyance. The decision applies equally to a unilateral contract, such as an option contract to buy land. Where the vendor repudiates the contract before the option becomes exercisable, the purchaser may nevertheless immediately apply for an order of specific performance.[1130] As noted previously, the institution of a claim for specific performance does not by itself constitute an affirmation. The victim might, therefore, subsequently terminate the contract and sue for damages if the order is not complied with by the contract-breaker.[1131] Indeed, the victim may sue concurrently for specific performance and, in the alternative, for damages, subject only to an election at the trial for the sake of avoiding double recovery.[1132]

In principle, there is no material difference in this regard between specifically enforcing a positive obligation and seeking an injunction against a breach of a negative obligation. The latter may thus be granted before performance of the negative obligation falls due or while it is continuously due. In fact, it is precisely in respect of a future breach that an injunction has a pre-emptive value. It has, therefore, been frequently sought as a remedy for an anticipatory breach.[1133] The availability of the injunction was explained on the ground that the anticipatory breach infringed 'an inchoate right to the performance of the bargain'.[1134] This must be taken to mean that an unaccepted anticipatory breach is capable by itself of triggering an injunction. There is no need to show either a right of action for

[1127] Canadian cases cited: *Roberto v Bumb* [1943] 2 DLR 613 (Ontario CA); *Kloepfer Wholesale Hardware & Automotive Co v Roy* [1952] 2 SCR 465 (SCC); American commentaries cited: *Restatement (Second) of Contracts* § 360; WHE Jaeger (ed), *Williston on Contracts*, 3rd edn (New York, Baker Voorhis, 1968) vol 5, § 3708–9. Similarly, in Australia: *Turner v Bladin* (1951) 82 CLR 463 (HCA).

[1128] *Hasham v Zenab* (n 116) 330.

[1129] *Ibid* 329–30.

[1130] *Cf McGibbon et al v Popoff* [1977] 4 WWR 685 (BCSC) 691 (McKay J).

[1131] *Johnson v Agnew* (n 180) 398 (Lord Wilberforce).

[1132] G Jones and W Goodhart, *Specific Performance*, 2nd edn (London, Butterworths, 1996) 14. *cf Ogle v Comboyuro* (n 696) 452 (Barwick CJ).

[1133] Eg *Denmark Productions v Boscobel* (n 435); *Decro-Wall* (n 201).

[1134] *Berkeley Community Villages Ltd v Pullen* [2007] EWHC 1330 (Ch), [2007] 3 EGLR 101 [81]–[82] (Morgan J), citing *Frost v Knight* (n 87) 114 (Cockburn CJ).

damages or an infringed proprietary right.[1135] Of course, it is not necessary for an injunction to be granted that a future breach must be fundamental and thus transformable to an anticipatory breach. There is nothing precluding the victim from seeking an injunction for a minor future breach.[1136]

Therefore, the victim of an anticipatory breach, even while not accepting the breach, may still have a number of remedies at its disposal. It may, subject to an extremely constricted rule of equity, continue to perform the contract and earn the contract price. It may also apply for an injunction to prevent the anticipated breach or seek an order of specific performance before the time for performance arrives.

[1135] Like an easement: *Goodhart v Hyett* (1883) 25 Ch D 182.

[1136] *Veracruz Transportation Inc v VC Shipping Co Inc and Den Norske Bank A/S (The 'Veracruz I')* [1992] 1 Lloyd's Rep 353 (CA) 361 (Sir John Megaw). Also, L Collins, 'The Legacy of the Siskina' (1992) 108 *LQR* 175.

Conclusion

This book presents a systematic, in-depth and critical review of the English doctrine of anticipatory breach. As a whole, the book challenges the doctrine for the misconceptions with which it was historically associated, the obscurity and precariousness in its theoretical foundation and the resulting inconsistency and inflexibility in its application. It is argued that the doctrine should be thoroughly reformulated pursuant to a more rational, coherent and refined theoretical framework.

The essence of the doctrine of anticipatory breach, as suggested in the introduction, is to prescribe the circumstances and manner in which present remedies (particularly the termination of a contract and a claim for expectation damages) might be sanctioned for a future breach. The concept of anticipatory breach has been devised to establish a linkage between the present remedies and the future breach. This concept, both theoretically and practically significant, has not as yet been subject to a systematic and in-depth treatment. This book fills the gap and reappraises and reconstructs the doctrine of anticipatory breach in a different light. Four major parts of the doctrine are examined separately.

Part I mixed an historical survey with a theoretical discourse. Chapter 1 traced some early developments of the doctrine of anticipatory breach. By a careful analysis of the decision in the landmark case of *Hochster v De la Tour*,[1137] this Chapter exposed two anomalies which arose in that case and which have since been associated with the doctrine. The first anomaly was the 'implied promise' theory, which characterised an anticipatory breach as a present actual breach of an implied obligation not to do anything inconsistent with the contractual relationship. Our survey showed that that theory was not supported by pre-*Hochster* case law. It was the reasoning in *Main's Case*,[1138] not the 'implied promise' theory, that dominated many of the earlier cases where an action was allowed for a disablement or renunciation that occurred before the time for performance. The disablement or renunciation was held to constitute a present actual breach not of an implied obligation, but of an accelerated future obligation. Prior to *Hochster*, the 'implied promise' theory in fact existed only in employment cases. It was not

[1137] n 1.
[1138] n 30.

extended to other types of contract until *Hochster* itself. The second anomaly is the breach-conversion rule, an important part of the principle of election. The rule states that an anticipatory breach is constituted only if and when the victim 'accepts' it as such. It probably stemmed from Lord Campbell's reliance in *Hochster* on *Planché v Colburn*[1139] as an authority and finally took central stage as a result of an error in reporting both *Avery v Bowden*[1140] and *Reid v Hoskins*.[1141] In each of the latter two cases Lord Campbell endorsed the breach-conversion rule in an obiter dictum, yet the headnote designated it as the only *ratio* of the case. The rule was subsequently followed by English courts in numerous cases. These two anomalies have greatly obscured the nature of anticipatory breach.

In view of this historical survey, Chapter 2 probed what ought to be the best theoretical explanation for an anticipatory breach. It was suggested that the breach-conversion rule should be discarded. An anticipatory breach should be recognised as a breach of contract in its own right. It does not require any act from its victim to be complete as a breach. It should not be viewed as either a tort or an infringement of property, as neither gives rise to a right to terminate the contract or to sue for expectation damages. Of the two competing analyses that characterise an anticipatory breach as a breach of contract, it was suggested that the inferential breach analysis should be adopted in preference to the actual breach analysis. The 'implied promise' theory was dismissed as artificial, impractical and outdated. It is, above all, not supported by the modern law of implied terms. Similarly, the reasoning in *Main's Case* was also rejected as it tends to enlarge the contract-breaker's contractual obligations without its consent. In contrast, it was suggested that an anticipatory breach should be recognised as distinct from an actual breach. An anticipatory breach is characterised as a present breach of one or more future obligations by way of a legal inference. It anticipates a future breach. The anticipated breach should be such as to justify an acceleration of the remedies for that breach. An acceleration of the remedies is justifiable only when the anticipated breach is fundamental. In such a case to hold the victim to the contract would encourage a waste of resources and an augmentation of losses. This Chapter lastly considered some terminological issues in relation to the doctrine of anticipatory breach. In particular, the use of the word 'repudiation' was examined. It was argued that that word should be used to refer only to a type of contractual wrong and, even in that sense, did not cover the whole ground of anticipatory breach. The original meaning of 'repudiation' contains an element of deliberateness but an anticipatory breach is not confined to a deliberate breach.

Part II suggested that the legal tests currently adopted by the courts in determining whether an anticipatory breach was committed should be replaced by a single test based on a reasonable inference of a prospective fundamental breach.

[1139] n 12.
[1140] n 73.
[1141] n 76.

Chapter 3 criticised the current dichotomy in this area of law. As illustrated by *Federal Commerce v Molena*[1142] and *Woodar v Wimpey*[1143] respectively, the House of Lords adopted two distinct approaches in determining the constitution of an anticipatory breach without even attempting to distinguish them. This has greatly vexed the law and has given rise to a pressing need for reform. The orthodox and dominant renunciation approach was closely examined in this Chapter. The Chapter analysed the application of that approach to instalment contract cases, disablement cases and wrongful termination cases. This analysis showed that the influence of the renunciation approach was actually waning despite the fact that it was constantly proclaimed to be the leading test and the courts have displayed a growing willingness to resort to the fundamental breach approach in dealing with anticipatory breach cases. More importantly, this analysis also exposed three major defects of the renunciation approach that justified its abolition: the approach suffers from an innate over-restrictiveness as it has been developed from and tailored for 'renunciation' and is thus unsuitable for other forms of anticipatory breach such as disablement; the application of the approach causes a great amount of uncertainty as the requisite 'intention' not only receives contradictory interpretations but also tends to bring unsettling factors such as good faith into the legal determination of an anticipatory breach; the approach is superficial as it fails to offer any explanation as to why a renunciation should entitle the victim immediately to terminate the contract and claim damages. It was thus suggested that the renunciation approach should not be adopted as the general test for anticipatory breach and is best discarded.

Chapter 4 proceeded to formulate a unified test for all types of anticipatory breach on the basis of the fundamental breach approach. It was argued that the fundamental breach approach successfully captured the 'fundamentality' of an anticipated breach but should be complemented by rules as to how an 'anticipation' of a future breach was established. Consequently, the unified test, termed the 'principle of inferred fundamental breach', is composed of both a test of reasonable inference and a test of fundamentality. Under the test of reasonable inference, the victim is required to show that the circumstances existing at the time of the alleged anticipatory breach give rise to a reasonable inference that a future actual breach is, on the balance of probabilities, likely to occur. Applied in *The Hermosa*,[1144] this test is necessitated by the prospective nature of an anticipatory breach. Despite the fact that there was scarce explicit acknowledgement from the courts, the test has consistently been applied in anticipatory breach cases. The test of fundamentality requires that the inferred breach should have the effect of depriving the victim of substantially the whole benefit intended to be acquired by it under the contract. Adopted by Lord Diplock in *The Afovos*,[1145] this test is

[1142] n 191.
[1143] n 205.
[1144] n 170.
[1145] n 168.

justified in that only when the inferred breach is fundamental does there arise a good justificatory reason for an acceleration of the legal remedies for that breach. The fundamentality of the inferred breach should be assessed by reference not to the time of occurrence of the inferred breach, but to the time of occurrence of the alleged anticipatory breach. Both the test of reasonable inference and the test of fundamentality should be satisfied on the basis of all evidence available at the trial. However, a reasonable inference drawn on the basis of pre-acceptance evidence, even if proved wrong by later evidence, would still justify the acceptance. In such a case the victim might not be entitled to claim damages. On the other hand, a reasonable inference, even unsupported by pre-acceptance evidence, might nevertheless be drawn on the basis of post-acceptance evidence and thereby retrospectively justify the victim's right to terminate the contract and claim damages. This rule of law was recognised in *Universal Cargo v Citati*[1146] and firmly supported by the *Taylor v Oakes*[1147] principle.

The issue explored in Chapter 5 was closely associated with the doctrine of anticipatory breach but was also distinct from it. The issue related to whether, and how, a party's future, anticipated breach might be used by the other party as a defence to exonerate the latter from liability for breach of contract. The Chapter started with a critical review of the Court of Appeal's difficult decision in *Braithwaite v Foreign Hardware Co.*[1148] Close examination showed that that decision entirely overlooked the fact that an anticipated fundamental breach on the claimant's part might be raised as a complete defence. Contrary to what was suggested by Collins MR in that case, it was argued that an anticipatory breach was incapable in itself of 'waiving' a contractual right or benefit and thus preventing an anticipated breach on the victim's part. 'Waiver' is actually a misnomer of 'estoppel'. Thus the defendant in a breach of contract action might raise the claimant's future, anticipated breach as a defence unless estopped from doing so. In order to mount a complete defence on that basis, the defendant may, but does not have to, establish an anticipatory breach on the claimant's part. The defence of anticipated breach is invoked once the defendant puts the claimant's willingness or readiness in issue. The claimant is then required to show that it would have been willing and ready to perform its part had it not been for the breach complained of. It was argued that a failure to show willingness and readiness as required would defeat a claim for damages or specific performance, but it should have no bearing on the claimant's right to terminate the contract.

Part III is a critique of the principle of election, which requires the victim of an anticipatory breach to make an 'election' between accepting the breach and affirming the contract before seeking remedies. It was suggested that acceptance and affirmation were best seen as two distinct acts which raised entirely different legal questions, rather than alternative acts governed by the same notion of

[1146] n 2.
[1147] n 237.
[1148] n 436.

'election'. Chapter 6 dealt with the constitution and legal characterisation of an acceptance. An exploration of case law showed that an acceptance was constituted once an unequivocal intention to bring the contract to an immediate end was manifested. An acceptance requires neither a particular form nor the victim's knowledge of the anticipatory breach or its right to terminate the contract. This leads to two important observations. First, an acceptance of an anticipatory breach is no more or less than a termination of the contract which is justified by that breach. The conceptual separation of an acceptance from a termination is both unnecessary and fictitious. Secondly, an acceptance is not required to be an informed or conscious choice and should therefore not be characterised as an act of election. The mere fact that an acceptance, once made, is irrevocable does not make it an act of election, because an irrevocable choice alone does not give rise to an election. Consequently, the only legal question raised by an acceptance is whether the victim has effectively terminated the contract and whether that termination is justifiable by the anticipatory breach. There is no need to resort to the notion of 'election'.

In Chapter 7, it was suggested that an affirmation gave rise to an entirely different legal question: has the victim relinquished its right to rely upon the anticipatory breach as a ground for terminating the contract? It was argued that there was a demonstrable failure by the courts to identify this legal question in the vast majority of cases where affirmation was in issue. The orthodox test adopted by the courts in general equates an affirmation with the mere continuance of the contract. As a result, the victim might too readily be held to have affirmed the contract and is thus likely to be unduly penalised for its reasonable efforts to rescue the contract. The courts have made several distinct attempts to avoid or rectify this problem. A survey of major cases exhibits three such attempts: a restrictive application of the orthodox test in *Yukong v Rendsburg*,[1149] the creation of a 'third option' in *Stocznia v Latvian Shipping*[1150] and the adoption of the 'continuing repudiation' theory in *Safehaven v Springbok*.[1151] None of them addresses the legal question properly. These attempts were all rejected as half-hearted and unsatisfactory. Consequently, it was suggested that the legal test for affirmation should be completely reformulated. The first step is to see if the victim makes an unequivocal representation not to rely upon the anticipatory breach as a ground for terminating the contract. The mere continuance of the contract is not sufficient to show such a representation. The second step is to ask whether such a representation alone binds the victim. A number of significant arguments in favour of an affirmative answer were examined. It was suggested that the fact that the victim faced a choice whether to accept the anticipatory breach did not create a situation of election and did not make a mere representation not to accept that breach irrevocable. The representation should be treated in the same way as

[1149] n 627.
[1150] n 384.
[1151] n 680.

any other promissory statement. Without being supported by valid consideration or being incorporated into a deed, the representation is best seen as operative only under the doctrine of promissory estoppel. It binds the victim only if the contract-breaker has relied upon it in such a way as to make it inequitable for the victim to retain, either temporarily or permanently, its right to accept the anticipatory breach. The characterisation of either an affirmation or an acceptance as an act of election is, therefore, equally inappropriate.

Part IV considered special issues arising when the victim of an anticipatory breach seeks legal remedies. Chapter 8 considered a claim for damages, the principal remedy available to a victim who has accepted the anticipatory breach. The victim's right of action for damages gives rise to three interconnected issues. First, the conditional damages rule, which requires the victim to accept the anticipatory breach before a right of action for damages accrues, was examined. The conditional damages rule was distinguished from the breach-conversion rule and was justified on the ground that the victim should not be allowed both to hold the contract-breaker to the contract and to recover for a loss of prospective performance. A different rule would cause an intolerable degree of inconsistency and uncertainty and would contradict the fact that an anticipatory breach is a retractable wrong. Secondly, the immediacy rule, which allows the victim to claim damages immediately after accepting the anticipatory breach, was explained. It was suggested that the immediacy rule was founded on practical considerations and should be upheld because it encouraged an early mitigation of loss and a timely settlement of the dispute. Thirdly, an appraisal was made of the American rule that the doctrine of anticipatory breach is not applicable where a party to a contract is under no outstanding obligation at the time when the other party commits an anticipatory breach. It was argued that this rule should not be accepted. The conditional damages rule could not be used to displace the immediacy rule in this context. The victim might terminate the contract and bring an immediate action for damages even though the contract is unilateral or executed on its side. The Chapter proceeded to consider special issues relating to the assessment of damages in anticipatory breach cases. A distinctive feature of the doctrine of anticipatory breach is that, if the loss of prospective performance is claimed, damages are generally assessed by reference not to the time of breach, but to the time for performance. Leaving aside the exception that, where a duty to mitigate arises, the time of acceptance might replace the time for performance as the time for assessment, this feature of anticipatory breach creates a natural gap between the time of acceptance and the time for performance. This gives rise to an issue whether a supervening event that would or might have occurred during that gap ought to be taken into account in assessing damages. A number of theories have been advanced to exclude such an event from the assessment of damages. The debate in the recent case *The Golden Victory*[1152] reflected some of these theories,

[1152] n 793.

which endeavour to promote certainty in assessing damages. Four major theories were examined and rejected. It was suggested that the fact that damages for an anticipatory breach compensated for a future loss of performance meant that any event that occurred before that loss was incurred and might thus either augment or diminish that loss should be taken into account. As far as the assessment of damages is concerned, certainty should in principle give way to fair and just compensation. The Chapter also briefly discussed how a lost chance was to be evaluated in anticipatory breach cases. It was suggested that, whilst a 51 per cent or more chance should be treated as a certainty, a 50 per cent or less chance should not be entirely disregarded and should be factored into damages according to the actual degree of probability substantiated on evidence.

Chapter 9 turned to the victim's remedies when the anticipatory breach is not accepted. The bulk of the Chapter revolved around the issue whether, where a party anticipatorily breaches a future obligation to pay a fixed sum of money, the other party might continue to perform its part and then commence an action in debt for that sum when it is due. The principal authority on this issue, *White & Carter v McGregor*,[1153] was closely analysed. It was suggested that the crux of the issue was not whether it was open for the victim to keep the contract alive or even whether the victim was entitled to bring an action in debt as such, but whether the victim's continuance with the contract, being wasteful, should be held to preclude an action in debt for the contract price. A solution was accordingly built on the basis of Lord Reid's two qualifications in *White & Carter*. Before any issue of wastefulness arises, the victim must satisfy the court that it is able to continue to perform the contract without co-operation from the contract-breaker. By virtue of this co-operation qualification, a claim for the contract price is ruled out in most cases. It is, however, the second (legitimate interest) qualification that constitutes the heart and soul of the principle, derivable from *White & Carter*, that determines the appropriateness of the victim's continuing performance in the face of the anticipatory breach. The nature and scope of this qualification was ascertained. It was suggested that the existence, or rather the absence, of a legitimate interest should not be determined in accordance with the test based upon the adequacy of damages in specific performance cases, the test of unreasonableness in association with a duty to mitigate losses or even the opaque test of 'wholly unreasonable', the currently prevailing test adopted by English courts. Instead, a new test was formulated to confine the courts' discretion to the question whether the wastefulness of the victim's continuing performance is so serious as to outweigh the certainty of preserving its right to earn the contract price by continuing performance. The court's discretionary power to preclude the victim from earning the contract price is exercisable only in exceptional cases. But a careful examination of relevant cases revealed that the existence of a further good reason, in addition to the fact that the victim had a bargained for right to earn the contract

[1153] n 976.

price, would militate strongly in favour of the exercise of that power. The Chapter also briefly accounted that the victim of an anticipatory breach might bring an action for specific performance or injunction before the time for performance.

In retrospect, the various Parts and Chapters of this book can be connected through a grand theme: an anticipatory breach is a breach present in form yet future in substance. It is a concept devised to recognise as a contractual wrong words or conduct that relate essentially to a future contractual obligation and to give effect to an acceleration of legal remedies for the anticipated actual breach of that obligation. A proper understanding of this grand theme will put the somewhat disoriented doctrine of anticipatory breach back on track and obliterate confusion and misconceptions. A renunciation is generalised into an inference of a future breach. An acceptance ceases to be seen as a necessary component of the anticipatory breach and is identified with a termination justified by that breach. Damages are assessed as an accelerated remedy for a breach at the future time for performance rather than on the basis of a fictitious acceleration of that breach. It is in the anticipation of a future breach that the doctrine of anticipatory breach finds its new, healthy life.

BIBLIOGRAPHY

Books

Atiyah, PS, *The Rise and Fall of Freedom of Contract* (Oxford, Clarendon, 1979)

——, *An Introduction to the Law of Contract*, 5th edn (Oxford, Clarendon, 1995)

Beale, HG (ed), *Chitty on Contracts*, 30th edn (London, Sweet & Maxwell, 2008) vol I 'General Principles'

Beatson, J (ed), *Anson's Law of Contract*, 28th edn (Oxford, OUP, 2002)

Birks, P, *An Introduction to the Law of Restitution* (Oxford, Clarendon, 1985)

——, *Unjust Enrichment*, 2nd edn (Oxford, OUP, 2005)

Bower, GS and Turner, AK, *The Law Relating to Estoppel by Representation*, 3rd edn (London, Butterworths, 1977)

Burrows, A, *The Law of Restitution*, 2nd edn (London, Butterworths, 2002)

——, *Remedies for Torts and Breach of Contract*, 3rd edn (Oxford, OUP, 2004)

Burrows, JF, Finn, J and Todd, S, *Law of Contract in New Zealand*, 3rd edn (Wellington, LexisNexis, 2007)

Carter, JW, *Breach of Contract*, 2nd edn (Sydney, Law Book, 1991)

——, Peden, E and Tolhurst, GJ, *Contract Law in Australia*, 5th edn (LexisNexis, 2007)

Chitty, TW, Denning, AT and Harvey, CP (eds), *Smith's Leading Cases*, 13th edn (London, Sweet & Maxwell, 1929) vol II

Cooke, E, *The Modern Law of Estoppel* (Oxford, OUP, 2000)

Corbin, AL, *Corbin on Contracts*, Interim edn (Matthew Bender, 2007) vol 10 'Breach of Contract'

Davies, JLR, Seddon, NC and Masel, G (eds), *The Laws of Australia: Contract* (Lawbook, 2003)

Ewart, J, *Waiver Distributed* (Harvard University Press, 1917)

Farnsworth, EA, *Farnsworth on Contracts*, 3rd edn (New York, ASPEN, 2004) vol II

——, *Changing Your Mind: The Law of Regretted Decisions* (New Haven, Yale University Press, 1998)

Feltham, P, Hochberg, D and Leech, T, *Spencer Bower: The Law Relating to Estoppel by Representation*, 4th edn (Tottel, 2004)

Fridman, GHL, *The Law of Contract*, 5th edn (Toronto, Thomson, 2006)

Furmston, M, *Cheshire, Fifoot and Furmston's Law of Contract*, 15th edn (Oxford, OUP, 2007)

Guest, AG, *Benjamin's Sale of Goods*, 6th edn (London, Sweet & Maxwell, 2002)

Handley, KR, *Estoppel by Conduct and Election* (London, Sweet & Maxwell, 2006)

Harris, D and Tallon, D (eds), *Contract Law Today: Anglo-French Comparisons* (Oxford, Clarendon, 1989)
Ibbetson, DJ, *A Historical Introduction to the Law of Obligation* (Oxford, OUP, 1999)
Jaffey, P, *The Nature and Scope of Restitution* (Oxford, Hart Publishing, 2000)
Jaeger, WHE (ed), *Williston on Contracts*, 3rd edn (New York, Baker Voorhis, 1968) vol 5
Jones, G and Goodhart, W, *Specific Performance*, 2nd edn (London, Butterworths, 1996)
Lord, RA (ed), *Williston on Contracts*, 4th edn (West, 2002) vol 23
Chaytor, AH and Whittaker, WJ (eds), Maitland, FW, *The Forms of Action at Common Law* (Cambridge, CUP, 1965)
Markesinis, BS, Lorenz, W and Dannemann, G, *The Law of Contracts and Restitution: A Comparative Introduction*, German Law of Obligations Series (Oxford, Clarendon, 1997)
——, Unberath, H and Johnston, A, *The German Law of Contract: A Comparative Treatise*, 2nd edn (Oxford, Hart Publishing, 2006)
McBryde, WW, *The Law of Contract in Scotland*, 3rd edn (Edinburgh, W Green, 2007)
McGregor, H, *Contract Code Drawn up on Behalf of the English Law Commission* (Milano, Dott A Giufferè Editore, 1993)
——, *McGregor on Damages*, 17th edn (London, Sweet & Maxwell, 2003)
McKendrick, E, *Contract Law: Text, Cases, and Materials*, 2nd edn (Oxford, OUP, 2005)
Perrins, B (ed), *Harvey on Industrial Relations and Employment Law* (London, LexisNexis, 1996)
Peel, E, *Treitel: The Law of Contract*, 12th edn (London, Sweet & Maxwell, 2007)
Pont, GED (ed), *Halsbury's Laws of Australia* (Sydney, Butterworths, 1992) vol 6
Reynolds, FMB, *Bowstead and Reynolds on Agency*, 18th edn (London, Sweet & Maxwell, 2006)
Seddon, NC and Ellinghaus, MP, *Cheshire and Fifoot's Law of Contract*, 9th Australian edn (LexisNexis Butterworths, 2008)
Simpson, AWB, *A History of the Common Law of Contract* (Oxford, Clarendon, 1975)
Simpson, JA and Weiner, ESC (comps), *The Oxford English Dictionary*, 2nd edn (Oxford, Clarendon, 1989) vol XIII
Smith, JC, *Smith and Thomas: A Casebook on Contract*, 11th edn (London, Sweet & Maxwell, 2000)
Smith, SA, *Atiyah's Introduction to the Law of Contract*, 6th edn (Oxford, Clarendon, 2006)
Stoljar, SJ, *A History of Contract at Common Law* (Canberra, Australian National University Press, 1975)
——, *The Law of Quasi-Contract*, 2nd edn (Law Book, 1989)
Treitel, GH, *The Law of Contract*, 11th edn (London, Sweet & Maxwell, 2003)
——, *Remedies for Breach of Contract: A Comparative Account* (Oxford, Clarendon, 1988)
Waddams, SM, *The Law of Contracts*, 5th edn (Toronto, Canada Law Book, 2005)
Walker, DM, *Principles of Scottish Private Law*, 4th edn (Oxford, Clarendon, 1988) vol II
Winfield, PH, *The Province of the Law of Tort* (Cambridge, CUP, 1931)
Weir, T (tr), Zweigert, K and Kötz, H, *An Introduction to Comparative Law*, 3rd edn (Oxford, OUP, 1998)

Articles

Baker, JH, 'The Use of Assumpsit for Restitutionary Money Claims 1600–1800' in Schrage, EJH (ed), *Unjust Enrichment: The Comparative Legal History of the Law of Restitution*, 2nd edn (Berlin, Duncker and Humblot, 1999)

Beale, H and Dugdale, T, 'Contracts between Businessmen: Planning and the Use of Contractual Remedies' (1975) 2 *British Journal of Law and Society* 45

Birks, P, 'The Concept of a Civil Wrong' in Owen, D (ed), *Philosophical Foundations of Tort Law* (Oxford, Clarendon, 1995)

Bridge, MG, 'Mitigation of Damages in Contract and the Meaning of Avoidable Loss' (1989) 105 *LQR* 398

Burrows, A, 'Limitations on Compensation' in A Burrows, A and Peel, E (eds), *Commercial Remedies Current Issues and Problems* (Oxford, OUP, 2003) 27, 37–43

Capper, D, 'A "Golden Victory" for Freedom of Contract' (2008) 24 *Journal of Contract Law* 176

Carter, JW, 'Regrettable Developments in the Law of Contract?' [1980] *CLJ* 256

——, 'The Embiricos Principle and the Law of Anticipatory Breach' [1984] 47 *MLR* 422

——, 'The Higher Altitudes of Contract Law' [1989] *Lloyd's Maritime and Commercial Law Quarterly* 81

——, 'Failure to Perform as "Acceptance" of a Repudiation' (1997) 11 *Journal of Contract Law* 255

—— and Peden, E, 'Damages Following Termination for Repudiation: Taking Account of Later Events' (2008) 24 *Journal of Contract Law* 145

——, Phang, A and Phang, SY, 'Performance Following Repudiation: Legal and Economic Interests' (1999) 15 *Journal of Contract Law* 1

Coote, B, 'Breach, Anticipatory Breach, or the Breach Anticipated?' (2007) 123 *LQR* 503

Collins, L, 'The Legacy of the Siskina' (1992) 108 *LQR* 175

Corbin, AL, 'Conditions in the Law of Contracts' (1918–1919) 28 *Yale Law Journal* 739

Dawson, F, 'Metaphors and Anticipatory Breach of Contract' [1981] *CLJ* 83

——, 'Waiver of Conditions Precedent on A Repudiation' (1980) 96 *LQR* 239

Dobbs, DB, 'Pressing Problems for the Plaintiff's Lawyer in Rescission: Election of Remedies and Restoration of Consideration' (1972) 26 *Arkansas Law Review* 322

Dobson, P, 'Late Payment of Instalments by Hirers' (1987) *Journal of Business Law* 147

Eisenberg, MA, 'Probability and Chance in Contract Law' (1997–1998) 45 *UCLA Law Review* 1005

Farnsworth, EA, 'Disputes over Omission in Contracts' (1968) 68 *Columbia Law Review* 860

——, 'Your Loss or My Gain? The Dilemma of the Disgorgement Principle in Breach of Contract' (1985) 94 *Yale Law Journal* 1339

Fine, BL, 'An Analysis of the Formation of Property Rights Underlying Tortious Interference with Contracts and Other Economic Relations' (1983) 50 *University of Chicago Law Review* 1116

Friedmann, D, 'The Performance Interest in Contract Damages' [1995] 111 *LQR* 628

FitzPatrick, TM, 'Contributory Negligence and Contract—A Critical Reassessment Part II: At Common Law' (2001) 30 *Common Law World Review* 412

Franklin, M, 'Equity as Form: A Study of Frost v Knight' (1955–1956) 30 *Tulane Law Review* 175

Furmston, MP, 'The Case of the Insistent Performer' (1962) 25 *MLR* 364

Goode, R, 'International Restatements of Contract and English Contract Law' (1997) *Uniform Law Review* 231

Goodhart, AL, 'Measure of Damages When a Contract is Repudiated' [1962] 78 *LQR* 263

Handley, KR, 'Exploring Election' (2006) 122 *LQR* 82

Harris, J, 'Anticipatory Breach—Innocent Party's Right to Terminate' (1988) 1 *Journal of Contract Law* 177

Hedley, S, 'Eloquent Silences and Reasonable People' [1996] *CLJ* 430

Kreitner, R, 'Speculations of Contract, or How Contract Law Stopped Worrying and Learned to Love Risk' (2000) 100 *Columbia Law Review* 1096

Lee, PW, 'Inducing Breach of Contract, Conversion and Contract as Property' (2009) 29 *OJLS* 511

Limburg, HR, 'Anticipatory Breach of Contracts' (1924–1925) 10 *Cornell Law Quarterly* 135

Lloyd, MG, 'Ready and Willing to Perform: The Problem of Prospective Inability in the Law of Contract' (1974) 37 *MLR* 121

Lubbe, G, 'Retraction of Repudiation: A Doctrine Writ in Water?' (1996) 7 *Stellenbosch Law Review* 147

Macaulay, S, 'Non-Contractual Relations in Business: A Preliminary Study' (1963) 28 *American Sociological Review* 55

Marston, G, 'The Cancelling Clause in Charterparties' [1969] *Journal of Business Law* 187

Mason, K, 'Commentary on "Conduct after Breach: the Position of the Party not in Breach' (1991) 3 *Journal of Contract Law* 232

McLauchlan, D and Hegan, N, 'Contract Damages: Fundamental Principle, Fundamental Disagreement' (2008) 46 *Canadian Business Law Journal* 89

McRae, DM, 'Repudiation of Contracts in Canadian Law' (1978) 56 *Canadian Bar Review* 233

Mitchell, P, '*Hochster v De La Tour* (1853)' in Mitchell, C and Mitchell, P (eds), *Landmark Cases in the Law of Contract* (Oxford, Hart Publishing, 2008)

Moses, PA, 'The Doctrine of Anticipatory Breach of Contracts, Theoretically and Historically Considered' (1900–1901) 1 *North Carolina Law Journal* 321

Mustill, M, 'Anticipatory Breach of Contract: The Common Law at Work' in *Butterworth Lectures 1989–1990* (London, Butterworths, 1990)

——, '*The Golden Victory*—Some Reflections' (2008) 124 *LQR* 569

Nicol, A and Rawlings, R, 'Changing Attitudes to Anticipatory Breach and Third Party Beneficiaries' [1980] 43 *MLR* 696

Nienaber, PM, 'The Effect of Anticipatory Breach: Principle and Policy' [1962] *CLJ* 213

Note, 'Tortious Interference with Contractual Relations in the Nineteenth Century: The Transformation of Property, Contract, and Tort' (1979–1980) 93 *Harvard Law Review* 1510

Oditah, F, 'Assets and the Treatment of Claims in Insolvency' (1992) 108 *LQR* 459

Opeskin, BR, 'Damages for Breach of Contract Terminated under Express Terms' [1990] 106 *LQR* 293

Peden, E, 'Policy Concerns Behind Implication of Terms in Law' (2001) 117 *LQR* 459

Peel, E, 'Affirmation by Termination' (2009) 125 *LQR* 378

Phang, A, 'Implied Terms, Business Efficacy and the Officious Bystander—A Modern History' [1998] *Journal of Business Law* 1

Porat, A, 'Contributory Negligence in Contract Law: Toward A Principled Approach' (1994) 28 *University of British Columbia Law Review* 141

Priestley, LJ, 'Conduct after Breach: the Position of the Party not in Breach' (1991) 3 *Journal of Contract Law* 218

Reynolds, FMB, 'Election Distributed' [1970] 86 *LQR* 318

Rogers, WVH, 'The Late Ship and the Non-Existent Cargo' (1971) 34 *MLR* 190

Rose, FD, 'The Effects of Repudiatory Breaches of Contract' (1981) 34 *Current Legal Problems* 235

Rossiter, CJ, 'The Doctrine of Election and Contracts for the Sale of Land' (1986) *Australian Law Journal* 563

Rowley, KA, 'A Brief History of Anticipatory Breach in American Contract Law' (2000–2001) 69 *University of Cincinnati Law Review* 565

Shea, AM, 'Discharge from Performance of Contracts by Failure of Condition' (1979) 42 *MLR* 623

Sheppard, AM, 'Demystifying the Right of Election in Contract Law' [2007] *Journal of Business Law* 442

Simon, D, 'A Critique of the Treatment of Market Damages in the *Restatement (Second) of Contracts*' (1981) 81 *Columbia Law Review* 80

Smith, JC, 'Anticipatory Breach of Contract' in Lomnicka, EZ and Morse, CGJ (eds), *Contemporary Issues in Commercial Law* (London, Sweet & Maxwell, 1997)

Stevens, R, 'Damages and the Right to Performance: A Golden Victory or Not?' in Neyers, JW, Bronaugh, R and Pitel, SGA (eds), *Exploring Contract Law* (Oxford, Hart Publishing, 2009)

Stoljar, S, 'Some Problems of Anticipatory Breach' [1974] 9 *Melbourne University Law Review* 355

Swanton, J, 'Discharge of Contracts for Breach' (1981) 13 *Melbourne University Law Review* 69

Tabachnik, E, 'Anticipatory Breach of Contract' (1972) 25 *Current Legal Problems* 149

Thomson, JM, 'The Effect of A Repudiatory Breach' (1978) 41 *MLR* 137

Tiplady, D, '*The Angelia*' (case note) [1973] 89 *LQR* 465

Treitel, GH, 'Damages on Rescission for Breach of Contract' [1987] *Lloyd's Maritime and Commercial Law Quarterly* 143

——, '"Conditions" and "Conditions Precedent"' (1990) 106 *LQR* 185

——, 'Affirmation after Repudiatory Breach' (1998) 114 *LQR* 22

——, 'Assessment of Damages for Wrongful Repudiation' (2007) 123 *LQR* 9

Vold, L, 'Repudiation of Contracts' (1927) 5 *Nebraska Law Bulletin* 269

——, 'Anticipatory Breach of Contracts and Necessity of Election' (1927–1928) 26 *Michigan Law Review* 502

——, 'The Tort Aspect of Anticipatory Breach of Contracts' (1927–1928) 41 *Harvard Law Review* 340

Wee, MS, 'Insolvency and the Survival of Contracts' [2005] *Journal of Business Law* 494

Wiesner, DA and Klotchman, J, 'Anticipatory Breach and the Unilateral Contract: A Decade of the Status Quo?' (1982–1983) 8 *University of Dayton Law Review* 61

Whittaker, S, 'How Does French Law Deal with Anticipatory Breaches of Contract?' (1996) 45 *ICLQ* 662

Waddams, SM, 'Damages for Failure to Return Shares' (1978–1979) 3 *Canadian Business Law Journal* 398

——, 'The Date for the Assessment of Damages' [1981] 97 *LQR* 445
——, 'The Valuation of Chances' (1998) 30 *Canadian Business Law Journal* 86
'*Woodar v Wimpey*' (case note) [1980] 96 *LQR* 321

Thesis

Tiplady, D, 'A Comparative Analysis of the Discharge of Contracts by Anticipatory Breach and Actual Breach with Particular Reference to the Terminology of Frustration' (M Litt thesis, Oxford University, 1973)

INDEX

acceleration
  future obligations accelerated, 17, 31–32
  immediacy rule, and, 162
  justification for accelerating legal remedies for inferred breach, 36–37, 221
  loan contracts, 166
  unilateral or one-sidedly executed contracts, 166–67
acceptance, 115–28, 223–25
  acceptance of anticipatory breach does not need knowledge of it, 115, 120–21
  constitution of acceptance, 115–21
  converting anticipatory breach into actual breach of contract, 122–23
  election, whether acceptance an act of, 123–28
    intention objectively assessed, 124
    irrevocability of election, 125–27
    knowledge, requirement of, 124–25, 127
    main reasons why acceptance not an act of election, 127–28
    onus of proof, 124–25
  intention
    failure to perform a contract, 119
    form intention manifested in, 117–19
    immediacy, 115, 117–18
    manifesting an intention to bring contract to an end, 115–20
    unequivocality, 115–17
  legal test for acceptance of intention, 115–20
  meaning of acceptance, 115
  nature of acceptance, 121–28
    acceptance as termination, 121–23
    whether acceptance an act of election, 123–28
  see also 'breach-conversion' rule
actual breach
  actual breach analysis, 31–33
    'implied promise' theory mainstream of analysis, 33, 37, 39
    'inferential breach' analysis preferred to, 37–39
    practical effectiveness doubted, 38
    present obligation must form subject of the breach, 31
    steps in approaching an anticipatory breach case, 33
  anticipatory breach distinguished from, 33–37, 47, 73, 124, 221
  time of breach dictating assessment of damages, 168
adequacy of damages test, 207–8, 226
affirmation, 129–51, 223–25
  act of election, as, 144
  elective view of, 144–48
    affirmation as act of election, 144–45
    anti-speculation principle, 147–48
    certainty and justice, 146
    irrevocable nature of 'election' to affirm, 145–46
    justification for, 145–48
    knowledge, 145–46
    windfalls by inconsistent actions, 146–47
  estoppel view, 141–51
    elective view, 144–48
    estoppel view, 148–51
    promissory estoppel, 148–51
    reliance, 148, 150–51
    unequivocal representation, 141–44
  nature and meaning of, 129–30
  orthodox test, 129–40
    consequences of 'affirmation', 130
    'continuing repudiation' theory, 136–40
    major defect, 139–40
    nature of orthodox test, 129
    restrictive interpretation, 130–32
    salvage, attempts to, 130–40
    third option outside acceptance and affirmation, 132–36
  unequivocal representation 141–44
    clear and unequivocal communication, 141
    election and estoppel, and, 143–44
    express or implied, 141
    knowledge, 144
    objective assessment, 141–42
anticipated breach as a defence, 93–112, 223
  averment of willingness and readiness, 105–12
    onus of proof, 108, 111
    types of willingness and readiness, 108–10
  Braithwaite conundrum, 93–99, 105, 112
    anticipatory breach by seller as exonerating buyers, 95–96
    application of doctrine not confined to 'wrongful' termination cases, 97–98
    termination on a wrong reason, whether wrongful, 95
    'waiver' theory, 98–99
  'waiver' theory, 98–99, 100–105, 223
    meaning of waiver, 100–101

estoppel, waiver as, 101
promissory estoppel brought into operation, 104–105
representation that fulfilling condition precedent is pointless, 104
wrongful termination triggering a waiver, 100
anticipatory, anticipated nature as meaning of, 39
anticipatory breach
actual breach, and *see under* actual breach
anticipatory repudiation or renunciation, as, 40
characterisation of *see* present actual breach of an implied promise; principle of election
constitution as key question, 3
contradictory approaches to determining existence of *see* prevailing test, critique of
core idea, 1–3
damages for *see* damages
evidential modes of establishing *see* evidential modes of establishing anticipatory breach
genesis *see* genesis of anticipatory breach
impure anticipatory breach in instalment contracts, 52–56
prevailing test *see* prevailing test, critique of
redefinition *see* redefinition of anticipatory breach
remedies *see* damages; specific relief
scope of concept, 3–4
specific relief for *see* specific relief
anticipatory repudiation, 42
anticipatory breach, as, 40
anticipatory repudiatory breach, 40, 42
anti-speculation principle, 147–48
assessing damages, 167–92
actual breach, 168
consequential loss, 168, 170–71
time of loss when loss actually sustained, 170
contract-breaker performing in most beneficial way to itself, 182–84
interest deducted, 166
normal loss, 168–70
default rule, 168, 169
time fixed for contract-breaker's performance, 168
time for performance fixed by contract or ascertained by court, 170
supervening events *see* supervening events
time for assessment, 168–73
'duty' to mitigate, 171–73
see also mitigation of loss
time of loss, 168–71
valuation of a chance *see* valuation of a chance
Atiyah, PS, 10
Australia, 80–81, 107, 149–50, 167, 189–91
Avery v Bowden (1855), 22–23, 156, 159, 221
balance of probabilities test, valuation of a chance and, 188, 189, 226
Bower, GS, 149
Braithwaite v Foreign Hardware Co (1905), 93–99, 105, 112, 175, 187, 223
'breach-conversion' rule, 122–23, 156, 221
anticipatory breach complete as a breach on acceptance, 28, 122–23
rule challenged, 28–30
rule obsolete, 29, 30
chain contracts, 29–30
characterisation of anticipatory breach as a breach of contract, and, 28–30
conditional damages rule, and, 156
constitution of a breach and accrual of right of action for damages, 29
error in reporting creating, 23, 24
historical development of anticipatory breach, 22–25
jurisdiction, and, 29
specific performance, and, 29
breach of contract
actual breach as usual nature of, 31
not automatically terminating a contract, 123–24
breach of future obligation *see under* future obligations
'business efficacy' test, 33, 38
'Bwllfa principle', 181

Canada, 79
Carter, JW, 95
chance, valuation of *see* valuation of a chance
civil wrong, anticipatory breach as, 26–27
claim for the contract price, 193–217, 226
building the solution, 203–17
adequacy of damages, 207–8
co-operation, 204–7
dependency of performance, 204–6
duty to mitigate, 209–11
legitimate interest, 207–17
new test, 212–17, 226
onus of proof, 203–4, 210
passive co-operation, 206–7
'wholly unreasonable', 211–12
identifying the issue, 196–203
automatic termination, 197–99
availability of specific relief, 199–201
wasteful performance, 201–3, 204
White and Carter principle, 193–97, 199–203, 205–216, 226
'co-operation qualification' *see* 'co-operation qualification'
'legitimate interest qualification' *see* legitimate interest qualification
compensatory principle, 175, 178, 191
certainty and finality in commercial cases, and, 181–82

conditional damages rule, 155–61
'breach-conversion' rule, and, 156
justification, 156, 158–61
major objections, 156, 157–58
illogicality, 157
immediate injury, 158
undue prejudice, 157–58
origins, 155–56, 158–59
practical implications of, 156
see also damages
conditions, 2
anticipatory breach of, 80–82
consequences of breach of, 80–81
future actual breach and reasonable inference, 80–81
implied, 33
breach of, 82–83
mere breach of, 41
non-promissory, 32
precedent, 14–17, 19, 31, 54
contract price as a debt payable if fulfilled, 199–201
co-operation qualification, and, 204
dispensing with, 101, 104
subsequent, 14, 16
conduct in determining anticipatory breach, consequences of *see* fundamental breach
'constructive performance', theory of, 18–19
'continuing repudiation' theory, 136–40
criticisms of theory, 138–40
contract price, claim for *see* claim for the contract price
'contractual property' theory, 26–28
impact on doctrine of anticipatory breach, 27–28, 30
tortious view of anticipatory breach doubted, 28
'co-operation qualification' 194–96, 200, 203–7, 226
dependency of performance, 204–6
passive co-operation, 206–7
Corbin, AL, 166
'crystallisation' theory, 177–82

damages, 155–92, 225–26
adequacy of damages, 207–8
assessing *see* assessing damages
compensatory principle, 175, 178, 191
certainty and finality in commercial cases, and, 181–82
expectation damages, 3, 28, 37, 113, 126–28, 220, 221
reliance damages, and, 191
interest deducted, 166
not allowed on basis of reasonable but incorrect inference, 87–88
primary remedy, 155
reliance damages, 170, 191
expectation damages, and, 191
right to claim damages, 155–67
conditional damages rule *see* conditional damages rule
immediacy rule *see* immediacy rule
unilateral or one-sidedly executed contracts *see* unilateral or one-sidedly executed contracts
disablement
cases, 14–18, 222
conditions precedent capable of being dispensed with 16–17
establishing on basis of post-acceptance evidence, 88–92
intention-based wrong, 60–61
irreparability of, 61
reasonable inference establishing, whether, 87–88
removing ability to perform, 60
renunciation approach, and, 60–65
transition from intention-based test to ability-based test, 62–64
due time, 31
'duty' to mitigate *see under* mitigation of loss

Elderton v Emmens (1853), 20–21, 32
election *see* principle of election
employment contracts
personal service contracts *see* personal service contracts
wrongful dismissal in, 20–21, 32, 220, 222
valid reason existing but not given, 89–90
wastefulness of continuation of contract, 201
English law, dichotomy of *see under* prevailing test, critique of
estoppel *see* affirmation; anticipated breach as a defence; promissory estoppel
evidential modes of establishing anticipatory breach, 85–92
establishing anticipatory breach on basis of post-acceptance evidence, 88–92
establishing anticipatory breach on basis of pre-acceptance evidence, 86–88
expectation damages, 3, 28, 37, 113, 126–28, 220, 221
reliance damages, and, 191

Farnsworth, EA, 40, 147
Federal Commerce & Navigation Ltd v Molena Alpha Inc, 48–51, 58, 67, 71–73, 222
'fictitious breach' theory, 174–77
criticisms of, 175–76
Freeth v Burr (1874), 52–55, 66–67
Frost v Knight (1871–72), 23–24, 27–28, 34, 140, 160, 171, 175–77
frustrating events, 124, 159, 198

fundamental breach
actual, 149
anticipatory breach, and, 79–83
application of test of fundamentality, 84–85, 222–23
approach *see* fundamental breach approach
definition of, 71, 72, 79, 84
principle of inferred fundamental breach: the dual tests, 73–85
inferred breach must be a fundamental breach, 37, 38–39
test of fundamentality, 79–85, 223–23
test of reasonable inference, 73–79
see also repudiatory breach
fundamental breach approach, 48–49, 54–55, 222
consequences of words/conduct in determining anticipatory breach, 42, 48–49, 58–59, 72
contexts in which concept used, 71–72
serious breach justifying termination, 71, 72
inadequacy, 72
inference, 73
intention, role of, 72–73
overshadowing renunciation approach, 54–56
rise of fundamental breach approach, 70–73
still encumbered by renunciation approach, 71
transition from renunciation approach, 62–64
future obligations
accelerated, 17, 31–32
actual breach of, 31
anticipatory breach as breach of, 34–37, 39
as present breach of, 35–36, 39, 75, 221
non-actual breach of, 34
anticipatory breach innately linked to, 36
'implied promise' theory, and *see* 'implied promise' theory
present words/conduct creating inference that obligations will not be performed, 36

genesis of anticipatory breach, 9–25
gestation of the 'implied promise' theory *see under* 'implied promise' theory
re-examination of *Hochster v De La Tour*, 10–14
rise of the principle of election *see under* principle of election
Golden Victory, The (2007), 179–82, 185–87, 189, 225

Hadley v Baxendale rule, 168
Harvard Law Review, 26
Hermosa, The (1982), 74–75, 76, 84, 86, 91, 222
historical development of anticipatory breach
'breach conversion' rule *see* breach conversion rule
'implied promise' theory *see* 'implied promise' theory
Hochster v De La Tour (1853), 9–14, 27, 32–33, 54, 120, 156, 161–62, 181, 220–21
'implied promise' theory 13, 16, 17, 19, 21
see also' implied promise' theory
'offer to rescind' theory rejected 12–13, 24
pre-*Hochster* disablement cases, 14–18
pre-*Hochster* renunciation cases, 18–20
promise to employ concept extended generally 20, 21, 32
termination of contract essential to anticipatory breach constitution, 13–14, 22

immediacy rule, 161–64
criticisms, 161–63
justification, 163–64
premised on conditional damages rule, 164
implication rules, 33, 38
'implied promise' theory 13, 24–25, 220–21
actual breach analysis, as, 33, 37, 39
anticipatory breach
actual breach of implied promise, as, 25
incomplete breach until acceptance, as, 25
'breach-conversion' rule sabotaging, 25
gestation of 14–21
pre-*Hochster* disablement cases, 14–18
pre-*Hochster* renunciation cases, 18–20
wrongful dismissal in employment contracts, 20–21, 32
'inferential breach' analysis preferred to, 37–39, 221
influence of theory waning, 33
precarious judicial basis for, 17, 20, 21, 24
steps in approaching an anticipatory breach case, 33
'impossibility' cases, 61–62, 160–61, 199
inference
anticipatory breach embodied in a legal inference, 30, 33–37
'inferential breach' analysis *see* 'inferential breach' analysis
inferred fundamental breach *see under* fundamental breach
present words/conduct creating inference that obligations will not be performed, 36
test of reasonable inference *see* reasonable inference, test of
'inferential breach' analysis, 30, 33–37, 221
anticipatory breach as inferential breach, 36
anticipatory breach distinguished from inferred future breach, 36
inferred breach converted into anticipatory breach, 36–37
inferred breach must be a fundamental breach, 37, 38–39

justification for accelerating legal remedies for inferred breach, 36–37
preferred to 'actual breach' analysis, 37–39
steps in approaching an inferential breach case, 37
injunctions, 218–19, 227
'innocence-guilt' dichotomy, 185–87
principal grounds for, 186–87
instalment contracts, 52–56, 222
intention
acceptance, and *see under* acceptance
determining existence of anticipatory breach, and, 42, 48, 49–51
disablement *see under* disablement
election, and, 124–25
fundamental breach, and *see under* fundamental breach
renunciation approach, and *see* renunciation approach
repudiation, and, 42
termination, and, 42, 56–60
transition from intention-based test to ability-based test, 62–64

'legitimate interest qualification', 194–96, 200, 203, 207–17, 226
duty to mitigate, 209–11
new test, 212–17, 226
restating 'wholly unreasonable' test, 212, 215–17
tests to determine, 207–12
adequacy of damages, 207–8
'wholly unreasonable', 211–12
'wholly unreasonable', 211–12
new test, 212–17
see also claim for the contract price
limitation periods, 35
conditional damages rule, and, 156
Statute of Limitations, 22, 36
Lovelock v Franklyn (1846), 16, 21
'implied promise' theory, adoption of, 16

Main's Case (1596), 15–19, 21, 27, 101, 105, 220–21
McGregor on Damages, 80
Mersey Steel and Iron Co v Naylor Benzon & Co (1884), 52–55, 67
mitigation of loss, 13, 24
conditional damages rule, and, 156
'crystallising' effect of duty to mitigate on quantum, 177–79
'duty' to mitigate, 171–73
claim to the contract price by continuing performance, 209–11
damages assessed by reference to time duty arises, 173
difficulty of forecasting loss relevant in assessing reasonableness, 172
duty arises when anticipatory breach accepted, 172, 173, 209
placing a ceiling on recovery of actual loss, 178
reasonableness/unreasonableness, 172, 210, 211, 226
encouraging, 37
principle preventing recovery of an aggravated but avoidable loss, 179
Mustill, M, 60

'obligation only' theory, 182–85, 190
criticisms of, 184–85
reasonable expectation test, and, 183–84, 185
'offer to rescind' theory 12–13, 24, 119–20
'officious bystander' test, 38
onus of proof
averment of willingness and readiness, 108, 111
claim for the contract price, 203–4, 210
principle of election, 124–25
outright refusal to perform as earliest from of anticipatory breach, 56–57, 65–66, 70
see also wrongful termination *under* termination

penal bond cases 14–16
personal service contracts, 20–21, 32, 200
automatic termination, 197–99
elective (or acceptance) view, 197
unilateral (or automatic termination) view, 197–99
see also employment contracts
Planché v Colburn (1831), 11–13, 22, 156
'offer to rescind' theory 12–13
present actual breach of an implied obligation, 9, 31, 220
present breach of a future obligation *see under* future obligations
prevailing test, critique of, 48–69
contradictory approaches determining existence of anticipatory breach, 48–52
dichotomy of English law, 48–52
Federal Commerce v Molena, 48–51, 58, 67
fundamental breach/renunciation approaches producing different results, 51
Woodar v Wimpey, 49–51, 54, 57–60, 66
renunciation approach *see* renunciation approach
prevention, concept of 18, 101
principle of election, 9–10, 14, 19
acceptance an act of election, whether, 123–28
intention objectively assessed, 124
irrevocability of election, 125–27
knowledge, requirement of, 124–25, 127
main reasons why acceptance not an act of election, 127–28
onus of proof, 124–25
affirmation, elective view of, 144–48

breach-conversion' rule *see* 'breach-conversion' rule
estoppel, and, 143–44
nature of election, 124–25
rise of 22–25
termination of contract essential to constitution of breach, 22
promissory estoppel, 104–105, 225
affirmation, and, 148, 150–51
not irrevocable until promis*ee* alters position, 151
proprietary view of contractual rights *see* 'contractual property' theory

reasonable expectation, 142
reasonable expectation test and 'obligation only' theory, 183–84, 185
valuation of a chance, and, 188
reasonable inference
conclusiveness of reasonable inference, 86–87, 222–23
claim for damages, and, 87–88
degree of likelihood required to establish, 76–77
establishing anticipatory breach on basis of pre-acceptance evidence, 86–88
requirement of anticipation concretising into, 75
source of reasonable inference, 76
supported by existing circumstances, 91–92
test must be applied objectively, 75–76
test of, 73–79
threats, 78
whether can be drawn dependent on circumstances, 77–79
'reasonable necessity' criterion, 38
'reciprocity principle', 178–79
redefinition of anticipatory breach, 26–43
anticipatory breach is a breach of contract, whether, 26–30
anticipatory breach as freestanding breach of contract, 30
'breach-conversion' rule, 28–30
'contractual property' theory, 26–28
anticipatory breach distinct from actual breach, whether, 30–39
anticipatory breach as actual breach of present implied obligation, 30, 31–33
anticipatory breach embodied in a legal inference, 30, 33–37
choosing between 'actual breach' and 'inferential breach' analysis, 37–39
nomenclature, 39–43
requirement of seriousness, 39–40
Reid v Hoskins (1855), 22–23, 156, 159, 221
reliance damages, 170, 191
expectation damages, and, 191
renunciation
actual breach as, 31–32
breach of an accelerated future obligation *see Main's Case*
implied obligation *see* 'implied promise' theory
anticipatory breach, as, 40
anticipatory repudiation, as, 40
approach *see* renunciation approach
cause of action, as, 10, 12, 24, 31
disablement and, 13
establishing on basis of post-acceptance evidence, 88–92
impairing an inchoate right to performance, 27
pre-*Hochster* renunciation cases, 18–20
repudiation constituting an anticipatory breach, as, 40, 42
renunciation approach, 49–51
classic statement of, 52
decline of, 52–65
disablement, 60–65
fundamental breach approach overshadowing, 54–56
impure anticipatory breach in instalment contracts, 52–56
wrongful termination, 56–60
defects of, 65–69
restrictiveness in scope, 65–66, 68, 222
superficiality in nature, 68–69, 222
uncertainty in application, 66–67, 69, 222
intention, 42, 49–51
exterior expressions, 65–66
good faith, 67
manifesting an intention not necessarily an anticipatory breach, 69
objective/subjective, 53–54, 65–67
negating willingness to perform contract, 60
subjective application, 53–54
transition to fundamental breach approach, 62–6
representation, unequivocal *see* unequivocal representation
repudiation
actual repudiation not existing, 43
'continuing repudiation' theory, 136–40
criticisms of theory, 138–40
intention, and, 42
meanings, 40–42
action of rejecting a debt (*Oxford English Dictionary*), 42
ending a contract prospectively only (termination), 40–41
equivalent to equitable rescission (rescission), 40
serious contractual wrong (repudiation), 41–42

measuring what amounts to an anticipatory breach, 39–40, 43
renunciation when constituting an anticipatory breach, as, 40, 42
termination, and, 39, 41
repudiatory breach, 40
meanings, 41–42
discharging breach, 41
serious breaches giving rise to right to terminate, 41
see also fundamental breach
rescission, 40
ending a contract retrospectively, 41, 122
termination, and, 41, 122
Reynolds, Professor FMB, 149

self-created incapacity *see* disablement cases
service and pay relationships, 20
Sir Anthony Main's Case see Main's Case
specific performance, 217–19
affirmation, and, 143, 218
availability of, adequacy of damages test and, 207–8, 226
claim for the contract price, 200–201
not dependent on accrual of cause of action for damages, 218
victim of anticipatory breach claiming when breach unaccepted, 29
specific relief, 193–219
claim for the contract price *see* claim for the contract price
specific performance and injunctions, 217–19
see also specific performance
Statute of Limitations, 22, 36
supervening events, 173–87
'crystallisation' theory, 177–82
'fictitious breach' theory, 174–77
criticisms of, 175–76
'innocence-guilt' dichotomy, 185–87
principal grounds for, 186–87
meaning of 'supervening event', 173
'obligation only' theory, 182–85, 190
criticisms of, 184–85
reasonable expectation test, and, 183–84, 185
relevant supervening events taken into account in assessing damages, 177–82, 187

Taylor v Oakes Roncoroni & Co (1922), 96–97
Taylor v Oakes principle, 90–91, 95, 120–21, 125, 127, 133, 223
qualifications, 91
termination of contract
acceptance as termination, 121–23
anticipated breach as a defence, and *see* anticipated breach as a defence
automatic termination, 197–99
breach of contract, repudiation for, 41
conditions, breach of, 81–82
essential to anticipatory breach constitution, 13–14, 22–24
fundamental breach granting, 39
see also fundamental breach
immediacy, 161
implication rules, and, 38
incorrect but reasonable inference, on, 86
commercial certainty, and, 87–88
intention, and, 42
justification for accelerating legal remedies for inferred breach, 36–37
repudiation, and, 39, 41
repudiatory breach, and, 41
rescission, and *see under* rescission
seriousness of breach giving rise to right to terminate, 84–85
valid reasons unknown but existing at time of, 89–90
wrongful termination, 23, 51, 56–60
requirement of intention, 57
whether constitutes an anticipatory breach, 78–79
tortious liability for interference with contractual relationships, 27
tortious view of anticipatory breach doubted, 28
Treitel, Professor GH, 149, 182
Treitel's Law of Contract, 87, 140

unequivocal representation *see under* affirmation,
unifying test, making, 71–92
evidential modes of establishing anticipatory breach *see* evidential modes of establishing anticipatory breach
principle of inferred fundamental breach *see under* fundamental breach
rise of fundamental breach approach *see under* fundamental breach approach
unilateral or one-sidedly executed contracts, 164–67
supposed exception to doctrine of anticipatory breach, 164–65
conditional damages rule, and, 166
exceptions to the exception, 165
justification for, 165–67
United States, 158, 164, 209
Universal Cargo v Citati, (No 1) (1957), 74–75, 87, 88–89, 91–92, 175–76, 223

valuation of a chance, 188–92
actual probability of occurrence (probabilistic test), 188, 189, 191, 226
courts preparedness to use, 189
balance of probabilities test, 188, 189

'waiver' theory *see under* anticipated breach as a defence
wastefulness of performance, 201–3, 204, 212–13, 226
  adequacy of damages test, and, 207–8
  restating 'wholly unreasonable' test, 212, 215–17
White & Carter (Councils) Ltd v McGregor (1962), 193–97, 199–203, 205–216, 226
  White and Carter principle *see under* claim for the contract price
'wholly unreasonable' test, 211–12, 226
  estating, 212, 215–17
Williston, S, 162
Woodar Investment Development Ltd v Wimpey Construction UK Ltd, 49–51, 54, 57–60, 66, 71, 78, 222
words/conduct in determining anticipatory breach, consequences of *see* fundamental breach
wrongful dismissal *see under* employment contracts

www.ingramcontent.com/pod-product-compliance
Lightning Source LLC
LaVergne TN
LVHW011753200926
848484LV00003B/689
* 9 7 8 1 8 4 9 4 6 1 1 2 2 *